THE THEORY OF PEASANT ECONOMY

# A. V. Chayanov

on

# THE THEORY OF
# PEASANT ECONOMY

Edited by

Daniel Thorner
Basile Kerblay
R. E. F. Smith

With a Foreword by
Teodor Shanin

THE UNIVERSITY OF WISCONSIN PRESS

Published 1986

The University of Wisconsin Press
114 North Murray Street
Madison, Wisconsin 53715

Published in Great Britain by
Manchester University Press
Oxford Road, Manchester M13 9PL

First Wisconsin printing

Printed in the United States of America

Library of Congress Cataloging-in-Publication Data
Chaĭanov, A. V. (Aleksandr Vasil′evich), 1888–1939.
The theory of peasant economy.
Translation of: Organizat͡sii͡a krest′i͡anskogo
khozi͡aĭstva.
Bibliography: pp. 279–296.
Includes index.
1. Agriculture—Economic aspects.   2. Agriculture—
Economic aspects—Soviet Union.   I. Thorner, Daniel.
II. Kerblay, Basile H.   III. Smith, R. E. F.
(Robert E. F.)   IV. Title.
HD1411.C414   1986      338.1′0947      85-40758
ISBN 0-299-10570-9
ISBN 0-299-10574-1 (pbk.)

# Contents

A. V. CHAYANOV

1888–1939

# Publisher's Note

This Wisconsin reprint includes a new foreword, "Chayanov's Message," by Teodor Shanin, written especially for this edition. It has been independently numbered and follows this note.

The original preface notes that Chayanov used the term "family farm" in a particular sense. By family farm, he referred only to those peasant households that relied almost exclusively on the labor of family members; if peasant farms used any hired labor, it was in order to establish their basic economic equilibrium between demand satisfaction and drudgery of labor at a more favorable point, not necessarily in order to make a profit. Readers accustomed to the Western European and Anglo-American use of the term "family farm" to mean a family-run enterprise aiming to make a profit are, therefore, urged to note particularly that as used by Chayanov *the term "family farm" means a farm normally run by a family without hired outside wage labor.* Further details are given in the Glossary (p. 271).

# Chayanov's Message: Illuminations, Miscomprehensions, and the Contemporary "Development Theory"

By Teodor Shanin

The first English edition of *The Theory of Peasant Economy* made history. The reactions following its publication in 1966 were remarkably strong. The book has been quoted right, left, and center, by those who gave it considerable thought as much as by those who clearly received only a garbled version. The author was hailed by some as peasantry's new Marx, a hero-inventor of a radically new political economy. He was attacked with equal heat by the defenders of the intellectual old regimes. For a time Chayanov was high fashion but even when the swing of academic attention moved to new names and "fads" many of his book's questions, insights, and even terms (e.g., "self-exploitation") have remained as fundamental points of reference of the contemporary social sciences, economic and noneconomic. For that reason, the book made history also in the sense of acquiring a life of its own—an influence which shapes perception, focuses attention, defines plausibilities and modes of analysis, offers symbols, and often underlies political programs, national as well as international.

The 1966 introductions and glossary by Thorner, Kerblay, and Smith did a fine job and their retention in the second edition makes unneccessary here any further summation of Chayanov's career and of the book's content and preliminary criticisms. We shall focus this preface on the book's own life and its place in the intellectual history of the dramatic two decades which followed 1966 and the subsequent scholarly as well as political attempts to

Acknowledgment. The author is grateful for advice and help, direct and indirect, from Eduardo Archetti, Göran Djurfeldt, Harriet Friedmann, Barbara Harriss, John Harriss, Mark Harrison, Gavin Kitching, Shuichi Kojima, Harold Newby, Michael Redclift, and David Seddon.

come to grips with the so-called development theory. At the core lay the issue of general analytical approach and of attempts at conceptual retooling by the contemporary social sciences in the face of social reality which has proved most predictions consistently and dramatically wrong. This problem of theoretical inadequacies reflected in consistent failures of prediction and planned intervention has not gone away and, indeed, has since acquired new depth. Chayanov's theoretical contribution should be judged vis-à-vis experience and usage as well as in the face of the contemporary projections of the future, as a potentiality.

## Usage, Experience, Meaning

The book's "own life" meant necessarily that in encounter with its audiences the significance of its different elements varied from that attached to it by its author. Application centered mainly on the rural conditions within the contemporary "developing societies." The book was extensively used by analysts of different persuasions, countries, and academic disciplines. Its misconceptions were often as significant in effect as its illuminations. Despite the consequent variety there was a pattern to the ways Chayanov's insights and examples were perceived and selected for use.

The least utilized or accepted of Chayanov's main suggestions were his consumption-needs/drudgery ratio, relating the operation of family farms to family consumption, labor, and demographic (or biological) regularities. Put in a rigorously scientistic form and accordingly mathematized, it was not substantiated by most of the available data drawn from Russia of the early part of the century or else from the "developing societies" of today. Nor was it particularly illuminating in an analytical sense. The reasons were partly spelled out by Chayanov himself. His formulas assumed the easy availability of farming inputs other than labor, especially of land (to which complex equipment, fertilizers, and credit should be added nowadays). This had seldom been the case; indeed, it was decreasingly so. Also, the demographic determinants act relatively slowly compared with the current trends of social transformations. The growing complexity, heterogeneity, and changeability of contemporary agriculture and of the peasant ways to make ends meet would make this demographically related model very limited as against the factors which do not enter it: state policies and markets of goods and labor (by now worldwide), new agricultural techniques, the extravillage cartelization of supply, demand, and credit, or the social construction of new needs. What was to Chayanov "not the sole determinant" shrank to barely a determinant at all, at least in the short term.

It is not surprising therefore that the major case when the discussed formula was put to use (and bore interesting fruits) was in a study by a leading anthropologist of the past within the present, expressed in the "Stone Age Economics" of the gatherers and hunters.[1] A broadly parallel suggestion that Chayanov's needs/drudgery ratio may prove increasingly realistic as we proceed back along the history of rural Russia was indeed made by one of Chayanov's Marxist critics already in the 1920s.[2] Following similar logic, D. Thorner suggested a higher significance of Chayanov's "ratio" for the thinly populated areas while E. Archetti assumed it for parts of Africa when compared to other "developing societies" of today.

The general aspect of Chayanov's analysis which captured contemporary attention was the depiction of peasant family farms as an economic form which differs from capitalist farming even in an environment clearly dominated by capitalism (and cannot be treated as feudal or "semifeudal" simply because it is noncapitalist). The analytical approach suggested was to begin the consideration of peasant agriculture "from below," that is, from the operational logic of the family farms rather than from the national and international flows of resources, goods, and demands. Of the two parallel specifications explored by Chayanov's book, the interpretation broadly adopted from his analysis of the particular economic structure and logic of the contemporary family farms was not the demographic one (related to the needs/drudgery ratio, with a possible autarkic extension of it). It was the one which defined a particular peasant economy by the characteristics of family labor and the relative autonomy of its usage at the roots of peasant survival strategies which are systematically different from those of capitalist enterprises.[3] A diverse calculus of choices when

---

[1] S. Sahlin, *Stone Age Economics* (Chicago, 1972), chaps. 1–3. (The author disassociated himself, however, from the marginalist mode of Chayanov's explanation.)

[2] G. Meerson, *Semeino-trudovaya teoriya i differentsiatsiya krest'yanstva v rossii* (Moscow, 1926).

[3] Kerblay stresses rightly the particular significance given to this position by B. Brutskus, but Chayanov has adopted it as well (if less exclusively), and it was through his work that this approach spread into the contemporary literature.

production, land-renting, labor out-of-farm, etc. are concerned meant different patterns of operation of the farm enterprises as well as different extraeconomic corollaries and different outflows into the political economy at the national and international levels. Evidence drawn from "developing societies" substantiated this; indeed, there are difficulties in interpreting much of it in any other way. This evidence documented the capacity of peasants to out-compete the often well-capitalized farming enterprises based on wage labor, to buy out large landholders, and to offer goods at cheapest price. Peasant farms often work at a consistent nominally negative profit yet survive—an impossibility for capitalist farming. Maximization of total income rather than of profit or of marginal product guides in many cases the production and employment strategies of peasant family farms. And so on. The message is one of difference of operational logic, of output, and of outcome as well as of the possibility, at times, of actual retreat of the classical capitalist forms of production in face of family farming. Chayanov's work offered an anticipation and analytical illumination of all these. The growing awareness of the significance of underemployment and employment patterns in the development of the contemporary rural economies facilitated the explicit as well as implicit popularity of this dimension of Chayanov's work.

Two recent sets of studies exemplify the relevance of peasant farm particularities and their interpretation in the light of the dominant usage of family labor. Djurfeld, Taussig, Friedmann, and others have documented for different environments the tendency of agrobusiness to withdraw from the process of production in agriculture, focusing their profit-making activities on credit, supply of inputs, contracting, and selling, while leaving farming to the small holders and "skimming" them rather than replacing them.[4] Capitalist profit-accountancy prevailed over the capitalist form of production. Second, the recent studies of the paradoxical simultaneity of "critical shortage of labor" said officially to be endangering or even demolishing the agriculture of Egypt and of the parallel evidence of production figures directly contrary to it.[5] Once the data concerning capitalist farming are

---

[4] J. Harriss, ed., *Rural Development* (London, 1982). Also H. Friedmann, "World Market, State and Family Farm" in *Comparative Studies in Society and History* (1978), vol. 20. The contemporary spread of the "putting out" system outside agriculture broadened the conceptual issues involved.

[5] B. Hansen and S. Radwan, *Employment Opportunities and Equity in Egypt* (Geneva,

selected from that of the peasant sector the initial puzzle dissolves. It is the capitalist farming which folds up despite the efforts of its owners and the government's attempts to help them survive. The family farms use family labor flexibly, draw on unwaged neighbors' help, and give priority to "home" when deciding on the times of family members' departure to work elsewhere (e.g., the Gulf) or to return. In result, family farmers advance their global production as well as their share of land held and produce compared with the capitalist farmers-employers. It means not a crisis of the agriculture of Egypt but its peasantization. (Insofar as capitalism is defined by its classical formula as commodity production for profit based on the use of wage labor, it is decapitalization as well.) One can multiply such examples.

This may be the place to refer to two standard misreadings of Chayanov linked to the issue discussed. First, his "analysis from below"—that is, the building up of the understanding of the social economy which commences with the operational logic of family farms—has often been treated as a substitution of the psychological and the subjective for the deterministic and the economic. This is wrong, for the material and structural determinants involved in the relations of production and exchange shape and restrict choices, even though more flexibility of possible and adopted strategies was built into Chayanov's explanatory scheme. What results is a combined explanation of some complexity, but the more realistic for it. In general terms there is little particularly "chayanovian" to it for a combination of the "objective" and the "subjective" at the roots of human action has been assumed by a broad gamut of schools of thought (from Marx's "men make their own history, but they do not make it as they please, etc."[6] to the contemporary phenomenological studies of intersubjectivity). The point is that an alternative general view, cross-cutting major conceptual divisions, adopts a different position. Within diverse schools of thought it assumed an archmodel of human action the determination of which is extrasubjective only—a puppet theater model of humans in society, associated with philosophical positivism. This view is necessarily misleading if applied to Chayanov's explanatory scheme.

---

1982); and E. Taylor, "The Egyptian Agricultural Labour Shortage: A Crisis for Whom?" (Manchester, 1985).

[6] K. Marx and F. Engels, *Selected Works* (London, 1973), p. 398.

Next, Chayanov's term "self-exploitation" is often understood simply in its most direct sense of excruciating labor by underfed peasant families damaging their physical and mental selves for a return which is below that of the ordinary wages of labor power (equating it therefore with K. Kautsky's "underconsumption" and Lenin's rural "plunder of labor").[7] To Chayanov this is not the whole story for it must be read together with his concept of "differential optimums," that is, his conclusion that in the different agrarian regions and sub-branches of farming and at any given stage of technology, there are different optimal sizes of enterprise and that the decrease *as well as* increase from these will make productivity decline. To this the social context of peasant farming and especially the resulting availability of the family, kinsmen, and neighbors' aid and unwaged labor should be added. Family economy is to Chayanov not simply the survival of the weak through their impoverishment which serves super-profits elsewhere, but *also,* the utilization of some characteristics of farming and of rural social life which may occasionally give an edge to noncapitalist economies over capitalist forms of production in a capitalist world.[8] The continuity and relative wellbeing of family farmers under capitalism can be therefore postulated as a possibility while self-exploitation (and indeed exploitation) takes place, even though *no* conclusion about a *necessary* survival of such economic forms can be deduced or should be assumed within this line of thought.

To return to the utilization of Chayanov's insights in contemporary scholarship, the effect of Chayanov's general view of "post-Euclidian" economics, which assumes the plurality of simultaneously operating economic systems and the need to match it by multiplicity of conceptual schemes, was characteristically ambivalent. It corresponded with the work of the more imaginative economic historians of precapitalism, especially K. Polanyi,[9] but those who were ready to quote Chayanov as their authority on contem-

---

[7] K. Kautsky in *The Agrarian Problem* (London, in print), chaps. 2c and 6b; and the study of U.S. agriculture in V. I. Lenin, *Polnoe sobranie sochinenii* (Moscow, 1968), vol. 19, p. 343.

[8] It has been pointed out by M. Harrison that selective preference for productivity of the small units does not explain on its own why capitalists do not react simply by decentralization of units owned by them. The answer seems to lie in the combination of economic or social patterns and effects as discussed.

[9] K. Polyani, K. Arensberg, and H. W. Pearson, *Trade and Market in the Early Empires* (Glencoe, 1971).

porary rural economics usually treated it with more respect than application. Disciplinary languages and academic training tend to disregard the submerged assumptions on which they are based with the conclusions drawn taken to be either universally true or universally false. In turn, eyes trained to universalist analysis of an ever-true *homo economicus* or of epochs which are uniformly capitalist or uniformly feudal tend to miss the centerpiece of Chayanov's assumptions, namely, that family farms are coincident with other economic "systems," responding to and/or being penetrated and influenced by the dominant political economy without their particularity dissolved (indeed, remaining particular also in their response). The consequent issue is not only one of multiplicity of forms but also of what results from multiplicities of types of interdependence and of analytical categories engaged. Such a logic of composites was explored more recently in a debate between Marxists concerning the "articulation of modes of production," but it carried there a significantly sharper stress on the hierarchy of socioeconomic systems, on their domination and exploitation by each other (which Chayanov recognized but accentuated to a lesser degree). On the other hand, much of the "articulation" debate was caught in the deadly trap of "if not capitalist, then feudal" to peter out with little analytical consequence. An attempt to introduce the concept of a particular Peasant Mode of Production, also made then, was a direct if not very successful attempt to incorporate theoretically the particular logic of peasant economy inserted into a dominant political economy.[10]

Finally, Chayanov's practical program of agricultural transformation was made remarkable little of directly, considering the extent to which both its positive and its critical parts were validated by further experience. Once again Chayanov's views on these matters were often misunderstood (and at times rediscovered through experience and at considerable social cost, or else used while their authorship and background remained hidden.)

Chayanov's actual program for the advancement of Russian agriculture, presented fully in the book which followed *The Theory of Peasant Economy* consisted of three interdependent conceptual

---

[10] The concept of "mode of production" loses much of its heuristic power without the inbuilt assumption of the intramode class conflict at its core rather than on its frontiers. For further discussion see T. Shanin, "Defining Peasants," *Sociological Review* (1983); for a general debate see A. Foster-Carter, "The Modes of Production Debate," *New Left Review* (1978).

elements: rural cooperatives, differential optimums, and vertical cooperation.[11] The first adopted the experience of Europe, especially of Denmark at the turn of the century, while accentuating grass-roots democracy and a "peasants are not stupid," antipaternalist and antibureaucratic view. The second element has already been mentioned. The third one concluded with a suggestion for a flexible combination, cooperative in form, of different sizes of units of production for different branches of farming. It had also shown that, historically, while the concentration of landownership was insignificant, merchant capital penetrated and transformed peasant agriculture through "vertical capitalist concentration" taking over selectively its extraproduction elements and creaming off incomes (as in the U.S. context where 65 percent of farmers' income from sales was taken then by railways, banks, traders, etc.). This process, however, is not a necessity. With the power of capital weakened by peasantry's organizations, and/or state policies, and/or internal contradictions between the capitalists, a different type of "vertical concentration," which is cooperative and run by the peasants, can be established and even play a central role in the socialist transformation of society. Chayanov linked it to a powerful and remarkably realistic precritique of Stalin's type of collectivization, code-named "horizontal cooperation," which substitutes maximization for the optimization of the sizes of units and bureaucratization for the suggested management "from below." The predicted result of such a "horizontal" reform was the stagnation or decline of productivity of the agriculture. "Horizontal" cooperation combined with the "milking" of agriculture's resources for the sake of urban growth and the ordering about of peasants would prove as counterproductive as it would be antidemocratic. It would thus court peasant resistance or apathy and destroy the local store of irreplaceable agricultural knowledge and capacity for communal self-mobilization for which bureaucratic pressure from above would prove a poor substitute. Shortage of resources would then be supplemented by their wastage, exploitive hierarchies by new ones as pernicious but less competent.

The typical misreading, especially by those who quoted Chayanov at second hand, tended to interpret his program as a dream

---

[11] Reproduced in B. Kerblay, *Oeuvres Choisis de A. V. Chayanov* (Paris 1967), vol. 5. Touched upon in short in the last chapter of *The Theory of Peasant Economy*.

of archaic peasant bliss stretching into the future, a "peasantism" from which no practical prescription for modern agriculture and rural change can be drawn. In fact the idea of peasant "vertical cooperation" included the need for large units of agricultural production and their further extension as the farming technology advances. It even accepted the "Grain Factories" idea of the day, subject to the right technology. Outside his *Travels of My Brother Alexis* (a novella defined by him as "a peasant utopia"), there was no "small is beautiful" message in Chayanov, only a sharp objection to a "the larger, the necessarily more effective" assumption then prominent, and a functional suggestion for a combined development intended to "optimize" (following the agronomists best choice for any regional context of natural conditions and the available labor and technology) plus democratic decision-making "from below." A relatively slow pace of change can be deduced, related once again to the wish to "optimize" rather than to maximize and to the characteristics of agriculture as understood. Agrarian reformers of different persuasion have encountered and documented ever since the dangers of excessive speed and bureaucratic zest when the transformation of agriculture is involved.

The peak of Chayanov's analytical work came in the 1920s, between the ages of 32 and 42, which for Russia will be mostly remembered as the years of the NEP—the new economic program which followed the revolution, civil war, and the egalitarian redivision of all Russia's arable lands by its peasant communities. The main economic issues of the country were those of postwar recovery, industrialization, and increase of agricultural production, which in the conditions given meant the increase of agricultural productivity and partial transfer of the rural labor force into towns. The political context was one of a postrevolutionary state intertwined with a socialist city-bound party facing a massive peasantry organized in rejuvenated peasant communes, in which 85 percent of the country's population held more than 95 percent of its arable land. This political economy was spoken of as one of "state capitalism" and socialist control of the "commanding heights of the economy" within a population most of whom were "middle peasants." Prognostication and planning by the rural specialists of Russia was defined by considerations which with hindsight is often referred to as the issue of the Collectivization. Chayanov's treble alternative and his precritique are relevant to agriculture and ruralites quite unrelated to Russia or to postre-volutionary states with Marxists in charge, but it can be tested most substantively vis-à-vis the Collectivization debate and results.

The last twenty years have seen a considerable amount of soul-searching and policy change concerning collectivized agriculture but nowhere more than in Hungary.[12] They first followed the So-viet "horizontal" pattern and after the 1956 revolution reorga-nized and tried it out again. What resulted was a decline or stag-nation of agriculture and chronic shortages of food supplies (to which, before 1956, harsh repressions meted out to a resentful rural population should be added). Neither mechanization nor the deportation of "Kulaks" and the arrest of the "saboteurs," nor bureaucratic orders and campaigns solved the permanent agri-cultural crisis. Then the Hungarian leadership demonstrated the courage of retreat, made a clean sweep, and began in a totally new manner. Village-scale units were now combined with both multi-village and single family ones. Those deported from their villages were permitted to come back and often to direct cooperative pro-duction. External controls declined, compulsory sales were abol-ished, and "vertical" chains of mutually profitable production ar-rangements were set up and facilitated (e.g., a small holder buying fodder at a price satisfactory to him from the large-scale collective enterprise of which he is a member, to produce within his family unit meat which is then sold on a "free market" or under a contract). The agricultural results were dramatic, moving the country rapidly to the top of the European league where in-crease in agricultural production and incomes are concerned, not only resolving the problems of supplies but establishing Hungary as an exporter of food. The case of Hungarian agriculture and many other experiments with Collectivization, positive and nega-tive, in Europe as well as in Asia, Africa, and Latin America, acted as an important validation of Chayanov's suggestions for agricul-tural transformation, of his prognostication, and, up to a point, of his more general theoretical constructs and approaches. It was clearly not the issue of size or of collectivism or even of Collectiv-ization *per se* but of the actual form of rural transformation and new organization of production as well as the way it combines with peasants-versus-bureaucrats relations, flow of resources, and the

---

[12] N. Swain, *Collective Farms Which Work* (Cambridge, 1985).

substantive issues of farming (and its peculiarities as a branch of production). In the face of all these issues, Chayanov's and his friends' superb understanding of agriculture, combined with that of rural society, made them unique. This makes his major project—what he called Social Agronomy—pertinent still. It is not that, on the whole, those who succeeded or failed have studied him directly in Hungary or elsewhere.[13] Such lines are seldom clear. But they would (or will) benefit and could lessen some pains if they would (or will) do so. The fact that this part of Chayanov's intellectual heritage is seldom considered or admitted has to do not with its content but with the nature of current ideological constraints to which we shall return.

We still know much too little about Chayanov's most direct topic of concern: the Russian countryside in the face of Stalin's Collectivization. We do know that contrary to the ideological myth to follow, it was not a natural deduction from Marxism or from Lenin but a fairly arbitrary result of the 1926–28 failure of rural policies and of interparty factional struggle.[14] It was outstandingly destructive of resources and humans, facilitated the brutalization of the country's political system and contributed to the current inadequacies of Soviet agriculture and arguably to a demographic crisis and industrial slow-down of the last decades. The first post-Stalin steps of the Soviet studies of Collectivization, relevant once again to the last two decades or so, indicated clearly that the flourishing of TOZ, that is, the self-help teams at its beginning ("vertical" rather than "horizontal" in its implications), was effective and actually well supported by much of the Russian peasant population.[15] It was the decision of "the Center" to sweep aside practically overnight the TOZ as well as the socialist communes and

---

[13] The Hungarian scholarship had its own tradition of peasant studies represented also on its Marxist wing especially by the works of I. Markus. Its views were condemned by the Soviet-like collectivizers as anti-Marxist but eventually won the day and were expressed in the country's third (and successful) collectivization. The impact of the implicit cross-influences cannot be ascertained but the views of Chayanov and his friends spread fairly broadly through Europe and Asia via the German professional literature of the 1920s.

[14] S. M. Lewin, *Russian Peasants and Soviet Power* (London, 1968). See also R. W. Davies, *The Soviet Collective Farm, 1929–1930* (London, 1980). The frequent use of Lenin's 1923 article "On Cooperation" to legitimate the 1929–39 Collectivization is an open falsehood. The article does not focus on production cooperatives.

[15] For example, see the item *Kolectivizatsiya* in *Sovetskaya istoricheskaya entsiklopediya* (Moscow, 1961), and also M. Vyltsan, V. Danilo, V. Kabanov, and Yu. Moshkov, *Kolektivisatsiva sel'skogo khozyaistva v SSSR* (Moscow, 1982), especially chaps. 1–3.

every other regionally specific form of rural cooperation stemming from local initiative,[16] and to impose the one and only form of a village-size Kolkhoz directed from above, which defined the destructive trend of the 1930s.[17]

## Methods and Labels

As stated, the misconceptions of Chayanov often played as important a conceptual role as the views he actually offered, and we have referred to a few of them. Two more, general in scope, will be considered to round out the picture: the status of conceptual models in Chayanov works and his "neo-populist" designation.

At the center of Chayanov's method of theoretical analysis, indeed, what made him the leading theorist of his generation, lie systematic exploration of alternative models and typologies. Abstraction and purposeful simplification are systematically used to define and test causal links. As is usual when theoretical models are concerned, purposeful simplification means the overstatement of some characteristics. The totally nonwaged family farm and the eight pure "economic systems" presented in the translation, find their farther equivalents in his *Experiments in the Study of an Isolated State, the Nomographic Elements of Economic Geography,* and even in his "science fiction": *The Travels of My Brother Alexis* and the 1928 discussion of "farming in a bottle" of the future scientific production of foodstuffs.[18] Chayanov's mastery and extensive use of Russian empirical evidence (and its wealth for the rural scene of the day), as well as his pronounced practical interests as an agricultural reformer, make many of his cursory readers miss the fact that his was an endless and highly imaginative experimentation with logic of analysis as a way to order the complexity of data in his grasp. He did not lack positive views of his own, made them clear, and can be criticized for them as well as for the

---

[16] Since the civil war there were a number of Socialist Communes which came to be considered "too collectivized" and dismantled in 1929–33 to provide for the homogeneity of the rural organization of production. There was also in 1928–30 some talk of gigantic-size Kolkhoz, but nothing came out of it.

[17] See footnote 14. The productive successes during the last two decades of the family plots and of the experiments with the *zveno* system of multifamily units (autonomous within a general kolkhoz system) in the Soviet Union and its current version under Gorbachev offer an interesting reference to the issue of "optimums" today.

[18] Kerblay, op. cit. As in the case of *Travels with My Brother Alexis*, this was also defined as "utopia," but this time a "scientific-technical" one.

methods he used to arrive at conclusions. This has been done by many, including the book's first editors and myself.[19] But Chayanov must be treated on his own terms, that is, with understanding of the way his mode of exploration and actual conclusion differed from each other. This is why it is unhelpful and often plainly ridiculous to express surprise or dismay at Chayanov's disregard of market relations, wage labor, or capital investment in the rural context. This "disregard" is a method, an analytical suspension used to explore causal links through the media of a conceptual model (which can be useful or less so). As to the issue of a conceptual model's realism, that is, its match with reality, it is important but provides only one element of theoretical thought. Chayanov experimented with a unicausal demographic model, with a bicausal model of agricultural development defined by population density and market relations intensity, and so on. Chayanov was also one of the leaders of the field of factual studies of market relations, monetarization, and wage labor, and was remarkably realistic when the day-to-day life of the Russian peasantry was concerned.[20] Recent studies by Soviet and other scholars have indeed shown that he was right as to the low commodity production and very low use of wage labor in rural Russian 1900–14 and 1921–28.[21]

Every model is selective, and Chayanov made his own choices on what to focus his attention and which causal links to "bracket" or deaccentuate. These were relevant, of course, to his views as well as to his conclusions. For example, Chayanov stated in a 1927 debate that he was only then beginning his own studies of peasantry's socioeconomic differentiation.[22] Considering what we know now about the relatively low class polarization of rural Russia of 1912 and 1921–28, the focusing of attention on the rural cooperation and optimal use of labor made good sense to a leader of a trend committed to the advance of what was called Social Agronomy. But it limited the grasp of the exploitive potentials of simple cooperation, state/peasants interaction, and some other is-

---

[19] In a section devoted to "biological determinism" in *The Awkward Class* (Oxford, 1972).

[20] For example, his detailed Budget Study of the family farms in the district *(uezd)* of Starobel'sk in Kerblay, op. cit., vol. 2.

[21] See A. M. Anfimov, *Krest'yanskoe khozyaistvo evropeiskoi Rossii* (Moscow, 1980); V. P. Danilov, *Sovetskaya dokolkhoznaya derevnya* (Moscow, 1979), vol. 2; T. Shanin, *Russia as a "Developing Society"* (New Haven, 1975).

[22] In a debate conducted by *Puti sel'skogo khozyaistva* (1927), nos. 4–9.

sues. (In parallel, the work by his major critic Kritzman and his assistants, who adopted from the young Lenin the model of peasantry's necessary polarization, overstated heavily their concern, arguably offering inducement to Stalin-type collectivization without sufficient awareness of its agrarian dimension and potential social pitfalls.) To recollect, one can criticize Chayanov for his priorities, or better still, consider their impact on his conclusions, but it is epistemologically naive to treat him as naive, blind to evidence, or overwhelmed by the ideological aberrations of "peasantism."

The positioning of Chayanov within an ideological context and vis-à-vis analytical and ideological taxonomies suffered mostly from two miscomprehensions. The first was less prominent, less significant, and less literate, resulting from limited knowledge of Chayanov's background, his range of publication, and from only cursory reading of Thorner and Kerblay's efforts to present its picture. It assumed Chayanov's singularity in inventing "chayanovism." The other classified him as a *Neo Populist* and derived his main characteristics from it.

The splendid tradition of Russian rural studies was rooted in the regional authorities' (*Zemstvo*'s) 1860s to 1917 effort that was introduced mostly by enlightened nobles and their employees within the "rural intelligentsia" to take account of and to improve the livelihood of the plebian populations in their charge, which was mostly rural and peasant.[23] Those studies reached maturity in late 1880 to 1906 (when Chayanov was being born or in school) to revive again after a failed revolution in 1909–14 (Chayanov began then, in 1912 at the age of 23, his spectacular public career.) As part of it, the conceptual family-farm focus can be traced back to A. Vasil'chakov's book of 1881, the Budget Studies development and initial usage to F. Shcherbina in the late 1890s, the Dynamic ("cohort") Studies to N. Chernenkov at the very beginning of the century, and the direct antecedents of Chayanov's assumption of structurally specific peasant economics to V. Kosinskii's book published in 1906. The expression "economics" is somewhat misleading, in fact, as was the usual occupational designation of most of those involved as "rural statisticians of the *Zemstvo*." What evolved were peasantry-focused social sciences in

---

[23] The best English source for coverage of those events is still G. T. Robinson, *Rural Russia under the Old Regime* (New York, 1949).

their broader sense, merging the contemporary Western disciplines of economics, history, anthropology, ethnography, sociology, demography, public medicine, agronomy, and ecology. Chayanov's originality is not in question. But his significance lay to a considerable degree in abilities of synthesis and presentation. In the best style of Russian intelligentsia he was a very literate man: well read, fluent in a number of foreign languages, skillful in his analytical presentation, and besides an author of essays, five romantic novellas à la Hoffman, a guide to West European drawing, a local history of Moscow and a book of poetry.[24]

The description of Chayanov's work and of the views shared by the so-called Organization and Production School as neopopulist, especially when used as a synonym of programmatic "peasantism" idealizing or hoping for a future peasant universe, is badly informed and misleading. A multistage miscomprehension is involved concerning populism, neopopulism, and Chayanov himself.

First, a few bothered to work out the actual characteristics of Russian populism over and above its descriptions by political foes (especially Lenin's attack on the SRs, which taken out of context, served its readers ill).[25] Russia's original socialism-for-developing-societies and its remarkable contemporaneous message which raised for the first time the issues of *Uneven Development, State Capitalism,* party *Cadres,* or *Social Ecology* is often being reduced to rural sentimentality. That it was they who created the first Russian socialist party of revolutionary type, its first urban Trade Unions and workers press, or that their Geneva branch permanent delegate to the General Council of the International was a man called Karl Marx, are simply left out of sight. The next stage in miscomprehension, the latter-day impact of populism—that is of its main theorists like Hertzen and Chernyshevskii and strategists like Zhelyabov or Kibal'chich of the Peoples Will—is treated as if it could

---

[24] Practically unknown, these novellas were recently published in Russian by Russica Publishers in the United States as A. Chayanov, *Istoriya Parikmakherskoi Kukly i Drugie sochineniya Botanika X* (New York, 1982). An introduction by L. Chertkov offers insightful commentary on Chayanov's literary career, but in reference to his economics repeats some of the mistaken assumptions of his Soviet critics.

[25] For discussion see T. Shanin, *Russia 1905–7: Revolution as a Moment of Truth* (New Haven, 1985). For studies available in English of the Russian Populism and its most manifest followers, the SRs' party (the PSR), see F. Venturi, *Roots of Revolution* (London, 1960); I. Berlin, *Russian Thinkers* (Harmondsworth, 1979); and A. Walicki, *The Controversy over Capitalism* (Oxford, 1969).

be disassociated from the rest of Russian intellectual history. To exemplify, Lenin's *What Is To Be Done?* manifestly modeled in context and in name on Chernyshevskii and the Peoples Will loses its intellectual roots becoming in turn a self-generated invention of a singular genius. The general interdependence of effects, the mutuality of borrowings, and the capacity to learn are "streamlined" to appear as a set of dogmatisms, eternally diverse and absolutely pure (and totally right or totally wrong, of course). Chayanov, being neither "a Marxist" nor a good bourgeois, must be assigned to one of the intellectual chains. A game for those not overburdened by knowledge of the actual context of Russian history asserts itself then, a world divided into "us" versus "them," while everything else is put into a leftover category of Populism due to trigger off images of sitting on the fence, sentimental attachment to obsolete archaism, utopian dreams, and manure. As to Chayanov, the easiest way not to dismiss outright his genius nor to surrender him to one's direct ideological enemies is to define him as a Populist (with a prefix "Neo" added for the benefit of those prone to point out that his views differed substantively from those of the main theorists of Russian Populism and from those who were defined in his generation as their most direct heirs be it Chernov, Aksentev, or Gershuni). Chayanov took his cues from the declared Marxists V. Kosinskii, V. Groman, and I. Gurevich (I must disagree here with Thorner, it was Gurevich who first suggested "demographic differentiation"), from the liberals N. Chernenkov and F. Shcherbina, as well as from the *bone fide* SR populist P. Vikhlyaev. His methods and conclusions paralleled in many ways those of the Bolshevik Central Committee member of 1905–7 P. Rumyantsev and later work of similar persuasion by A. Khryashcheva. His tolerance of different ideas was known; in the 1920s he helped the careers of N. Kondratiev, the brilliant pioneer of the studies of global economic systems, as well as of the Marxist "young Turks" like V. Anisimov. He also often disagreed with those of his own "school," for example, A. Chelintsev, but proceeded to work closely with them. There is no way to define his possible guilt by heritage or association.

The only way to resolve the question of Chayanov's populism is to consider his actual views vis-à-vis the contemporary Russian Populists' main articles of faith concerning rural Russia. He did not accept the view of some right-wing populists in the 1890s that capitalism must fail to establish itself in poverty-ridden rural Russia. He did not adopt the most significant proposition-cum-program of Populism's left wing in 1906–22, the PSR, to turn peasant communes in control of all available land into the core structure of postrevolutionary rural Russia. He shared with the Russian Populists, but not only with them, the wish to have Russia transformed along lines which would see autocracy abolished and democracy established (with much peasant coloring to it in a population which was 85 percent peasants). The idea of "service to the people" by the Russian intelligentsia was also "populist," but by this time, not only so. Chayanov's political party animus was low. In the dramatic year of 1917 he was closest to the Popular Socialists, a mildly populist, markedly academic party of little following. Throughout his life he was to stay the nonparty Muscovite intellectual at his best: erudite, hardworking, broadminded, and deeply committed to humanitarian causes, scholarship, and aesthetics. This approach and those capacities were met in the 1920s by a remarkable laxity toward him by the authorities (said to be ordered by Lenin himself).[26] It was to cost him his life in the decade to follow and to end with his posthumous "rehabilitation" for what it was worth.

As to their goals and predictions, Bolsheviks, SRs, and Chayanov shared hostility to rural capitalism, especially in its extra-production forms (the "Kulaks"). In common with the SRs Chayanov believed more in peasants undifferentiated socioeconomic advance or decline ("agregate shifts") versus capitalist and/or state capitalist economy than in the significance of interpeasant polarization processes. He was attacked because of that by many of the Russian "orthodox Marxists," but some other "orthodox" Marxists, for example, Kautsky, were far from sure on that score.[27] So were some of the Bolsheviks.[28] Chayanov's distrust of the "large is beautiful" proposition accepted then by most adherents of Progress did not relate this to a peasantist dream à la Proudhon; in the hungry Moscow of War Communism he depicted a small-holder's universe in a text described as "utopia" (and a peasant one at

---

[26] Chertkov speaks of Lenin's order in 1921 to let Chayanov be "because we need wise heads, we are left with too few of them" (Chayanov, op. cit., pp. 23–25). The extensive publication of Chayanov's works, even then highly controversial, and his frequent travels to Europe in the 1920s substantiate the assumption of particular tolerance displayed toward him in those days.

[27] See K. Kautsky, op. cit., chaps. 7, 9, and 10.

[28] For N. Bucharin's place in this debate see M. Harrison in Harriss, op. cit.

that), but suggested something very different in concluding chapter of the book he called in 1925 The *Theory* of Peasant Economy. One should best take as true Chayanov's own explanation of his views as rooted in study of Russian agriculture of which he had so superb a knowledge. On balance Chayanov was being defined as neopopulist mostly by default, a shorthand description which hides more than it reveals.

Why then the persistence of the neither-us-nor-them neopopulist designation in our own times? The reason lies in the ideological confrontations of our own generation to which the already discussed reductionism should be added. The admirers of Green Revolution who believe in its antisocialist potentials often interpreted the "from below" approach as "let it be as it is" for "those above" and then used "peasantism" as a handy ideological device to forget the agrobusiness. Once one moves from the form to substance Chayanov is unacceptable to them: he is sharply anticapitalist, with no trust in "free market" processes, and devoted to the cooperatives' warfare against the "entrepreneurs." Moreover he was clearly loyal to the Russian postrevolutionary state, refused to emigrate, and even prospered temporarily in his career under the new regime. For the orthodox Marxists of the "developing societies" his method of analysis was equally unacceptable for it challenged head on Lenin's 1899 study which had acquired the status of supramodel as to what peasant society is and/or is becoming. (Kautsky's position, definitely "orthodox" and legitimated by Lenin's admiring references, yet in no necessary contradistinction with Chayanov's view of peasant economy's possible survival under capitalism, is still barely known.) But the crux of the "need" to define Chayanov as Neo-Populist lay there in the very assumption of one and only finite Marxism. As to Chayanov, he was neither "a Marxist" nor a rich farmers lover, but neither was he simply a Populist thereby. He learned from many sources but stayed his own man.

Why then did not Chayanov become a contemporary guru, a patron saint of a new sect of admirers who would use his books to enforce and validate their own separateness and ideological purity? He has been quoted admiringly but nobody has claimed his mantle while those called Neo-Populists have usually disclaimed such designation. The answer lies partly in the ideological dualizations described above but it was caused also by a fundamental limitation of Chayanov's mode of analysis, itself explicable in terms of the experience available when he wrote as against that of our own time. The most significant of the social transformations of the twentieth century was the advancing integration of increasingly complex social forms. Rural society and rural problems are inexplicable any longer only in their own terms and must be understood in terms of labor and capital flows which are broader than agriculture. To understand the diversity of the results of Collectivization one must look at the countryside *as well as* at industry and at the political elite. And so on. Chayanov's analysis "from below" is incomplete not only because its author was precluded from its completion. It cannot be completed by simply proceeding along the same road. Not accidentally it was his most exclusively family-centered model, the demographic one, which first fell into disuse. The only way to handle effectively contemporary social reality is through models and theories in which peasant family farms do not operate separately and where peasant economy does not merely accompany other economic forms but is inserted into and usually subsumed under a dominant political economy, different in type. Also peasant economies are being transformed (or even reestablished) mostly by "external" intervention, especially by the state and the multinational companies, intervention which outpaced by far Chayanov's experience as well as his theoretical schemes. This makes combined "from above" and "from below" models necessary for further exploratory advance. In this, Chayanov's analysis did play a major but restricted role. Some of his views were clearly mistaken (and invalidated by further evidence), but in the main his weakness lies in an analysis which was not incorrect but insufficient. For the increasingly complex rural world of today it has clear limits, hence, no "chayanovism" but there are many of Chayanov's illuminating insights, explicit and implicit, in the contemporary rural studies.

## Historiography and Future

At its 1966 beginnings the effect of Chayanov's book's first English edition was the direct result of a major crisis, of what was called the Third World and of its conceptualization within the Modernization Theory and its political corollaries, conclusions, and predictions.[29] The post–World War II rapid decolonization, the Cold War, and the expanding U.N. as a focus of new hopes, have redrawn maps as well as redefined and dramatized the problem of world inequality between "The West" and what was then called "the Backward Nations." This global gap between states and societies became a fundamental issue of the day. A new terminology was coming into being representing new concerns. The *global gap* was part of it. The confrontation of the "world" led by the United States with the one led by the Soviet Union (extending its impact to the native revolutionaries elsewhere) made the issues of the *development* in the *Third World* into a matter of utmost political urgency. Fortunately the solution seemed at hand—*a take off* into the *self-sustained economic growth* along the lines tried out by the forerunners of industrialization.[30] Western-style parliaments, markets, ideas, and education plus some aid or loans and investments were to facilitate it all. An assumed natural law of social equilibrium was to secure international equalization, stability, and homogeneity (the larger the discrepancy the more powerful its tendency for self-eradication).[31] Rationalization embodied in science was to help it along for it is seemingly faster to import experts and expertise than to produce them first hand. The assumedly inevitable Progress was to close the First/Third worlds gap, to eradicate poverty and to keep revolutionaries at bay.

By the turn of the 1950s the optimistic assumptions were proving shockingly wrong. The "gap" was increasing. Pauperization advanced through most of the Third World. Postcolonial independence, economic spontaneity of local and international markets, literacy campaigns, and charitable aid did not resolve "the problems of development." The West and especially its slow-to-take-the-hint colonizers and budding neocolonizers clearly faced situations no longer describable as riots of despair but massive popular wars and coalitions between resentful governments of the "backward" nations: the Algerian war and the Bandung Conference of the Nonaligned Nations, Congo, Vietnam, and a new UNESCO majority. On the intellectual scene Paul Baran, Gunnar Myrdal, and Paul Prebish savaged the Modernization Theory pre-

---

[29] For further discussion see H. Alavi and T. Shanin, *Introduction to Sociology of the "Developing Societies"* (London: 1982).

[30] W. W. Rostow, *Process of Economic Growth* (London, 1962).

[31] A position advanced by the Functionalist School in sociology and by the simpler versions of Neoclassical economics particularly influential in the 1950s.

scriptions and methods.[32] Against the old registers of correlates and determinants of *economic growth* came the new pessimism of focusing at the *bottlenecks* explaining the growing gap in a catchy phrase which swept the world—*the development of underdevelopment*.[33] This was increasingly defined by the international dependency of the peripheries on the exploitative metropolitan centers. It was also defined intranationally by dependent plebeian populations which were structurally marginalized and excluded from the benefit of modernity—nowadays often called *the subaltern classes*. This conceptual box was increasingly being filled by peasants—the large majority of the population of the *developing societies* (the "backward nations" of yesterday). But peasants appeared now not only as victims or an object of development. The dramatic impression of the victory of Mao's peasantry revolutionary army was spreading and being reinforced by guerrillas all through the Third World. Also, the peasantry was increasingly being seen as a potential political actor—a subject of history. In the 1960s they came to spell new hopes of sweeping away oligarchy in Latin America, outfacing an imperial army in Vietnam, helping to balance failures of industrialization or of the egalitarian program attached to the Green Revolution.

Chayanov's emergence into the English-speaking world coincided with a dramatic "face to the peasants" realignment of attention which took place in the 1960s. The World Bank officials and Marxist revolutionaries, politicians and scholars, not forgetting the committed student masses, rapidly turned peasantologists. From a piece of anthropological exotica, peasants have moved into the center of debate about the most significant contemporary issues. Overnight the discussion of peasantry in books, theses, and programs has shot up from next to none to hundreds and then thousands of items. The very word "peasant" became "hot" and "with it"; like sex and crime it was by now selling manuscripts to publishers and books to readers. The trouble was that this academic avalanche was theoretically very thin. The freshly collected "facts" about peasants, mostly localized, and the speculations

---

[32] P. Baran, *The Political Economy of Growth* (New York, 1957); and G. Myrdal, *Economic Theory and Underdeveloped Regions*. The work of P. Prebish became known in the 1950s mostly through the Reports of UN ECLA he directed.

[33] Introduced by A. G. Frank, *Capitalism and Underdevelopment in Latin America* (New York, 1969), to become for a moment arguably the most read book on theory of development.

about them, mostly very grand and abstract, found themselves like Pirandello characters searching for a conceptual framework which could relate and transform them into a branch of systematic knowledge. Of the available older writings of relevance only Lenin and Redfield could be put to partial use,[34] while the more contemporary efforts to make theoretical sense of the peasants were only then beginning to come through.[35] Chayanov's 1966 book entered this void (together with Marx's *Grundrisse* presented first in English by Hobsbawm in 1964, and a more conventional economics text by Schultz published in the same year).[36] The richness of the data and the sophistication of the methodology put forward by Chayanov, the contemporaneity of his concerns, and his broad theoretical sweep took the breath away from scores of peasantology beginners. Some declared allegiance, more used it to cut their teeth defending or reestablishing the orthodoxies of old, but the most numerous utilized Chayanov's evidence and insights in their own analyses and schemes concerning peasants the world over.

It would seem that the very positioning of Chayanov as "the man who knew about peasants" or his more literate designation as a social scientist who helped us see better the analysis of family farming as a particular form or element of economy should lead to the gradual decline of his significance in the future. Peasants still form a major part of mankind but their numbers are stationary while their share in the population of the "developing societies" is rapidly in decline. They are also being "incorporated" while the livelihoods of those who survive as rural small holders increasingly include what has been considered as "nonpeasant" characteristics. A decline in the significance and the particularity of peasantries leading to a parallel depeasantation of the social sciences can be predicted, with Chayanov assigned eventually to the archives. Or is it?

---

[34] Translations of V. I. Lenin, *Development of Capitalism in Russia* (Initially 1899) were particularly well known and used by the Marxists as the archmodel of analysis and of conclusions concerning peasantry's demise. R. Redfield, *Peasant Society* (Chicago, 1956), offered the usual starting point for many U.S. anthropologists.

[35] E. R. Wolf, *Peasants* (New York, 1966); T. Shanin, *Peasants and Peasant Societies* (Harmondsworth, 1971); and B. Galeski, *Basic Concepts of Rural Sociology* (Manchester, 1972). Two early journals specifically devoted to peasantry began publication in the early 1970s in the United States and the United Kingdom: *Journal of Peasant Studies* and *Peasant Studies*.

[36] K. Marx, *Pre-Capitalist Economic Formations* (London, 1964); and T. W. Schultz, *Transforming the Traditional Agriculture* (New Haven, 1964).

The crisis of the 1960s has not been resolved but has actually broadened in its substance and its implications. The predicament of the Third World, made morally unacceptable and politically dangerous by the way the better-off have prospered, extended into a socioeconomic crisis which includes "us." Massive structural unemployment at the lower pole of the First World has grown sharply and is increasingly being recognized as irreversible. A crisis of the Second World, both economic and moral, is visible and self-admitted, diminishing its ability to offer alternatives—the impact of a major model and determinant of development in the past generations is declining. All through the 1980s a parallel crisis of capitalism and of its actually existing alternatives has been growing, economically and politically but also conceptually; we face a reality we decreasingly know how to extrapolate or to grasp.

A central element of contemporary global society is the failure of the capitalist economies as well as of state economies to advance unlimitedly and to secure general welfare in ways expected by the nineteenth-century theories of progress, liberal and socialist alike. Control and extent of profits by capitalist multinational companies is advancing side-by-side with the retreat of standard capitalist forms of production and of social organization linked to the extension of unemployment and "underemployment," of "informal economies," and other networks of survival. Sluggish state economies are intertwined with the massive "second" and "third" (or "black") economies, increasingly recognized as irreducible. While in the "developing societies" islands of precapitalism disappear, what comes instead is mostly not the industrial proletariat of Europe's nineteenth century but strata of plebian survivors—a mixture of increasingly mobile, half-employed slum-dwellers, part-farmers, lumpen-traders, or pimps—another extracapitalist pattern of social and economic existence under capitalism and/or third-worldish types of state economy. The populations involved in the informal and/or family-bound and/or "black" and/or mixed economies are growing around the globe and one cannot understand without reference to this either the way national economies work or the way people actually live. While exploitive relations are preserved and enhanced, the functional organization of economy changes, extending rather than concealing those elements of it which call for modes of analysis alternative to those ordinarily in use. By now a new "green" radicalism has begun increasingly to respond politically to these experiences, new exploitative patterns, and conceptual insights. Theoretically the analysis of modes of incorporation by a dominant political economy is in increasing need of being supplemented by the parallel study of modes of nonincorporation operating in the worlds we live in.

It is against this context that Chayanov's analysis of alternative and complimentary economies, of family labor, of the nonmonetarized calculus of choices and of patterns of physical production (rather than their prices only) of differential optimums, of modes, and of utilities of cooperation—an analysis "from below" attempting to relate structure to choice—will have to find its future possible echo and uses. So will the method of exploring models of alternative realities and rationales. In fact there are still hundreds of millions of peasants and as many may exist in the year 2000 but, paradoxically, Chayanov's fundamental methods and insights may prove particularly enriching for worlds of fewer peasants as well as of fewer "classical" industrial proletarians while the subject of his actual concern, the Russian peasantry, has all but disappeared. In no way would future theorizing be a simple replication of Chayanov, but it might carry important elements of his achievements and that of the Russian rural analysis of 1880s–1928 as part of the body of new development theories aiming to understand more realistically our environments and to improve future worlds. Which will make a good epitaph for a memorial of a great scholar when his countrymen remember to build him one.

# Chayanov's Concept of Peasant Economy

By Daniel Thorner

Most of those who are today seeking to understand the economic behavior of the peasantry seem to be unaware that they are traversing much the same ground trod from the 1860's onward by several generations of Russian economists. The problems that are today plaguing economists in countries like Brazil, Mexico, Turkey, Nigeria, India, and Indonesia bear striking similarities to those that were the order of the day in Russia from the emancipation of the serfs in 1861 down to the collectivization of agriculture at the end of the 1920's, to wit:

How to transform traditional rural society so as to overcome the misery, squalor, and illiteracy of the peasantry;
How to get the peasants to modernize their agriculture, especially their farming technique;
How to carry out this transformation and modernization so as to permit—indeed, to facilitate—the development of the entire national economy.

One of the first methods young Russian idealists tried for dealing with these problems was direct action. Hundreds upon hundreds of college students, doctors, nurses, university teachers—including economists and statisticians—quit their urban life and attempted to "go to the people." Establishing themselves in villages, they tried to be of use to the peasantry, to get them into motion; revolutionaries among these idealists preached the virtues of socialism. The police smoked them out and rounded them up, sometimes tipped off by the peasants themselves, suspicious of outsiders from other orders of society.

Chastened by their experiences, many of these action-oriented intellectuals deemed it wise, before undertaking further adventures in rural philanthropy, to obtain a more precise knowledge of village realities. Scores of them offered their services when in the 1870's the new provincial and district assemblies, the zemstvos—set up to help implement the land reforms of 1861—launched a vast program of economic and statistical investigation into peasant economic problems. It would be difficult to exaggerate the value of these field inquiries, which continued through four decades down to World War I. In sheer bulk, they add up to more than 4,000 volumes. These constitute perhaps the most ample single source of data we have on the peasant economy of any country in modern times.

More significant than the quantity is the quality of these data. From the outset, the field investigators included some of the ablest men of the day. Sympathetic to the peasantry and anxious to gain insight into their problems, they were determined to carry out their inquiries with utmost thoroughness. In presenting their results, they took great pains to choose suitable categories and to design statistical tables so as to bring out clearly the basic relations among the various economic and social groups in the villages. Some of their reports were so striking that in 1890 the government passed a law forbidding any further inquiries into landlord–peasant relations, but, nonetheless, the work went on.

In the decades from 1880 onward, Russia's leading economists, statisticians, sociologists, and agricultural experts assessed, analyzed, and fought over the materials furnished by the successive zemstvo inquiries. Their articles and books provide the richest analytical literature we have on the peasant economy of any country in the period since the Industrial Revolution. Among the Russian scholars who participated in the debate over the zemstvo statistics, N. A. Kablukov, V. A. Kosinskii, A. N. Chelintsev, N. P. Makarov, and G. A. Studenskii stand out for their attempts to formulate a theory of peasant economy. Alexander Vasilevich Chayanov, from 1919 to 1930 the leading Russian authority on the economics of agriculture, synthesized the theoretical ideas of his predecessors and contemporaries, and developed them along original lines. Translations into English of two studies by Chayanov form the core of the present volume.

The first and by far the larger of these works is Chayanov's masterpiece, *Organizatsiya krest'yanskogo khozyaistva*, the title of which may be rendered in English as *Peasant Farm Organization*. It provides a theory of peasant behavior at the level of the individual family farm, i.e., at the micro level. The second, much shorter study—"Zur Frage einer Theorie der nichtkapitalistischen Wirtschaftssysteme,"[1] which may be translated as "On the Theory of Non-Capitalist Economic Systems"—sets forth the proposition that at the national, or macro, level, peasant economy ought to be treated as an economic system in its own right, as a noncapitalist system of national econ-

---

[1] *Archiv für Sozialwissenschaft und Sozialpolitik*, Vol. 51 (1924), part 3, pp. 577–613.

omy. The brief remarks that follow will be concerned chiefly with Chayanov's theory of the peasant farm, his micro theory, which Constantin von Dietze has termed the most noteworthy creative synthesis so far achieved in this field down to the present day.[2]

### Chayanov's Theory of the Peasant Farm

The sure and certain way to misunderstand the peasant family farm, Chayanov held, was to view it as a business, that is to say, an enterprise of a capitalistic sort. To him, the essential characteristic of business firms or capitalistic enterprises was that they operated with hired workers in order to earn profits. By contrast, peasant family farms, as Chayanov defined them, normally employed no hired wage labor—none whatsoever. His family farms were pure in the sense that they depended solely on the work of their own family members.

Chayanov's definition of the family farm may surprise us by its narrowness when compared with the much wider usage of the term in recent decades.[3] Present-day economists familiar with model building might assume that for his purpose Chayanov framed a special model or ideal type. In fact, Chayanov considered his category a real one drawn from life. He contended that 90 percent or more of the farms in Russia in the first quarter of the twentieth century had no hired laborers, that they were family farms in the full sense of his definition. In so far as his contention was correct, his model was far from being "ideal"; quite the contrary, it stood for the most typical farm in what was then the largest peasant country in the world.

From this starting point, Chayanov proceeded to challenge head on the validity of standard economics for the task of analyzing the economic behavior of peasant farms that relied on family labor only. The prevailing concepts and doctrines of classical and neoclassical economics, he wrote, had been developed to explain the behavior of capitalistic entrepreneurs and business undertakings in which hired hands worked for wages. The economic theory of the behavior of such firms turned on the quantitative interrelationship of wages (of labor), interest (on capital), rent (for land), and profits (of enterprise). To find out whether a given business firm was making a *profit*, it was necessary to set down the value of gross annual output, deduct outlays

---

[2] C. von Dietze, "Peasantry," in *Encyclopaedia of the Social Sciences*, Vol. XII (1934), p. 52; and personal communication from Professor von Dietze, Summer, 1964.

[3] The term family farm is sometimes even used for capitalistic enterprises producing essentially for export, as long as these are family-operated.

for *wages*, materials, upkeep, or replacement of capital and other usual expenses, including *rent*, and then compare the sum left over with the *interest* that might be earned at prevailing rates on the total fixed and circulating capital. These four factors—wages, interest, rent, and profits—operated in close functional interdependence and were reciprocally determined. The moment one of the four factors was absent, it became impossible to establish just what was to be included in each of the remaining three; hence there was no way of determining their magnitudes. Take away any one of the four factors, Chayanov argued, and the whole theoretical structure went awry, like a cart that has lost one wheel. This was precisely what happened, according to Chayanov, when economists tried to apply the analysis in terms of wages, profit, rent, and interest to peasant family farms.

Since peasant family farms had no hired labor, they paid no wages. Accordingly, the economic category "wages" was devoid of content and the economic theory of wages irrelevant to family activity. Carrying the argument further, Chayanov posed the question whether in the absence of wages the net gain, the rent, and the interest on capital could be worked out for such peasant farms. His answer was a flat no. In the absence of wages, these calculations could not be made. Hence, the behavior of these farms could not be accounted for in terms of standard theories of the four main factors of production.

Furthermore, Chayanov saw no validity in circumventing the absence of wage data by imputing values to unpaid family labor. He insisted on taking the entire family household as a single economic unit and treating their annual product minus their outlays as a single return to family activity. By its very nature, this return was unique and indivisible. It could not be meaningfully broken down into wages and the other factor payments of standard economic theory. In Chayanov's view, the return to the peasant family was *undifferentiable*.

Professional economists, Chayanov conceded, would balk at this, for they would somehow prefer, as Alfred Weber had told him in Heidelberg about 1924,[4] to encompass these family units together with the more tractable business enterprises within a single system, a universal economics, the standard economics on which they had been brought up. Such an attempt, Chayanov insisted, was foredoomed to failure.

---

4 Alfred Weber was the distinguished German economist who, together with Joseph Schumpeter and Emil Lederer, then edited the leading German social science periodical, *Archiv für Sozialwissenschaft und Sozialpolitik.*

Economists would have to face the fact, he held, that economies made up of family units in which the category of wages was absent belonged to a fundamentally different economic structure and required a different economic theory. Such a theoretical system, he wrote, would have the same relationship to present-day economics as Lobachevskii's geometry bore to that of Euclid. In his day, Lobachevskii gave up the assumption of parallel lines; we would have to drop wages.

Chayanov's own theory—or, if the expression be permitted, his non-Euclidean economics—was not restricted to peasant agricultural production. He was concerned with the total income of the peasant family from agriculture and also from crafts and trades. The economic unit for which his theory was devised was the peasant family taken as a whole in all its works, or, alternatively, the total economic activity of family labor. Thus, he saw his exposition of peasant economy as a particular form of a larger doctrine—the theory of family economy.[5]

## The Labor–Consumer Balance

Chayanov's central concept for analyzing family economics was what he called the labor–consumer balance between the satisfaction of family needs and the drudgery (or irksomeness) of labor. Once grasped, this concept furnishes the key to his entire position and mode of presentation. It was one of the chief weapons he wielded in his severe critiques both of Marxian economics in Russia and of orthodox classical and neoclassical economics in the West.

In developing his concept of the labor–consumer balance, Chayanov began with the *gross* income or gross product of a peasant family household at the end of an agricultural year, assumed to be at a given level (say, 1,000 rubles). From this annual gross income, certain expenses had to be deducted so as to restore the farm to the same level of production it possessed at the beginning of that agricultural year, i.e., seed, fodder, repairs, replacement of expired livestock and worn-out equipment, etc. Once these expenses had been deducted, the family was left with a *net* product or net income that constituted the return for its labor during that agricultural year. How was that net

---

[5] Cf. the title of Chayanov's book in German, *Die Lehre von der bäuerlichen Wirtschaft: Versuch einer Theorie der Familienwirtschaft in Landbau (The Theory of Peasant Economy: Test of a Theory of Family Economy in Agriculture)* (Berlin: P. Parey, 1923).

income or net product to be divided among family budget for consumption, capital formation for raising the farm's potential level of production, and savings (if there was any possibility of savings not invested in the farm)? Put more simply, what should the family eat, what fresh capital should it invest in the farm, what should it put by?

A *capitalistic* enterprise, Chayanov pointed out, can get objective, quantitative evidence about how to proceed. By deducting from its gross product the outlays on materials and wages, a business concern can ascertain its net profits. If it wishes to increase its profits, the concern can put in more capital and obtain, in due course, an exact quantitative statement as to the increase, if any, in net profits. For a peasant family farm, however, there are neither wages nor net profits. The family members know roughly how many days they have worked, but Chayanov insisted there is no *valid* way of estimating in money the value of their work. All they can see before them is the net product of their work, and there is no way of dividing days of labor into bushels of wheat.

According to Chayanov, the peasant family proceeds by subjective evaluation based on the long experience in agriculture of the living generation and its predecessors. Most peasant families, Chayanov showed, are in a position either to work more hours or to work more intensively, sometimes even both. The extent to which the members of the family actually work under given conditions he called the degree of self-exploitation of family labor. The peasants would put in greater effort only if they had reason to believe it would yield an increase in output, which could be devoted to greater family consumption, to enlarged investment in the farm, or to both. The mechanism Chayanov devised for explaining how the family acted is his labor–consumer balance. Each family, he wrote, seeks an annual output adequate for its basic needs; but this involves drudgery, and the family does not push its work beyond the point where the possible increase in output is outweighed by the irksomeness of the extra work. Each family strikes a rough balance or equilibrium between the degree of satisfaction of family needs and the degree of drudgery of labor.

In itself, Chayanov hastened to add, there was nothing novel or remarkable about this concept. What is of interest and gives value to Chayanov's book is the way he handled the concept. He showed how for different families the balance between consumer satisfaction and degree of drudgery is affected by the size of the family and the ratio of working members to nonworking members. He traced the "natural history" of the family from the time of marriage of the young couple through the growth of the children to working age and marriage of this second generation. In relating this natural history of the family to the changing size of peasant farms from generation to generation, Chayanov developed the concept of "demographic differentiation," which he asked his readers to contrast with the Marxian concept of class differentiation among the peasantry.

But his analysis is far from being primarily demographic. Using the bases of the zemstvo statistics, the studies of these by his predecessors and colleagues, and fresh field inquiries, Chayanov examined the effects on the labor–consumer balance of a wide range of factors. He took account of size of holdings, qualities of soil, crops grown, livestock, manure, location, market prices, land prices, interest rates on capital loans, feasibility of particular crafts and trades, availability of alternative work, and relative density of population. Chayanov was not so much concerned with the individual effects of each of these factors as with their mutual effects as they changed through time.

In weighing the influence of these *several* elements on the delicate balance between urgency of family needs and drudgery of labor, Chayanov employed some of the concepts and techniques of marginal utility analysis. His terminology included, for example, demand satisfaction and marginal expenditure of work force. For factors not subject to any precise measurement, such as willingness to put in greater efforts, he constructed equilibrium graphs showing interaction under varying assumptions.

Chayanov foresaw, quite correctly, that his use of these tools of "bourgeois" economics would shock many of his contemporaries in Soviet Russia of the mid-1920's. He countered that his work should be judged not by the genealogy of his techniques but, rather, by the results he had been able to obtain through the application of those techniques to the Russian data in the light of economic postulates firmly anchored in peasant behavior.

Summing up his findings, Chayanov wrote that "available income was divided according to the equilibrium of production and consumption evaluations or, more accurately, a desire to maintain a constant level of well-being."[6] Generally speaking, an increase in family gross income led to increases in both family budget and capital forma-

---

[6] See below, p. 218. For an earlier discussion of a balance between "need" and "labor," see W. Stanley Jevons, *The Theory of Political Economy* (4th ed.; London: Macmillan & Co. Ltd., 1911), chap. v.

tion. The precise way the gross income was divided up in each family was a question of subjective judgment by the head of the family and, hence, could not be expressed in objective, quantitative terms.

According to Chayanov, the basic characteristics of the peasant family's economic behavior fundamentally differed from those of capitalist farm owner's in price they were prepared to pay for buying land, interest they were willing to pay in borrowing capital, rent they would pay for leasing in land, price at which they would sell their produce, etc. In conditions where capitalist farms would go bankrupt, peasant families could work longer hours, sell at lower prices, obtain no net surplus, and yet manage to carry on with their farming, year after year. For these reasons, Chayanov concluded that the competitive power of peasant family farms versus large-scale capitalist farms was much greater than had been foreseen in the writings of Marx, Kautsky, Lenin, and their successors.

### Viability of Peasant Family Farms

In proclaiming the viability of peasant family farming, Chayanov set himself against the mainstreams of Marxist thought in Russia and western Europe. Marx had termed the peasant who hires no labor a kind of twin economic person: "As owner of the means of production he is capitalist, as worker he is his own wage worker." What is more, Marx added, "the separation between the two is the normal relation in this [i.e., capitalist] society." According to the law of the increasing division of labor in society, small-scale peasant agriculture must inevitably give way to large-scale capitalist agriculture. In Marx's own words:

> . . . [the] peasant who produces with his own means of production will either gradually be transformed into a small capitalist who also exploits the labor of others, or he will suffer the loss of his means of production . . . and be transformed into a wage worker. This is the tendency in the form of society in which the capitalist mode of production predominates.[7]

Marx and Engels believed that the advantages of concentration and centralization lay with the capitalist farmers who would, in the course of time, swallow up the small peasants. Two outstanding followers of Marx who adhered to this position were Kautsky, whose mono-

---

[7] Marx, *Theorien über den Mehrwert*, in the translation of G. A. Bonner and Emile Burns, *Theories of Surplus Value* (London: Lawrence and Wishart, 1951), pp. 193–94.

graph, *Die Agrarfrage*, was published in Stuttgart in 1899, and Lenin, whose work, *The Development of Capitalism in Russia*, appeared later in the same year in Moscow. The analyses by Kautsky for western Europe and Lenin for tsarist Russia were each sharply challenged in a large body of literature. It is out of the question for us to discuss these works here.[8] Of interest to us is that Chayanov rejected both the terms in which Marx analyzed the peasant farm and the assessment by Lenin of the importance of family farms in the Russian economy of his time.

At the outset of his book on *Peasant Farm Organization*, Chayanov assailed the characterization of the peasant as having a twofold nature, combining in himself the attributes of both a capitalist and a wage worker. Chayanov termed this bifurcation an unhelpful fiction—what is worse, a purely "capitalist" kind of fiction in the sense that it was made up entirely of capitalist categories and was conceivable only within a capitalist system. For understandable reasons, Chayanov did not explicitly state that he was criticizing Marx. It was all too easy, however, for anyone familiar with what Marx wrote, or with what Lenin wrote about Marx, to discern who was at least one of Chayanov's targets.[9]

Chayanov's position vis-à-vis Marx, it should be noted, was not altogether his own creation but reflected the cumulative work of the Organization and Production School of Russian agricultural economists onward from the time of Kosinskii's 1905 treatise. A neat statement of the position of this group can be found in the well-known

---

[8] Even before the appearance of Kautsky's book, the position and policy of the German Socialists with regard to the small peasantry had given rise to sharp dispute within the party. Some of the original documents are conveniently assembled and translated into English by R. C. K. Ensor in his useful collection, *Modern Socialism* (2d ed.; London and New York: Harper and Bros., 1907), especially items xv, xvi, and xxii. Convenient discussions of the controversy in central and western Europe are given in the works by A. Gerschenkron, *Bread and Democracy in Germany* (Berkeley: University of California Press, 1943), and in George Lichtheim, "Kautsky," *Marxism* (London: Routledge & Kegan Paul, 1961), chap. v. For the controversy in tsarist Russia, see Kerblay's article below, pp. xxviii–xxx.

[9] Where Chayanov found Marx in agreement with him, he of course did not hesitate to quote him by name. Thus, he cites both in Chap. 5 and in Chap. 6 the celebrated passage in which Marx states: ". . . with parcellated farming and small scale landed property . . . production to a very great extent satisfies own needs and is carried out independently of control by the general (i.e., the capitalist) rate of profit." See below, Chap. 5, p. 222 and Chap. 6, p. 240.

It should be noted that in the 1870's Marx learned Russian primarily in order to read the zemstvo reports on the peasantry. He followed these closely and, as was his habit, took extensive notes. Three volumes of these notes have been translated into Russian and published, and a fourth has been announced. See the *Arkhiv Marksa i Engel'sa* (Moscow, 1948, 1952, and 1955), Vols. XI, XII, and XIII.

treatise on *The Accumulation of Capital* by Rosa Luxemburg, the most dynamic force in German socialism in the period of World War I. Luxemburg had been born in Poland under tsarist rule and was thoroughly familiar with Russian literature on the peasantry.

It is an empty abstraction [she wrote] to apply simultaneously all the categories of capitalistic production to the peasantry, to conceive of the peasant as his own entrepreneur, wage labourer and landlord all in one person. The economic peculiarity of the peasantry, if we want to put them . . . into one undifferentiated category, lies in the very fact that they belong neither to the class of capitalist entrepreneurs nor to that of the wage proletariat, that they do not represent capitalistic production but simple commodity production.[10]

Chayanov's differences with Lenin were, if anything, even sharper than his divergences from Marx. As early as 1899, Lenin had written that in Russian agriculture the capitalist farmers—the peasant bourgeoisie—were already in the saddle. They were in a small minority, Lenin wrote, perhaps no more than 20 percent of the farm households. Nonetheless, in terms of the total quantity of means of production, and in terms of their share of total produce grown, "the peasant bourgeoisie are predominant. They are the masters of the countryside."[11]

By what criteria did Lenin separate capitalist farmers from non-capitalist peasants? In his view, the decisive step toward capitalism came when laborers had to be hired, when ". . . the areas cultivated by the well-to-do peasants exceed the family labor norm (i.e., the amount of land a family can cultivate by its own labor), and compel them to *resort to the hiring of workers*. . . ."[12] For Lenin, the hiring of workers had become widespread, and Russia was well on its way toward a capitalist agriculture with a peasant bourgeoisie and a rural proletariat. Chayanov's numerous references to the very small part hired laborers played on Russian farms (e.g., his assertion that 90 percent had no hired laborers in the period 1900–1925) constitute, therefore, a direct, if implicit, refutation of Lenin.[13] In fact, Chayanov's

---

[10] Rosa Luxemburg, *Die Akkumulation des Kapitals* (Berlin, 1913, as reprinted in 1923), p. 368. I have followed the English translation of 1951, *The Accumulation of Capital* (London: Routledge, 1951), but have made it more literal.

[11] V. I. Lenin, *The Development of Capitalism in Russia* (Moscow: Foreign Languages Publishing House, 1956), pp. 177–78.

[12] *Ibid.*, p. 52.

[13] See below, p. 112.

whole approach—his selection of the pure family farm as the typical Russian unit, his insistence on the survival power of such family farms, and his treatment of rural differentiation in terms of demographic cycles rather than class antagonisms—was diametrically opposed to that of Lenin.

## Wider Relevance of Chayanov's Theory

Chayanov's micro theory, as he was able to elaborate it before his career was cut short, is essentially a theory of one kind of individual family farm in Russia—the family farm that employs no hired labor whatsoever. There were other kinds of peasant farms in Russia, and there were capitalist farms as well. Once we step out of Russia we find peasant family farms elsewhere in Europe and in Asia, Africa, and the Americas. Chayanov's theory was devised to take account of Russian conditions, where the kind of peasant family farm that he discussed was predominant. Does his micro theory apply to peasant family farms in other countries?

Chayanov himself conceded that his theory worked better for thinly populated countries than for densely populated ones.[14] It also worked better in countries where the agrarian structure had been shaken up (as in Russia after the emancipation of the serfs in 1861) than in countries with a more rigid agrarian structure. Where the peasants could not readily buy or take in more land, his theory would have to be seriously modified.[15]

Since Chayanov did not work out these modifications, he did not elaborate a full-blown theory of peasant family farming for any country other than Russia. Nonetheless, he indicated that he thought one single universal theory of the peasant family farm at the micro level could be devised. In his view, the Russian case, which he developed so fully, was only an illustration of this larger theory.

One wonders whether he may not have been overoptimistic about the possibility of a universal micro theory of peasant family farming. We will recall that in calculating the springs of peasant decisions in Russia Chayanov took account of the interaction of a very large number of factors, including family size and structure, land tenures, climate, access to markets, and possibility of getting extra jobs in off-seasons. He was able to construct his models more easily, since he

---

14 See below, p. 111.
15 See below, p. 112.

assumed the existence of a single "pure" type of family farm, free of hired wage labor. Extending the theory outside Russia would at the very least involve preparation of alternative models for "impure" peasant households employing hired labor.

Although it encompassed a very wide range of possibilities, Chayanov's theory of peasant farming remained essentially a static one. From the 1860's through the 1920's, the Russian agricultural economy underwent a rapid series of fundamental changes. There were marked sectoral and regional differences in rates of growth. Chayanov often referred to the existence of these differentials, but pitched his theory at a level of abstraction well above them.

With regard to the broader institutional framework, Chayanov was fond of saying that capitalism was only one particular economic system. There had been others known to history, and perhaps more were to come in the future. In his 1924 article, the title of which we have translated as "On the Theory of Non-Capitalist Economic Systems," Chayanov cites six major kinds of economies. Three of these are familiar—capitalism, slavery, and communism. The fourth, "family economy," Chayanov divided into two subtypes—"natural" economy and "commodity" economy. These two names may be taken as roughly equivalent to "self-subsistent" and "market-oriented." In Chayanov's two additional categories—the "serf economy" of tsarist Russia and the "feudal economy" of medieval western Europe—the "commodity" economy of the lords was superimposed on the "natural" economy of the peasants. The chief difference between the two systems, according to his schema, was that in Russia the peasants worked on their own fields but had to make payments in kind to the lord, whereas in the West the peasants had to put in certain days of work directly on the home farm of the lord. Both of these lord-and-peasant systems were essentially symbiotic mixtures of the two subtypes within the basic category "family economy." In effect, therefore, Chayanov postulated only four major systems—capitalism, slavery, communism, and family economy.

Will one universal economics, Chayanov asked, suffice for all these systems? One could be erected, he conceded, but at the price of containing only vague and lofty abstractions about scarcity and optimalization. That would scarcely be worth the trouble. Properly speaking, each separate system required its own theory, its own body of theoretical economics. Each such theory should explain the functioning of the economy at the aggregate level, i.e., the economics of the nations or states falling within its purview.

The major system with which Chayanov was most familiar was, of course, the family economy of his native Russia. He referred repeatedly to his desire to show the significance of agriculture based on peasant family farming for the entire Russian *national* economy. In the Introduction to his book, *Peasant Farm Organization*, he announced his intention to go into the subject thoroughly at a later date, but he does not seem to have found the time to do so. Hence, we do not have from him any systematic exposition of his theory of family economy at the national level, nor any case study of the economic functioning of a predominantly peasant country taken as a whole. Nonetheless, we find scattered through his works many suggestive remarks on peasant economy at the national level.

When Chayanov was arrested in 1930, together with a number of his colleagues, his research teams were dispersed. The most fertile and sophisticated group of scholars then working in any country on peasant economy was shattered. The quality of Chayanov's writings from 1911 to 1930 permits us to believe that had he been able to continue with his scientific work he would have contributed even more significantly to the understanding of peasant economic behavior both in and out of Russia.

# A. V. Chayanov: Life, Career, Works

By Basile Kerblay[1]

Alexander Vasil'evich Chayanov is a name familiar to a whole generation of Russian agricultural economists who from the reforms of Stolypin until the collectivization campaign had the heavy responsibility of modernizing the traditional peasant economy and training the leaders of this new agriculture. Nevertheless, Chayanov is a name virtually forgotten today both in the U.S.S.R. and in the West.[2]

---

[1] The author wishes to express his gratitude to Professor Daniel Thorner for the stimulation and cooperation which made this study possible. He would also like to thank Professor Simon Kuznets and Dr. Fr. Schlömer for having placed at his disposal copies of Chayanov's works from their personal libraries.

[2] Among current Soviet authors, S. M. Dubrovskii (*Voprosy istorii sel'skogo khozyaistva, krest'yanstva i revolyutsionnogo dvizheniya v Rossii* [Moscow, 1961], p. 358), merely mentions his name in conjunction with the article from *Bolshevik*, No. 3–4 (1924), which condemned Chayanov's theories; A. L. Vainshtein, *Narodnoe bogatstvo i narodnokhozyaistvennoe nakoplenie predrevolyutsionnoi Rossii* (Moscow, 1960), p. 469, and N. A. Savitskii, *Zemskie podvornye perepisi* (Moscow, 1961, new edition of the same work, 1926), p. 352, are among the few to refer to works of Chayanov, though to ones written before 1913. In the West, among those who have appreciated the significance of Chayanov's work are:

Werner Sombart, *Der Moderne Kapitalismus, Das Wirtschaftsleben im Zeitalter des Hochkapitalismus* (München and Leipzig, 1928) Vol. III, Part 2, p. 1020.

A. Gerschenkron, "Alexander Tschayanoff's Theorie des landwirtschaftlichen Genossenschaftswesen," in *Vierteljahrschrift für Genossenschaftswesen*, Halle (Saale), Vol. 8 (1930), pp. 151–66.

Pitirim A. Sorokin, Carle C. Zimmerman, and Charles J. Galpin, *A Systematic Source Book in Rural Sociology* (Minneapolis: The University of Minnesota Press, 1931), Vol. II, pp. 144ff.

C. von Dietze, "Peasantry," *Encyclopaedia of Social Science* (New York, Macmillan Co., 1934), Vol. 12, p. 52.

J. H. Boeke, *The Structure of the Netherlands Indian Economy* (New York: Institute of Pacific Relations, 1942), pp. 31–32.

A. Gerschenkron, *Bread and Democracy in Germany* (Berkeley: University of California Press, 1943), p. 192.

Naum Jasny, *The Socialized Agriculture of the U.S.S.R.* (Stanford: Stanford University Press, 1949), pp. 27, 242–46, 429.

M. M. Postan and J. Titow, "Heriots and Prices on Winchester Manors," *Economic History Review*, Ser. 2, Vol. XI (April, 1959), p. 410.

N. Georgescu-Roegen, "Economic Theory and Agrarian Economics," *Oxford Economic Papers*, Vol. XII (February, 1960), pp 1–40.

Lazar Volin, "The Russian Peasant from Emancipation to Kolkhoz," in *The Transformation of Russian Society*, ed. Cyril E. Black (Cambridge, Mass.: Harvard University Press, 1960), p. 299.

Despite this neglect, the works of Chayanov—60 books and brochures alone, not counting innumerable articles—represent the culmination at the time of the Revolution in theory and practice of several decades of research and discussion on agrarian questions in Russia. As Daniel Thorner has shown, the problems raised over 40 years ago by Chayanov are just as pertinent today for developing countries where peasant economy remains a predominant factor.[3] Even in the U.S.S.R., the discussion he initiated has still not been concluded. For these reasons, the theories of Chayanov represent a turning point not only for historians and students of agrarian theory in Russia at the beginning of the twentieth century, but also for economists and sociologists seeking in the Russian model elements for a theory of peasant economy or illustrations for more concrete problems.[4]

## Biography

The available information concerning Chayanov's life is too fragmentary and uncertain to permit a reconstruction of his *curriculum vitae*.[5] However, the volume of writings that Chayanov has left behind is sufficiently large to enable one to trace the genesis of his thought and thereby to outline his personality. A cultivated man, he was not only interested in diverse realms of economics, sociology, and agricultural policy, but was also involved in art, literature, and history. Under various pseudonyms,[6] he wrote plays and novels in which are reflected his open and tolerant mind, his frequent travels abroad,[7] and his intimate knowledge of Western thought. It is these character-

---

3 Daniel Thorner, " 'L'Economie Paysanne': Concept pour l'Histoire Economique?" *Annales* (Paris), No. 3 (May–June, 1964), pp. 417–32. For the English text of this paper, see "Peasant Economy as a Category in Economic History," *Second International Conference of Economic History, 1962* (Paris and The Hague: Mouton & Co., 1965), Vol. II, pp. 287–300.

4 Professor Benedikt Korda of the Institute of Economics in Prague has emphasized the importance of some work of the Russian economists of the 1920's, including Chayanov's school, and has regretted that they are unavailable today (*Hospodárské Noviny*, special edition devoted to the scientific session, November 8–12, 1963).

5 The last edition of the *Great Soviet Encyclopaedia* leaves blank the date of his death, asking its readers to provide information on this matter. Professor Albert Vainshtein has kindly informed us by letter that Chayanov died in 1939.

6 X. Botanik, "Moskovskii Botanik X.," Ivan Kremnev.

7 His first travels brought him in 1908 to Lombardy to study the irrigation system and to Belgium to observe the organization of cooperatives. His last trip abroad was to Berlin in 1928 in connection with the German edition of his study on the size of agricultural enterprises (*Die Optimalen Betriebsgrössen in der Landwirtschaft*, Berlin, 1930). B. Seebohm Rowntree, *Land and Labour: Lessons from Belgium* (London: Macmillan & Co., Ltd., 1910), pp. 225–54, points out the significance of the Belgian cooperatives at the time Chayanov was interested in their development.

istics—common to his generation of the intelligentsia—which imply that he did not come from peasant stock. Yet, unlike the aristocratic dilettantes and aesthetes who sought to escape the realities of Russian life of that period, Chayanov devoted all his intelligence and generosity to the service of the peasantry. It was not simply the romantic idealism of the movement, "Back to the people," but, rather, a desire for objective analysis and for immediate results that guided his research and his agricultural activity.

His brilliance was recognized early. When in 1913 he was appointed assistant professor at the Agricultural Institute of Petrovskoe Razumovskoe, near Moscow (today the Timiryazev Agricultural Academy), he was only 25 and had already published 13 studies. His reports had been mentioned at various agricultural and cooperative congresses since 1910. In 1919, he took charge of the seminar on agricultural economy of the Timiryazev Academy, later to become the Institute of Agricultural Economy, which he directed until 1930.[8] His penetrating mind enabled him to pass with remarkable ease from fact to theory and from theory to empirical verification.

This dialogue between theoretical discussions and practical research was encouraged by the rapid and, at certain times, dramatic evolution of Russia from 1908 to 1930—a period which offered Chayanov an exceptional opportunity for experiment and reflection. The years preceding World War I, the period of the war itself, of the Revolution, the years of N.E.P., and, finally, the beginnings of collectivization provide convenient stages for following the trend of Chayanov's thought and the development of his theory of peasant economy.

## *The Place of the Organization and Production School in the Evolution of Agrarian Doctrine in Russia*

Throughout the eighteenth century and until about 1880, Russian agricultural officers were interested only in the problem of the large estates of the nobles.[9] By the beginning of the twentieth century,

---

8 It is now Vsesoyuznyi nauchno-issledovatel'skii institut ekonomiki sel'skogo khozyaistva, detached from the Timiryazev Academy and attached to the Ministry of Agriculture of the U.S.S.R.

9 The first Russian books on agronomy were the *Domostroi*, which were meant to be commonsense books for running an estate. One of the oldest was translated into French, *Le Domostroj, Ménagier Russe du XVI^e Siècle* (Paris: Picard, 1901). For a masterly contribution to the understanding of the economic thinking of the Russian landlords at the end of the eighteenth century, see M. Confino, *Domaines et Seigneurs en Russie* (Paris: Institut d'Etudes Slaves, 1963), 310 pp.

however, their attention was directed to the problems of peasant farms. The crisis of the years 1880–1890 was a cruel blow to those large estates based on extensive agriculture using cheap labor. It was the same crisis that initiated the debate in Russia among Populists, legal Marxists, and revolutionary Marxists concerning the relative merits of small- and large-scale farming.

During this period, expansion of the agricultural colleges had increased the supply of agricultural specialists.[10] Unable to find employment in the few large estates, they had no alternative but to accept posts in the zemstvo organizations. This explains why the Russian agricultural officers suddenly turned their attention to peasant economics, the principal preoccupation of the zemstvos. After 1905, this new generation of agricultural economists became powerful enough to gain intellectual control of the principal agricultural societies of the country. The agricultural associations of Moscow, St. Petersburg, Kharkov, and, to a large degree, the Free Economic Society, were directed no longer by the nobility but by the leftist intelligentsia whose role was to be decisive in the orientation of Russian agrarian thought up to World War I.

In the years leading to the outbreak of hostilities in 1914, Stolypin's reforms had neither appeased the intelligentsia divided on the agrarian question nor satisfied the poorer levels of the peasantry. The creation of *khutors*, peasant enclosed farms separated from the rural communities, had reinforced the social division within the villages. The Social Democrats and the Social Revolutionaries considered that the agrarian question could be solved only by the nationalization or socialization of the land, thereby presupposing a political revolution. On the other hand, those who propounded the organization and production current of thought,[11] mainly the agricultural officers and teachers in the zemstvo administrations, felt that land redistribution was an insufficient palliative, and that, furthermore, such a solution implied a social upheaval whose consequences would be unpredict-

---

10 The number of agricultural colleges passed from 2 in 1895, with 75 students, to 8 in 1912, with 3,922 students. The number of agricultural officers employed by the zemstvos progressed from 124 to 2,701 in the same period. This meant there was one agricultural officer per *uchastok* (canton or subdistrict) instead of only one per *uezd* (district), which brought the agricultural officer to the peasant (V. V. Moratsevskii, *Agronomicheskaya pomoshch' v Rossii* [St. Petersburg: Ministry of Agriculture, 1914], 607 + 35 pp.).

11 The phrase used in Russian is *organizatsionno-proizvodstvennoe napravlenie*. For a detailed discussion of this school, see N. Makarov, *Krest'yanskoe khozyaistvo i ego evolyutsiya* (Moscow, 1920), Vol. 1, pp. 1–160. For a brief summary, see S. V. Utechin, *Russian Political Thought, a Concise History* (New York: Frederick A. Praeger, Inc., 1963), pp. 138–39.

able. Their own solution consisted of a series of agricultural and economic proposals designed to intensify the production of the peasant
farms. Their aim was to transform the entire *organization* of the peasant economy without waiting for political changes; hence, the name
"organizational" was attached to this school of thought.

It was no longer a question, as at the time of Herzen and Cherny-
shevsky, whether Russia could achieve socialism without passing
through a capitalist stage. Nor was it one of mere social or fiscal
change, as it had been in 1894 at the Ninth Congress of Russian
Doctors, which had concentrated on the peasant family's standard of
living.[12] The problem that preoccupied these administrators, inspired
by such Western innovations as improvement of breeds, mechanization, fertilizers, and cooperatives, was the suitability of economic and
technical progress. Their problem was how to adapt certain Western
agricultural or economic advances (theory of location, marginal analysis) to peasant farms based entirely on family labor and oriented
only in part toward a money economy.

The 1904 course of lectures given by A. I. Chuprov at the École
Supérieure Russe des Sciences Sociales at Paris on the advantages of
small-scale production and the methods needed to modernize it is
one of the first manifestations of this current of thought.[13] But V. A.
Kosinskii went much further by putting the problem of the distinc-
tions between peasant and capitalist economy in terms which re-
kindled the debate with the Marxists, not so much on the political
plane as on the plane of economic theory. It is for this reason that
Chayanov considered him the spiritual father of the school of peasant
economy.[14]

In peasant economy, Kosinskii noted, "there is neither a question
of rent nor of profit."[15]

The peasant providing simultaneously land, capital and labor, he does
not divide the value created in the process of production between costs of
production and surplus value. All the value thus created returns to him to
be used as a whole and is the equivalent of wages and the capitalist's
surplus value. This is why the idea of surplus value and of interest on

---

[12] This congress marks an important date in the evolution of social surveys in
Russia, for methodological problems were discussed there by a committee that contained
the best statisticians of the period—A. I. Chuprov, Shcherbina, Kablukov, L. N. Maress.

[13] *Mel'koe zemledelie i ego osnovnye nuzhdy* (St. Petersburg, 1907), republished in
Berlin, 1921.

[14] A. Chayanov, "Gegenwärtiger Stand der Landwirtschaftlichen ökonomie in Russland," *Schmollers Jahrbuch*, Vol. 46 (1922), p. 731.

[15] V. Kosinskii, *K. agrarnomu voprosu* (Odessa, 1906), Vol. 1, p. 167.

capital is foreign to him. He considers his net income as the product of his own labor using material resources of his own.[16]

According to Kosinskii, this explained how the peasant could pay high rents relative to net income, for he tried to maximize the utilization of his labor by intensifying production in conditions of limited availability of land. Thus, by 1906 an essential notion already had been formulated: the concepts of rent and surplus value are not applicable to the peasant farm in the way used by the Marxists to assimilate it to their traditional model.[17]

It was with this school that Chayanov affiliated himself. Like other colleagues—Chelintsev, Brutskus,[18] Markov, etc.—he very quickly apprehended two fundamental facts: first, the sterility of much of the immense statistical information collected by the zemstvo organizations, because of the lack of an appropriate method for the economic analysis of peasant agriculture; second, the inapplicability of the concepts of classical economics based on the capitalist mode of production. It was Chayanov's genius to be able to create from these difficulties not only a method of inquiry adapted to the solution of organizational problems on which he was doing research but also a theory of peasant economy capable of explaining the specific character of this unique mode of production, thereby directing the agricultural officer in his daily contact with the peasantry.

## First Studies of Chayanov and Origin of His Theory of Peasant Economy

For the agricultural officers of this generation, the Agricultural Congress of 1901 and the Congress of the Cooperative Movement of 1908 provided the catalyst for this appreciation of the specific character of the peasant economy.[19] At this time, Chayanov was too young

---

16 *Ibid.*, pp. 165–66.

17 N. Kablukov, *Ob usloviyakh razvitiya krest'yanskago khozyaistva v Rossii* (Moscow, 1908), pp. 377–84, analyzes in the same way the specific characteristics of the utilization of capital and profit-making in the peasant economy.

18 B. Brutskus, *Ocherki krest'yanskago khozyaistva v zapadnoi Europe*, 1913, contrasts the peasant and capitalist economies (the peasant based on *values* considered *subjectively*, the capitalist on *costs* objectively *quantifiable*). He points out in the same terms as Chayanov the arbitrary nature of the accounting methods of the Swiss agronomist E. Laur.

19 One must also note the part played by the agricultural journals such as *Zemskii Agronom*, of Saratov; *Moskovskii Vestnik Sel'skogo Khozyaistva*, directed by A. G. Doyarenko; and especially the *Agronomicheskii Zhurnal*, of Khar'kov, whose editorial committees contained the movement's chief spokesmen.

to make his mark, but in 1911 he was chosen by the First Congress of the All-Russian Union of Linen Producers to carry out a survey on the role of flax in peasant incomes in the district of Volokolamsk, Moscow guberniya.

That same year, the theories of the organizational school were finally accepted by the Congress of Agricultural Officers of Moscow guberniya. Pervukhin attacked the methodological basis used by the zemstvos for their surveys of peasant budgets. These periodical questionnaires contained a very large number of subdivisions often too complex to be understood by the peasant and often too much for the powers of his memory.[20] To make the surveys conducive to economic analysis, Pervukhin demanded simplified accounts which a peasant could keep himself. Chayanov backed up Pervukhin with a report on the "District Agricultural Officer and the Organizational Plan of the Peasant Economy," in which he emphasized the usefulness of the budget analysis of peasant *farms*—not merely of *family* consumption —as an accounting instrument that would furnish the agricultural officer with information relevant to the organization of the farms for which he was responsible. Brutskus approved this declaration: "Chayanov has been able to express what all agricultural officers are thinking."[21]

Chayanov's first field surveys supported the theories he had formulated at the congress. In the course of the inquiry on flax producers' incomes, which he had conducted in the Volokolamsk flax district,[22] together with the inquiry in Smolensk guberniya with the assistance of A. N. Grigoriev, made in June and July, 1911, in order to extend the sample to a poorer region, he had discovered the impossibility of applying the accounting methods used in western Europe at the time. For example, E. Laur's method, studied by Chayanov,[23] tried to identify the gross income of a given farm; then, by

---

[20] Shcherbina's model, adopted in 1900 for the inquiry in Voronezh guberniya, consisted of 677 questions. It took from a day and a half to two days for a researcher to fill out a single family's questionnaire.

[21] *Trudy s"ezda*, Moskovskii oblastnoi s"ezd deyatelei agronomicheskoi pomoshchi naseleniyu, Moscow, 1911.

[22] *Len i drugie kul'tury v organizatsionnom plane krest'yanskago khozyaistva nechernozemnoi Rossii* (Moscow), Vol. 1 (Volokolamsk uezd, 1912), 198 pp., Vol. 2 (Smolensk guberniya, 1912), 209 pp.

[23] A. Chayanov, *Krest'yanskoe khozyaistvo v Shveitsarii* (Moscow, 1913). Professor Ernst Laur, Secretary of the Union of Swiss Peasants had perfected a complicated accounting system which required keeping five different books in order to record the monetary and financial flows from one account to another (one account each for the enterprise, for the family house, for labor, for subsidiary income, and for the owner).

*(cont.)*

deducting the costs of the farm and those of the family, the remuneration of labor and of capital, he obtained a net profit or loss. In weakly monetized economies like those in Russia, Chayanov observed, such a capitalistic approach would be arbitrary, their evaluations being essentially qualitative and subjective. A given product exists in sufficient or insufficient quantity relative to the peasant's needs, but the products are not interchangeable as in a market economy.[24]

He pointed out, in addition, that the marginalist theory explaining the behavior of a capitalist entrepreneur in his choices cannot be transferred to a peasant family unit, for in this type of farm the decreasing returns of the value of marginal labor do not hinder the peasant's activity so long as the needs of his family are not satisfied. "Decreasing returns do not stop work until an equilibrium between needs and the drudgery of effort has been achieved."[25] In other words, the optimum in a peasant family labor farm[26] is defined in terms different from those of a capitalist economy. Thus, the premises of what was to be his theory of peasant economy were already formulated by 1911.

That very year, the Moscow Committee of the Credit and Savings Cooperatives set up a commission, in which Chayanov took part, to inquire into the monetary elements of the Moscow guberniya peasant economy in order to establish credit plans related to the money returns and expenditure of the region's cultivators. In 1912, the commission worked out the first accounting system adapted to Russian conditions and simplified for the use of agricultural officers.[27] Chayanov's monograph, *Opyt anketnago issledovaniya denezhnykh elementov krest'yanskago khozyaistva moskovskoi gubernii* (1912), describes the difficulties encountered by this first experiment. Of the 7,000

---

The labor of members of the family was evaluated at the same rate as hired labor. (*Landwirtschäftliche Buchhaltung bäuerliche Verhältnisse*, 1904; 5th ed., 1913). Moreover, E. Laur inspired a peasant movement whose ideals were similar to those of the Russian Populists. He developed them in *Politique Agraire* (Paris: Payot, 1919).

[24] A. Chayanov, *Opyt razrabotki byudzhetnykh dannykh po sto odnomu khozyaistvu Starobel'skago uezda Khar'kovskoi gub.*, *Istoriya byudzhetnykh Issledovanii* (Moscow, 1915), Vol. 1, chap. vi.

[25] *Len i drugie kul'tury, op. cit.*, pp. 13–14.

[26] A family farm that does not employ outside labor. Cf. the Glossary, below, for further discussion.

[27] A Chelintsev's *Uchastkovaya agronomiya*, published in 1914, was a first attempt to provide a practical manual for agricultural surveys and simplified accounting in the spirit of the organizational school. In *The Theory and Practice of Peasant Economy*, a course of lectures he gave to the agronomists of Kiev in 1912, one can find the same aims and often the same concepts as those of Chayanov.

questionnaires sent out, 300 replies were received, of which only 164 were usable. How was it possible to interpret them, to obtain averages, or to verify the results? Chayanov's contribution was the priority given to analysis of the family's expenses considered as the expression of its monetary needs, for it is in relation to these needs that the activity of the family is organized, both inside and outside the farm (external wages).

These two experiments inspired in Chayanov a first attempt at a theoretical formulation.[28] In *Ocherki* (1913) he begins by analyzing, first, the relation between the drudgery (or irksomeness) of labor and the satisfaction of family needs in a peasant economy, and, second, the different elements in peasant consumption budgets and their elasticity compared to workers' budgets.[29] But this first effort left the author unsatisfied. He was aware that his first observations were mostly based on poorer peasant groups and that it was equally necessary to study the behavior of the peasant groups at the top of the agricultural pyramid. Most of all, he wanted to analyze the relation between the peasant family's consumption and farm expenses, for the "organization and production" aspect of the peasant farm was the chief object of his research.

Friends from the Khar'kov zemstvo who were agricultural officers helped him in this venture by providing him with the unsifted material of a detailed survey made in 1910 in the Starobel'sk uezd of Khar'kov guberniya. In analyzing these statistics, Chayanov tried to verify whether the relationship between size of family (in particular, the relation between number of active workers and number of mouths to feed during the cycle of the family's reproduction and upbringing) and size of farm confirmed the hypothesis that the needs of the family at the different stages of its evolution provide the chief motive force of the peasant's activity. The statistics of Starobel'sk corroborated his first theoretical attempt, for they confirmed that the size of a farm is not so much the determining factor of peasant activity as it is the expression of this activity.[30]

By extending his analysis to the nonmonetized as well as the monetary elements of the peasant holding, Chayanov was able to establish

---

[28] *Ocherki po teorii trudovogo khozyaistva* (Moscow, 1912–13), 2 Vols., 24 and 91 pp.

[29] This essay was to appear later as the first chapter of *Die Lehre*, 1923, and *Organizatsiya*, 1925.

[30] In a report submitted to the Free Economic Society on January 17, 1912, Chayanov had already called attention to this point.

the movements in money and in kind by which the family achieved the volume of resources necessary for its needs. Once again, but this time with more confidence, Chayanov emphasized his disagreement with Laur. Chayanov did not claim, as did Laur, to identify, after deducting the costs of production, what could be considered as payment for capital, labor, or land in the mass of goods produced by a farm. For a peasant family, he maintained, there is no valid way of estimating the value of labor in monetary terms. Any attempt to evaluate it at the rate of agricultural wages is arbitrary, as is the calculation of land rent on the basis of the rate of return on the capitalized market value of the land, a method valid for capitalist farms.[31] The results of the Starobel'sk study, fundamental to Chayanov's intellectual development, were published in 1915, republished in 1922, and then integrated in several chapters of *Die Lehre* (1923) and *Organizatsiya* (1925).

## World War I and Chayanov's Activity in the Cooperative Movement

Russia's participation in the war directed Chayanov's activity to the concrete problems of organizing the flax market. This experience was decisive in the formulation of his theories of cooperation.

Russia in 1914 was the chief exporter of flax on the world market; this product provided many northern and central provinces with an essential part of their agricultural income. But Russia's conquest of the flax market was not definitive, since it rested on the low levels of peasant living. In addition, the market was constantly threatened by the competition of overseas cotton (which had already seriously damaged flax cultivation in Belgium and France) and by foreign producers' demands for "quality." Thus, from their first congress in 1911 the Russian linen producers were concerned not merely with the stability of flax cultivation if the world market worsened[32] but also with the organization of cooperatives to improve the quality of the flax in its initial processing, since treatment of the flax was the principal winter occupation of the peasants in certain areas.

At the Second Congress of Linen Producers in Moscow (April 4–7, 1913), Chayanov, who had already made a field survey on the economic stability of flax production in 1911, showed the difficulties in-

---

31 *Byudzhety krest'yan Starobel'skago uezda* (Khar'kov, 1915), pp. 116–21.

32 The *pud* (16.38 kilograms) of flax priced at 234 kopeks at Volokolamsk in 1894 had risen to 493 kopeks by 1913.

volved in organizing a system of cooperatives ex nihilo. The peasants would not be interested in cooperatives unless cooperatives offered higher sales prices for their produce. Even from its inception, then, the organization must be sufficiently powerful to overcome the established commercial buyers and dealers; but how could the organization become powerful without a massive peasant enrollment? To break this vicious circle, Chayanov proposed the organization of the "downstream" cooperative—that is, a *central* cooperative for exports rather than a network of local producer cooperatives. The interruption of communications with foreign countries which created a marketing crisis for flax production gave Chayanov a unique opportunity to put his ideas into practice.[33]

The 16 million tons of flax produced in Russia in 1914 left, after interior markets were satisfied, a surplus of 6 million tons which threatened to cause a price crash if it was not absorbed. Chayanov used the existing cooperative structures—the rural credit banks and the powerful Siberian Union of Cooperative Creameries—to export this surplus flax to England via Archangel or Norway.[34] He obtained the cooperation of the State Bank to finance the operation; the cooperative credit bank branches were to be the buyers and collectors at the production level, while the Creameries Union with its London agent, the Moscow Narodny Bank, was responsible for the sale abroad. For the first year, the operation could hardly have been called successful. After a roundabout trip of 12 months, the flax arrived at its destination in such a condition that 75 per cent of it was unsalable. The only benefit of this venture was that the Russian peasant became accustomed to selling his flax to a cooperative. This was enough encouragement for founding a Central Cooperative Association of Flax Growers the following year; Chayanov was one of its member-directors. The association undertook flax-selling both inside Russia, where it offered manufacturers a guarantee of quality, and abroad in France, England, and Japan. Under the direction of V. Anisimov, A. Chayanov, S. Maslov, and A. Rybnikov, the association managed to group 150,000 producers into 350 cooperative societies and 11 controlling unions. After an agreement signed in 1916-17 with the capitalist firm RALO (Russkaya assotsiatsiya l'novodcheskikh obshchestv), it gained an export monopoly in Russian flax.

---

[33] This experiment is described in detail in Chayanov, *Russkoe l'novodstvo, l'nyanoi rynok i l'nyanaya kooperatsiya* (Moscow, 1918), 177 pp.

[34] E. N. Kayden and A. N. Antsiferov, *The Cooperative Movement in Russia during the War* (New Haven: Yale University Press, 1929).

## The Revolution of February–October, 1917—
## Chayanov and the "Agrarian Question"[35]

The revolutions of February and March, 1917, caused a ferment of ideas and a realigning of opinions on the agrarian question on the part of the left-wing agricultural officers and economists. Until then, the Organization and Production School had tried to adapt itself to the pattern of evolution caused by Stolypin's decree; now they believed the ground was prepared for more radical measures. The proposed solutions were varied. Those more to the left advocated the socialization or nationalization of land; the Socialist Revolutionaries wanted to give it to peasant societies, the Bolsheviks wanted to give it to the state. Those to the right believed that a fixed agricultural land tax, wiping out land rents, would make the expropriation of the capitalists unnecessary, since the rent abolition would cut off their raison d'être.

Despite these disagreements, the Free Economic Society, the Agricultural Society of Moscow, the Agricultural Society of Khar'kov, the All-Russian Zemstvo Union (*Vserossiiskii zemskii soyuz*) brought together economists and agricultural officers of differing tendencies, such as the Marxist B. P. Maslov, the Socialist Revolutionary N. Oganovskii, the Populists S. Maslov and N. Makarov, and the Conservative A. Stebut.[36] In April, 1917, they agreed on certain fundamental principles and on creation of the League for Agrarian Reform. Chayanov was a member of the executive committee.[37]

While Lenin's April Theses demanded prompt confiscation of the large estates (which were to serve as large model farms) and nationalization of the land, including that of the peasants,[38] the league was content to propose the transfer of all land to peasant farms. In this, it followed the S.R. (Socialist Revolutionary) program, except that the league wanted this operation done within the framework of a central

---

[35] Chayanov played an important part in organizing the food supply both during the war and the Revolution through the All-Russian Zemstvo Union. His knowledge of the problems of peasant consumption was indispensable for establishing ration levels both in the cities and in the country. See A. Chayanov, *Normy potrebleniya sel'skogo naseleniya* (Moscow, 1916), which was followed in 1919 by a study on consumption in Moscow.

[36] Brutskus had prepared the ground by submitting a series of reports on the agrarian question to the Free Economic Society in 1916 and 1917. There were published as *Agrarnyi vopros i agrarnaya politika* (Petrograd, 1922).

[37] During 1917, two members of the committee filled posts as undersecretary of state for agriculture.

[38] For the evolution of Lenin's tactics in 1917, see Pierre Sorlin, "Lénine et le Problème Paysan en 1917," *Annales* (Paris), March–April 1964, pp. 250–80.

state plan, while the S.R. wanted a decentralized administrative system. Moreover, the league differed with the general proposals of the political parties in its insistence that the reforms should take into account regional requirements. According to the principles adopted by the league, agrarian reform—i.e., modification of the property system—was only one element of the question. The solution of the agrarian problem demanded a new "organization" of the peasant economy in order to adapt it better to the conditions of the world market. The league's object was to define for each region the types of reforms appropriate to its economic and social structure and to popularize these results in a series of pamphlets.

The first study, Chayanov's *What Is the Agrarian Question?*,[39] was a commentary on the principles enunciated above, and it leads us to believe that he had a major role in creating the program of the league. In what terms did Chayanov in 1917 envisage the solution of the agrarian problem?

Politically, he believed it was simply a matter of passing legislation that would conform to the proposed social ideals. But because economic life obeyed its own laws rather than the will of individuals, it was necessary to consider the economic development and, in particular, the specific characteristics of agriculture, lest the proposed solutions be stillborn.

Chayanov emphasized that it was the diversity of regional characteristics which distinguished the Russian situation. In central Asia and southern Russia, there was nomadic herding and fallow land; in Siberia, the land was plentiful and the right of property in it did not exist as such; in the central regions, the density of the population imposed intensive farming and a unique system, the *obshchina*—property held in common, and an equilibrium between the population and the land available maintained by a periodic redistribution of the land. With such diversity, solution of the agrarian problem could not be the same for all regions.[40]

Nevertheless, the reforms were not to be left to the regional authorities—the uezds or volosts. They were to be determined by the requirements of the national economy taken as a whole. This would avoid a situation in which, for example, the peasant Cossacks of Orenburg and Samara guberniyas, already possessing 10 desyatinas of land

---

[39] *Chto takoe agrarnyi vopros?* (Moscow, 1917), 63 pp.

[40] To answer these needs, the league published an atlas produced by S. A. Klepikov under Chayanov's direction. *Atlas diagramm i kartogramm po agrarnomu voprosu* (Moscow, 1917), 40 pp.

per household, might decide to divide among themselves the large private estates, whereas from a national point of view it would clearly be more desirable to transplant the surplus agricultural population from the guberniyas of Kiev, Podolie, etc., to this region, rather than to encourage extensive farming by the peasants who already had land there.

The second distinguishing characteristic of the Russian situation, Chayanov stated, was the predominance of the peasant farm based on family labor. The peasantry had evolved a great deal in the previous decades: agriculture had been monetized; peasants had bought 27 million hectares of land as personal property, often at the cost of great effort; cooperatives had developed on a commercial basis. Even if private property was not ideal, it was a reality, dangerous to attack as long as the peasants' ideas remained unmodified. Chayanov did not think that the old Populist slogan, "Land and Liberty," was enough to solve the agrarian problem. Certainly, giving back "the land to those who work it" was a moral necessity, but the socialization or nationalization of the land would cause only an insignificant quantitative increase in peasant land—for example, of 100 million hectares sown in 1916, 89 million belonged to the peasantry and only 11 million to the nobility. The moral obligation was, therefore, not sufficient,[41] because no political power was able to force the peasant to change the nature of his farming. Chayanov felt that the solution to the agrarian problem lay essentially in the patient work of reorganizing the peasant economy. It was a question of finding the principles of organization which would increase the *productivity of agricultural labor,* while at the same time safeguarding the principle of a more egalitarian distribution of national income among those who participated in its formation.[42]

In this school of thought, the consolidation of *peasant* lands and the work of land improvement were to play an essential role. The results one can expect from a bringing together of production units are not the same in agriculture as in industry. This explains why the superiority of large-scale farming over small is not apparent in the same

---

41 Chayanov was in favor of nationalizing the large private estates which played a leading role in animal and plant selection. As they also produced an important share of the marketed crop, nationalization would avoid the running down of this irreplaceable capital and prevent a decline in the surplus available for export and the internal market. See *Chto takoe agrarnyi vopros?, op. cit.*

42 He recognized that these principles were not easy to reconcile, which the experience of the agricultural "communes" was to show after 1917. See Robert G. Wesson, *Soviet Communes* (New Brunswick, N.J.: Rutgers University Press, 1963).

way in all sectors of agriculture. In an area of extensive cultivation where 2,000 to 8,000 hectares of grain land can be farmed with the appropriate machinery, the optimal dimensions of productive units will not be the same as they are in a region of sugar beet cultivation where the more intensive use of machines makes transport costs grow disproportionately beyond an optimum of 200 to 250 hectares.

In other words, natural conditions themselves impose certain limits on the possibilities of a horizontal concentration of agricultural production. These difficulties disappear, however, for vertical integration: small farms can benefit from all the advantages of scale by using the formula of cooperatives. Thus, the peasant sector can organize in unions to obtain on the market the same conditions for price and credit as does the large producer or merchant.

But what means were to be used to achieve these transformations? Chayanov did not believe in the virtues of force. The authoritative methods used by Catherine II at the time of enlightened despotism were not to be imitated. It was necessary to find a system of state regulation that would influence the conditions in which agriculture was to develop rather than to impose certain structures a priori. Chayanov defined four instruments for this action. Legislation would, first, suppress all land transactions without abolishing private property. Only the state would be able to acquire land if anyone wanted to sell it. Second, a fiscal system of discriminatory land taxes would encourage and accelerate transfer of land to the state. The tax would be set for the large capitalist estates at a level higher than the land rents, but at a lower level for the peasant farms. Next, the state could decide to expropriate certain large estates when the national interest required this; the former owners would be compensated by state bonds redeemable over a period of 50 to 100 years. Finally, the land thus bought or expropriated would form a land reserve to be used to effect the structural reforms required. This reserve land could be rented to peasants to finance the payment of the expropriation indemnities.

These measures would be integrated in a financial plan to avoid the danger of inflation, and they should extend over a long period, since successful structural reforms require a transitional stage. The state could use this period to create the conditions for a gradual transition either to a socialization or to a nationalization, but it would have to combat the impatience of the democratic masses and of those who would want to impose an accelerated rate on the transformations. For Chayanov, land reform was not simply a division of wealth among different groups of the population but a recasting of the whole country's economic structure. In this work of renovation, the agricultural officer must play a dynamic part to organize and direct the energy of the peasantry.

### *The Social Role of the Agricultural Officer in the Transformation of the Agrarian Structure (1918)*

Chayanov had already organized, in 1913, a seminar in Petrovskoe Razumovskoe on the theme, "The Agricultural Officer and the Cooperative Movement," which had provoked a general confrontation of ideas with the great Russian agricultural authorities of the period—Vladimirskii, Matskevich, Levitskii, and his mentor Fortunatov. In the same way, his study of the fundamental principles of social agronomy,[43] which the Cooperative Press published in 1918, summarized the prewar experience of the Russian agricultural officers,[44] and at the same time it suggested new paths of development.

Chayanov defined this social agronomy as "the totality of social measures which attempt to orient a country's agriculture toward more rational forms taking into account considerations of time and place." In a sense, this was the principles outlined in *What Is the Agrarian Question?* applied to the elaboration of a concrete program of action for raising a given region's level of agricultural productivity.

Generally, the passage from one type of agriculture to another is spontaneous and unplanned. Peasants imitate methods that have been proved. For example, in Siberia the colonists tried at first to use the same agricultural system they had known in their home province. After a period of 10 or 20 years of adaptation, the variety of initial methods had given way to a single system.

Thus, the agricultural officer must pay close attention to the organizational forms of local agriculture, since they are the fruit of long experience. The art of agriculture is to find the combinations best able to exploit the peculiarities of a given soil. From Moscow, one cannot predict the general methods valid for Voronezh or Chernigov. On the other hand, the area agricultural officer is not the director of one farm; he is responsible for a vast sector containing thousands of

---

43 *Osnovnye idei i metody raboty obshchestvennoi agronomii* (Moscow, 1918), 111 pp. Republished, 1922; translated into German by Dr. Fr. Schlömer under the title *Die Sozialagronomie* (Berlin, 1924), 96 pp. A literal translation of the original Russian title into English is: *Basic Ideas and Work Methods in Agricultural Advice to the Public.*

44 The work in the West of Paul de Wuysta and A. Bizzozzero also had an influence.

independent cultivators. Being social, his sphere of action is neither machines nor fields but, rather, individuals; he must inspire a new consciousness in their minds and wills; it is from this new awareness that a modern agriculture can be born.

However, this activity will not be efficacious until its psychological effect strikes the mass of the peasantry and not just this or that farm. For this, it would be necessary to discover two or three fundamental local needs of vital interest to all the peasants and easy to satisfy with simple and inexpensive innovations, such as replacement of the wooden scratch plow by the true iron plow, or methods of insect control. After several years of work in the area, the success gained in this first step will gain the peasants' confidence; they will then come of their own accord to ask the advice of the agricultural officer. At this point, the problem must be considered from the point of view of the farmer, because the measures recommended in the second stage of local activity should no longer be on a large scale but should differentiate between the various types of farms which the agricultural officer's growing familiarity with the area should now enable him to recognize.[45] In short, Chayanov believed that there is first a population, then an agriculture; the role of the agricultural officer is to nourish the human forces that will, in turn, give birth to a new rural culture.

## The Institute of Agricultural Economy of Petrovskoe Razumovskoe at the Time of War Communism (1919)

A group of young economists and agricultural officers who agreed with these principles worked under Chayanov's direction at his seminars in the Academy of Petrovskoe Razumovskoe. From the spring of 1919, these seminars rapidly acquired the form of an autonomous institution, which shortly became the Institute for the Study of Economics and Agrarian Policy. In the beginning, it consisted of 18 teachers and 30 research students,[46] and had the collaboration of

---

45 The experience acquired during numerous years of survey in the field was used to evolve the method of analysis for each region. This could still be profitably used today by technical assistance experts working in new regions to develop concrete programs of agricultural advice. A. Chelintsev, "Opyt postroeniya mestnoi sel'skokhozyaistvennoi politiki," *Krest'yanskaya Rossiya* No. VII (Prague, 1924), p. 55, describes the practical experiment tried by the Union of Cooperatives of Khar'kov from 1918 to 1919.

46 Among whom were N. P. Nikitin, F. I. Semenov, S. A. Klepikov, A. L. Vainshtein, V. N. Knipovich, N. I Kurochkin, A. N. Grigoriev, G. Studenskii. Later, many others, of whom V. S. Nemchinov was one of the most prominent, joined the institute.

many scholars of different political tendencies.[47] The research department inherited or acquired several private libraries[48] to which the library of the Cooperative Institute was added. By 1920, the library of the Institute of Agricultural Economy, with 140,000 volumes, was considered the biggest economics library in Moscow.

At the same time, in Chayanov's seminars and under his authority, a department for the study of the economic situation in Russia and abroad was set up on the model of similar departments at Harvard and Berlin. N. D. Kondrat'ev, who was named its director,[49] thus began with Chayanov a very close collaboration that was to continue until they both became victims of a Stalinist purge in 1930.

The orientation of the work undertaken at the institute was from the beginning both theoretical and practical. On the theoretical level, interest centered on the development of a theory of peasant economy as well as a theory of location in agriculture—a theory which would be the adaptation to Russian conditions of Weber's theory for industry. On the practical level, the problems dealt with were those which the Commissariat of Agriculture submitted to the institute—a study of consumption, of credit, of irrigation, of optimal sizes for agricultural enterprises. The institute became, in effect, the research center of the commissariat. Chayanov was particularly preoccupied by concrete problems. How, for instance, could economic calculation, basic for all decisions in agriculture, maintain its effectiveness in a period of galloping inflation? How could an accounting system be established when a horse bought for 30,000 rubles in January would be worth 10 times as much in December? To answer this, Chayanov finished, in October, 1920, *Methods of Non-Monetary Calculation in Economic Undertakings*, which was published by the People's Commissariat of Agriculture of the R.S.F.S.R.[50] Despite the title, the practical applicability of this method appears limited today, because the calculation recommended by the author is not applicable at the level of the individual farm. He postulates the existence of a central plan and an administrative pyramid, with a group of offices responsible for calculating input–output norms in physical quantities for each type

---

[47] S. N. Prokopovich, A. Rybnikov, Brutskus, Gatovskii, Pervushin, Litoshenko.

[48] Such libraries as those of V. I. Semevskii, V. N. Grigoriev, A. P. Levitskii, S. A. Klepikov, A. I. Chuprov, P. P. Dyushen, S. A. Muromtsev, N. V. Yakushkin.

[49] It marks the beginning of the studies of Pervushin, Lubimov, and Kondrat'ev on the agricultural cycles in Europe and Russia.

[50] *Metody bezdenezhnogo ucheta khozyaistvennykh predpriyatii, Trudy vysshego seminariya sel'sko-khoz. ekonomiki i politiki* (Moscow, 1921), Vypusk 2, 98 pp.

of agricultural production and then establishing the balance sheet of each unit by weighing the results by each production branch with these preestablished norms.

From the historical point of view, however, Chayanov's study is excellent, not only because it is a vigorous application to agriculture of the whole model for planning in kind, which is still one of the characteristics of the Soviet type of planned economy, but also because the author raised theoretical and political problems which must be placed in the context of the discussions of his day.

These discussions were mainly concerned with the possibility of substituting a "labor equivalent" for the monetary unit. Such was the title of the well-known article by V. G. Strumilin,[51] in which he urged generalization of the experiment carried out in several Moscow factories—the institution of a "nonqualified unit of labor," which would serve as a basis for a system of prices in labor equivalents. In the same number, Vainshtein, a member of Chayanov's team, showed that this presupposed previous studies of the timing of each production cycle, but these studies would often be useless because the conditions of war communism would not be the same as those in peacetime. Moreover, labor units are not interchangeable as is money in real terms: an engineer's labor, for instance, is by several units qualitatively different from nonqualified labor. Thus, a balance sheet of labor units does not eliminate the necessity of keeping the material balances in physical terms. Chayanov went even further in his criticism: if each product is measured by a constant value of labor units, there are no longer deficit products and the analysis of a decision's rationality is no longer possible. In addition, in agriculture where the peasant thinks in concrete terms of produce per hectare or per animal the labor unit is an abstract notion ill-adapted to the needs of a farm.[52]

On the theoretical level, Chayanov's study takes a stand on the specific character of economic laws in a socialist regime—an extension of his previous theses on the inapplicability of the concepts of capitalist economics to a peasant economy. The criterion of profitability measured in market terms is meaningless in a "natural" economy (a cow doesn't make a profit or loss); it is therefore necessary to substitute technical criteria. Chayanov considered the socialist economy, regulated by the single will (that of the state), as a natural economy governed by the requirement of satisfying society's needs with the

---

51 "Trudovoi ekvivalent," *Ekonomicheskaya Zhizn'*, No. 167 (July 31, 1920).

52 *Metody* . . . , *Trudy, op. cit.*, p. 40.

available resources. Moreover, the economy's organization rests on a network of labor "cells" whose rationality can no longer be evaluated in terms of the economic units which are the criteria of the capitalist market, but is evaluated at the macroeconomic level by determining the best use of the labor force for the increase of national income. Classical economics were no longer applicable to the socialist regime.

One cannot help but notice the close affinity these statements have with Bukharin's theses in *The Economics of the Transition Period*, which also appeared in 1920. However, apart from their common condemnation of political economy, the radicalism of the *ABC of Communism* is poles apart from the cautious attitude of the agricultural experts. Chayanov took good care to emphasize that a lasting form of Socialism could not be built on enthusiasm alone. Socialist society, according to Chayanov, had not yet found the stimuli that would impel the production units to attain their optimal organization. The intensification of work could result only from internal stimuli. As long as this key remained undiscovered, the economy was destined to be the victim of a gigantic bureaucracy. The principle of necessary equality between labor intensity and satisfaction of needs cannot be violated without harmful consequences: the socialist economy should not be that of Sparta. Here, Chayanov seemed to be condemning, in scarcely veiled terms, war communism's agricultural policy which, by its requisitioning, had cut off the source of personal initiative.

## Refuge in the Peasant Utopia, Moscow, 1984

In this difficult period when the black market of Sukharevka in Moscow was the principal source of provisions, Chayanov amused himself by dreaming, like the shepherds in the famous painting of Breughel the Elder, of a land of plenty. Under the pseudonym Ivan Kremnev, he invited the reader on the *Journey of My Brother Alexei to the Land of Peasant Utopia*.[53] This work, published in 1920 by the state press, with a preface by Orlovskii, rapidly became a bibliographical rarity. Under the cover of fiction it expresses a whole school of political thought tending toward populism or anarchism, while at the same time it provides certain insights into Chayanov's artistic tastes and philosophical inclinations.

---

[53] *Puteshestvie moego brata Alekseya v stranu krest'yanskoi utopii* (Moscow, 1920), 62 pp.

Citizen Kremnev wakes up in Moscow in 1984, but the world he discovers is quite different from that which George Orwell later imagined. It was Arcadia. "The era of urban culture has passed away"; the large cities have disappeared. Moscow itself has only 100,000 inhabitants, whole blocks have been razed, all the old monuments have been preserved. Urban centers are no bigger than 10,000. The factories have been relocated in the country, which looks like a vast checkerboard cultivated by peasant families organized in cooperatives.

This pastoral universe is the logical conclusion which, following the fall of the Bolsheviks, brought the peasant labor party to power in 1934. "The generation of the weak has been covered by a layer of stones . . . a new generation of barbarians carried socialism to the limits of absurdity," but the Communists failed because they wanted to impose nationalization of the land in a land where the peasant masses predominated. On the international level, the Communist movement has been divided by the action of centrifrugal forces. In 1984, of all the nations, Germany alone has kept the systems of the 1920's, for it is within the gates of the German capitalist factory that socialism was born as the antithesis of capitalism.

In a chapter which Chayanov–Kremnev directed "to the attention of the members of the Communist Party," he reproached the ideologists of the working class for claiming to monopolize all creative initiative, for considering the peasant economy as an inferior stage of development, and for "trying to apply their ideals by the methods of an enlightened despotism which provoked Russian society to an anarchic reaction." Here, utopia is simply a fable to denounce the errors of the present and especially the efforts made to destroy the family, considered as a survival of capitalism, and to substitute for the peasant family large-scale units of production. The notion of a bread and meat factory "is a monstrosity for the socialist peasant ideologists," for it makes the peasant passive instead of making him the motive force of spiritual and cultural progress. The author defended a pluralism that permits all the possibilities of life to express themselves and a planned economic system that preserves the chief individual incentives of prices and wages.[54] "The art of planning is not one of constructing the plan but is essentially one of animating the economy."

---

[54] But Kremnev foresees a tax system which mops up all income that is not the fruit of labor, such as land rent and dividends.

This political and literary essay tried, moreover, to define an ideology which could be opposed to communism and which would take root in the peasant cultural tradition. In effect, the ideology Chayanov proposed continues a whole current of thought, borrowing from Kropotkin, with his ideals of urban decentralization, local autonomy, and alternating activities, as well as from theosophy and anthroposophy, in fashion at that time. It falls in with the experiments tried at that period by the anarchist and theosophist communes of which Kremnev gives an idealized picture in his visit to a "fraternity" in Archangel in 1984.

In other words, his ideals were those of the cosmopolitan Russian intelligentsia rather than an expression of the peasant tradition. His conception of the peasants' future way of life is also very conservative; the fairs, cuisine, songs, and traditional costumes will not have disappeared in 80 years. Art exhibitions—here one finds the ideal of the school of *Peredvizhniki*[55]—productions of Hamlet, art books, and exotic fruit within reach of the peasants living in the agrocities of the future are the only signs of change. This peasant existence thus appears to reflect bourgeois ideals.

In his preface, Orlovskii underlined the "petty bourgeois" character of the book, mixed with artistic pretensions and with a peasant conservatism, and emphasized at the same time Chayanov's outmoded conception of technical progress. Kremnev recommends formulas of peasant microproduction units and of increasingly intensive agriculture at a time when the machine must liberate man from slavery to the soil. Orlovskii recognized, however, that Kremnev was a cultured and well-intentioned man. He did not hold against Kremnev the prophecies about the triumph of the peasant party—a joke, no doubt—which were to prove so fatal to Chayanov in 1930.

### The Model of the Isolated State

This peasant utopia was closely linked to the *Essay on the Study of the Isolated State*,[56] issued the year after, thereby inaugurating a long series of studies in the higher seminar of rural economy and policy.

---

55 Alain Besançon has pointed out the links that existed between the Populists and the disciples of this school of "traveling exhibitions." Cf. "La Dissidence de la Peinture Russe, 1860–1922," *Annales*, March–April, 1962, pp. 259–65.

56 A. Chayanov, "Opyty izucheniya izolirovannogo gosudarstva," *Trudy, op. cit.* (Moscow, 1921); certain fragments had already been published as "The Population Problem in an Isolated State," *Agronomicheskii Zhurnal*, No. 2 (1915).

The vision of the pastoral future of Russia described by Kremnev was based implicitly on an optimal equilibrium between town and country and on a system of agricultural intensification to which the "isolated state" provides the theoretical key.

Why this title? Undeniably, the isolated state is the image that best renders the situation of Russia at the time, but it seems that the concept especially marks the author's debt to von Thünen.[57] Chayanov differed from von Thünen, however; von Thünen was mainly concerned with research on land rent and the influence of prices on location, while Chayanov was interested in the relation between agricultural and nonagricultural activities. Although his research had previously considered peasant farming detached from the rest of the economy, Chayanov was now trying to relate it to the whole economy, in particular to the context of Russia's future relations with the world market. Moreover, the proposed "model" was intended to help define the degrees of optimal intensification for the study of agricultural regionalization, a problem on which several of Chayanov's collaborators had been working.[58]

The model was based on several hypotheses. Property in land did not exist. The territory is divided into five concentric agricultural zones around a single town. Each of these zones can have six different degrees of intensification of production (that is, the amount of labor input per hectare doubles, triples, etc., but production does not increase by the same progression because of the law of diminishing returns). Exchanges between the town and the surrounding country are limited to a single product on both sides; the country product, A, is a foodstuff with inelastic demand, while the city product, B, with elastic demand is not subject to the law of diminishing returns (product increases in proportion to labor). Finally, the transport costs of product A rise in direct proportion to its distance from the town, whereas such costs are considered nonexistent for product B.

From this, Chayanov studied the chronological order (in 21 stages)

---

57 J. von Thünen, *Der Isolierte Staat in Beziehung auf Landwirtschaft und National-ökonomie* (3d ed.; Berlin, 1875). Cf., *Von Thünen's Isolated State*, trans. [with some abridgements] by Carla M. Wartenberg, ed. with an intro. by Peter Hall (London: Pergamon Press, 1966), liv + 304 pp.

58 V. Knipovich and Nikitin published in the works of the Institute of Agricultural Economy two studies on regionalization of agriculture which drew conclusions from a series of important studies in this field by the organizational school: Chelintsev in Tambov guberniya, Brutskus and Kotov in Voronezh guberniya, Makarov in Siberia. See V. Knipovich, "K metodologii raionirovaniya," *Trudy*, Vypusk 5 (Moscow, 1921), and Nikitin, "Sel'skohozyaistvennoe raionirovanie Moskovskoi gubernii," *Trudy*, Vypusk 6 (Moscow, 1922).

of the cultivation of the different zones and of their degrees of intensification, both factors varying with the increase of the agricultural and
urban populations and product A's surplus (net product) available for
the town. The conclusion showed that intensification would support
an ever-growing population but that past a certain optimum level this
population increase would be more and more absorbed by agriculture, thus reducing the possibilities of urban expansion and industrialization because of the diminution of the net product in the last
phases of intensification. Chayanov also showed the relative level at
which the prices of A and B would be fixed and the population movements these prices would provoke between country and town, or vice
versa, as long as there remained a discrepancy between the standards
of living in town and in country.

In a second analysis, the author examined the modifications
wrought on the model given a new hypothesis of private ownership of
land in a capitalist frame of reference. The dominant motivation
would no longer be the optimum for the population but the earning
of the highest net income per hectare, using hired workers. It was
assumed that the wages of these workers were fixed, for each phase of
cultivation, to the corresponding level of marginal income that the
worker would obtain if in place of hiring out his labor he used it to
cultivate new land. One can thus establish the net income represented
by the absolute and differential rent appropriated by the capitalist
owner at the different phases of intensification. Since this income is
all the higher when the wages are lower, the income of peasant labor
diminishes proportionately to the degree of intensification. On the
other hand, a system based on the peasant family labor farm without
the hired labor would permit an optimal agricultural intensification
from the viewpoint of population density and of the growth of gross
national income.[59]

Does this mean that land rent does not exist in a peasant labor
farm? Some economists such as Chelintsev and Makarov who belonged to the same "organizational" school maintained this thesis[60]
by applying to the peasant economy Ricardo's analysis of the minimum subsistence level for a worker family. They considered that the

---

59 Chayanov's study on the economic basis of potato-growing, *Ekonomicheskie osnovy
kul'tury kartofelya, Trudy*, Vypusk 4 (Moscow, 1921), is a verification in the field of the
theoretical model. Potatoes being a type of intensive cultivation which develops in
areas of high population density, the author analyzed the factors that determine the
evolution of this production, especially potato-growing for industrial use.

60 A. N. Chelintsev, *Opyt izucheniya organizatsii krest'yanskogo sel'skogo khozyaistva*
(Khar'kov, 1919), pp. 40, 116–17.

income of a peasant family and the number of farms in a given area became established at the minimum level as a result of the growth of the population density, incomes staying proportionate to the family's expenses. At this point, they would have had to admit that the rules of the market economy do not apply to the peasant farm, particularly the rent-forming mechanism. From this, there was but a step to make the peasant economy a distinct economic system, a mode of production in the Marxist sense. Did Chayanov really make this step?

## Theory of the Organization of the Peasant Labor Farm

To reply to the preceding question, we must now examine how Chayanov reworked his initial studies on the peasant economy, first in *Die Lehre* (1923), then as an essay, *Ocherki* (1924), before he arrived at his general theory of the peasant economic system, translated below under the title, "On the Theory of Non-Capitalist Economic Systems" (1924), and of its specific mode of organization, *Peasant Farm Organization* (1925), also presented below in translation.[61]

When in 1923 Chayanov resumed the elaboration of his theory begun in 1913 on the basis of the Starobel'sk survey, he had to consider more recent studies published in the first years after the October Revolution.[62] Some of these studies brought into question his first hypotheses, according to which the basic concepts of classical economics work differently in a peasant economy. The article published by G. Raevich, "On the theory of peasant economy and the concept of worker (*rabotnik*)," in *Na Agrarnom Fronte* (1925, No. 11, pp. 23–24) gives a good survey of the debate around 1924–25. The so-called "subjective" approach, according to which the consumption level of the family was the key factor determining the drudgery of the labor in a peasant farm, was severely challenged. It was not possible, on the basis of statistical evidence provided by budgetary inquiries, to relate the intensity of peasant labor to a single factor and to consider the peasant working family as a pure biological unit free from any social

---

61 *Die Lehre von der bäuerlichen Wirtschaft: Versuch einer Theorie der Familienwirtschaft in Landbau* (Berlin: P. Parey, 1923), 132 pp. *Ocherki po ekonomike trudovogo sel'skogo khozyaistva* (Moscow, 1924), 152 pp. "Zur Frage einer Theorie der nichtkapitalistischen Wirtschaftssysteme," *Archiv für Sozialwissenschaft und Sozialpolitik*, Vol. 51 (1924), pp. 577–613. *Organizatsiya krest'yanskogo khozyaistva* (Moscow: The Co-operative Publishing House, 1925), 215 pp. These last two works are presented below in English translation.

62 In particular, A. Chelintsev's work, *Oypt izucheniya, op. cit.*, a study of the organization of the peasant economy, based on a survey carried out in Tambov guberniya.

interference. That is why Chayanov had to deepen his first analysis. In *Die Lehre*, he maintains that the peasant economy has a unique conception of profitability which is not the search for the highest net profit. The degree of intensification of agriculture or the self-exploitation of family labor is determined not only by the needs of the family but also by its possession of draft animals and productive equipment. He defined again the peculiar roles played by labor, capital, and land in the peasant economy, and he refined his earlier position concerning the problem of social differentiation of the peasantry.

Two chapters in *Ocherki*[63] are worthy of notice—one on the role of machinery in the peasant economy and one on land improvements. The author tried to calculate in what conditions the machine is preferable to manual labor for a peasant farm. He underlined that the method and the criteria used for a capitalist economy were not applicable, for it was necessary to consider the inequalities of the use of the labor force available during the year. Thus, the area that two active laborers can harvest in 10 days constitutes a boundary that mechanization (a reaper) can surpass, whereas in the dead season a machine (thresher) would be inappropriate because there is underemployment of labor.[64]

Land improvements were also to play an increased part in a more intensive agriculture, especially irrigation in regions where water, not land, was the limiting factor. Chayanov analyzed in detail the mechanisms of this singular water "rent," contrasting it with land rent. Water rent is not marginal, since it is not tied to the land's condition. On the other hand, when water rent rises because water is scarce, land rent falls because the poor ground is no longer cultivated. From this, he drew practical recommendations for agricultural officers responsible for field rotations in irrigated regions, allocating the water throughout the year and setting the price of irrigation water. He emphasized particularly that calculations of the limits of possible land improvements for a peasant economy must take into account the cost of the land and not the foreseeable increase of the rent, for in a peasant economy the prices agreed for the purchase of land or for land im-

---

[63] The publication of *Ocherki* was delayed till 1924, although it was written before *Die Lehre*, which was published in 1923. The title, *Ocherki po ekonomike sel'skogo khozyaistva*, was revised and a preface by Kritsman added to the original version. The other chapters were not new; they can be found in Chayanov's earlier publications.

[64] This phenomenon had already been observed in Russia in Perm' guberniya by D. I. Kirsanov in 1900.

provements are not set at the level represented by the capitalization of the rent, as in a capitalist economy. This is why Chayanov concluded that the practical range of land improvements is larger for a peasant than for a capitalist economy.

*Die Lehre* tried to make a synthesis of his observations on the interplay of factors (labor, land, capital) in the organizational system of the family economy. In the capitalist economy, land and capital are the variable factors which the entrepreneur tries to combine to obtain the maximum remuneration from his capital, considered as a fixed factor. In a peasant economy, labor, proportionate to the size of the family, is the stable element which determines the change in the volume of capital and land area. To support this thesis, Chayanov showed (*a*) that it is not a lack of land and capital which makes a peasant find work outside his farm, and (*b*) that capital does not play the same part in a peasant economy as in a capitalist one. The family's contribution to production consists less in capital than in labor. The result of this is that what can be isolated in a capitalist economy as an income from capital is used here for the family's consumption. The frontier between wages and income from capital which can be objectively determined in a capitalist exploitation (this income being smaller as wages are higher) has only a subjective value in a peasant holding where there is no conflict between income from capital and consumption.

The social implications of the organizational details of the peasant economy were more specifically analyzed in "On the Theory of Non-Capitalist Economic Systems," below, and in *Peasant Farm Organization,* also below. The first considered these implications from the perspective of macroeconomics and the system, whereas the second regarded them from the point of view of microeconomics. But in both studies, the concept of rent was the central theme.

The historical school's contribution had been to relativize in time the concepts of classical economics founded on the functional dependence of the categories price, land rents, and interest rates, but it had not tried to develop a theory of noncapitalist systems. In his essay, "On the Theory of Non-Capitalist Economic Systems," Chayanov tried to discover such a theory, using the methods of analysis that had been so rewarding for the study of the family economy. Was it possible to establish a universal economic theory on the basis of factors common to all the known systems? Doesn't this "generalized" economy (to employ Professor F. Perroux's phrase) presuppose theoretical studies describing each of the pure systems—family economy, slave-based economy, feudal economy, collectivist economy? In what measure and form do the categories of wages, rent, and profit appear in each of these modes of production, and what is the role of economic and extraeconomic stimulants in each of them?

For example, even if the rent is not always visible, as a separate and autonomous income, the formative factors of rent undeniably influence the product level obtained by the family (family economy), the master (slave economy), or the lord (feudal system). In the peasant family economy, the interest paid for renting land does not obey the rules of marginal productivity of capital, and the land prices are not the expression of the capitalization of rent but of the labor force used to satisfy family needs. This explains why the rents became higher in the poorer and more densely populated regions. In a slave economy, slave rent is the profit made by the slave owner on the difference between price of the slave and cost of maintaining him; this rent is all the bigger when capture reduces the acquisition price to zero or when the fertility of the soil greatly reduces the costs of upkeep. Equilibrium is reached between the marginal product obtained and production costs of the marginal slave. In the quitrent economy, the lord no longer has to bear the costs of upkeep and reproduction of human capital, but he is no longer able to determine the number of serfs, as in the slave economy. Overpopulation lowers the standard of living of the serf and the degree of taxation; the rent can be negative unless there occurs an exodus of the population to colonize new land. In these examples, as well as in the collectivist economy, Chayanov emphasized the importance of constraint in determining the use of the land, irrigation, and obligations in kind or in labor.

To reply to the criticisms evoked by these two essays,[65] Chayanov decided to publish a new version of his theory under the title *Peasant Farm Organization.* Apart from a few additions to the ends of chapters, it differed from the preceding version (*Die Lehre*) only in the last chapters, which dealt with the social implications of the peasant organization. Retreating from his former positions, Chayanov speci-

---

[65] Chayanov was sensitive to the criticism of A. Weber, who regretted seeing superfluous categories break the unity of economic theory. Chayanov reports a personal conversation with Weber to this effect in *Organizatsiya, op. cit.,* p. 10 (cf. p. 41, below). Professor August Skalweit, of Kiel, felt that Chayanov's observations were perhaps valid for the peasant's situation in Russia but, as they were not verified in Germany's case, did not have a universal significance. The peasant economy was not a kind of *Reinkultur* but a variation of the capitalist economy, since it had close relations with the market and was subject to all the effects of competition, such as prices and interest rates determined by these markets. See "Die Familienwirtschaft als Grundlage für ein System der Socialökonomie," *Weltwirtschaftliches Archiv,* Vol. 20 (1924), pp. 231–46. We shall outline below the main criticisms that Chayanov received in Russia.

fied in his preface that his theory concerned the organization of the farm; it was a chapter of *Betriebslehre*, the theory of organizational forms, that he intended to write, not a description of a system or a type of national economy. In short, he did not deny that the peasant farm, like the capitalist farm, shared the same macroeconomic area which the author had declared himself ready to call capitalist because of the privileged role of the dominant economy.[66] However, given the difference in organizational type between the capitalist and the peasant enterprise, it was important to discover what was, in reality, the respective balance between these two sectors. On the other hand, if the unique organizational peculiarities of peasant farms were admitted, was it not necessary to deduce a distinctive mode of social relations? The resulting problems of rent and of social differentiation were raised again.

Chayanov did not deny the existence of rent in a peasant economy. Like Ricardo, he considered only the differential rent[67] and, like Ricardo, conceded a historical progression in land cultivation,[68] but, following Fr. Aeroboe,[69] he emphasized the difficulty in agriculture of calculating a net income, particularly of identifying rent in a peasant economy where only the following categories could be isolated: gross income, money spent for capital reproduction and family maintenance, savings. It is true that the land's relative fertility and distance from the market either reduce or increase the necessary labor, but rent did not entail a profit or loss as it did for the capitalist. The result was not necessarily expressed in monetary income but, rather, "in kind" by greater or lesser family consumption and by lesser or greater labor intensity. Thus, the rent here was independent of other economic categories, while capitalist land rent did not exist isolated from the market.

Moreover, the level of the rent could be evaluated in different ways. For the peasant economy, the factors establishing consumption and labor levels were subjective, being largely determined by the density of the population. For this reason, the land rents or prices (capitalized rent) were higher in more populous regions. Thus, the state of the market was not a determining factor as in the case of capitalist rent. This explained why the peasant economy was able to

---

66 A. Chayanov, *Organizatsiya, op. cit.*, p. 72 (cf. p. 49, below).

67 He does not discuss the absolute rent or scarcity rent that appears when all the land is occupied and when even marginal land produces rent.

68 Carey's studies have shown that this law is not verified in the agrarian history of the United States.

69 Fr. Aeroboe, *Die Beurteilung von Landgütern und Grundstücken* (Berlin, 1921).

win out over capitalist farming in intensive cultivations, such as flax, at a time of falling prices; a fall of economic activity caused an intensification of peasant labor, whereas a capitalist farm, on the contrary, reduced its production when the market was unfavorable. A peasant economy does not take interest rates into consideration when making its decisions to invest in land improvements or machines. For this reason, Chayanov considered the possibility for the intensification of capital to be greater in a peasant than in a capitalist economy.

### The Dynamics of the Peasant Economy and the Social Differentiation in the Countryside

Chayanov felt it necessary to reply to the criticism that his analysis of the peasant economy was static, not taking into account the dynamics of social differentiation. He had never maintained that demographic differentiations were the only motive forces; nevertheless, they were, in his opinion, decisive.[70] The state of the market has either accelerating or braking effects on social polarization, which originates in such demographic disparities as family sizes. He supported his proof with regional statistics of the evolution of peasant holdings and families from 1882 to 1911. He felt that the dynamics of changes in farm areas was not a sufficient criterion to detect a process of proletarianization or of capitalist development in the country. These changes were, rather, to be seen in the analysis of the type of agricultural organization—for example, the percentage of wage labor employed. Moreover, this process could only be very slow in the U.S.S.R., since nationalization of the land and the division of the large estates had put an obstacle in the way of the spontaneous concentration of properties.

The budget surveys that had given rise to Chayanov's theoretical inquiries were taken up again under his direction after 1924.[71] But the new research was not simply organizational; it had to study the farms' grain and fodder balance,[72] the degree of commercialization of

---

[70] This means that situational differences between one peasant family and another are primarily the result of sizes of the families: larger families cultivate more land than others.

[71] This was the point of departure for a series of surveys in Penza, Volokolamsk, and other guberniyas in 1925, in the beetroot-growing guberniyas in 1926, and in Yaroslavl' guberniya in 1927.

[72] A. E. Lositskii, who was director of the consumption section of the Central Statistical Office, was responsible for this survey, which borrowed a great deal from the analysis of the consumption budgets.

the peasant economy, and especially the social differentiation in the villages. A committee chaired by A. N. Chelintsev was set up within the Institute of Agricultural Economy to work out a methodology for these inquiries. Chayanov recounts the development of these survey methods in a book published in 1929 as volume 47 of the institute's studies.[73]

The official surveys accomplished between 1920 and 1924, such as that done by Litoshenko, had adopted the criteria of social differentiation used by G. I. Baskin in his study of Stavropol' guberniya in 1913. Baskin had distinguished 17 social groups according to the share in their budget of external income, wages, and the hiring of labor. The young Marxist, V. S. Nemchinov, who was a collaborator at Chayanov's institute, tried to use a different approach on the basis of a survey made in the Urals in 1925. His aim was to achieve a quantitative evaluation of the surplus value gained by each group (he distinguished 30, counting the subgroups), depending on the degree of dependence or independence of the cultivator vis-à-vis the land, the basic capital, the variable capital, and the labor force.[74]

Other young Marxist colleagues tried to develop this analysis by calculating the arithmetical relationship between labor force and the means of production in each group. This survey was carried out in the Volokolamsk region by Anisimov, Vermenichev, and Naumov,[75] who used the theoretical propositions of Kritsman. With his concern for objectivity and pluralism, Chayanov wanted to proffer his advice and encouragement to his young colleagues who were, however, embarrassed to acknowledge the help and authority of their director, as they were obliged to contribute to the growing criticism of Chayanov's theories. As we will see, the Marxists reproached him for approaching the peasant economy from the inside without taking the social environment into account.[76] Chayanov tried to react by evolving a statistical method of inquiry that would show the different external relations of the peasant economy, such as the importance of land renting and credit. To apply this method, he chose the regions

---

[73] A. Chayanov, *Byudzhetnye issledovaniya: istoriya i metody* (Moscow, 1929), 331 pp.

[74] V. Nemchinov's studies were criticized by Kritsman in *Na Agrarnom Fronte*, No. 2 (1926).

[75] Published under the title, *Proizvodstvennaya kharakteristika krest'yanskikh khozyaistv razlichnykh sotsial'nykh grupp*, 1927, with a preface by Chayanov and a translation of the summary into English by V. V. Williams, who was to give his name to a ley rotation system.

[76] This was Kautsky's reproach to the historical school.

of beetroot cultivation—in other words, the areas most influenced by the market economy.[77]

These theoretical positions had political repercussions because of the discussions inside the party on the social evolution of the Soviet countryside. After the somersaults of war communism, and the scissors crisis during the first years of N.E.P., the Soviet economy by 1924 had achieved a price stability similar to that in 1914. It could be expected that the traditional fiscal and financial mechanism would regain its power to stimulate peasant activity. In December, 1924, the price of wheat had been raised to accelerate sales. In addition, Lenin's articles on cooperation of January, 1923, signified a truce with the cooperative movement—a truce regarded with suspicion by the Bolsheviks.

The radical elements of the party felt these concessions to the peasantry were a return to the policy of support for the "strong" peasants; raising agricultural prices benefited only the rich peasants who dominated the cooperatives. On the other hand, Zinoviev and Bukharin recommended a more flexible policy; it was under their inspiration that the decree of May, 1925, was adopted to allow the peasants to rent land. The controversy over the party's attitude toward social differentiation had taken a new turn with the difficulties of the grain collections in 1925–26 and the increase of unrest in the countryside—revolt in Georgia, murders of the sel'kor, i.e., rural reporters who were pro-Communist. As of April, 1926, the indulgent policy toward the kulaks was over.

The evolution of the political climate explains both the success of Chayanov's school at the beginning of the N.E.P. and its difficulties after 1926. In the last years of his scientific career, he kept up a struggle on the optimal size of agricultural enterprises and the most suitable methods of agricultural integration for accelerating technical transformation.

## The Optimal Size of an Agricultural Enterprise

The problem of the optimum size of the agricultural enterprise had from the start been on the program of the Institute of Agricultural Economy. In 1922, Chayanov published his first essay on this

---

[77] Anisimov refers to the manuscript of this survey in an article in *Byulleten' Nauchno-Issledovatel'skogo Instituta sel'skokhozyaistvennoi ekonomii*, No. 1, pp. 4, 105. A part of this text probably was the basis of Chayanov's study on the cost of beetroot production, *Sebestoimost' sakharnoi svekly* (Moscow, 1928), 131 pp.

subject in the collection *Problemy zemleustroistva* (*Trudy*, Vypusk 7). Two other editions of his essay, *Optimal'nye razmery zemledel'cheskikh khozyaistv*, appeared subsequently, with several important revisions. The last edition was published in 1928, at a time when the Soviet authorities were more than ever convinced of the advantages of large agricultural units. Chayanov's point of view was much more cautious on this point, being opposed to those who were recommending large wheat factories.

On the question of optimum size of an enterprise, one finds the old debate between the advocates of small- and large-scale enterprise. But this time the problem is examined from a quantitative point of view. Chayanov was careful to point out that his calculations referred only to capitalist enterprises and not a peasant economy. His reference point was the German school (Thünen, Werner, Dr. V. Stebel[78]), which had been the first to calculate the limits for the use of machinery in an agricultural space; beyond a certain optimal boundary, varying from 1 kilometer with Werner to 3 kilometers with Stebel, transport costs absorb the net profit made by using machinery. Chayanov divides the different operating costs as a function of distance: (*a*) constant costs (seed grain, cost of domestic labor), (*b*) decreasing costs (amortization of machinery), (*c*) costs increasing with distance or, in other words, with the size of the enterprise (transportation expenses). In this last category, he distinguished regular transport, seasonal transport, the frequency of trips to be made each day, etc., so as to draw the series of curves that would determine the optimal dimensions of an enterprise. He arrived at the conclusion that the limits vary according to the type of crop: 2,000 hectares for extensive cereal cultivation, 800–900 hectares for a system of three-yearly crop rotation, 500–600 hectares for intensive cereal growing, 200–250 for sugar beet cultivation.

In his last edition of 1928, Chayanov observed that the price changes between 1922 and 1928 as well as the lower agricultural salaries permitted higher optimum levels: 3,000 hectares for extensive cultivation, 500 hectares for intensive crops. Besides, the optimum can be raised if the farthest fields are cultivated in a less intensive way than the nearer fields. Thus, Chayanov's revisions tended to increase his optimum limits. He pointed out that the calculations for crop growing were not adaptable for establishing the size of livestock

---

[78] Werner, *Uber zeitgemässen Landwirtschaftsbetrieb*, 1904. Dr. V. Stebel, "Einfluss der Grundstückentfernung auf Wirtschaftsaufwand," *Frühlings Landwirtschaft Zeitung*, Nos. 1 and 2 (1909).

farms, and that his institute was engaged in studying the specific problems of the different types of animal husbandry (livestock ranching, dairy farming), since the transport costs for forage were not the same in each case.

On the other hand, Chayanov wanted his methods to be used to determine the size of rural communities, i.e., taking into consideration the specific characteristics of peasant farms where optimal limits were lower than those for large enterprises.[79] In his conclusion, Chayanov considered that the method of optimum calculation should be applied for each enterprise to each of its branches and that the solution lay in the organization of each of these branches according to the laws of its own optimum. This idea of *differentiated optima* was central to all Chayanov's thinking on cooperation.

### Chayanov's Theory on Agricultural Cooperation and Collectivization

Chayanov's study, *Basic Ideas and Organizational Forms in Peasant Cooperatives*, dates back to 1919[80] and was often republished, the last edition being issued in 1927. It was based on the experience in the cooperative movement described above. But in the last years of N.E.P., Chayanov's theses were put to a severe test, since massive collectivization, despite its cooperative disguise, was the antithesis of his recommendations. Chayanov maintained that horizontal concentration of production offered only limited advantages in agriculture, as the studies of farm sizes showed; on the other hand, vertical concentration allowed agriculture to achieve a revolution comparable to that of the steam engine in industry. The whole point of this vertical integration was to reconcile the maintenance of peasant farms in the biological processes of intensive cultivation and livestock breeding, where they were more productive than capitalist farms, and with the requirements of technical progress, where the large enterprise had an advantage in mechanization, production, and marketing. The agricultural cooperative was to be the instrument of that integration.

Another advantage of the cooperative formula for the technical transformation of agriculture was its being a movement sprung spon-

---

[79] The land is split up into a large number of lots and holdings; the tools and draft animals not being fully used thus increase transport costs.

[80] *Osnovnye idei i formy organizatsii krest'yanskoi kooperatsii* (Moscow, 1919), 343 pp. But Chayanov's first ideas go back to *Kratkii kurs kooperatsii* (1st ed., 1915), the result of his teaching at the Shanyavskii public lectures.

taneously from the peasantry. For Chayanov, it was essential to keep the democratic and voluntary character of cooperation, opening it to all the peasantry and thus making it a *mass movement*. It was on this condition alone that cooperation had a chance to succeed. Every restrictive measure that would limit the freedom of membership in the cooperatives in the name of some ideological principle would lessen their strength as a mass movement. But, on the other hand, it would be wrong to consider cooperation as a movement isolated from the organizational forces that gave birth to it. This is why those who wanted to amalgamate in the same institution both agricultural productive cooperatives and workers' consumption cooperatives were wrong, since the interests of each were not the same. Because cooperation was a spontaneous mass movement, it could do much better than the other types of collective enterprises, such as the communes and artels which had never shown much progress in the task of successfully transforming Soviet agriculture.[81]

Chayanov had doubts about "collective" agriculture (communes and artels), because the incentive problem had been solved more flexibly by the cooperatives based on the small family farm, with its individuality intact, than by the artels. For where the artel or commune was founded on an ideological or religious basis that maintained the corporate spirit and the incentive to work in spite of the egalitarian division of the product, it was too narrow to allow an expansion of cooperation. More frequently, where no ideological tie bound the members of a collective farm, salaries had to be introduced to stimulate work—close to capitalism, but with the disadvantage of substituting for a single employer a collective authority without the employer's powers of constraint.

Differing from the state farm, the collective farm did not have the same facilities for hiring additional outside labor; thus it was condemned either to underemployment if it kept on the personnel necessary for its needs at peak periods, or to labor shortages.

Chayanov was not, however, systematically opposed to all forms of horizontal integration. Horizontal and vertical integration were complementary rather than contradictory. The limits of horizontal integration—the desirable dimension of the production unit—were not identical at all stages of production and for all products. Chayanov

---

[81] On June 1, 1929, i.e., before the outbreak of the campaign of forced collectivization, the total area under collective farming did not exceed 3.9 percent of the agricultural land.

admitted that collectivization could reach to extensive cultivation and to pasturing where processes were easily mechanized. On the other hand, collectivization could not give good results where biological processes were dominant (livestock, intensive farming). For marketing, vertical integration gained an advantage with zones of application that went far beyond the limits envisaged for the collective farm, as the dairy societies showed. From this was developed the idea of optimum differentiation for each branch of production, which, by forecasting different levels of integration, implied the possibility of breaking up the links of an organizational plan of enterprise. The cooperative was the system best adapted to combine the advantages of large-scale commercial mechanical or processing activities with those of the family farms for intensive production.

It is not necessary to emphasize the gap that separated these ideas from the positions adopted by the Soviet government. Need one recall the government's efforts to take over the cooperative movement which at the beginning of the Revolution had been controlled by the S.R. (Social Revolutionary Party)?[82] The official directives excluding the rich peasants from the cooperatives and the measures of constraint used for collectivization are well known. For the Bolsheviks, cooperation was only a stage in the socialist transformation of agriculture; for Chayanov, cooperation was an ideal compromise, combining the advantages of small peasant property with the technical advantages of large-scale farming.

### The New State Farms and the Techniques of the Future

The problem of optimal size of the agricultural enterprise was again a question of the day for the last years of Chayanov's activity as the head of the Agricultural Economy Institute during the state farms campaign. Since April, 1917, Lenin had recommended forming state farms out of the old feudal domains. From 1928, the state farms drive was extended to new regions to create veritable cereal factories, which were to deliver the marketable surplus that was harder and harder to obtain as the peasant, lacking incentive, retreated into his shell.

Chayanov's last works on the state farms were concerned with defining an organizational policy and a method for planning their pro-

---

[82] The decree of August 6, 1918, made membership in cooperatives obligatory, but at the Ninth Party Congress, 1920, Lenin opposed the fusion of worker and agricultural cooperatives in single institutions.

duction. In an article on the "Technical Organization of Grain Factories,"[83] he tried to answer the following questions.

1. In what region of the U.S.S.R. could 25 million hectares of land be found to accommodate the creation of new state farms? It was impossible to crowd them into the traditional agricultural regions which were already overpopulated; therefore, it would be necessary to concentrate on the territories situated on the periphery of the peasant economy, especially on the Volga, in Siberia, and in Kazakhstan, where, according to Chayanov's calculations, 12.3 million hectares could be newly cultivated or, in some cases, recultivated. It was a kind of virgin land program drawn up 25 years before Khrushchev. The difficulty was that the lands were situated in regions where there was insufficient rainfall and a poorly developed communications infrastructure. The average distance of the new enterprises from a railway or port would be 20–40 kilometers, sometimes even 70.

2. What type of agriculture would be best adapted to these marginal regions to insure stable production? Until then, these lands had been used for livestock pasturing or had been left uncultivated because the primitive peasant tools had not been able to work the land, given the shortness of the season. The tractor and truck would overcome this difficulty, but it would also be necessary to vigorously combat plant disease and to perfect methods of conserving winter humidity and soil fertility in order to avoid summer drought and soil erosion. Chayanov had thus foreseen the main dangers which were to confront the virgin land experiment. To remedy these difficulties, he recommended American dry farming methods—wheat-growing followed by a year of fallow. But not everyone agreed on this point. Other experts advocated cereals rotated with grass, which implied livestock and, thus, more complex farms and larger investments.

3. What was the degree of mechanization and the optimum size envisaged for these specialized farms? Chayanov was in favor of 100 percent total mechanization to limit the number of workmen and to make the most of farming on vast areas—10,000–12,000 hectares, all in one block. Chayanov was now far from the ceilings he had set previously, but he explained his change of mind. His previous calculations establishing maximum dimensions of 800–1,500 hectares in extensive cereal farming had been based on the use of horses and of machines which would have to return to the farm each evening, but if the machines stayed in the fields and if the men could return to

83 *Ekonomicheskoe obozrenie*, No. 12 (1929), pp. 95–101.

the farm by truck these limits could be modified. Technical progress would allow production units of 8,000 to 12,000 hectares, so that by joining together several of these units state farms of 60,000 to 100,000 hectares could be created; several production units would form a state farm for administrative purposes. The main bottleneck, according to Chayanov, would be trained personnel rather than capital. He concluded by calling for an accelerated program for training agricultural officers and state farm administrators.

Among the other problems of the cereal factories were the methods of elaborating production plans for the state farms. The plenary session of the institute, March 16, 1928, discussed the report Chayanov presented on this subject.[84] The method he advocated for working out agricultural plans is still used in Soviet practice, although his conception of the state agricultural enterprise was very different from the state farm of today.

To set up a production plan, Chayanov started with the regional targets defined by the higher authorities. These targets would determine the orientation of the enterprise's production, taking into account costs and market conditions as profitability criteria for the possible production alternatives. The organizational plan of the enterprise would be the logical consequence of the chosen orientation; it would try to strike a balance between the principal production (cereals, for example) and the complementary activities (livestock, fodder, food for workers) which, in turn, would determine, first, the land utilization of the area (the sown–pasture ratio), second, the number of traction units required, and third (taking into account the available manpower), the required addition of seasonal labor. The availability of fodder would determine the composition of the stock, and this, in turn, the volume of fertilizer needed; the practicable degree of intensification would be deduced from this need. This intensification would set the income level, which would determine the possibilities of accumulation and of enlarged reproduction. The objectives of the plan were thus like links of a chain, hence the term "key links," given to this now classic method of Soviet planning.

However, to conceive a state agricultural enterprise along capitalist lines by basing the direction of the state farm production not only on the plan's targets but also on profitability criteria was to provoke criticism from several of Chayanov's colleagues—K. I. Naumov, V. N.

---

84 "Metody sostavleniya organizatsionnykh planov sel'skokhoz. predpriyatii v usloviyakh sovetskoi ekonomii," *Byulleten' Nauchno-Issledovatel'skogo Instituta sel'sko-khozyaistvennoi ekonomii*, No. 1–2 (1928), pp. 5–14.

Lubyakov, and I. S. Kubshinov.[85] It is known that the authorities scarcely followed Chayanov's advice in organizing the state farms and that the profitability of these enterprises has long been one of the weak spots of the Soviet state sector.

In all his later writings, one can detect a noticeable revision of Chayanov's previous positions, not only on the problem of optimal size of enterprises but more generally in his understanding of the basic evolution of Soviet agriculture.

Chayanov's early studies, which had provided the basis for his first theoretical formulations, were related to Russian agriculture little touched by technical progress. At that point, Chayanov was unaware of the revolution wrought in American agriculture by the tractor, the truck, and the combine. In 1929, he hailed these innovations as comparable to the effect of the steam engine on industry, and he implied by this that agricultural science would have to be wholly rethought. "This revision," he wrote, "obliges us to relegate to the background much of what we have hitherto considered as fundamental."[86] The theory of peasant economy had been developed on the assumption of a preindustrial technical world. "To defend peasant economy is to defend several generations destined to slow death."[87] It would be just as unrealistic to defend the artisan's workshop against the factory at the end of the eighteenth century. The problem was simply to know what form the inevitable agricultural revolution would take in the present conditions. Would there be a Russian equivalent of the development of capitalist agriculture in England? The Soviet regime offered another solution—the organized transformation of peasant farms grouping themselves in large units by a process of self-collectivization (*samo-kollektivizatsiya*).

In other words, agricultural cooperation, previously restricted to the marketing sphere, was to be extended to the production sphere. *There would no longer be a peasant economy,*[88] but vast collective farms stretching over thousands of hectares. These collective farms would be distinguished from large capitalist units not by organization and technology but by their social implications. In a planned socialist economy, where the state controlled all the resources, it would be possible to avoid the social catastrophe of an agricultural revolution's

85 *Ibid.*, p. 14.

86 "Segodnyachnii i zavtrashnii den' krupnogo zemledeliya," *Ekonomicheskoe obozrenie*, No. 9 (1929), p. 40.

87 *Ibid.*, p. 52.

88 *Ibid.*, p. 80.

destroying the personnel of the old peasant economy. In short, Chayanov hailed the new orientation of Soviet agriculture toward the creation of state farms and collective farms as "the only realistic path for agricultural development,"[89] on the condition that the heritage of peasant experience be preserved and that self-collectivization be achieved without external pressure.

The chapter that Chayanov wrote in 1928 for the collection of essays on *Life and Technology in the Future*, "The possibilities of Agriculture,"[90] was an act of faith in scientific progress. He foresaw the upheavals which the progress of research would impose on agriculture in a more or less distant future. The prospects offered by soilless agriculture (thanks to factory-produced syntheses of albumen and the mastery of certain biological processes) were described in terms that were utopian for the time. Chayanov visualized factories for food products and synthetic textiles; the plants would be used purely for their decorative purposes and natural fruits for their inimitable perfumes. He also predicted that man would be able to control climate and forecast harvests. One can hardly accuse him of turning his back on progress.

But side by side with these predictions was a whole program for agronomic research in the U.S.S.R. which again revealed Chayanov's deep knowledge of the regional realities of his country. He emphasized the need for studies of plant selection to acclimatize the species to very short growth cycles in northern regions, the problems of different methods of combating drought in southern regions, and so on. One finds there an enumeration of the principal difficulties Soviet agronomists have encountered in the past decades.

## A Synthesis of Chayanov's Contribution

As one can see from this chronological presentation of the main trends in Chayanov's thought, his work displays such a remarkable unity that one may consider it to constitute a theory of peasant economy just as well worked out as his own book on the subject. The principal stages and the logical developments of this theory can be summarized as follows.

Until the end of the nineteenth century, the debate on the agrarian problem between slavophiles and westernizers and later between

---

89 *Ibid.*, p. 51.

90 "Vozmozhnoe budushchee sel'skogo khozyaistva," *Zhizn' i Tekhnika Budushchego (Sotsial'nye i nauchno-technicheskie utopii)*, ed. A. Kolman (Moscow, 1928), 503 pp.

Populists and Marxists had been seen in the light of social relations in agriculture. Against the idealization of the peasant commune and the vitality of the traditional community were opposed the theory of the decomposition and proletarianization of rural society under the impact of capitalism. The Organization and Production School, of which Chayanov became the most eminent theoretician after the Revolution, directed the debate, not on the social relations, but on the organizational forms of the peasant economy. He tried to show that to the categories and modes of production Marx had recognized (slavery, feudalism, capitalism, socialism) there should be added a distinctive form—the peasant labor economy ("On the Theory of Non-Capitalist Economic Systems").

While in Marxist eyes the chief motivation of the peasant economy —the search for maximum income—allowed it to be assimilated into the capitalist system, Chayanov claimed that consumption, or the family's subsistence, was the motive force determining the peasant's activity. From this, he showed that the arrangement of the factors of production in a peasant farm obeyed subjective criteria (*Peasant Farm Organization*). In addition, the comparison of peasant and worker budgets in Belgian, German, and Swiss surveys showed that the consumption trends were not identical in these two categories, thus confirming the specific nature of the peasant economy (cf. *Ocherki*).

From analysis of the theory of peasant economy, Chayanov went on to analysis of various types of farming. Classical theory used the criteria of land, capital, and labor to characterize the degree of agricultural intensity of a given region; it used the law of diminishing returns to explain the general evolution of the different agricultural systems. But the studies of Aeroboe in Germany and Laur in Switzerland showed that the orientation of a farm's production—i.e., its principal produce—was more important in characterizing a given type of farm than was the combination of its factors of production. This explains why the surveys of Russia's rural economy by sector of production were in such favor. Chayanov's studies on the economy of flax, the potato, beetroot, and irrigation completed the work of Chelintsev and Brutskus, undertaken at the same time. Chayanov's principal contribution was to attempt a synthesis of the main factors determining the development of agricultural systems and thereby of social relations in agriculture.

Von Thünen had been one of the first to point to the market as the determining influence on the degree of intensity of an agricultural unit. Specialization decreases and the type of produce alters progressively as distance from the city increases, taking account of transport costs, the perishable quality of produce, and local prices. Ricardo's teaching on land rent which forms the basis of Marxist analysis of agricultural development also contributes to treatment of the market as the essential factor. It is for this reason that the discussion between legal Marxists and Social Democrats on the possibility and signs of the development of capitalism in Russia was focused on the problem of the market.[91] For the Social Democrats, the market was to play a "progressive" role in transforming the natural peasant economy; without modifying the market, one could not expect significant changes in the organization of the farm.

The German historical school of Schmoller and a few Russian theoreticians, such as Chelintsev, tried to show that population density plays a more important role than the market in directing the development of systems. For his part, Chayanov tried to analyze the relationships between population density and organizational forms in agriculture. However, he went further than his predecessors by combining in the same model (in an isolated state) both factors—market and population density. In a natural economy, intensification is determined by population density. For this intensification to arrive at specialization—i.e., at an even greater intensification—a market was needed. Local markets could be the result of the population density of a region, but the density factor was insufficient to explain the action of distant markets on regional specialization. Thus, since agricultural development is not determined by any single factor, social relations in the village are complex and differ from one region to the other.

It would be an exaggeration to claim that it was exclusively due to Chayanov that progress has been made in understanding the peasant farm. The German revisionists and the work of the historical school have contributed their share.[92] But Chayanov wanted to transcend both the abstract generalizations of the classic and neoclassic

---

91 Vl. Ilin (Lenin), *Razvitie kapitalizma v Rossii, protsess, obrazovaniya vnutrennego rynka dlya krupnoi promyshlennosti* (2d ed.; St. Petersburg, 1908).

92 *Der Moderne Kapitalismus* was translated and published in Russia in 1905. For W. Sombart, the variety in the structure of the peasant economy is greater, because the uniformity of capitalist motivation is replaced by the diversity of peasant needs and because the peasant economy can avoid the activity of the market more easily. See W. Sombart, *Apogée du Capitalisme*, Vol. 2, p. 475. According to N. Makarov, *op. cit.*, Chayanov transposed Sombart's "precapitalist" type of consumer or handicraft economy to the peasant economy. However, analysis of Chayanov's writings does not confirm this statement, as he never cites Sombart.

theoreticians, such as the marginalists, and the relativism of the historical school. The notion of organizational types and systems allowed him to bridge the gap between abstract theory and history.

Doubtless not all Chayanov's ideas were equally original. Who can dispute today, however, that his major views, based on a thorough knowledge of the Russian situation, would have facilitated some of the changes and avoided many of the trials that its peasantry and agriculture have endured since then?

The proof can be seen that now, with the perspective of the years, the Soviet Marxist school approaches agricultural problems with much less dogmatism and sometimes with an attitude close to that of Chayanov 40 years ago when the two were opposed to each other.

## Russian Critics of Chayanov's Theories

Among the leftist economists not affiliated with the Bolshevik party, S. N. Prokopovich was at least as influential as Chayanov. *Krest'yanskoe khozyaistvo* (Peasant Economy),[93] Prokopovich's reply to *Die Lehre*, was therefore disappointing, since it did not live up to its claims. It was not, in fact, a new theory of peasant economy but a collection of more or less connected essays on different aspects of this economy before the Revolution. Prokopovich wanted to show that the "subjectivist" view of the peasant farm—i.e., Chayanov's theory that its principal impulse came from consumption—was compatible with the "objective" Marxist position, which considered production needs to be decisive. To make this synthesis of the two schools, Prokopovich used, as had Chayanov, the budget surveys, establishing correlation coefficients that showed the connections among land, capital, and labor. He tried to show that the factors of production, and especially the area used by a peasant, have a higher correlation coefficient vis-à-vis the level of family income than the number of mouths to be fed. He thus rejects the theory that consumption needs determine the size of the peasant holding.[94] He does not, however, conclude that the peasant economy can be described as a capitalist economy, although he questions Chayanov's criteria of differentiation.[95] Unfortunately, the constructive part of his proof errs in the method of correlations he used: today we are better aware of the risk involved in using correlations to support a theory.

---

[93] S. N. Prokopovich, *Krest'yanskoe khozyaistvo* (Berlin, 1924), 246 pp.

[94] *Ibid.*, p. 36.

[95] *Ibid.*, p. 41.

Similarly, Brutskus, who was a professor at the Agricultural Institute of St. Petersburg from 1907 to 1922 and who emigrated to Berlin at the same time as Prokopovich, adopted an intermediary position between Chayanov and the Marxist school in his treatise on rural economy.[96] A peasant farm tries "to satisfy the needs of the family *by trying to obtain the maximum income* from the land through a better utilization of the peasant's and family's labor."[97]

As for Chayanov, his work subsequent to *Die Lehre* (1923) had very little effect among the Russian émigrés, despite the presence among them of his old friends Chuprov and Kosinskii. One looks in vain for a reference to Chayanov in the Prague periodical, *Krest'yanska Rossiya*, edited by S. Maslov.

It is in Chayanov's own Institute of Agricultural Economy that one finds echoes of the discussions which put him into conflict with some of his close collaborators. Thus, in a work on land rents, published by the institute, G. A. Studenskii took exception to his director's ideas on the subject.[98] It is to be remembered that although Chayanov did not deny the existence of rent in the peasant economy he believed that it was not to be thought of as separate from the total revenue obtained by a peasant family's labor. Studenskii tried to formulate a method that would allow the calculation of rent in a peasant economy by using Vainshtein's studies on land rent.[99] He tried to discover the principles of a fiscal policy that would allow the elimination of rent while leaving the remuneration of labor and capital intact.[100] Like Chayanov, however, he hoped that with land taxes the mechanics of the market would be able to play a stimulating role in intensifying agricultural production without upsetting the peasant economy from the outside.

Later, in 1928, the rent question arose again in the institute's discussions of the law of diminishing returns in agriculture. Chelintsev

[96] B. D. Brutskus, *Ekonomika sel'skogo khozyaistva* (Berlin, 1923), 360 pp. Chelintsev acclaimed it as the first treatise of wide scope, and regretted that "Chayanov's numerous and precious studies do not form a complete course." *Krest'yanskaya Rossiya*, No. 5–6 (1923), p. 237.

[97] On the advantages of small scale holdings and cooperation, Brutskus agreed with Chayanov. Like him, he was familiar with the theories of marginal utility and productivity. In the criticism of the dynamics of social evolution, the positions of Prokopovich and Chayanov are also identical. See *Krest'yanskoe khozyaistvo, op cit.*, chap. vi, pp. 157–92.

[98] G. A. Studenskii, *Renta v krest'yanskom khozyaistve i printsipy oblozheniya*, *Trudy*, Vypusk 15 (Moscow, 1925), 114 pp.

[99] A. L. Vainshtein, *Oblozhenie i platezhi krest'yanstva* (Moscow, 1924).

[100] Chayanov discussed the same problem in *Sel'sko-khozyaistvennaya taksatsiya* (Moscow, 1925), 186 pp.

was opposed to Chayanov, who adopted the Marxist point of view. But it was the problem of differentiations in peasant society that was to provoke the greatest commotion in the institute as well as, according to Sylkovskii,[101] a schism in the Organization and Production School from 1927 on. Makarov and Kondrat'ev felt that social differentiation was beneficial and "progressive," because it tended to develop the efficient peasant productive forces. Chayanov (supported by Chelintsev) questioned this differentiation and denied the "progressive" character of "capitalist" development in peasant economy, advocating an agriculture based on small peasant property organized in cooperatives.[102]

The opposition of the party's Marxist theoreticians to Chayanov's thesis appeared very early—for example, in the preface to Ivan Kremnev's *Peasant Utopia*. In his introduction to *Peasant Farm Organization*, Chayanov himself cited the major arguments of the Marxist school against his theory of peasant economy.

1. *The method used by Chayanov was not Marxist.* He was considered a spokesman of the Austrian marginalist school, whose theory was based on current market prices and who considered value subjectively as a function of needs. But for a Marxist, prices were merely variables determined by the level of production forces and modified in relation to labor productivity,[103] whereas value had for them an objective content. In the 1924 preface to *Ocherki*, Kritsman particularly attacked Chayanov for ignoring the role of the material productive forces as a factor in the development of the peasant economy. Meerson followed with this criticism: the importance of activity was measured by the labor *and* the means of production, not by labor alone; because the means of production were not divided equally, there was a redistribution of the labor force itself, as Marx had shown in his introduction to the *Critique of Political Economy*.[104]

2. *Peasant economy was considered as a static entity*, independent of the economic environment. Chayanov's school refused to see that the peasant economy was in conflict with capitalism and the prey to social differentiation. Lenin's work, *The Development of Capitalism in Russia*, was the Soviet Marxists' reference book to illustrate this

---

101 *Na Agrarnom Fronte*, No. 11–12 (1929), pp. 75–96.

102 Extracts from the "verbatim" report used by party theoreticians in attacks against Chayanov's school give only an imperfect account of this debate. See I. Vermenichev, *Na Agrarnom Fronte*, No. 4 (1927).

103 G. Gordeev, *Na Agrarnom Fronte*, No. 4 (1927), pp. 162–71.

104 D. Meerson, *Na Agrarnom Fronte*, No. 3 (1925).

breakdown. According to his critics, Chayanov had mistakenly grouped together middle peasants and kulaks under the category of farmers with more than 15 hectares. A further breakdown by farm size would have shown that renting land and employing labor were very frequent in the group cultivating more than 25 hectares. Also, increase in family size was more rapid in the last categories than in those where it was necessary, because of lack of land, to look for outside wages. Finally, the drudgery of labor inside the peasant family varies not only in relation to the size of the family but also in relation to the social group to which the given family belongs.[105]

It was not correct to claim that the small farm could compete successfully with capitalist farms. This reasoning, based by Chayanov on an equality in technical levels of the two sectors, was refuted by the facts; capitalist enterprises used more perfected techniques and therefore obtained greater returns. The inability of the small farm to adopt technical progress or its underutilization of machinery because of its size proved the contradictions between this social form and the production forces. Continuing in this defense of technical progress, the theoreticians of the party attacked Chayanov's "optima" theory, accusing him of failing to see the evolution of the optima in relation to this progress and of confusing the optimal dimension of an enterprise with the optimal dimension of cultivated areas.[106]

3. *Chayanov tended to idealize peasant economy by attributing to it well-intentioned motives.* Facts prove that the mentality of a peasant is no different from that of a capitalist farmer. This idealization was a reflection of the petty bourgeois ideology which justifies the reactionary policy of support for the kulaks.[107] "Neopopulism" was a new version of the ideology of the Stolypin reform, an "American style" development without revolution. In other words, Chayanov's policy would stabilize the peasant economy by cooperation and encourage the efficient elements of the peasantry, considered as "progressive."[108]

The school had adopted in some measure the pre-Revolutionary thesis of the Social Democrats—a thesis that considered the evolution of capitalism in agriculture inevitable, and even desirable, as a step in the transition toward socialism. But (and in this the neopopulism

---

105 L. Kritsman, Preface to the 1924 edition of *Ocherki*.

106 Sulkovskii, *Na Agrarnom Fronte*, No. 4 (1928).

107 This reproach was aimed more at Kondrat'ev than at Chayanov. See Vermenichev, *Na Agrarnom Fronte*, No. 4 (1927).

108 Sylkovskii, *Na Agrarnom Fronte*, No. 11–12 (1929), pp. 78–96.

conformed to the former populism) they continued to think that a peasant economy could attain socialism without going through forced collectivization, and that the creation of large production cooperatives had no future except in certain regions where an extensive mechanized agriculture was possible.

When the right opposition in the party was liquidated, the gulf between Chayanov and his opponents became unbridgeable.[109] The criticism, which initially had been relatively courteous, gained in intensity from 1929 on and became increasingly political. In 1930, Chayanov was accused of counterrevolutionary conspiracy.[110]

"A group of bourgeois and petit bourgeois scholars: Kondrat'ev, Yurovskii, Doyarenko, Oganovskii, Makarov, *Chayanov*, Chelintsev and others to which are joined Groman, Sukhanov and Bazarov, representing the anti-marxist tendency in agrarian economics, these last Mohicans of the populist ideology, are now unmasked as being leaders of a counter-revolutionary organization aimed at overthrowing the Soviet régime."[111] According to the same author, this organization was trying to slow down the growth of agricultural production and foster the development of capitalist elements in the countryside; the scholars belonging to it inspired right-wing deviationism (*pravyi uklon*), and were trying to deflect the party line toward a bourgeois ideology.

These accusations were based on the "confessions" of Professor Karatygin, who had admitted participating in an organization to sabotage the workers' food supply.[112] Thus, the difficulties of the procurement campaign were attributed to these scholars.

## The Present Importance of Chayanov and the Evolution of Social Science in the U.S.S.R.

Chayanov's ideas have, nevertheless, survived him, and many of the problems debated by him in the twenties are now receiving a

---

109 Kulikov, *Na Agrarnom Fronte*, No. 1 (1931), p. 36, but Nicholas Bukharin disclaimed belonging to "these petty bourgeois princes who protect agriculture against all the changes envisaged in favor of industry. They are in essence supporting the conservation of the small enterprise with its family structure, its backward techniques. . . . These ideologists of petty bourgeois conservatism do not manage to understand that the development of agriculture depends on that of industry." "Notes of an Economist," *Pravda*, October 30, 1928.

110 I. Vermenichev, "Burzhuaznye ekonomisty kak oni est (Kondrat'evshchina)," *Bol'shevik*, No. 18 (1930), pp. 38–55.

111 *Ibid.*

112 *Pravda*, September 22, 1930.

new illumination. It would doubtless be an exaggeration to say that official positions on the political level have been changed, but it would be no less incorrect to underestimate the noticeable evolution in Soviet theses in scientific and historical studies as well as in rural economics.

The most interesting changes of the young school of Soviet historians on the problem of agricultural development in twentieth-century Russia are shown in the analysis of the development of capitalism in Russian agriculture before the Revolution and the social composition of the Russian peasantry after it. Without entering into a discussion that is far from concluded,[113] certain historians, such as A. M. Anfimov,[114] want to go beyond the works of Lenin in their studies of economic types in Russian agriculture at the beginning of the twentieth century. By adopting more sophisticated criteria and by better distinguishing the different regional developments,[115] Anfimov separates the sector of capitalist farming from the sector of peasant economy. In the upper levels of the peasantry, Anfimov succeeds in separating those that do not hire labor and those evolving toward capitalism because they employ outside labor. In other words, he thus tends to minimize the importance of capitalism in agriculture.

In the same way, the most recent historical studies of the social structure of Russian villages in the twenties before collectivization tend to emphasize the importance of the middle peasantry. I. Malyi cites Lenin at the Tenth Party Congress (1921):

The peasantry has become much more "middle" than before, opposition is reduced, the use of the land is much more equally shared . . . the statistics show in general and in detail that the village has incontestably been levelled, i.e., that the pronounced polarization between the kulak on the one hand and the landless peasant on the other has been mitigated. The peasantry has become stabilized on the whole at the situation of the middle peasant.[116]

113 N. Rubinshtein, *Voprosy Istorii*, No. 8 (1961); *Istoriya S.S.S.R.*, No. 4 (1962); I. D. Koval'chenko, *Istoriya S.S.S.R.*, No. 1 (1962); P. Ryndzyunskii, *Istoriya S.S.S.R.*, No. 4 (1963); V. Yatsunskii, *Istoriya S.S.S.R.*, No. 1 (1963); A. Anfimov, *Istoriya S.S.S.R.*, No. 2 (1963).

114 "K voprosu ob opredelenii ekonomicheskikh tipov zemledel'cheskogo khozyaistva," *Voprosy Istorii Sel'skogo Khozyaistva, Krest'yanstva i revolyutsionnogo dvizheniya v Rossii* (Moscow, 1961), pp. 362–79.

115 *Ibid.*, p. 367. The 1913 survey of Starobel'sk and the concept of the "peasant consumer economy" are used, but Chayanov is not named.

116 I. Malyi, "Voprosy agrarnoi statistiki v posleoktyabr'skikh trudakh V. I. Lenina," *Vestnik statistiki*, No. 4 (1964), pp. 15–16.

The same author mentions a study by V. S. Yastremskii[117] which demonstrates the correlations between land area and family composition. There again, one of Chayanov's fundamental theses has returned to the surface.

The analyses of V. Yakovtsevskii[118] on the social structure of Soviet agriculture between 1921 and 1925 also emphasize the role of the middle peasantry, classified, not as capitalist, but as belonging to the "small market economy." There is but a step from this point to considering the peasant economy as a specific category. It appears that this step has been taken by the economists.

In fact, the recent *Course of Political Economy*, published in two volumes in 1963 by the University of Moscow, under the editorship of Professor N. A. Tsagolov, devotes a paragraph in the chapter on land rent to rent in a "peasant economy" (*V krest'yanskom khozyaistve*, p. 452). Many sentences could easily have been signed by Chayanov:

The chief motivation of the small market peasant economy is not the increase of value; the necessary condition for its functioning is not the obtaining of an average profit; prevailing prices are not necessarily equal to the price of the factors of production for a peasant economy. In the peasant economy there are no costs of production $(C + V)$ for it does not buy labor. Nevertheless to the extent that the capitalist form of production dominates, the categories of capitalist economics can be applied in a conventional way (*uslovno*) to the peasant economy.

In other words, they seem to admit that the peasant economy presents characteristics different from those of the capitalist form of production and that the use of capitalist concepts in this case has only conventional value.

More decisive is the return to favor of mathematical methods in

---

117 V. S. Yastremskii, "Svyaz' mezhdu elementami krest'yanskogo khozyaistva," *Vestnik statistiki*, No. 9–12 (1920), pp. 51–53.

118 In the collection published under the direction of I. A. Gladkov, *Sovetskoe narodnoe khozyaistvo v 1921–1925* (Moscow, 1960), pp. 267–80. In the volume, *Postroenie fundamenta sotsialisticheskoi ekonomiki v S.S.S.R. 1926–1932* (Moscow, 1960), p. 272, the same V. Yakovtsevskii cites the following statistics to support his thesis.

Dynamics of social evolution in the country:

|  | Before the Revolution | 1928–29 |
|---|---|---|
| Poor peasants (bednyak) . . . . . | 65% | 35% |
| Middle peasants (serednyak) . . | 20% | 60% |
| Kulaks . . . . . . . . . . . . . . . . . . | 15% | 5% |

On p. 274, he adds: "One criterion alone, such as the area, is not sufficient to determine whether a peasant farm belongs to one or the other group . . . our statistics do not provide global facts on the distribution of the cultivated area, yields, gross production and marketed production for each socio-economic group of the peasantry."

Soviet economics, thanks to the work of Kantorovich, Nemchinov, and Novozhilov. The notions of scarcity and marginal calculus are tending to perfect and modify both Marxist value theory and the practice of economic decisions. In this revision, whose importance transcends the boundaries of agricultural economics, it is interesting to note the role played by two former colleagues of Chayanov—V. S. Nemchinov, who has been mentioned already, and A. L. Vainshtein,[119] who is now working in the department of econometrics and economic models of the Academy of Sciences.

The application of marginal calculus to agricultural economics is reopening the problems of optimal size of the agricultural enterprise and location of production which preoccupied Chayanov in the 1920's. It is significant that the studies recently completed in this area[120] link up with some of Chayanov's former work. I. A. Borodin's proposal for deciding the size of an enterprise repeats with improvements Chayanov's conclusions in his article on the state farms: "The problem of optimal size of the state farm and its subdivisions must be solved simultaneously with the rational allocation of the divisions on the state farm's land."[121] The optimal subdivision depends on the type of produce: 2,500 to 3,000 hectares for cereals in the Volga regions; 100 to 120 hectares (northwest), 300 to 400 hectares (central region) for the intensive cultivation of vegetables. These dimensions are close to those Chayanov advocated from 1922 to 1928.

This development of the social sciences in the U.S.S.R. in areas touching the peasant economy more or less directly does not, of course, imply that the official political positions have been modified. The correctness of collectivization and the fight against the kulaks is not questioned. Only the speed of the transformations and the methods practiced by Stalin are severely judged by historians of this period.[122] For this reason, it would still seem premature for Chayanov

---

119 See biographical note on V. S. Nemchinov by A. L. Vainshtein, *Vestnik statistiki*, No. 4 (1962), p. 81.

120 For the application of linear programming to planning the regional distribution of production, see the studies of A. G. Aganbegiyan, V. S. Mikheeva, and I. G. Popov in *Problemy optimal'nogo planirovaniya proektirovaniya i upravleniya proizvodstvom* (Conference at the University of Moscow, March, 1962) (Moscow: University of Moscow, 1963), pp. 373–409.

121 "Ob optimal'nykh razmerakh sovkhozov," *Voprosy ekonomiki*, No. 12 (1963), pp. 34–51. See, also, *Voprosy ratsional'noi organizatsii i ekonomiki sel'sko-khozyaistvennogo proizvodstva* (Moscow, 1964), pp. 261–328.

122 V. P. Danilov, N. A. Ivnitskii in *Ocherki istorii kollektivizatsii sel'skogo khozyaistva v soyuznykh respublikakh* (Moscow, 1963), pp. 3–67. V. P. Danilov is the leading scholar of Soviet agrarian history.

to be rehabilitated, even if, in practice, some of the research he pioneered is being carried on today with new means.

The continuing vitality of many of his ideas is surely the best homage that can be paid to Chayanov today. Even if he often showed more indulgence to the traditional peasant economy than to the future industrial agriculture, it is no less true that to understand the problems posed by the Russian peasant economy in the period preceding collectivization Chayanov's contributions and especially his work on the organization of the peasant economy constitute a turning point in the development of his country's agrarian thought which it is impossible to ignore.

# On the Theory of Non-Capitalist Economic Systems

In modern theory of the national economy, it has become customary to think about *all* economic phenomena exclusively in terms of a capitalist economy. All the principles of our theory—rent, capital, price, and other categories—have been formed in the framework of an economy based on wage labor and seeking to maximize profits (i.e., the maximum amount of the part of gross income remaining after deducting material costs of production and wages). All other (noncapitalist) types of economic life are regarded as insignificant or dying out; they are, at any rate, considered to have no influence on the basic issues of the modern economy and, therefore, are of no theoretical interest.

We shall have to accept this last thesis in regard to the indisputable dominance of finance and trading capital in world commerce and the unquestioned part it plays in the present organization of the world economy. But we must by no means extend its application to all phenomena in our economic life. We shall be unable to carry on in economic thought with merely capitalist categories, because a very wide area of economic life (that is, the largest part of the agrarian production sphere) is based, not on a capitalist form, but on the completely different form of a nonwage family economic unit.[1] Such a unit has very special motives for economic activity and also a very specific conception of profitability. We know that most peasant farms in Russia, China, India, and most non-European and even many European states are unacquainted with the categories of wage labor and wages. Even superficial theoretical analysis of their economic structures shows that their specific economic phenomena do not always fit into the framework of classical economics and the modern theory of the national economy derived from it. We must go beyond

---

[1] The terms, family economic unit, labor economic unit, family labor economic unit, and labor family economic unit, in this article mean the economic unit of a peasant or artisan family that does not employ paid workers but uses solely the work of its own members, even where this characteristic has not been explicitly stated.

this conceptual framework of the national economy if we are to conduct a theoretical analysis of our economic *past*.

The late systems of serfdom in Russia and slavery in America raise the question whether the concepts of contemporary economic thought (capital, interest, economic rent, wages) are applicable. Wages, as an economic category in the modern meaning of the word, is obviously absent in the systems mentioned above; and, together with this category, the customary theoretical content of other categories of our national economic systems drops out, because rent and interest as theoretical constructs are indissolubly connected with the category of wages. On the other hand, we acquire from such observation a new category, completely unknown to modern theory, *the price of slaves*.

We are in an even more difficult position regarding the economic systems of primitive peoples. In these systems, a basic category like the market price (fundamental to our theoretical thought) often does not exist. In this, the economic structure of the Roman Colonate, as well as that of the natural economy of primitive people, lies completely outside the framework of present economic theory. Even with regard to the Middle Ages, we would have difficulty in analyzing price formation with our existing equipment. How, for example, does one price the products that the feudal lord exacts as payment in kind and exports for sale to faraway markets?

The German historical school undoubtedly has the extremely great merit of having written about the economic past (especially the Germano-Roman and the ancient world) and of having disclosed their detailed morphology; but even the most thorough and exact description as such is unable to provide a theory of the economic facts described. Economics, however, urgently needs a theoretical analysis of our economic past; for each of the economic types we have already partly depicted, an economic system should be constructed corresponding to its peculiar features. It occurs to me that research in this direction, even if it may appear to be an amateurish collecting of antiques, could achieve much. Merely as economic paleontology it would not only further comparative analysis of existing economic formations, but would also be of great use for the purely practical aims of economic policy. For not only the family labor economic unit type (which we shall define in more detail later) but also other older types still exist in great numbers to the present day in non-European countries. Theoretical analysis with categories really adequate to their characteristics would contribute more to colonial policy than, for example, forcing the economy of Zambeziland into the Procrustean bed of the modern Manchester School's economic categories.

We regret that neither Aristotle nor other ancient writers have left us an economic *theory*, as we would understand the word today, of the economic reality surrounding them. The Fathers of the Church, as contemporaries of the feudal regime, often touched on economic problems in their treatises; but, as we know, they devoted all their attention to the ethical side of economic life. Russian economic literature at the turn of the seventeenth and eighteenth centuries, as represented by Sylvester, Pososhkov, and Volynskii, dealt mainly with private economic affairs or with problems of state administration. Neither the slave economy in the United States nor the economy of the serf period in Russia has left us a complete economic theory corresponding to their special structures. As we have little knowledge of the Japanese and Chinese literature, we cannot judge the state of their theoretical attempts to explain past forms of economic life. Since past epochs have failed of their own to evolve any theories about former economic systems, we are compelled to try to construct them in retrospect.

We know that the key to understanding economic life in capitalist society is the following formula for calculating economic profitability: an enterprise is considered profitable if its gross income, *GI*, after the deduction of the circulating capital advanced (i.e., of the annual material expenditure, *ME*, and of the wage costs, *WC*), makes a sum, *S*, which is as large or larger than the whole of the (constant and circulating) capital, *C*, of the enterprise at interest calculated according to the rate prevailing in that country at that time (*a*).

$$GI - (ME + WC) \gtreqless C \cdot \frac{a}{100}$$

All calculations of theoretical economics start with this formula, explicitly or tacitly. The elements of this formula—the exchange value (market price) of gross income and of material expenditure, the wages, and the interest on capital—in this case are not any accidental private economy magnitudes but basic phenomena of a social and economic order. The content and task of the theory of the national economy is the scientific explanation of these basic phenomena.

The economic theory of modern capitalist society is a complicated system of economic categories inseparably connected with one another—price, capital, wages, interest, rent, which determine one another and are functionally interdependent. If one brick drops out of this system, the whole building collapses. In the absence of any one of these economic categories, all the others lose their specific character and conceptual content, and cannot even be defined quantitatively.

Thus, for example, one cannot apply, in their usual meanings, any one of the economic categories mentioned above to an economic structure that lacks the price category (an entire system of units on a natural economy basis and serving exclusively to meet the needs of the laboring families or collectives). In a natural economy, human economic activity is dominated by the requirement of satisfying the needs of each single production unit, which is, at the same time, a consumer unit. Therefore, budgeting here is to a high degree *qualitative:* for each family need, there has to be provided in each economic unit the qualitatively corresponding product *in natura.*

Quantity here can be calculated (measured) only by considering the extent of each single need: it is sufficient, it is insufficient, it is short in such and such a quantity—this is the calculation here. Owing to the elasticity of the needs themselves, this calculation does not have to be very exact. Therefore, the question of the comparative profitability of various expenditures cannot arise—for example, whether growing hemp or grass would be more profitable or advantageous. For these plant products are not interchangeable and cannot be substituted for each other; therefore, no common standard can be applied to them.

According to this, all economics of natural economy, its conception of what is economic and profitable as well as the strange "laws." which dominate its social life, are, we shall prove below, very different in character from the basic ideas and principles of our usual economics which are customarily presented in manuals on the national economy. Only with the development of an exchange and money economy does managing lose its qualitative character. Now, the interest in mere quantity comes to the fore—the concern *to obtain the maximum quantum* which can adopt any qualitative form through exchange. As exchange and money circulation (the commodity nature of the economy) increases, quantity becomes more and more independent of quality. It begins to achieve the abstract value of being independent of quality and its specific significance for given demands. The price category becomes prominent, and, together with other categories if these are available, it forms the economic system which is the only one considered by national economics.

A similar fate threatens theoretical economics if any other category drops out of the system—for example, that of *wages*. Even if out of all the possible economic systems lacking this category we choose one in which exchange and credit (and thus the categories of price and capital) are present (for example, the system of peasant and artisan family labor units held together economically by monetary and exchange processes), we shall still find that the structure of such an economy lies outside the conceptual systems of an economics adapted to capitalist society.

On the family labor farm, the family, equipped with means of production, uses its labor power to cultivate the soil and receives as the result of a year's work a certain amount of goods. A single glance at the inner structure of the family labor unit is enough to realize that it is impossible without the category of wages to impose on this structure net profit, rent, and interest on capital as real economic categories in the capitalist meaning of the word.

Indeed, the peasant or artisan running his own business without paid labor receives as the result of a year's work an amount of produce which, after being exchanged on the market, forms the gross product of his economic unit. From this gross product we must deduct a sum for material expenditure required during the course of the year; we are then left with the increase in value of material goods which the family has acquired by its work during the year, or, to put it differently, their *labor product*. This family labor product is the only possible category of income for a peasant or artisan labor family unit, for there is no way of decomposing it analytically or objectively. Since there is no social phenomenon of wages, the social phenomenon of net profit is also absent. Thus, it is impossible to apply the capitalist profit calculation.

It must be added, of course, that this indivisible labor product will not always be the same for all family economic units. It will vary according to market situation, the unit's location in relation to markets, availability of means of production, family size and composition, quality of the soil, and other production conditions of the economic unit. But, as we shall learn below, the surplus the economic unit achieves by better location or by relatively better availability of means of production is neither in its nature nor in its amount identical with the rent and the interest on capital of capitalist economy.

The amount of the labor product is mainly determined by the size and composition of the working family, the number of its members capable of work, then by the productivity of the labor unit, and

—this is especially important—by the degree of labor effort—the degree of self-exploitation through which the working members effect a certain quantity of labor units in the course of the year.

Thorough empirical studies of the peasant farms in Russia and other countries have enabled us to substantiate the following thesis: the degree of self-exploitation is determined by a peculiar equilibrium between family demand satisfaction and the drudgery[2] of labor itself.

Each new ruble of the growing family labor product can be regarded from two angles: first, from its significance for consumption, for the satiation of family needs; second, from the point of view of the drudgery that earned it. It is obvious that with the increase in produce obtained by hard work the subjective valuation of each newly gained ruble's significance for consumption decreases; but the drudgery of working for it, which will demand an ever greater amount of self-exploitation, will increase. As long as the equilibrium is not reached between the two elements being evaluated (i.e., the drudgery of the work is subjectively estimated as lower than the significance of the needs for whose satisfaction the labor is endured), the family, working without paid labor, has every cause to continue its economic activity. As soon as this equilibrium point is reached, however, continuing to work becomes pointless, as any further labor expenditure becomes harder for the peasant or artisan to endure than is foregoing its economic effects.

Our work, as well as the numerous studies of A. N. Chelintsev, N. P. Makarov, and B. D. Brutskus, have shown that this moment of equilibrium is very changeable. It is reached as follows: on the one hand, through the actual specific conditions of the unit's production, its market situation, and through the unit's location in relation to markets (these determine the degree of drudgery); on the other hand, by family size and composition and the urgency of its demands, which determine the consumption evaluation. Thus, for example, each increase in labor productivity results in gain of the same quantity of products with less labor. This allows the economic unit to increase its output and to satisfy family demands in full. On the other hand, the significance of each ruble of gross income for consumption is increased in a household burdened with members incapable of work.

---

2 Editors' note.—Chayanov introduced a Russian term, *tyagostnost'*, to indicate labor inputs as subjectively assessed by the peasant. The term might be translated by "laboriousness" or "irksomeness," but "drudgery" seems preferable and has the advantage of being etymologically parallel to the Russian form. (Cf., the Glossary, Drudgery of Labor.)

This makes for increased self-exploitation of family labor power, so that the family's standard of living, threatened by increased demand, can be kept up in some way.

Starting with the nature of the basic consideration described above, the family labor farm has to make use of the market situation and natural conditions in a way that enables it to provide an internal equilibrium for the family, together with the highest possible standard of well-being. This is achieved by introducing into the farm's organizational plan such labor investment as promises the highest possible labor payment per labor unit.

Thus, the objective arithmetic calculation of highest possible net profit in the given market situation does not determine whether or not to accept any economic action, nor does it determine the whole activity of the family economic unit; this is done by the internal economic confrontation of subjective evaluations. True, some consideration is given to the particular objective conditions of the economic unit.

An economic unit working on the principles outlined above does not necessarily need to be extravagant in its economic conduct; for *usually* the objects that yield the highest labor payment per labor unit invested and those that guarantee the highest net profit to a capitalist unit are roughly the same. But empirical studies show that in a number of cases the structural peculiarities of the peasant family labor farm make it abandon the conduct dictated by the customary formula for capitalist profit calculation.

Such differences become very clear, for example, in densely populated areas where land shortage does not permit the peasant family to develop its full labor power under optimum organization forms, i.e., forms rendering the highest possible labor payment. For the capitalist economic unit, these optimum forms of economic organization (the optimum state of business intensification is expressed in it) are an *absolute norm*. With each additional intensification, the effect of extra labor input decreases steadily according to the law of decreasing returns to land; consequently, net profit falls as well. In farms greatly short of land, on the other hand, the concern to meet the year's needs forces the family to turn to an intensification with lower profitability. They have to purchase the increase of the total year's labor product at the price of a fall in income per labor unit.

Professor E. Laur, for example, has investigated Swiss farms with little land. These farms trebled their intensity. They suffered a big loss in income per labor unit, but they gained the opportunity to use their labor power fully, even on the small plot, and to sustain their families. In the same way, small farms in the north and west of Russia increased the growing of potatoes and hemp, which are often of lower profitability than oats but are more labor-intensive and thereby increase the farm family's gross product.

In other words, a capitalist business can only increase its intensity above the limit of its optimum capacity if the changed market situation itself pushes the optimum in the direction of greater intensity. In the labor family unit, intensification can also take place without this change in the market situation, simply from pressure of the unit's internal forces, mostly as a consequence of family size being in an unfavorable proportion to the cultivated land area. The peculiar features of the peasant family labor unit pointed out above inevitably make themselves felt on the whole economic system if it is exclusively based on family economy and, therefore, lacks the category of wages.

This peculiarity is especially clear when analyzing the element of economic rent under the conditions of the labor family unit. Rent as an objective economic income category obtained after deducting material costs of production, wages, and the usual interest on capital from gross income cannot exist in the family economic unit because the other factors are absent. Nevertheless, the usual rent-forming factors like better soil and better location in relation to the market do surely exist for commodity-producing family labor economic units, *too*. They must have the effect of increasing output and the amount of payment per labor unit.

Deeper analysis indicates the following: the family's single indivisible labor product and, consequently, the prosperity of the farm family do not increase so markedly as does the return to a capitalist economic unit influenced by the same factors, for the laboring peasant, noticing the increase in labor productivity, will inevitably balance the internal economic factors of his farm earlier, i.e., with less self-exploitation of his labor power. He satisfies his family's demands more completely with less expenditure of labor, and he thus decreases the technical intensity of his economic activity as a whole.

According to Professors A. N. Chelintsev and N. P. Makarov, this rent factor, which is expressed in a slightly increased level of prosperity, cannot exist for very long, for the regions with such an increased level of prosperity will inevitably attract population from less favored regions. This will reduce the land holdings of individual farms, force them to intensify cultivation, and depress prosperity to the usual traditional level.

If in such circumstances the leasing of land and a free land market develop, land prices naturally cannot be determined by capitalizing the rent, since the category of rent itself (as we understand it today) does not exist in the economic system just investigated, as has been shown above. Nevertheless, in a monetary land market properties do not change hands unpaid for. Thus, we are faced with the basic problem of the economics of the family labor unit: What determines the land price? What can the peasant farm pay for land? For what sum will it sell it?

We can answer these questions if we approach them with the notion of the specific concept of profitability which we have defined for the labor family unit. This shows that tenancy or land purchases are obviously advantageous to the peasant family only if, with their help, the family can reach the equilibrium of its economic unit, either with an increased level of living or with decreased expenditure of labor power.

Peasant farms that have a considerable amount of land and are, therefore, able to utilize the family's whole labor power at an optimum degree of cultivation intensity need not lease or buy land. Every expenditure on it appears irrational to them as it does not increase family prosperity but decreases their resources. If a family can dispose of only a small plot which allows them to use only part of the given labor power, acquiring a new item with a view to using unemployed labor power is extremely significant, for this allows them to bring the unit's intensity nearer the optimum and to utilize working hours previously lost in forced inactivity. In both cases, the increase in payment per labor unit, with the resultant rise in the level of prosperity, can be so important that it enables the family unit to pay for the lease or purchase a large part of the gross product obtained from the newly acquired plot.

We can even maintain, disregarding the apparent paradox, that the more the peasant farm will be ready to pay for land, the less it owns already, and, therefore, the poorer it is. In conclusion, we must consider that the land price as an objective category depends on the given situation in the land market, i.e., on the extent and urgency of land demand among peasants with little land and on the number of offers of land available for some reason or other.

In the family labor farm system, the land price level does not depend only on the market situation for agricultural produce and on the profitability of land cultivation resulting from it, but to a greater extent depends on the increase in local rural population density.

Studies on movements in land prices and leases in Russia carried out by Professor V. Kosinskii and the corresponding data from Professor Laur's studies about peasant farms in Switzerland have confirmed that peasants with little land pay land prices that significantly exceed the capitalized rent. These data can, therefore, serve as an empirical substantiation of our theoretical proposition.

It is extremely interesting that other mutually dependent economic categories, such as the market rate of interest on capital, behave in an analogous way in the system of the family labor economy. It is obvious that the family labor unit considers capital investment advantageous only if it affords the possibility of a higher level of well-being; otherwise, it reestablishes the equilibrium between drudgery of labor and demand satisfaction.

In all cases where prospective new capital expenditure, be it through increased labor productivity or through expansion of the area, promises to achieve this increase in prosperity, the family can pay an unusually high interest for the capital required. Yet, this interest must not be so high that it offsets all the advantages achieved by the new investment of capital. On the one hand, the demand at the moment resulting from this situation, and on the other hand, the supply of capital then available determine the market price in the form of the loan interest normal at that time.

In other words, according to this we must suppose that the "circulation of capital" in the family labor unit does not result in an income from capital in the form of a special objectively available source of income, but it exercises an important influence on labor product and thus on the level of the single indivisible labor product and on the critical moment of internal economic equilibrium. The normal level of the market rate of interest is not determined by the whole productive capital turnover in the country (which obviously does not conform to the classical [Marxian] formula, $M-C-M + m$)* but only by the market situation of demand and supply in that part of the nation's capital in the credit system.

Its internal capital circulation is also very peculiar for the family labor unit. If the family does not seek loan credit from outside persons, it will always have to consider not only that each expenditure of capital on the economic unit, by new capital formation and by capital renewal, is advantageous but also that the family will have to be able to find an amount for this expenditure from its labor income, and

---

* EDITORS' NOTE.—The formula $M-C-M'$ comes from Vol. 1 of Marx's *Capital*, Part II, ch. iv. $M$ = Money, $C$ = Commodities, and $M'$ = the original sum advanced, plus an increment.

this would, of course, be at the expense of immediate consumption. Naturally, this will be possible only if the consumption value of the amount intended for production appears in the eyes of the family to be less than its value for production.[3]

It is obvious that the larger its annual product, the easier it is for the family to find from it the means for capital formation. In hard times, with bad harvests or disadvantageous market situations, it will be difficult for the family to extract from its small payment a part intended for consumption in order to use it to form new capital or merely for ordinary replacement of circulating capital.

Thus, the following categories can be defined for the economic system of the labor family unit or, in other words, for the economic structure of a society where production is in the form of peasant and artisan units and where the institution of wage labor is lacking.

1. The single, indivisible labor income of the family which reacts on the rent-forming factors.[4]
2. Commodity prices.
3. The reproduction of means of production (capital formation in the wider sense of the word).
4. Prices for capital in credit circulation.
5. Land prices.

We get an even more peculiar picture if we complicate the form of the family economic unit here under consideration by assuming that there is no category of market price—that is, no factor of commodity exchange. At a quick glance, it would appear that the fully natural family farm would not display any phenomena of an economic kind. A closer look, however, shows that it is not at all like this. It seems possible to find a whole number of social and economic relations in the social and economic bloc consisting of several integral labor farms which meet their demands *in natura*. These control the organization of each of the separate natural farm units and standardize their production structure.

---

[3] The comparative confrontation of the subjective evaluations of the consumption and production value of the nth unit of the labor product is among the most complicated problems in the family labor unit theory; it is thoroughly dealt with in the fourth chapter of my book; *Die Lehre von der bäuerlichen Wirtschaft* (Berlin: P. Parey, 1923). [TRANSLATOR'S NOTE.—Cf. Chapter 5 of *Peasant Farm Organization*, p. 195 of the present volume.] In our analysis, we take as a measure of production value that degree of drudgery which has to be suffered if the nth unit of income is not used for capital renewal or formation.

[4] We number this single indivisible labor income of the family among the economic categories because it is determined not only by technical but also by a whole range of social factors: the development of a habitual traditional level of demand, the local population density, and, finally, the particular rent-forming factors.

In fact, the internal private economic structure of the individual natural family farms is the same as those of farms with commodity exchange, with the exception of some peculiarities in calculating profitability, which we have indicated at the beginning of this article. The same notion of profitability is the determining factor; it becomes even clearer that it is impossible to apply the profitability formula of a capitalist enterprise. The economic equilibrium between demand satisfaction and drudgery is also determined in the same way. The same can be said about the formation and replacement of means of production. Even if the rent-forming factor of market location is absent here, the various soil and climatic conditions undoubtedly introduce into the system of the natural economic unit something like the factor of rent.

Most significant for the structure of the natural farm is that the intensity of cultivation and its organizational forms depend to a very great extent on the amount of land for use, the size of the labor family, and on the extent of its demand, i.e., on internal factors (family size and composition and its relation in proportion to the amount of cultivated soil). Thus, population density and forms of land utilization become extremely important social factors which fundamentally determine the economic system. Another less important, yet essential, social factor is the traditional standard of living, laid down by custom and habit, which determines the extent of consumption claims, and, thus, the exertion of labor power.

In other words, if we think of one region of the natural economy and analyze this social and economic bloc, we see that in spite of the lack of interrelationships and in spite of the economic dissociation of the individual economic units a number of complicated economic processes take place in this region, the main factor for which is demographic—population density and migration. These determine land utilization, level of prosperity, and, thus, the ever-varying amount of capital accumulation and taxability of the population; the last forms the basis for organizing the nation's state and culture.

Independently of demographic factors, very prosperous regions will stand out where rent-forming factors—higher quality of soil, etc. —are especially effective. Empirical studies of seminatural agrarian countries show that the *noneconomic* constraint—in default of a regulating influence from the market situation and its economic constraint—becomes very important in the form of administrative control of land utilization and sometimes in the form of the "warlike settlement" of population migration.

Thus, even in a country with an absolutely natural economy structure we can find the following social and economic categories determining the structure of the individual economic units.

1. The indivisible labor product of the family, constituted according to: (*a*) population density; (*b*) the habitual, traditional demand level; (*c*) the rent-forming power of better soil and more favorable climatic conditions.
2. The population's capacity to form capital and its taxability, depending on the level of prosperity.
3. The economic and political measures of the state power which by noneconomic constraint controls the mode of land utilization and popular migration.

In complete contrast to the family economic system is another type of economy which also lacks the category of wages—the slave economy system. The difference becomes quite distinct when we confront the structures of their two economic units in respect of their private economic morphology. The peasant and the artisan manage independently; they control their production and other economic activities on their own responsibility. They have at their disposal the full product of their labor output and are driven to achieve this labor output by family demands, the satisfaction of which is constrained only by the drudgery of the labor. None of these factors exists in a slave economy.

The slave labors in a production dominated by a stranger's will; he is only a blind tool and has no right to dispose of his labor product. He is driven to labor output only by threat of punishment and satisfies his demands at the discretion of his owner only as much as is necessary to maintain his labor power.

For the slave-owning entrepreneur, keeping slaves is rational only when it leaves him a surplus product after deducting expenses and the expenditure of keeping the slaves; this, after being realized on the market, makes for an objective income from slave-keeping. *Niebuhr* pointed out that the institution of slavery came into existence only at the moment when the productive power of human labor had developed so far that this surplus product could be achieved.

The expenditure on keeping slaves is determined by physiological norms and by the labor tasks allotted; it cannot be taken as an economic category behind which hide complicated social and economic relations analogous to those connected with the category of wages. Therefore, the slave hardly differs from the beasts of burden as far as organization of the enterprise is concerned if we disregard the ethical norms shaping patriarchal life, which were of special significance, for example, in Muslim slavery.

The peculiar features of the private economic organization of a slave enterprise pointed out above affect a whole number of fundamental economic categories. The slave owner receives a certain sum as income after deducting from the gross product of his enterprise the material costs of production and the expenses of keeping the slaves. When the customary interest calculated on invested fixed and circulating capital, but not on the value of the slaves, has been deducted, the rest can be attributed to slave utilization.

In capitalist society, this residual attributed to the worker would be that part of his wages exceeding the value of board, clothing, and housing provided in kind by the entrepreneur. In the slave economy system, the part of the product attributed in economic terms to slave labor is not taken by the slave but by his owner on the strength of his slave ownership; it becomes a new sort of unearned income which is the raison d'être for slave-owning.

This income, which is no longer a mere technical norm as, for example, is the cost of maintaining slaves, is determined by a complicated structure of a whole number of social and economic interrelations. It is an economic category and constitutes the *slave rent* the owner receives on the strength of his property right. If the slave economic unit is agrarian, the unearned income from slave-owning will grow, together with the progression from less advantageous conditions of production and transport to relatively more advantageous ones. Since the slave and his labor output remain the same and the slave-keeper's income would not fall by substituting some slaves for others, the extra income we are examining here cannot be connected with slave-owning as such but must be attributed to the soil and results from its better quality or more advantageous market location, and it has to be considered as ordinary differential rent. Insofar as it is possible to achieve the same technical results based on slave labor as those on paid labor, this economic rent will also correspond quantitatively to that of capitalist agriculture.

Thus, all the social and economic categories of the capitalist economy can retain their places in the theoretical system of the slave economy; it is necessary only to substitute the category of slave rent for that of paid labor. The slave rent is appropriated by the slave owner, and its capitalized value constitutes the slave price as an objective market phenomenon.

The quantitative amount of the slave *rent* is determined by the productivity of his utilization, analogous to the determination of wages by the productivity of the marginal worker as calculated by Anglo-American theoreticians in their systems. The quantitative determination of the *market price* for a slave is more complicated. We have already pointed out that it tends to be an amount similar to the capitalized rent of the marginal slave. In a way, this is the demand price, while, on the other hand, the prime cost of "slave production" forms the supply price. In this context, we must distinguish between two systems of slave economy.

1. A system in which the supply of slave material occurs by capturing in war from foreign peoples slaves who are already adult. The exploitation of their labor is complete and leads to its quick consumption; this avoids the cost of raising children (reproduction), as well as prolonged maintenance of the adults.

2. A system in which the supply occurs in a natural way by reproduction of slave material within the slave family itself; this, of course, necessitates costs for raising the coming generation, as well as for the reduced degree of exploitation of slave labor power, especially that of the female part.

In the first case, the prime cost of slave production is the cost of capture; in the second, the cost of raising and educating, which, as a rule, is much higher. In historic periods favoring capture of human material in war—as in ancient Rome, in the Middle Eastern states of antiquity, and even, for the first decades, in Spanish America—the prime cost—the cost of slave production—was very low. The customary capitalized slave rent surpassed it many times. Good evidence for this is the high market price of the Spanish crown's slave patents with which it issued licenses for the capture and importation of slaves during the first period of the importation of negroes into America.

The human material was cheap, and this allowed ownership to increase in extent and allowed slaves to be used for work with ever-decreasing labor productivity, up to the point, of course, where the steadily falling slave rent became identical with the prime cost of acquiring them. This factor determined the market price of the slave and the extent of a slave-based economy. As the sources for capture of slaves in war became exhausted by frequent attacks, the prime cost of acquiring slaves grew; their market price increased quickly, and many slave uses that generated a small slave rent were no longer profitable and were gradually dropped. As a result, the slave-based economy decreased in extent.

From this, we can conclude that an important factor in the decline of the ancient system of slavery was that in order to insure the supply of slaves war and capture had to be abandoned for peaceful production by means of natural reproduction. Here, the ancient economic unit faced prime costs so high that they started to overtake the capitalized slave rent.

In any case, the slave price, as a phenomenon subject to the laws of the market, is an objective category which determines slave production in a private economic calculation. It is obvious that the slave economic unit, from the private economic viewpoint, can appear advantageous only as slave production yields a net product that does not amount to less than the slave rent that exists at the time as an objective economic fact and, through the market, is realized in the slave price.

We must also stress that slavery or, to put it more generally, human bondage as an economic phenomenon displays a number of variations differing widely from one another. Thus, for example, Russian serfdom in its quitrent form differs very much from the system described above.[5] The quitrent form, a peculiar combination of a family labor farm and a slave farm, is of extraordinary theoretical interest.

The farm of a quitrent peasant was organized in the form usual for a family labor unit. The laboring family dedicated its whole labor power only to its own agricultural or other economic activity. But a noneconomic constraint forced such a unit to hand over to the owner of the laboring serf family a definite amount of the produce won by its labor. This amount was called quitrent [*obrok*] and represented the serf rent.

Despite similarities in the legal position of slave and serf, the economic structures of the slave economic unit on the one hand and the serf economic unit on the other hand are of a completely different nature. Quitrent neither qualitatively nor quantitatively coincides with slave rent.

---

5 Russian serf law distinguished three different sorts of serfs. (1) They could be in-servants (*dvorovye*), i.e., destined to meet the needs of the landlord's household, the landlord himself, and his family by personal domestic service, or, without running their own farms, to be used on the demesne [home farm] insofar as that existed on the manor. (2) They could be paying labor-rent (*barshchina*), i.e., managing their own farms but at the same time obliged to render services on the landlord's estate in the fields or in the manor on a certain number of weekdays. (3) They could be quitrent peasants, i.e., using their labor power on their own holding but obliged to pay part of their produce to the landlord.

In its internal private economic structure, the farm of a serf quit-rent peasant is in no way different from the usual form of the family labor unit we already know. In this regime, the family runs its own farm on its own responsibility and has the resulting produce at its disposal. The family is stimulated by its needs to force up its labor power, and the quantity of the product is determined by the equilibrium, peculiar to the family labor farm, between the amount of the family's drudgery and the degree of its demand satisfaction. In the quitrent system, however, the family is forced by noneconomic factors to reach this equilibrium in such a way that the product obtained not only meets its own demands but also the quitrent to be paid to the owner.

Therefore, the demand for material values is much higher compared with the free peasant farm. As a consequence, the equilibrium between the amount of labor drudgery and the degree of demand satisfaction is achieved with a much higher degree of self-exploitation of labor than in the free peasant farm. Yet, the increased labor input mentioned above will not yield so great an additional product as the quitrent requires; thus, part of it must inevitably be covered at the cost of the family's demand satisfaction. Consequently, the family paying quitrent has a lower level of well-being than the free peasant family.

By paying quitrent to the landlord, partly at the price of an increased labor effort, partly at the price of a lower degree of demand satisfaction, the serf farm creates another economic income category—the unearned income from serf ownership, the serf rent. Disregarding this rent payment, the farm paying quitrent remains in all other aspects an ordinary family labor unit with all the peculiar organizational features pointed out above.

If we want to turn to the factor determining the amount of the quitrent, we must start off with its particular nature. The amount of quitrent brought in by means of noneconomic constraint is determined by the will of the owner. It is in his interest to maximize the quitrent; the only natural barrier is the danger that the serf farm may be ruined and thus be deprived of its ability to pay.

The amount of quitrent can be considered normal as long as it is paid at the cost of the serfs' increased labor input and a lowering of their consumption, but not at the cost of upkeep and necessary capital renewal. If pressure from paying the quitrent brings capital renewal on the farm to a standstill, the quitrent system begins to destroy its own roots.

Those quitrent-liable farms that are in relatively better rent-forming conditions are, of course, able to pay relatively much higher amounts to their landlords. Such an increase in quitrent cannot be attributed to human labor input but to the soil, and it constitutes ordinary differential rent.

In a free land and serf market, that part of the quitrent attributed to the soil and forming the rent derived from the soil is capitalized and produces the land price; the remainder, attributed to serf labor and forming the serf rent, is capitalized and produces the serf market price. It seems unnecessary to prove that the serf rent is determined by the ability of the marginal peasant, producing under unfavorable conditions, to pay the quitrent, while the differential rent is in such circumstances determined by the difference between the marginal peasant's ability to pay and that of any other peasant farm. Considering the great qualitative difference in the ways the quitrent and the slave rent are formed and paid, as well as the difference in the production organization of the large-scale slave economic unit and the small-scale serf unit, we cannot expect that serf rent and slave rent will be quantitatively the same.

Differences in the process of price formation for serfs on the one hand and slaves on the other are still greater. We have already pointed out that the prime cost of slave acquisition plays a considerable part in forming the slave price. With the quitrent serf economic unit, however, the owner has no economic costs in reproducing the human material. Therefore, the number of serfs is not determined by the equilibrium between the serfs'[6] marginal product and the marginal prime cost, as is the case in the slave economic unit; the increase through procreation, and thus the number of serfs, is left to themselves. Consequently, the ability to pay and, thus, the rent of the marginal serf is determined by the actual number of serfs in a certain country at a certain time.

What has been said above is sufficient for a morphological description of the quitrent farm. By confronting this system with the economic type of the slave farm, we can convince ourselves by illustration that both systems differ completely and are determined by very different objective elements in their economic relations, in spite of some exterior legal similarities.

This confrontation makes clear the fundamental differences in the two types of economy. It is to be noted that both systems are also quite

6 TRANSLATOR'S NOTE.—The German text reads slaves'.

ECONOMIC CATEGORIES IN THE SLAVE AND QUITRENT SYSTEMS

| *Slave Economic System* | *Quitrent Serf Economic System* |
|---|---|
| 1. Commodity prices. | 1. Commodity prices. |
| 2. Capital, which is advanced by the slave owner and circulates in capitalist form in the production process $(M-C-M+m)$. Part of this capital is the cost of maintaining the slaves. | 2. [Capital goods in the possession of the serfs (production takes place in the forms of the labor family economic unit, cf. p. 4 ff.); not an economic but purely a natural category.] |
| 3. [Maintenance cost of slaves—not an economic but purely a natural category.] | 3. Indivisible labor product of the family. |
| 4. Profit from capital (interest). | 4. Interest on borrowed capital. |
| 5. Slave rent. | 5. Serf quitrent. |
| 6. Slave price. | 6. Serf price. |
| 7. Differential rent. | 7. Rentlike income which the landowner receives due to the effect of rent-generating factors on the amount of the quitrent. |
| 8. Land price. | 8. Land price. |

different in their conception of profitability and economic calculation.

The entrepreneur in the slave economic unit comes close to a slightly changed formula of capitalist profitability calculation as regards the concept of profitability for his enterprise. On the outgoings account, in place of wages he puts the technically and physiologically determined cost for slave maintenance. He divides his net product into three heads: interest on capital, rent, and slave rent.

It is completely different in the serf economic unit that pays quitrent. A very peculiar feature of this unit is a certain division of the economic subject in which the peasant family concept of profitability is in the form we find in the family labor unit; apart from this, the calculation of the man who owns serfs and land is that of a typical rentier and expresses the search for a capital investment as profitable as possible.

The difference in the nature of the quitrent and slave economic units pointed out above leads to two very peculiar economic consequences. The owner of peasants paying quitrent has property rights and claims to rent, but at the same time, unlike the entrepreneur of the slave economic unit, he does not have his own production unit. This fact becomes clear in the peculiar and interesting way the quitrent is to a large extent subject to the influence of demographic factors, whereas rent in the slave economic unit is independent of them.

Moreover, in the organization of the slave economic unit the number of slaves can be and is adapted to the unit's optimum labor demand, i.e., that optimal degree of intensity promising the maximum slave rent. In the serf economic unit, however, the relation of available labor power to the amount of cultivated land cannot so easily be directed toward an optimum by the owner of the land and the peasant, because, disregarding rare exceptions, the population movement in this regime is of a purely natural and elemental character. Therefore, we have here the possibility of relative overpopulation, which, as we have already pointed out in our analysis of the family labor economic unit, causes intensification beyond the optimum and decreases the population's level of living as well as its ability to pay tax.

As a result, we get the peculiar phenomenon of negative overpopulation rent which eats up a large part of the quitrent. The only way out of this state of affairs is to move part of the serf population from the overpopulated land and to use them to colonize sparsely populated areas. In this case, of course, we get a marked increase in serf rent yielded by the transferred population, which has now achieved an optimum relation to land. Together with rent, the serf price resulting from the capitalization of the rent increases. This makes every population and colonization movement very advantageous, both for the owner of a quitrent economic area and for the peasants concerned.

Concluding our confrontation of the slave and the serf economic units, we would like to stress most emphatically that given the same market situation and the same natural and historical conditions the rents achieved in both cases (that of the slave and of the serf) are not always of the same magnitude; rather, they can differ considerably in level. To go into all the details of this extremely interesting problem would require mainly an empirical analysis of extensive material. Hence, we confine ourselves to mentioning in accordance with that difference that in old Russia of the serf epoch we are able to recognize regions with a predominantly quitrent form of economy and others where *labor rent* was dominant, which meant economically a certain trend to slave economy organization. In course of time, these regions changed their geographical outlines under the pressure of various factors. At times here, at times there, the slave rent respectively fell below or rose above the serf quitrent; adapting themselves to these changes, landlords transferred their peasants, according to the "market situation," from labor rent to quitrent and vice versa.

The imposition of a fief system on an agrarian natural economy region, a frequent occurrence in history, is of great interest for theoretical analysis. This is a special form of feudal economy in which the basic stratum of primary producers—the tributary peasants—continues to be in a completely natural economy and pays tributes to the feudal lord in kind, while the recipients of the tributes—the dukes, counts, monasteries, etc.—"realize" as commodities on distant markets the economic rent and serf rents they have drawn off in kind.

In this system, with a general economic structure corresponding to the type of the quitrent serf economy we have just investigated, price formation for those products collected by the feudal lord in the form of payment in kind and realized on distant markets is especially interesting. Obviously, the cost-of-production element cannot play any part in this, unless one regards as a prime cost the upkeep of a (noneconomic) coercive apparatus to collect tribute and suppress rebellion.

We know that the owner of a serf paying quitrent and of a feudal tenure takes very little part in the actual organization of production. The amount of produce that forms his feudal rent is for him an amount given in kind, limited by the tribute-paying capacity of the estate's dependent population, and this cannot be forced up with impunity. However, the feudal lord can, to a certain extent, initiate changes in the composition of produce collected from the dues-paying population as payment in kind. He will try to adapt them to the market situation. But, considering the limited flexibility of peasant farms, significant barriers also hinder this form of the feudal lord's economic activities. Therefore, the economic activities of the feudal lord and his intervention on the market are almost always condemned to be passive. The prices of his goods are not connected with their production and are wholly determined by the receptiveness of the market; they are realization prices of a given amount of certain commodities.

Given this particular exchange and monetary orientation, the *rent* going to the feudal lord on the strength of his feudal tenure is dependent not only on the amount of payment in kind but also on the market situation for selling the products received. Fluctuations in the market situation can, in spite of a constant amount of payment in kind, favorably or unfavorably influence the rent and, thus, the price of the tenure. The only possible economic activity of a feudal lord must, therefore, be confined to certain measures of an economic and political kind which seem appropriate to him for increasing his tenants' prosperity and, thus, their ability to pay taxes.

Besides these five main types of economy organized in a noncapitalist way, there have been in our economic past, and are still, a whole
number of other forms, both transitional and independent. Thus, in
the broad grouping of peasant agriculture we can distinguish between
the family labor farm type and the half-labor farm (farmer unit[7]),
which uses paid labor in addition to family labor power, but not to
such an extent as to give the farm a capitalist character. Theoretical
study of this case shows that the presence of the wages category somewhat changes the content of the labor farm's usual categories but does
not entirely succeed in substituting for them the categories of a
capitalist farm.

Without doubt, it must also be admitted that labor in Russia's serf
epoch did not mean slavery in the sense of negro slavery in America,
nor only that of the ancient world, even though it may have approxi-
mated to it and though the economic laws regulating the labor rent
no longer coincide with those we pointed out for the quitrent serf
farm. Neither can we fit the household of antiquity [Oikos] into the
framework of any of the pure economic types we have studied.

The trustification of capitalist industry now progressing and developing, as well as the forms of state and municipal capitalism recog-
nizable at the beginning of the twentieth century, most probably will
not fit into the finished scheme of classical theory of the economy but
will demand revision of doctrines. Very interesting complications
must also result for economic theory from the system of agricultural
cooperatives rapidly evolving before our eyes. Yet, we prefer to confine ourselves to what we have already said; the analysis made of the
five different economic types is sufficient to clarify the inapplicability
of the customary categories of national economics to all instances of
economic life. It cannot be the task of this short article to give a complete theory of noncapitalist economic forms.

We must make one exception for an economic system that has not
yet found its full realization but, to a great extent, has attracted the
attention of our contemporary theoreticians. We are talking of the
system of state collectivism or communism as regards the way in
which its foundations have been evolved in the treatises of its theoreticians and the attempts to realize it which have taken place at various
epochs in the course of human history.

---

7 TRANSLATOR'S NOTE.—*Halbarbeitswirtschaft* or *farmerwirtschaft*. See FARMER UNIT
in the Glossary.

Unfortunately, in their critique of capitalist society Marx and the more significant of his adherents have nowhere fully developed the positive fundamentals of a socialist economy's organizational structure. Thus, we ourselves must try to build a theory of such a structure by taking as a starting point some of Marx's observations in *La misère de la philosophie*,[8] as well as some studies by N. Bukharin and E. Varga and, most of all, the ideas that have been effective in the practical attempts to create a communist society in various European states during the period 1918–20.

According to these attempts, communism is an economic system in which all the economic fundamentals of capitalist society—capital, interest on capital, wages, rent—are completely eliminated, while the whole technological apparatus of the present economy has been preserved and even further improved.

In the communist economic order that must fulfill this task, the national economy is conceived as a single, mighty economic unit of the whole people. The people's will directs through the state organs, its tools, and the state administers the economic unit according to a unified economic plan that fully utilizes all technical possibilities and all favorable natural conditions. Since the economy is conceived as a single unit, exchange and price as objective social phenomena drop out of the system.[9] Manufactured products cease to be values with meaning in a money or exchange sense; they remain only goods distributed according to a state consumption plan. The whole peculiar economics of this regime is reduced to drawing up state plans for consumption and production and to establishing an equilibrium between the two.

The exertion of social labor power is here, obviously, as in the family unit, taken to the point where the equilibrium between drudgery of labor and social demand satisfaction has been reached. This point is, obviously, fixed by those state organs that work out the state production and consumption plans and must bring the two into harmony. Since each individual worker's standard of living determined by the state has no connection, if taken by itself, with his labor output (the amount of production he achieves), he has to be driven to labor by his social consciousness and by state sanctions, and perhaps even by a premium system.

---

8 TRANSLATOR'S NOTE.—*The Poverty of Philosophy*.

9 Taxes are not prices in the sense of an economic phenomenon subject to its own laws.

In contrast to all the economic systems hitherto discussed, which can exist purely automatically and elementally, a communist economic order requires for its maintenance and continuation in accordance with the state plan a continuous social exertion and, to prevent the rise of economic activity not intended in the state plan, a number of economic and noneconomic sanctions. According to this, we do not get here in the system of state communism a single one of the economic categories set out in the analysis of the economic systems we earlier considered. An exception is the purely technical process of production and reproduction of means of production.

Our presentation, which lays bare the morphology of the system, contributes little to understanding its dynamics, but achieving this is probably impossible before observation of the regime and how it functions, and before its ideologists and theoreticians have provided a fully developed theory of organization.[10]

Summing up the results of our analysis, we obtain the following table that tells us for each of the various economic systems studied here which categories are lacking and which are present.

Having summed up in this table the systems of economic categories we have presented, we are able to deduce from our analysis certain theoretical conclusions.

First of all, we must take as an unquestionable fact that our present capitalist form of economy represents only *one* particular instance of economic life and that the validity of the scientific discipline of national economics as we understand it today, based on the capitalist form and meant for its scientific investigation, cannot and should not be extended to other organizational forms of economic life. Such a generalization of modern economic theory, practiced by some con-

---

10 It seems to me that we must wait for the theory of organization to give the answers to the following three questions, the solutions of which might make more specific the notions of the mechanism of socialist economics.

1. With the help of which method and according to what principles will the degree of social labor exertion and the required amount of demand satisfaction, as well as the necessary equilibrium between the two, be determined when state production and consumption plans are established?

2. By what means is the individual worker to be driven to labor so that he does not consider as drudgery the input expected of him under the production plan and really carries it out in practice?

3. Which measures make it possible to prevent in the socialist society on the basis of new production relations the danger of a new class stratification being created that might start forms of distributing the national product which would deprive the whole regime of its original high ideals?

Without solving these problems, the regime of socialist economy can be sketched only in its most general morphological form.

ECONOMIC SYSTEMS

| Economic Categories | Capitalism | Family Economy | | Slave Economy | Quitrent Serf Economy | Feudal System* | | Communism |
|---|---|---|---|---|---|---|---|---|
| | | Commodity Economy | Natural Economy | | | Landlord Economy | Peasant Economy | |
| Commodity price | + | + | − | + | + | + | + | − |
| Single indivisible family labor product | − | + | + | − | + | − | + | − |
| Technical process of production or reproduction of the means of production | + | + | + | + | + | − | + | + |
| Capital advanced by the entrepreneur and circulating in production according to the formula $M–C–M+m$ | + | − | − | + | − | − | − | − |
| Interest on capital in the form of rentier's income | + | + | − | + | + | + | − | − |
| Wages | ++ | − | − | − | − | + | + | − |
| Slave rent or serf rent | − | − | − | ++ | ++ | + | − | − |
| Slave price or serf price | − | − | − | ++ | + | + | − | − |
| Differential rent | ++ | ++ | − | ++ | +† | +‡ | − | − |
| Land price | ++ | + | − | + | +† | +‡ | − | − |
| State production plan | − | − | − | − | − | − | − | + |
| Regulation by noneconomic constraint necessary to maintain the regime | − | − | + | + | + | + | + | + |

* The feudal economy is a symbiosis of the natural labor economy of tribute-paying peasants and the monetary and exchange economic orientation of the commodity-trading feudal lords. Therefore, it has two economic objects of a different kind and two systems of economic categories, the elements of which do not coincide. This circumstance made us allocate two different columns in this table.

† Rent does not occur here as a special independent income category; nevertheless, rent-generating factors affect the amount of the single indivisible labor product of the family.

‡ Rent is present here as an economic income category, but its genesis is different from that in the capitalist system.

temporary authors, creates fictions and clouds the understanding of the nature of noncapitalist formations and past economic life.

Some scientific circles have obviously become aware of these facts, and recently it has often been said that it is necessary to establish a universal economic theory, the concepts and laws of which would embrace all possible formations of human economic life. We shall try to clarify the question of whether it is possible to construct such a universal theory and whether it is necessary as a tool for scientific understanding.

First, we shall compare the various kinds of economic formation we have previously investigated and sort out the principles and phenomena common to all. We obtain five.

1. The necessity to equip human labor power with various means of production for the purpose of organizing production, and to devote part of the annual output of production to the formation and replacement of means of production.

2. The possibility of considerably increasing labor productivity by applying the principle of division of labor both as regards technique of production and in the social sense of the word.

3. The possibility of running agriculture with different amounts of labor exertion and with different amounts of concentration as far as means of production per unit of soil area are concerned, and to increase by intensifying farm activity the amount of produce per unit of soil area and per labor unit. It must be taken into consideration that the product does not increase so quickly as the labor and means of production inputs.

4. The increase in labor productivity and in the amount of produce per unit of soil area resulting from better soil quality, more favorable surface configuration, and more favorable climatic conditions.

5. The opportunity, provided by a relatively high level of human labor productivity, for a laboring man to produce in the working year a larger amount of products than is necessary to maintain his labor capacity and to secure his family's opportunity to live and reproduce. This circumstance is the presupposition for the possibility of any social and state development.

Looking closely at these five universal principles of man's economic activity, we notice without difficulty that they are all phenomena of a natural and technical order. It is the economics of things in kind (*in natura*).

These phenomena, even though often ignored by economic theoreticians and considered by them interesting only from the point of view of production *technique*, are extremely important. Now, in the chaos of the postwar period, their whole significance is revealed especially distinctly, since the complicated structure of the economic apparatus of capitalist society has been destroyed, and money has lost the quality of an abstract, stable expression of value.

The five principles we have brought forward do not contain an element for evaluating things. If this evaluation should once emerge and the social and economic phenomenon of objective value be created on its basis, all things would adopt, so to speak, a second mode of existence. They would become values, and the production process would acquire, besides the expression *in natura*, the new expression *in valore*.

Then only would emerge all the economic categories stated by us above. These would join together, in accordance with the social and legal structure of the society, in *one* of the particular value economic systems which we have analyzed. The "valoristic" system with its categories takes over the prior, natural production process and submits everything to its characteristic economic calculation in value terms.

Each of these systems is very individual in its nature. Attempts to cover them by any generalizing universal theory could yield only very general doctrines void of content, e.g., the ideal type "exaggerating" way of stating that in all systems the economic unit strives for the greatest possible effect with the least input, or analogous phrases.

Therefore, it seems much more practical for theoretical economics to establish for each economic regime a particular national economic theory. The sole difficulty in carrying out these ideas is that only very rarely in economic life do we come across any economic order like a pure culture, to use a term borrowed from biology. Usually, economic systems exist side by side and make for very complicated conglomerations.

Even today, significant blocs of peasant family labor units are interspersed in capitalist world economy. Economic formations that resemble slave or feudal economic types are still interspersed in the colonies and the states of Asia. Analyzing the economic past, we more frequently, one may say constantly, come across the fact of such coexistence, sometimes the beginnings of capitalism together with the feudal or serf system, sometimes the slave economy next to serfdom and the free family labor economy, etc.

In these cases, since each system was a closed one it would communicate with the others only by those objective economic elements they had in common, as shown in our table of economic systems. This contact usually occurred on the plane of commodity and land market prices. Thus, for example, from the peasant emancipation (1861) to the Revolution of 1917, the peasant family farm existed in Russian agriculture alongside capitalist large-scale enterprise. This led to the destruction of capitalism because the peasants, relatively short of land, paid more for the land than the capitalized rent in capitalist agriculture. This inevitably led to the sale of large landed property to the peasants. Conversely, the high ground rent achieved by the large capitalist sheep farm in eighteenth-century England caused the plundering of peasant tenancies, which were not able to pay the same high rent to the estate owners.

Just as characteristic is the substitution of labor rent by quitrent and vice versa during certain periods of Russian serfdom. This was caused by the raising of slave rent over quitrent and vice versa. And perhaps the economic cause for the abolition of slavery has to be sought in the fact that the rent of the capitalist economic enterprise based on wage labor exceeded the amount of rent and slave rent. These as well as a number of analogous examples remove any doubt about the preeminent importance of the problem of coexistence among different economic systems. Today, our world gradually ceases to be only a European world. As Asia and Africa enter our lives and culture more and more often with their special economic formations, we are compelled to turn our interest again and again toward the problems of noncapitalist economic systems.

Therefore, we have no doubt that the future of economic theory lies not in constructing a single universal theory of economic life but in conceiving a number of theoretical systems that would be adequate to the range of present or past economic orders and would disclose the forms of their coexistence and evolution.

A. V. Chayanov

# Peasant Farm Organization

One of the works of the
Agricultural Economics Scientific Research Institute,
Moscow

1925

MOSCOW

The Co-operative Publishing House

# Contents

peasant farm organization and their solutions (106): (1) What determines the
quantitative division of labor between crafts and trades and agriculture (107)?
(2) What determines the capital the peasant family has available (110)? (3) What
is the effect of surplus labor and unsatisfied family demand on the organization
of the agricultural undertaking (113)? The effect of surplus labor on intensity in
Swiss and Czechoslovak farms (115). The objections of Professor Skalweit and
Kurt Ritter to the term labor farm (117).

# *Foreword*

The basic ideas put forth in this book are not completely new to the reader of economic literature. The author first expounded some of them in 1912, i.e., more than ten years ago; others were gradually formed in the course of research and were published in various articles and other works. Finally, in 1922 and 1923, the author had the opportunity to bring them together, with the addition of some work on problems not hitherto analyzed, and to publish them, in German in the first instance, in the form of a certain coherent whole.[1]

As is known, the theory evoked many critical notes and articles. These have been particularly abundant of recent years when a whole cluster of economists—Litoshenko, Prokopovich, Kritsman, Brutskus, Dubrovskii, Manuilov, Kondrat'ev, Bazykin, and others—have attempted to question many of the arguments.

Such a variety of critics, and the fierceness of the criticism itself, has shown us that the theory has achieved a certain maturity. I and my colleagues in this trend of economic thought no longer have to suffer from having our theories ignored; we must try in every way to defend our arguments, drawing up our formulations with the help of this varied criticism, rejecting elements that have been found wanting, amending and adding to that which has shown itself sound and correct in our theory.

Unfortunately, our critics for the most part used our early works for their analyses, and sometimes even simply popular pamphlets, which had been written with the necessary simplification and crude schematization. Due to this, the criticism contains many misunderstandings. This circumstance obliges us to proceed apace with the publication of this work, and to consider that its formulations and arguments alone correspond to the present state of the theory. All earlier works can be regarded as preparatory phases in this respect, of interest only as regards the theory's origins.

---

[1] A. Tschajanoff, *Die Lehre von der bäuerlichen Wirtschaft* (Berlin: P. Parey, 1923).

In a very extended Introduction to this book, the author deals in detail with the more important criticisms and tries to remove the often very unfortunate misunderstandings that have arisen. With the publication of the present text, all other "criticism" of itself misses the mark.

The German text of this work, compared with the author's earlier works, contained completely new chapters on the relationship of land, capital, and the family, on capital circulation on the peasant farm, and on the consequences for the national economy which follow from the nature of the peasant farm.

In the present Russian edition, an extensive chapter on the peasant farm's organizational plan and an Introduction have been added, the last chapters have been considerably extended, and the whole text has been reedited.

The author feels obliged to express his deep gratitude to Professors L. Bortkiewic, E. Laur, A. Weber, M. Sering, O. Auhagen, as well as to his German translator Fr. Schlömer, for numerous criticisms that the author has considered in working on the Russian text.

BARVIKHA, MOSCOW RIVER                    THE AUTHOR
Summer, 1924

# Introduction

For many decades now, peasant farming has been the subject of careful and detailed study. This study has more than once led to sharp arguments and divergent currents of economic thought. One might think it would be impossible to find any other theme in Russian economic literature to which has been devoted such an immeasurable quantity of books and pamphlets with varied approaches to the problem and very different trends of thought.

Therefore, in coming forward with a new work on the peasant farm it is absolutely essential to orient oneself with regard to all theories that formerly existed and problems that have been posed, and to determine as strictly as possible one's tasks and method of work. If this is not done, it will be difficult to avoid unfortunate misunderstandings and quite incorrect interpretations of the results obtained.

These precautions were ignored by those who carried out research on the school of thought to which the author belongs. As a result, before beginning an exposition of the results of his work, which has extended over many years, he must expend no small effort to prove the mere right of the school to exist, and must spend no little time on exactly formulating the methodological bases of his work, a common understanding of which is the only thing that will give the author, his critics, and the reader the opportunity of speaking the same language.

The current of Russian economic thought, which has, not entirely happily, been called the Organization and Production School and to which belong A. N. Chelintsev, N. P. Makarov, A. A. Rybnikov, A. N. Minin, G. A. Studenskii, the author, and others, was formed not long before the war and was brought forth by those deep social and economic changes observed in the life of our countryside after the 1905 revolution.

Prior to this period, people approached the study of peasant farming solely from the standpoint of the level of national economic development that then existed, as a seminatural, elemental feature in the economy; they were interested in it as a source for tax collection, as an internal market for the products of the urban industry which was to be encouraged, or as an inexhaustible source of cheap labor to be sent to the towns by the social strata in the countryside which were

35

being proletarianized. On the other hand, some students of social and political thought, who wanted to find in the roots of country life elements capable of resisting the threatening "calamity of capitalism," studied the peasant commune and the forms of day-to-day labor gangs, attempting to discover in them the defense they were seeking. However, this populist research, too, set itself social and economic problems. It was precisely on this plane that the whole well-known populist and Marxist argument about the fate of agriculture, the development of capitalism in it, and the differentiation and proletarianization of the peasants arose and was carried on. And, we repeat, it was impossible even to expect other approaches to the peasantry at that time.

Matters gradually begin to change in that a radical turning point is observed at the grass roots of our agriculture and, indeed, of the whole economy at the beginning of this century. The world market situation shifted favorably for agriculture. In Russia, an internal market for agricultural produce was formed, thanks to the development of industry; market relations and the commodity nature of peasant farming rapidly developed; trading capitalism grew rapidly; the cooperative movement grew without restraint; all bodies assisting agriculture and, in particular, groups offering agricultural advice to the population continually increased. All this, which appeared completely unnoticed in the form of every sort of "experiment," "initiative," and "interesting phenomenon," grew *quantitatively* more and more each year, and became a mass phenomenon. By the start of the war, our countryside *qualitatively* bore little resemblance to the countryside of the last century. It is self-evident that later, in the Soviet period of our history, all these processes went still further, and the gulf between new and old became still wider.

What was particularly important in this exceedingly deep historical process, for us at the present moment, was that many thousands of agricultural officers and cooperative workers appeared in the depths of the countryside. They not only observed and studied, but in their professional work were obliged to organize peasant farming, to enter in detail into the basis of its organizational plan, to seek and find ways to change it, and to build a new Russian countryside by means of their molecular work.

Of course, in this work, completely new for all Russian society, the agricultural officers and cooperative workers were frequently in the dark and often confused. A great number of half-technical, half-economic problems faced them—problems not envisaged by any book and not yet reviewed by any learned school. Recording the profitability of chemical fertilizers in the conditions of the Russian countryside, rates of payment for fodder, the normal composition of the herd, the advantages of one or another crop rotation, the economic evaluation of various systems of feed-getting, the basis of petty credit, labor organization on the farm, the limits for the use of agricultural machinery, and many more in which techniques and economics intermingled in the most varied combinations—all these questions were very pressing. Without some solution or other, even a somewhat crude one, the continuation of agricultural advisory work itself became unthinkable.

It is, therefore, not surprising that in the most varied corners of the country all sorts of authors began to solve different *organizational* problems of agricultural *production*. One has only to read articles in local agricultural journals, the minutes of debates at uezd and guberniya meetings of agricultural officers, reports of agricultural officers, and statistical handbooks of the portentous years of the second decade of our century to see clearly the subsoil of the Organization and Production School in economic thought. The authors with whose names this school is linked, mostly agricultural officers, partly cooperative workers and statisticians, first met personally, if I am not mistaken, at the 1911 Moscow Oblast Agriculture Congress, and from that year the school of thought itself gradually crystallized out in the course of fierce internal polemics. The Khar'kov *Agricultural Journal*, edited by K. A. Matseevich, was the main citadel of the school; here, N. N. Sukhanov and P. P. Maslov worked together with the adherents of the school. The secretary, if I am not mistaken, was M. A. Larin.

Recently, for some reason, it has been commonly considered that the scientific research work of the Organization and Production School amounts to the construction of a particular peasant farm theory. This is one of the deepest delusions. In answering the practical demands of agricultural officers and cooperative workers, our group has worked out a wide range of topics:

1. Methods of agricultural regionalization.
2. Use of railway transport statistics to give a description of regions.
3. Bookkeeping analysis for peasant farms.
4. Methods of research on budgets and by means of questionnaires.
5. A minute study of special crops and cottage crafts.
6. Analysis of the work of petty credit institutions.
7. Monograph descriptions of the butter, potato, flax, and milk cooperatives.

8. Study of the evolution of agricultural organization forms.
9. The basis of water management on irrigated lands.
10. Establishment of the optimal sizes for agricultural undertakings.
11. Methods of technical accounting for agricultural production.
12. The theory of agricultural cooperation.
13. Methods of agricultural assistance to the population.

Such is a far from complete roundup of the topics elucidated in the works of A. N. Chelintsev, N. P. Makarov, A. A. Rybnikov, and other authors belonging to this school.

Peasant farm theory was but one of these topics. True, it was perhaps the most controversial, since all the other work has not usually encountered criticism. Nonetheless, in accordance with the subject of the present work we should leave aside all the other researches of this school and focus our attention on its theory of peasant farm organization.

The problem of the theoretical foundations of peasant farm organization gradually emerged in the heat of practical work in agricultural advice and cooperation, and was initially posed in the form of numerous isolated doubts and consideration of individual organizational problems.

Two streams of research work have merged to form our views.

1. An enormous quantity of empirical material on problems of peasant farm organization, obtained partly by work on zemstvo and state statistics, partly by independent researches, mostly on budgets, was gradually accumulated. Simple inductive generalization of this material has led to a whole series of incontestable empirical conclusions which, as the reader will see from subsequent chapters, forms two thirds of the contents of the present book.

2. Numerous facts and dependent relationships that did not fit into the framework of the usual conception of the organizational basis of private economic undertakings and that demanded some special interpretation have been established, also empirically. At first, special explanations and interpretations were given separately in each specific instance. But this introduced into the usual theory of the private economic undertaking such a number of complications that, finally, it seemed more convenient to generalize them and to construct a separate theory of the family undertaking working for itself, differing somewhat in the nature of its motivation from an undertaking organized on the basis of hired labor. This hypothesis freed the theoretical analysis of peasant farm organization from numerous corrections, exceptions, and complications, and allowed us to construct a

more or less harmonious, logical generalization of the whole empirical material.

Thus it was that a "particular understanding of the nature of the peasant farm" was created; many unfortunate misunderstandings are connected with it. Since only the second of these two sources of our views on peasant farm organization is of methodological and theoretical interest, we shall try to illuminate these stages in as much detail, and as concretely, as possible.

The chief facts and empirical dependent relationships which called attention to the peculiarities in peasant farm organization and which are of decisive significance for the development of the theory may be summed up as follows.

1. At the end of the last century, Kirsanov, a Perm' agricultural officer engaged in the popularization of improved equipment among the peasants, came up against extreme difficulties in popularizing the threshing machine, despite its great advantage when calculated in bookkeeping terms. He saw the chief cause of this failure in that, in this instance, the labor displaced by the machine was unable to be used on other tasks in winter in Perm' guberniya. Thanks to this, the undoubted reduction in output costs here came up against the fact that the introduction of an improved and advantageous machine not only failed to increase the total amount of the peasant's income, but also reduced it by the amount of the machine's annual depreciation. If by analogy with the organizational basis of the usual private undertaking we consider that the peasant farm is an undertaking in which entrepreneur and worker are combined in a single person, in this case the benefit to the peasant as entrepreneur is entirely canceled out by his losses as a hired worker obliged to lengthen his seasonal unemployment.

2. Not long before the 1905 revolution, the Kiev professor, V. Kossinskii, wrote a fat book, *On the Agrarian Problem*. In it, he showed with very great care and extensive material that the rents paid by peasants for arable land leased from private owners were considerably higher than the net profit that might be obtained with capitalist exploitation of these same lands. About the same time, P. P. Maslov noted this circumstance in the first volume of his *Agrarian Problem*. He established the concept of "consumer rent," in which land-hungry peasants, under pressure from consumption needs and avoiding forced unemployment, pay not only economic rent and total net income for the leased land but also a considerable part of their wages. In this instance again, the peasant's interests as a worker distressed by

unemployment on his farm prevail over his interests as an entrepreneur. Subsequently, it was shown that the pecularity noted applied not only to rent payments but also to land prices paid by peasants in amounts considerably exceeding the capitalized economic rent.

3. In analyzing the economic basis of peasant flax- and potato-growing, an explanation similar to the case of produce rents should have been given. Empirical materials collected on these labor-intensive crops have shown that frequently—compared with oats, for example—they give a very small net profit according to bookkeeping analysis and, therefore, are hardly ever widespread on private landowners' and large-scale peasant farms. The land-hungry peasants, though, proportionately losing some net profit, grow them quite widely, since this gives them the opportunity to increase the amount of labor they expend on their farms and to reduce seasonal unemployment.

4. Budget studies in Vologda, Voronezh, and a number of other guberniyas have shown us an inverse dependence between amount of land held and size of income from crafts and trades. The smaller the area of land for use, the greater the volume of craft and trades activity. Moreover, it is interesting that the total income from farming, crafts, and trades taken together, while not constant for those sowing different acreages, is, at any rate, more constant than income from crafts and trades and agricultural income taken separately. In other words, when our peasant as worker-entrepreneur is not in a position to develop an adequate sale of his labor on his own farm and to get for himself what he considers sufficient earnings, he temporarily abandons his undertaking and simply converts himself into a worker who resorts to someone else's undertaking, thus saving himself from unemployment in his own.

5. In one of his works in A. F. Fortunatov's seminar, Professor N. P. Nikitin succeeded in establishing that in Russia, unlike in England, wages were not directly but inversely proportional to the price of bread. Since bread prices were determined by the harvest, the natural explanation of this phenomenon was that in years of harvest failure and, consequently, of high prices the peasants as worker-entrepreneurs, unable to make ends meet by means of their own farming activities, threw themselves as workers onto the labor market and reduced wages by the mass influx of offers of working hands.

6. An analysis of budget materials for small-scale peasant farms in Switzerland and in Vologda, Moscow, Khar'kov, Novgorod, and Tambov guberniyas has established without any doubt that the peasant family labor force is far from fully utilized, and not at one degree of

intensity. The level of gross productivity of this labor to a great extent influences the level of this self-exploitation.

Thus, for example, if as a result of an improvement in the market situation or a more advantageous location of a farm each labor unit begins to give greater earnings, the total earnings of the farm will increase, of course, but not at the speed at which the productivity of a labor unit increases; consequently, the number of labor units sold falls. This is also confirmed by direct observations. In this case, the peasant as worker, having made use of the favorable situation of the farm and his unearned income, obliges the peasant as entrepreneur to offer him better labor conditions in the sense of a reduced working year, despite the natural tendency of the entrepreneur to extend the scope of his economic activity to make use of a favorable market situation.

This list of peasant farm violations of entrepreneurial rules may be considerably expanded, as the reader will see in subsequent chapters. The latest investigators have shown that they are all particularly vividly expressed in areas of agrarian overpopulation; these materials also served us for our first works. However, in view of the mass nature of agrarian overpopulation, the phenomena which have been noted are equally widespread and can give sufficient material for study.

As is seen from our incidental analysis, all these instances can be interpreted with the aid of the categories of the capitalist farm based on hired labor. To do this, however, we have to create an exceedingly doubtful concept; we must unite in the peasant both the entrepreneur capitalist and the worker he is exploiting—the worker who is subject to chronic unemployment and who obliges his master, in the name of his worker interests, to break up his farm and behave disadvantageously from an entrepreneurial viewpoint. It is possible that this fiction ought, in fact, to be preserved in the interests of the monism of economic thought, as was indicated, for example, by Professor A. Weber during a conversation I had with him concerning the German edition of this book.

To me personally, however, this seems too strained and artificial, and, moreover, in practice will rather confuse than explain the facts that have been observed. Therefore, I am more inclined to use another hypothesis to explain theoretically the organizational peculiarities that have been observed—a hypothesis based on the concept of the peasant farm as a family labor farm in which the family as a result of its year's labor receives a single labor income and weighs its efforts against the material results obtained.

In other words, we take the motivation of the peasant's economic activity not as that of an entrepreneur who as a result of investment of his capital receives the difference between gross income and production overheads, but rather as the motivation of the worker on a peculiar piece-rate system which allows him alone to determine the time and intensity of his work. The whole originality of our theory of peasant farm organization is, in essence, included in this modest prerequisite, since all other conclusions and constructions follow *in strict logic* from this basic premise and bind all the empirical material into a fairly harmonious system.

The whole key to the problem is in the confrontation of these two hypotheses. We ought to accept either the concept of the fictive twofold nature of the peasant, uniting in his person both worker and entrepreneur, or the concept of the family farm, with work motivation analogous to that of the piece-rate system. No third possibility is offered.

We have chosen the second as a hypothesis that is less fictive and more simply explains all the phenomena observed. Moreover, a certain extension of the theoretical statement of the peasant farm problem has influenced our choice to a considerable extent.

The concept of the peasant farm as an entrepreneurial one in which the head of the farm hires himself as a worker is conceivable only in a capitalist system, since it consists entirely of capitalist categories. The peasant farm as an organizational form, however—and at the moment, that is all that interests us—is also completely conceivable in other systems of national economy—namely, serf feudal or peasant and artisan countries and, finally, purely natural economy, i.e., economic systems in which the categories of hired labor and wages are logically, if not historically, completely absent.

In accordance with this, if we wish to have a single organizational concept of the peasant labor farm independent of the economic system into which it enters we ought inevitably to base our understanding of its organizational essence on family labor.

It is self-evident that for each system of the economy and even for each phase of its development the part played by peasant farms in the national economy, the interrelationship of these farms with other types of economic units and the interrelationships and struggle of the peasantry as a class with other coexisting classes, and, finally, the way in which they participate and share in the distribution of the national income will vary to a great extent. Yet, the organizational shape of the basic cell, the peasant family labor farm, will remain the same, always changing in particular features and adapting to the circumstances surrounding the national economy, as long as the peasant farm exists as such, of course, and has not begun to be reconstructed into other organizational forms.

Such is the genesis and such the essence of our theory of the peasant farm *as views on one of the organizational forms of private economic undertakings.*

So far, I am claiming only what I have expounded and nothing more—only the particular chapter from the course on farm organization, the celebrated German *Betriebslehre.*

And those critics are quite incorrect who, not understanding the modesty of our intentions (and for this we also are guilty through some excessively bombastic phrases in our early works), accuse us of exceedingly bold attempts from which we ourselves are quite far removed. The criticisms that usually accompany the development of the Organization and Production School, if they are not to be considered random, are usually based on misunderstandings that naturally disappear on detailed acquaintance with a really systematic work. They usually amount to five serious accusations. We shall list them all.

1. They point out to us that the Organization and Production School treats the peasant farm statically and surveys it in isolation from the surrounding social and economic historical reality. After the latest Marxist and other works, this is naive and cruelly incorrect.

2. The Organization and Production School does not use Marxist method and is, in essence, an offspring of the Austrian marginal utility school.

3. At the present time, the peasant labor farm we have described, with its noble labor motivation, is not found in nature. The whole of the peasantry is agitated by entrepreneurial activity, and the capitalist farming type of organization is the proximate stage of our agriculture; therefore, it is not of practical interest to study outmoded forms.

4. The Organization and Production School completely ignores the fact that the peasant farm has been drawn into the worldwide capitalist economic system, is struggling with it, and of itself is not a homogeneous, ideological, sweet little collection of patriarchal labor farms, but is a series of differentiated groups carrying on a fierce struggle with one another.

5. The Organization and Production School idealizes the pulverized peasant farms imbued with the petty bourgeois spirit, hammers out their ideology, and thus supports reactionary, precapitalist forms of the economy.

It is exceedingly simple to show that all these accusations are incorrect and based on the crudest misunderstandings. We shall try to review each one separately.

1. If we were to set ourselves the task of analyzing the peasant farm as a national economy phenomenon, we would undoubtedly have to review it dynamically in connection with the historical setting in which it exists and to do it as a historical, and not as a logical, category.

We have not yet set ourselves this task. We are not concerned with the fate of the peasant farm, nor its historical and national economy conception, nor even with the historical development of economic systems. Our task is incommensurably more modest. We simply aim at understanding what the peasant farm is from an organizational viewpoint: What is the morphology of the production machine called the peasant labor farm? We are interested in how the proportional nature of the parts is achieved in this machine, how the organizational equilibrium is achieved, what are the mechanics of the circulation and replacement of capital in a private economic sense, what are the methods for determining the degree of satisfaction and profit, and what are the ways it reacts to the influences of the external natural and economic factors we have taken as given.

In all this, we are interested not in the system of the peasant farm and forms of organization in their historical development but, rather, in the mere mechanics of the organizational process. But this organizational analysis by its very nature ought to be static, just as the analysis of the construction of a compound steam locomotive or some turbogenerator is static.

They can tell us that morphological study is not needed for a national economic understanding of the peasant farm and that this is the task, not of an economist, but of a technologist. We will not argue, and agree beforehand to be called agricultural officers; but, to our mind, a static organizational and agricultural study of the peasant farm is just as essential to understand at the level of the national economy as is a dynamic study of it in the whole historically developing system of the economy.

Every science should include both dynamic and static elements. In order to understand plant life, we should now study geobotany—the life of plant forms from excavated remains—acquaint ourselves with the theories of Darwin and de Vries, and study the whole chemistry of plant physiology. Yet, all this not merely permits, but also demands, an insistent and yet preliminary study of the anatomy of the plant cell and the morphology of, let us say, the leaf. Yet no one, of course, will suspect a stem morphologist of deducing the laws governing the distribution of the Compositae in the botanical zones of Europe on the basis of an analysis of the cambial layer.

It is the same in economics. In the system of K. Marx, who can by no means be reproached with disdain for dynamics, numerous static elements and techniques of static analysis may be found. The theory of value, the morphology of capital circulation and of the processes of expanded and simple capital renewal are static and constructed by logical analysis in order to subsequently use them as a weapon for a historical, dynamic analysis of reality. In short, *for the time being* we are elaborating the morphological static elements of the science of peasant farms. And for this reason alone, they can not be contrasted with any other dynamic national economy concept of the peasant farm.

In their present form, these elements are exceedingly useful to agricultural officers and organizers in exactly the same way the statistically constructed courses on farm organization by Goltz, Waterstradt, and Aereboe are of use to the organizers of the large-scale German farms. In all probability, our morphological analysis will in the future serve as a very valuable tool for the dynamic analysis of the peasant farm in the full complexity of its historical setting.

In all instances—not many, it is true—when economists of the Organization and Production School have approached general economic problems they have always adopted a dynamic viewpoint. To be completely convinced that these books are constructed on a plane of doubly dynamic analysis, it suffices to read N. P. Makarov's *The Peasant Farm and Its Evolution* or A. A. Rybnikov's work on commercial flax-growing.

2. In our explanations regarding the first accusation, we have to some extent also replied to the second. Since the organizational analysis of the peasant farm production machine is our task, we inevitably ought to remain within the limits of static methods of organizational analysis. The methods of Marxist national economy analysis, however, have been elaborated and are applied to the practice, not of private economy, but of national economy research, and it is exceedingly difficult to transfer them to, for example, agricultural valuation surveys or bookkeeping, and equally to analysis of the organization of the undertaking.

Many Marxist methods long ago received general recognition and were organically included in the social sciences, and it would be exceedingly curious if we avoided them and approached peasant farm analysis as a national economy category. We think that in the next few years, on the basis of research into national economy problems, we will be able to explain to ourselves and to others what we will take up in our practical research work from the rich experience of Marxist methods.

Matters are a bit more complicated as regards the accusation of allegiance to the "Austrian house." This accusation, however, is personal rather than having anything to do with a school. Economists of the most varied general economic allegiances are included in the Organization and Production School as they are included, too, among its critics. I, for example, am completely unable to recall A. N. Chelintsev's views on the problem of value; I know only that he is a vehement opponent of the law of diminishing returns. No line written by N. P. Makarov, nor A. A. Rybnikov, still less by A. N. Minin affords a basis for suspecting them of the Austrian sin.

Expressions such as "subjective evaluation," "marginal labor expenditure," and even "the utility of the worker's marginal ruble of earnings" are to be found in the works of the present author and even, in fact, in the present book. Here, it is difficult to make a disavowal. I nevertheless consider this accusation incorrect and, to use the words of a French prisoner: "Being a murderer I don't at all want them to call me a poisoner."

I use the hypothesis of the subjective labor–consumer balance to analyze the on-farm processes and to establish the nature of the motivation of the peasant family's economic activity. Beyond its limits in the sphere of interfarm relations, the peasant farm appears, and can only appear, through its objective actions. It is from the mass interrelations of these actions with those of others composing the system of national economy that the objective social phenomena of price, rent, and so on are formed.

In the first volume of *Capital*, K. Marx recognizes the possibility of a consumer's evaluation of benefits, but asserts that it is impossible to deduce from it the social phenomenon of price. In analogous fashion, I have disclosed the presence of a labor–consumer balance in the peasant farm's economic practice and the great part it plays in determining the volume of family economic activity, but I do not at all consider it possible to deduce from this a whole system of the national economy.

As regards the Austrian school, the author of the present book stands in approximately the same position as does J. H. von Thünen, for whom the marginal principle has also played no small part.

3. Our critics sometimes point out that the subject of our analysis, the peasant labor farm, is at the present time being outmoded as a phenomenon on the scale of the national economy, and for the next few decades it will be an anachronism. They assert that even at the present time numerous quite varied forms may be distinguished within the limits of the historically existing peasantry, and, of these, farms based on own labor are only a part. Finally, they state that labor farms themselves, when they are viable, are filled with acquisitive and entrepreneurial activity, and at the first opportunity become semicapitalist farms.

All this may be true or, more accurately, almost true. In the historical development of an economy, various economic forms now develop, now fall into decline, and sometimes completely disappear and are borne away into the past. It is quite possible that at some time or other the forms of peasant labor farms we have studied will exist only in historical chronicles and folk songs. Research into the fate of the peasant farm at the level of the national economy* at present does not concern us.

Yet it is clear that within the limits of the next decade peasant labor farms will, nevertheless, remain an unalterable fact in numerous countries, including the U.S.S.R. We who are concerned with the practice of agriculture must construct its future forms from the existing forms of peasant farming; therefore, we are, in practice, concerned with the deepest possible study of the peasant farm.

It is quite true that peasant farming is not homogeneous; apart from peasant labor farms it includes numerous semiproletarian and semicapitalist farms to which Professor L. N. Litoshenko's description would fully apply. We do not propose, however, to consider our organization theory a universal one embracing all forms of undertakings labeled peasant. We are investigating only the *organizational forms of the family farm in agriculture,* and will extend our results only to this still quite considerable sector of the national economy.

It is true that L. N. Litoshenko doubts that the psychology of the labor–consumer balance is characteristic of those in this sector and insistently suggests avarice as the basic feature of peasant psychology. In this instance, however, we must agree on precisely what is the psychology of avarice and what is the labor–consumer balance. Of course, our critics are free to understand the labor–consumer balance

---

* EDITORS' NOTE.—Reading *narodno-khozyaistvennogo,* instead of *nauchno-khozyaistvennogo.*

theory as a sweet little picture of the Russian peasantry in the likeness of the moral French peasants, satisfied with everything and living like the birds of the air. We ourselves do not have such a conception and are inclined to believe that no peasant would refuse either good roast beef, or a gramophone, or even a block of Shell Oil Company shares, if the chance occurred. Unfortunately, such chances do not present themselves in large numbers, and the peasant family wins every kopek by hard, intensive toil. And in these circumstances, they are obliged not only to do without shares and a gramophone, but sometimes without the beef as well. It seems to us that if Rothschild were to flee to some agrarian country, given a social revolution in Europe, and be obliged to engage in peasant labor, he would obey the rules of conduct established by the Organization and Production School, for all his bourgeois acquisitive psychology.

But, apart from this, we have to remember that, as has already been noted, the labor–consumer balance theory was created not out of the head of some theoretician but as a result of observing features in the economic conduct of the masses of peasants, which were successfully explained only with the help of this hypothesis.

Nevertheless, we must, of course, recognize that our constructs reduce life to a scheme and, like any abstract theory, have as their subject an imaginary farm much purer in type than those we must encounter in reality. Incidentally, we have included in the present work an extensive new chapter dealing with the organizational plan of the peasant farm in all its concrete detail, and it will not be difficult for the reader to see to what extent the organizational features we have noted appear in reality.

4. The accusation that we consider peasant farming apart from any connection with world capitalist circulation, apart from the class struggle, and, as it were, apart from all social and economic features which are the essence of the economy's development in the present period is also based on a misunderstanding and disappears for the same reasons as the accusation of static analysis.

Although we do not deny their importance and we support the necessity for a careful study of them, all the problems listed are outside our consideration, since our subject is the internal organizational foundation of the individual family farm, working in its given conditions. We consider this point, misunderstood by our critics, one of the most important in explaining the problem, and thus allow ourselves to deal with it in greater detail.

As we have already noted in passing, the peasant farm as an organizational type of producing machine has existed historically and has been theoretically considered as entering into various economic systems. With certain changes in its internal structure, it may be the basis of a natural economy system, be an item in a national economy system consisting of peasant farms and family units of urban artisans, or become the basis for a feudal economy. In each of these economic regimes, the peasant farm occupies a specific place, different in each particular instance, is bound in different ways with other social classes, and conducts itself in different ways in the ups and downs of class struggle characteristic of each regime.

At the present time, the peasant farm almost everywhere has been drawn into the system of the capitalist commodity market; in many countries it is influenced by finance capital, which has made loans to it, and it coexists with capitalistically organized industry and, in some places, agriculture also. Peasant undertakings have exceedingly complex social interrelations with all these elements of the present-day economy. After Professor Lyashchenko's works on the evolution of Russian farming and Lenin's on the American farm, we can see with great clarity that we should not necessarily expect the development of capitalist influence and concentration in agriculture to take the form of the creation and development of latifundia. More probably, we should expect trading and finance capitalism to establish an economic dictatorship over considerable sectors of agriculture, which as regards production will remain as before, composed of small-scale family labor peasant undertakings subject in their internal organization to the laws of the labor–consumer balance.

We distinctly recognize the need for the Organization and Production School to indicate in individual investigations the place occupied by the peasant farm in the total system of the present-day national economy, and to give the theoretical tie-up of our organizational concept with the principle views on the national economy and its development.

We deal at the end of this book with certain consequences for the national economy which seem to us to follow from the organizational nature of the peasant farm, which we have established. These observations, however, do not have the significance of a theory of the national economy but only approach one. They are static, and describe the peasant farm as material relevant to the national economy rather than establish the historical national economy concept of the peasant farm. Their relation to national economic analysis of the historically existing economy is like A. Weber's views on the *Standort* of industry to the study of the development of present-day industry.

An all-around analysis of peasant farming as a phenomenon of the national economy and in all its concrete historical detail will be the next stage in the development of the school, and I should think that this analysis will be made in the next few years by one of the authors belonging to this school.

5. After all that has been said above, it would be essentially super-fluous to dwell on the fifth point of the criticisms made of us; the more so since not a word is said about any ideology in the course of the whole of the present investigation. However, remembering that this point is of special interest to many of our readers and that our opponents have on many occasions pointed out, "it's not what they say, but what they don't say that's important," we consider we must also deal with this point.

Can you accuse an agricultural officer who in his district has atten-tively studied the very pitiful livestock breeds and the ways in which they are kept, the local crop rotations and weed varieties, on these grounds, of being an adherent of three-course tillage and an enemy to agricultural progress? I think hardly anyone would decide to do this. But can you accuse economists who have worked for many years on a molecular analysis of the basis of present-day peasant farming, on these grounds, of being reactionaries, ideologists of petty bour-geois, property-owning peasant farming, pulverized and individualis-tic, demarcated from any social forms of production, obscurantists denying any agricultural progress and scientific achievements? Evi-dently, you can. You can, even if the authors being criticized are active workers in the cooperative movement and leaders in agricul-tural assistance to the population. I say you can, because that is how some of our critics behave.

The economists of the Organization and Production School, work-ing all their lives in one connection or another with peasant farming, are naturally accustomed to looking at much of economic life from the point of view of the interests of peasant farming. The whole ques-tion, however, is: *What sort of* peasant farming?

By carefully studying present-day peasant farming *as it is*, we have primarily studied the initial material from which the new country-side, in our opinion, should historically evolve in the next decade, having converted, by means of cooperatives, a considerable part of its economy into socially organized forms of production. It should be a countryside industrialized in all spheres of technical processing, mechanized, and electrified—a countryside that has made use of all the achievements of agricultural science and technology.

Anyone acquainted in practice with the present-day peasantry knows that the embryonic, initial elements of this new countryside are already evident, and their gradual quantitative growth should, in a number of decades, qualitatively improve our countryside, both in an economic and equally in a social sense. We deal with the development of this idea in great detail at the end of this book, and suppose that acquaintance with this system will once and for all destroy any possibility of counting us as opponents of agricultural progress and reactionary ideologists of outmoded economic forms.

All that has been said above fully and clearly outlines to sufficient degree the task before our study. An organizational analysis of peasant family economic activity is our task—a family that does not hire outside labor, has a certain area of land available to it, has its own means of production, and is sometimes obliged to expend some of its labor force on nonagricultural crafts and trades.

We will start our study with a detailed survey of the biologically developing family itself as a cooperative of worker and consumer units, and also of the influence that the peculiarities of the family as a producing machine may have on its economic activity. We will devote special attention to the character of work motivation of family members, and to production and other features which determine the degree to which the labor force exploits itself. After discussing these problems, we will handle with particular care the interrelations and influence on the farm's organization of three basic items—land, capital, and labor—and, at the same time, the machinery for achieving economic equilibrium among these factors. After thus establishing the basic organizational foundations of the peasant farm, we will discuss in great detail, link by link, all the elements of an organizational plan of a peasant agricultural undertaking, and will attempt to show, in a series of concrete examples, the application of our principles to the practical work of organization. Having thus finished an organizational survey of the peasant farm, we will deal with an exceedingly important problem, still little worked on—the forms of circulation and capital renewal in the family farm. We will end our study by pointing out certain consequences for the national economy which follow from the organizational nature of the peasant farm, without at the same time claiming to establish a national economy concept of the peasant farm taken in its historical and concrete detail.

Such are our tasks. We hope that our work, if it does not solve them, will in any event be able to help in perhaps correctly posing the problem of the organizational basis of the peasant farm.

CHAPTER 1

# The Peasant Family and the Influence of
# Its Development on Economic Activity

On turning to a study of the labor farm's organization, we ought inevitably to begin our investigation with an all-around analysis of the constitution and laws governing the composition of the subject of this farm—the family that runs it.

Whichever factor determining peasant farm organization we were to consider dominant, however much significance we were to attach to the influence of the market, amount of land for use, or availability of means of production and natural fertility, we ought to acknowledge that work hands are the technically organizing element of any production process. And since, on the family farm which has no recourse to hired labor, the labor force pool, its composition, and degree of labor activity are entirely determined by family composition and size, we must accept family makeup as one of the chief factors in peasant farm organization.

In fact, family composition primarily defines the upper and lower limits of the volume of its economic activity. The labor force of the labor farm is entirely determined by the availability of able-bodied family members. That is why the highest possible limit for volume of activity depends on the amount of work this labor force can give with maximum utilization and intensity. In the same way the lowest volume is determined by the sum of material benefits absolutely essential for the family's mere existence.

As we shall see, these limits are far from being this broad, and, as will be shown below, within these limits family size and composition will further influence farm organization, not only quantitatively, but also qualitatively. It is absolutely essential, therefore, to study the labor family as fully as possible, and to establish the elements in its composition, on which basis it develops its economic activity, before we touch any question about the labor farm.

Leaving aside the semiclan, semifamily formations we have out-lived and limiting ourselves merely to present-day forms of everyday life in civilized countries, we shall, nevertheless, find very great variety in the basic family structure of different peoples and of social strata.

First of all, there is no doubt that the concept of the family, particularly in peasant life, is far from always equated with the biological concept underlying it and is supplemented in content by a series of economic and household complications. In attempting to apportion the contents of this concept in the peasant's mind, Russian zemstvo statisticians, for example, when carrying out household censuses established that to the peasant the concept of the family includes a number of people constantly .eating at one table or having eaten from one pot. According to the late S. Bleklov, peasants in France included in the concept of the family the group of persons locked up for the night behind one lock.

To a still greater extent, we will find variations in family size. In many agricultural districts of Slavonic countries, you may frequently encounter living together several married couples of two or even three generations, united in a single complex patriarchal family. On the other hand, in many industrialized districts we see every young member of the family striving before manhood to branch off from the paternal home and win economic independence and a life for himself.

Nevertheless, however varied the everyday features of the family, its basis remains the purely biological concept of the married couple,[1] living together with their descendants and the aged representatives of the older generation. This biological nature of the family determines to a great extent the limits of its size and, chiefly, the laws of its composition; although, of course, daily circumstances may introduce numerous complications.

Thus, for example, comparing peasant family size by area, we can observe considerable variation. Table 1–1, showing average peasant family size according to zemstvo census data compiled by Mr. Blagoveshchenskii at the end of the nineteenth century, gives us a characteristic picture in this respect.[2]

---

[1] The married trio or quartet in countries with polygamous family structure.

[2] Blagoveshchenskii, *Svod stat. sbornikov khozyaistvennykh svedenii po zemskim podvornym perepisyam* [Summary of statistical handbooks giving economic information on zemstvo household censuses], M., 1893 g.

TABLE 1–1

PEASANT FAMILY SIZE

| Guberniya | Number of Families (000) | Persons Both Sexes (000) | Persons per Family |
|---|---|---|---|
| Leningrad .................... | 71.5 | 385.5 | 5.4 |
| Tver' ...................... | 114.7 | 646.7 | 5.6 |
| Smolensk .................... | 97.7 | 573.7 | 5.9 |
| Novgorod .................... | 25.6 | 140.3 | 5.5 |
| Moscow ...................... | 19.3 | 102.4 | 5.3 |
| Vyatka ...................... | 211.8 | 1238.6 | 5.8 |
| Nizhnii Novgorod ............. | 60.0 | 316.4 | 5.3 |
| Perm' ...................... | 59.7 | 307.3 | 5.1 |
| Ryazan' .................... | 81.3 | 530.0 | 6.5 |
| Tambov .................... | 317.0 | 2108.6 | 6.6 |
| Saratov .................... | 295.7 | 1747.8 | 5.9 |
| Samara .................... | 346.1 | 2026.9 | 5.8 |
| Orel ....................... | 113.0 | 732.5 | 6.5 |
| Kursk ...................... | 294.8 | 1897.8 | 6.4 |
| Voronezh .................... | 226.8 | 1569.8 | 6.9 |
| Chernigov ................... | 89.7 | 523.1 | 5.8 |
| Khar'kov ................... | 20.0 | 114.1 | 5.7 |
| Poltava .................... | 212.9 | 1168.2 | 5.5 |
| Ekaterinoslav ................ | 85.1 | 536.3 | 6.3 |
| Kherson ·................... | 82.2 | 420.8 | 5.1 |
| Bessarabia .................. | 37.4 | 168.2 | 4.5 |

This variation acquires still greater significance if instead of taking the total number of persons we make a slightly deeper analysis. We estimate the family labor force and consumer units, counting, in accordance with the rates now accepted in budget statistics, different age groups that compose the family as equivalent to a full worker and male consumer; then we compare the number of consumers a worker in each family has to maintain. For families included in budget descriptions, which later we shall be mainly using, we have the figures in Table 1–2.

TABLE 1–2

| Area | Persons | Consumers | Workers | Consumers ÷ Workers |
|---|---|---|---|---|
| Starobel'sk .......... | 7.7 | 5.1 | 3.6 | 1.40 |
| Volokolamsk ......... | 7.8 | 5.2 | 3.9 | 1.40 |
| Gzhatsk ............. | 7.7 | 5.8 | 4.3 | 1.47 |
| Porech'e ............ | 7.6 | 5.3 | 3.8 | 1.40 |
| Sychevka ............ | 7.0 | 4.9 | 3.7 | 1.38 |
| Dorogobuzh ......... | 7.7 | 5.2 | 3.9 | 1.35 |
| Vologda ............. | 6.3 | 3.9 | 3.0 | 1.28 |
| Tot'ma ............. | 5.9 | 4.0 | 3.1 | 1.28 |
| Novgorod .......... | 6.9 | 4.7 | 3.7 | 1.28 |

When comparing the figures in the table which describe family size and composition, we should not forget that we have before us averages describing the total group of families analyzed and not a concrete typical family of a particular area. It is enough to glance more deeply at the material to see that, at least for European Russia where semiclan life is now a thing of the past and patriarchal families are rarely found, families of quite varied size occur in any area.

Thus, for example, the average figures from budget investigations quoted above were arrived at by combining families composed as shown in Table 1–3.

TABLE 1–3

DISTRIBUTION OF BUDGET SURVEY FAMILIES BY FAMILY SIZE

| | Persons in Family | | | | | | | | | | | 13 or more | Total No. of Families |
|---|---|---|---|---|---|---|---|---|---|---|---|---|---|
| | 2 | 3 | 4 | 5 | 6 | 7 | 8 | 9 | 10 | 11 | 12 | | |
| Starobel'sk Uezd, Khar'kov Guberniya .... | 8 | 9 | 7 | 8 | 9 | 9 | 16 | 8 | 8 | 5 | 3 | 12 | 102 |
| Novgorod Guberniya .... | 2 | 5 | 5 | 14 | 16 | 17 | 10 | 11 | 4 | 6 | 1 | 1 | 92 |

In delving into the cause of such variation, we ought to explain it mainly as a fact of the biological development of the family, breaking the total group of families down into a series of subgroups by age and, consequently, both by size and by composition.

Among families of small size, we have a number of young ones, often consisting of the newlyweds alone—the husband and wife who have only just become separate from the paternal home. We have a number of families consisting of the married couple and young children, and we have mature families in which the second generation is already working. Many families consist of several related married couples living together. Finally, we always have several decaying old families that consist of two old people living out their days, their descendants having gone off or been lost. In other words, we have before us all the phases of development through which the family passes. In order to understand the composition of the total group of families and of each one separately, we ought inevitably to follow the theoretically normal family development and establish the basis of its composition at each age. Only by taking the family in the full extent of its development, starting at birth and finishing at death, can we understand the basic laws of its composition.

If we take it that a surviving child is born every third year in a young family that has just been established, the future family composition and development is shown *in a rough scheme* in Table 1–4.

TABLE 1–4

FAMILY MEMBERS' AGES IN DIFFERENT YEARS

| Year of Family's Existence | Husband | Wife | Age of Children | | | | | | | | | Number of Persons |
|---|---|---|---|---|---|---|---|---|---|---|---|---|
| | | | 1st | 2nd | 3rd | 4th | 5th | 6th | 7th | 8th | 9th | |
| 1 ..... | 25 | 20 | — | — | — | — | — | — | — | — | — | 2 |
| 2 ..... | 26 | 21 | 1 | — | — | — | — | — | — | — | — | 3 |
| 3 ..... | 27 | 22 | 2 | — | — | — | — | — | — | — | — | 3 |
| 4 ..... | 28 | 23 | 3 | — | — | — | — | — | — | — | — | 3 |
| 5 ..... | 29 | 24 | 4 | 1 | — | — | — | — | — | — | — | 4 |
| 6 ..... | 30 | 25 | 5 | 2 | — | — | — | — | — | — | — | 4 |
| 7 ..... | 31 | 26 | 6 | 3 | — | — | — | — | — | — | — | 4 |
| 8 ..... | 32 | 27 | 7 | 4 | 1 | — | — | — | — | — | — | 5 |
| 9 ..... | 33 | 28 | 8 | 5 | 2 | — | — | — | — | — | — | 5 |
| 10 ..... | 34 | 29 | 9 | 6 | 3 | — | — | — | — | — | — | 5 |
| 11 ..... | 35 | 30 | 10 | 7 | 4 | 1 | — | — | — | — | — | 6 |
| 12 ..... | 36 | 31 | 11 | 8 | 5 | 2 | — | — | — | — | — | 6 |
| 13 ..... | 37 | 32 | 12 | 9 | 6 | 3 | — | — | — | — | — | 6 |
| 14 ..... | 38 | 33 | 13 | 10 | 7 | 4 | 1 | — | — | — | — | 7 |
| 15 ..... | 39 | 34 | 14 | 11 | 8 | 5 | 2 | — | — | — | — | 7 |
| 16 ..... | 40 | 35 | 15 | 12 | 9 | 6 | 3 | — | — | — | — | 7 |
| 17 ..... | 41 | 36 | 16 | 13 | 10 | 7 | 4 | 1 | — | — | — | 8 |
| 18 ..... | 42 | 37 | 17 | 14 | 11 | 8 | 5 | 2 | — | — | — | 8 |
| 19 ..... | 43 | 38 | 18 | 15 | 12 | 9 | 6 | 3 | — | — | — | 8 |
| 20 ..... | 44 | 39 | 19 | 16 | 13 | 10 | 7 | 4 | 1 | — | — | 9 |
| 21 ..... | 45 | 40 | 20 | 17 | 14 | 11 | 8 | 5 | 2 | — | — | 9 |
| 22 ..... | 46 | 41 | 21 | 18 | 15 | 12 | 9 | 6 | 3 | — | — | 9 |
| 23 ..... | 47 | 42 | 22 | 19 | 16 | 13 | 10 | 7 | 4 | 1 | — | 10 |
| 24 ..... | 48 | 43 | 23 | 20 | 17 | 14 | 11 | 8 | 5 | 2 | — | 10 |
| 25 ..... | 49 | 44 | 24 | 21 | 18 | 15 | 12 | 9 | 6 | 3 | — | 10 |
| 26 ..... | 50 | 45 | 25 | 22 | 19 | 16 | 13 | 10 | 7 | 4 | 1 | 11 |

Undoubtedly, due to the death rate of grown children or a somewhat higher birth rate than we have taken, family development in reality will differ from our figures. We will always meet families that consist of only three or four persons, despite having lasted fifteen years. Families will frequently break down prematurely, taking the full cycle as 25 years, as we have done, more or less. However, the type of normal family development which occurs without catastrophe will always resemble these figures, and the scheme is adequate for a theoretical description of family development.

In future, the family is of interest to us as an economic and not as a biological phenomenon. So in looking at our table, we ought to express its composition regarding consumer and worker units at different phases of its development. We should try to explain how the relationship of the family labor force to its consumer demands changes as the family develops, and to what extent at different phases of this development it is possible to apply the principle of complex cooperation, since it is precisely these elements in its makeup which are important in organizing its economic activity.

If we adopt the rates established in the Vologda budget studies in accounting consumer and worker units, simplifying them somewhat and retaining division by sex only for the parents, then the development of the family will be as shown in Table 1–5, in which family members engaging in work of an economic nature are shown in boldface.

TABLE 1–5

| Years of Family's Existence | Married Couple | Children | | | | | | | | | Total in Family Consumers | Workers | Consumers ÷ Workers |
|---|---|---|---|---|---|---|---|---|---|---|---|---|---|
| | | 1 | 2 | 3 | 4 | 5 | 6 | 7 | 8 | 9 | | | |
| 1 ... | 1.8 | — | — | — | — | — | — | — | — | — | 1.8 | 1.8 | 1.00 |
| 2 ... | 1.8 | 0.1 | — | — | — | — | — | — | — | — | 1.9 | 1.8 | 1.06 |
| 3 ... | 1.8 | 0.3 | — | — | — | — | — | — | — | — | 2.1 | 1.8 | 1.17 |
| 4 ... | 1.8 | 0.3 | — | — | — | — | — | — | — | — | 2.1 | 1.8 | 1.17 |
| 5 ... | 1.8 | 0.3 | 0.1 | — | — | — | — | — | — | — | 2.2 | 1.8 | 1.22 |
| 6 ... | 1.8 | 0.3 | 0.3 | — | — | — | — | — | — | — | 2.4 | 1.8 | 1.33 |
| 7 ... | 1.8 | 0.3 | 0.3 | — | — | — | — | — | — | — | 2.4 | 1.8 | 1.33 |
| 8 ... | 1.8 | 0.3 | 0.3 | 0.1 | — | — | — | — | — | — | 2.5 | 1.8 | 1.39 |
| 9 ... | 1.8 | 0.5 | 0.3 | 0.3 | — | — | — | — | — | — | 2.9 | 1.8 | 1.61 |
| 10 ... | 1.8 | 0.5 | 0.3 | 0.3 | — | — | — | — | — | — | 2.9 | 1.8 | 1.61 |
| 11 ... | 1.8 | 0.5 | 0.3 | 0.3 | 0.1 | — | — | — | — | — | 3.0 | 1.8 | 1.66 |
| 12 ... | 1.8 | 0.5 | 0.5 | 0.3 | 0.3 | — | — | — | — | — | 3.4 | 1.8 | 1.88 |
| 13 ... | 1.8 | 0.5 | 0.5 | 0.3 | 0.3 | — | — | — | — | — | 3.4 | 1.8 | 1.88 |
| 14 ... | 1.8 | 0.5 | 0.5 | 0.3 | 0.3 | 0.1 | — | — | — | — | 3.5 | 1.8 | 1.94 |
| 15 ... | 1.8 | 0.7 | 0.5 | 0.5 | 0.3 | 0.3 | — | — | — | — | 4.1 | 2.5 | 1.64 |
| 16 ... | 1.8 | 0.7 | 0.5 | 0.5 | 0.3 | 0.3 | — | — | — | — | 4.1 | 2.5 | 1.64 |
| 17 ... | 1.8 | 0.7 | 0.5 | 0.5 | 0.3 | 0.3 | 0.1 | — | — | — | 4.2 | 2.5 | 1.68 |
| 18 ... | 1.8 | 0.7 | 0.7 | 0.5 | 0.5 | 0.3 | 0.3 | — | — | — | 4.8 | 3.2 | 1.50 |
| 19 ... | 1.8 | 0.7 | 0.7 | 0.5 | 0.5 | 0.3 | 0.3 | — | — | — | 4.8 | 3.2 | 1.50 |
| 20 ... | 1.8 | 0.9 | 0.7 | 0.5 | 0.5 | 0.3 | 0.3 | 0.1 | — | — | 5.1 | 3.4 | 1.50 |
| 21 ... | 1.8 | 0.9 | 0.7 | 0.7 | 0.5 | 0.5 | 0.3 | 0.3 | — | — | 5.7 | 4.1 | 1.39 |
| 22 ... | 1.8 | 0.9 | 0.7 | 0.7 | 0.5 | 0.5 | 0.3 | 0.3 | — | — | 5.7 | 4.1 | 1.39 |
| 23 ... | 1.8 | 0.9 | 0.9 | 0.7 | 0.5 | 0.5 | 0.3 | 0.3 | 0.1 | — | 6.0 | 4.3 | 1.39 |
| 24 ... | 1.8 | 0.9 | 0.9 | 0.7 | 0.7 | 0.5 | 0.5 | 0.3 | 0.3 | — | 6.6 | 5.0 | 1.32 |
| 25 ... | 1.8 | 0.9 | 0.9 | 0.7 | 0.7 | 0.5 | 0.5 | 0.3 | 0.3 | — | 6.6 | 5.0 | 1.32 |
| 26 ... | 1.8 | 0.9 | 0.9 | 0.9 | 0.7 | 0.5 | 0.5 | 0.3 | 0.3 | 0.1 | 6.9 | 5.2 | 1.32 |

Looking at the table and figure 1–1, which illustrates the development of the basic elements, we see that in the first years as the family grows it becomes ever more burdened with children unable to work,

FIGURE 1-1

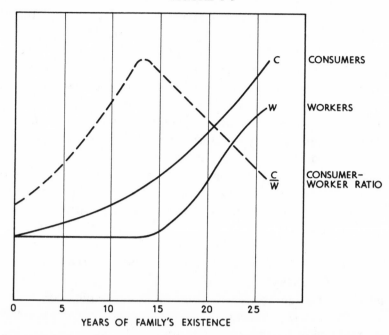

and we note a rapid increase in the proportion of consumers to work-ers. In the fourteenth year of the family's existence, this proportion reaches its highest point, 1.94. But in the fifteenth year, the first child comes to the aid of the parents when he has reached semiworking age, and the consumer–worker ratio immediately falls to 1.64. In reality, of course, no such sharp leap occurs, since the transition from the child unable to work to the half-time worker is made more gradually. But it is nonetheless true that about this time the burden of con-sumers on the workers of the family becomes lighter, since each year the children take a greater and greater part in the work. In the twenty-sixth year of the family's existence, the ratio falls to 1.32.

If after this year we take it that no further children are born to the head of the family, as the children grow up the consumer–worker ra-tio will fall rapidly, approaching unity and reaching it in the thirty-seventh year of the family's existence, provided that none of the sons marry and the old people do not lose their ability to work.

If daughters-in-law enter the household and have children, a cer-tain increase in the consumer–worker ratio will again commence in the complex family which has been formed. This increase rises sharply when the original parents become unfit for work. Parallel to the changes in family composition that have been noted in connection with its growth, we must notice the increase, as it matures, of the number of working hands; this gives the chance of applying the principles of complex cooperation in work and, thus, increases the power of each of them. At some moment in its development, for some internal reasons, the family that has thus matured meets with catastrophe and splits into two or more families. Each of these young families then begins afresh to pass through the phases of family development we have described, if they have not already passed through the first of them while still in the paternal patriarchal family.

Thus, *every family*, depending on its age, is in its different phases of development a completely distinct labor machine as regards labor force, intensity of demand, consumer–worker ratio, and the possibility of applying the principles of complex cooperation.

In accordance with this, we can pose the first problem of our inquiry: *Does the state of this continually changing machine affect the economic activity of a family running its labor farm, and if it does, how and to what extent?*

Since the labor family's basic stimulus to economic activity is the necessity to satisfy the demands of its consumers, and its work hands are the chief means for this, we ought first of all to expect the family's *volume of economic activity* to quantitatively correspond more or less to these basic elements in family composition.

By the volume of economic activity here and throughout this book we understand all forms of family economic activity, both in agriculture and in the total group of crafts and trades. Any other approach to family economic activity will be mistaken, since the basic economic problem of the labor farm is a correct and joint organization of the year's work, stimulated by a single family demand to meet its annual budget and a single wish to save or invest capital if economic work conditions allow. Therefore, any sector analysis of economic work— analysis of peasant family farming by itself, for example—will be production, but by no means economic analysis. It will become economic only when problems of agricultural organization are analyzed in connection with the problem of the total economic activity of the family as a whole.

However, in taking the volume of economic activity as an economic concept we ought to make use of farm elements which cover all its joint nature in order to measure it quantitatively. Unfortunately, thanks to the dualism of peasant economic activity—agriculture and crafts and trades—such elements are very limited (labor and income), and empirical investigation of them has started only in the last few years. Therefore, if we wish to adduce mass empirical material to solve the problem we ought to make use of any production element *as a measure* of the volume of economic activity. The *sown area* has usually been taken as such in practice in agricultural statistics. Since we are dealing with peasant farms in which *crafts and trades and commercial livestock farming are weakly or equally developed*, this *measure* may be applied and offers the opportunity of drawing numerous conclusions; though one must, of course, deal with it critically and constantly take account of the nature of this measure. In this particular case, we may conditionally take the sown area as a measure of the volume in order to establish the connection between family size and volume of economic work.

FIGURE 1–2

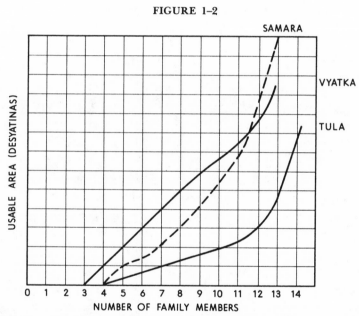

In reality, the first zemstvo statistical workers, who approached the analysis of household censuses by classifying the material by number of livestock, size of arable, sown area, or other farm elements, long ago noted that this connection for Russian peasant farms could be a quantitative measure of the family's volume of economic activity. Table 1–6 and Figure 1–2, which we have drawn up on the basis of B. N. Knipovich's summary, show us the nature of this connection.

In following the development of the functions we can establish a clearly expressed dependence between family development and size of area for use. The character of this dependence is not the same for different areas, depending on variations in the form of general economic life.

## TABLE 1-6

### VOLUME OF ECONOMIC WORK AND FAMILY SIZE

| Sown Area (Desyatinas) | VYATKA Desyatinas of Suitable Land Per Farm | VYATKA Persons of Both Sexes Per Farm | Sown Area (Desyatinas) | TULA Desyatinas of Suitable Land Per Farm | TULA Persons of Both Sexes Per Farm | Sown Area (Desyatinas) | POLTAVA Desyatinas of Suitable Land Per Farm | POLTAVA Persons of Both Sexes Per Farm | Sown Area (Desyatinas) | SAMARA Desyatinas of Suitable Land Per Farm | SAMARA Persons of Both Sexes Per Farm |
|---|---|---|---|---|---|---|---|---|---|---|---|
| 0 | 1.2 | 2.8 | 0 | 0 | 1.0 | 0 | 2.5 | 4.9 | 0 | 0 | 3.5 |
| 0 – 1 | 4.5 | 3.5 | 0– 1 | 0.4 | 3.4 | 0– 1 | 1.5 | 4.9 | 0– 3 | 1.8 | 4.4 |
| 1 – 2½ | 8.9 | 4.4 | 1– 2 | 1.4 | 4.4 | 1– 2 | 2.5 | 5.1 | 3– 6 | 4.5 | 5.2 |
| 2½– 5 | 12.6 | 5.3 | 2– 5 | 3.4 | 6.2 | 2– 3 | 3.6 | 5.4 | 6– 9 | 7.5 | 6.1 |
| 5 – 7½ | 16.6 | 6.2 | 5–10 | 6.9 | 8.4 | 3– 6 | 5.2 | 6.0 | 9–12 | 10.5 | 6.9 |
| 7½–10 | 21.0 | 7.2 | 10–15 | 11.0 | 11.0 | 6– 9 | 9.5 | 6.8 | 12–15 | 13.5 | 7.5 |
| 10 –15 | 27.7 | 8.6 | 15–25 | 17.7 | 12.6 | 9–15 | 15.8 | 7.5 | 15–20 | 17.4 | 8.2 |
| 15 –20 | 36.5 | 10.7 | >25 | 43.9 | 14.4 | 15–25 | 28.0 | 8.5 | 20–30 | 24.1 | 9.4 |
| >20 | 51.2 | 12.8 | – | – | – | 25–50 | 54.5 | 9.5 | 30–40 | 34.2 | 10.9 |
| – | – | – | – | – | – | >50 | 144.0 | 11.2 | >40 | 65.9 | 113.0 |

| Sown Area (Desyatinas) | VLADIMIR Desyatinas of Suitable Land Per Farm | VLADIMIR Persons of Both Sexes Per Farm | Sown Area (Desyatinas) | KALUGA Desyatinas of Suitable Land Per Farm | KALUGA Persons of Both Sexes Per Farm | Sown Area (Desyatinas) | YAROSLAVL' Desyatinas of Suitable Land Per Farm | YAROSLAVL' Persons of Both Sexes Per Farm | Sown Area (Desyatinas) | VOLOGDA Desyatinas of Suitable Land Per Farm | VOLOGDA Persons of Both Sexes Per Farm |
|---|---|---|---|---|---|---|---|---|---|---|---|
| 0 | 0.2 | 3.2 | 0 | 0 | 3.6 | 0 | 1.4 | 2.8 | 0 | 7.1 | 2.5 |
| 0 – 3 | 4.9 | 5.3 | 0– 3 | 2.0 | 4.8 | 0– 1 | 4.6 | 4.1 | 0– 2 | 7.4 | 4.1 |
| 3 – 6 | 9.4 | 6.6 | 3– 6 | 4.3 | 6.0 | 1– 2 | 7.3 | 5.1 | 2– 3 | 12.0 | 5.3 |
| 6 – 9 | 14.2 | 8.3 | 6– 9 | 7.1 | 7.3 | 2– 3 | 10.5 | 6.0 | 3– 6 | 16.6 | 6.2 |
| 9 –12 | 20.1 | 9.8 | >9 | 11.3 | 8.4 | 3– 4 | 14.4 | 6.9 | >6 | 19.1 | 7.5 |
| >12 | 31.1 | 12.0 | – | – | – | >4 | 21.2 | 8.6 | – | – | – |

Thus, in the northern guberniyas—Vyatka, Yaroslavl', Vologda—where earnings from crafts and trades are well developed, the area of land for use is directly proportional to the development of the family. In agricultural areas—Tula, Samara, and Poltava—the land use curve noticeably increases in rate of growth as it develops. But in both instances, the development of the curves so conforms to a pattern that for many guberniyas it could easily be expressed by a mathematical formula. Thus, for example, for Samara guberniya if family size (number of persons) is $x$, the quantity of suitable land per household in the groups we have analyzed is $y$:

$$y = 0.36x^2 - 0.52x - 2.6.$$

For Vyatka guberniya, it is even simpler:

$$y = 4.38x - 10.5.$$

Table 1–7 indicates how far these formulas accurately express the curves.

TABLE 1–7

| No. of Persons in Family (x) | SAMARA GUBERNIYA Sown Area (Desyatinas) per Household (y) According to: | | No. of Persons in Family (x) | VYATKA GUBERNIYA Sown Area (Desyatinas) per Household (y) According to: | |
|---|---|---|---|---|---|
| | *Formula* | *Observation* | | *Formula* | *Observation* |
| 4.4 | 2.0 | 1.8 | 3.5 | 4.8 | 4.5 |
| 5.2 | 4.4 | 4.5 | 4.4 | 8.8 | 8.9 |
| 6.1 | 7.6 | 7.5 | 5.3 | 12.7 | 12.6 |
| 6.9 | 10.7 | 10.5 | 6.2 | 16.7 | 16.6 |
| 7.5 | 14.7 | 13.5 | 7.2 | 21.1 | 21.0 |
| 8.2 | 17.3 | 17.4 | 8.6 | 27.2 | 27.0 |
| 9.4 | 24.3 | 24.1 | 10.7 | 36.3 | 36.5 |
| 10.9 | 34.5 | 34.1 | | | |

The significance of the formulas we have given should not be exaggerated, since they are based on the group processing of tens of thousands of farms, with the elimination of all other factors save those connected with farm size. Therefore, our formulas *can not be applied* to individual farms, since apart from family size and sown area a number of other factors operate which can considerably alter the correlation of the figures. Nevertheless, they definitely establish a tendency. S. N. Prokopovich's detailed inquiries have also indicated without any doubt that a high degree of correlation exists between the family and the measure of agricultural activity. In other words, this method of processing the material also shows us that these two phenomena are related to each other to a considerable extent.

Thus, S. N. Prokopovich established the following correlation coefficients for farm agricultural income and family size.[3]

Starobel'sk uezd, Khar'kov guberniya:
Gross agricultural income and number of workers ........ 0.64
Gross agricultural income and number of consumers ...... 0.61

Even in Vologda uezd, where crafts and trades are exceedingly well developed and a considerable part of family income is derived from such activities, agricultural income, although sometimes subordinate to earnings from crafts and trades, nevertheless shows a noticeable relationship to family size.

Gross agricultural income and number of workers ....... 0.42
Gross agricultural income and number of consumers ...... 0.41

These coefficients, of course, are lower than the technical connection between production factors within agricultural activity itself; but they statistically justify a close connection between family size and volume of economic and even agricultural activity. Yet, while acknowledging the fact of this dependence we can dwell on the question of the internal character of this relationship and suppose that it is not family size which determines volume of family economic activity, as we formerly thought; on the contrary, the measure of agricultural activity, let us say, determines family composition. In other words, the peasant provides himself with a family in accordance with his material security.

The solution to this dilemma is far from being as simple as it may appear at first glance. On the one hand, European scholars in numerous demographic studies have noted that birth and death rates depend on the material conditions of existence, and there is a clearly expressed reduced net population growth among those underprovisioned. On the other hand, it is also known that practical Malthusianism in France is most highly developed in well-to-do peasant circles. In all probability, several years' painstaking research is required to give a final solution to this problem.

We may consider, on the basis of the materials at our disposal, that this problem has no uniform answer. It is evident that at a low level

---

3 S. N. Prokopovich, *Proizvoditel'nost' krestyanskogo khozyaistva po byudzhetnym dannym* [Peasant farm productivity according to budget data].

of material security, when there is the mere possibility of physical existence, material conditions influence family size with the force of a determinant. N. P. Makarov, for example, came to such a conclusion when studying the Voronezh budgets of the dismally remembered 1880's. We are not going to review this state of affairs, however, since we are concerned with the peasantry of the present century, which is at an immeasurably higher standard of well-being than in the 1880's.

Indeed, for this situation to be correct it would be absolutely essential that the peasants on small-scale farms artificially lower the birth rate of their families compared with the birth rate of families holding larger farms. Otherwise, it ought at least to be shown that child mortality in families with little or medium amounts of land is so far above the norm in peasant life that even with equal birth rates it considerably reduces the family, lessening it two- or threefold compared with the well-to-do groups.

Both elements can be statistically established. Unfortunately, however, our registration of births and deaths takes no account of material security. In accordance with this, we will make an analysis that simultaneously takes account of the two phenomena of interest to us —that is, the presence of children up to six years of age and their percentage composition in the family. In this instance, we record the number of births in six years, less children born in these years who died. Limiting ourselves to the materials before us, we obtain the rates shown in Table 1–8 for juniors (0–6 years) in peasant families by sown areas.

TABLE 1–8

| Tot'ma Uezd | | Novgorod Guberniya | |
|---|---|---|---|
| Sown Area per Farm (Desyatinas) | Children 0–6 as % of Persons in Family | Sown Area per Farm (Desyatinas) | Children 0–6 as % of Persons in Family |
| 0.1–1.0 | 20.6% | 0.1–2.0 | 25.7% |
| 1.1–2.0 | 19.1% | 2.1–3.0 | 21.6% |
| 2.1–3.0 | 17.7% | 3.1–4.0 | 13.5% |
| 3.1–4.0 | 17.8% | >4.0 | 17.1% |
| 4.1–6.0 | 18.1% | | |
| >6.0 | 17.1% | | |

The figures of a (combined) estimate of a 1916 Kostroma guberniya census are of a similar character. Table 1–9 gives percent of adults.

As the table shows, there is no basis for asserting that family-forming factors in households with small farms operate more weakly than

TABLE 1-9

| Desyatinas of Sown | Men | Women |
|---|---|---|
| 0.1–1...... | 37.4 | 52.0 |
| 1–2...... | 39.1 | 52.8 |
| 2–3...... | 43.2 | 55.2 |
| 3–4...... | 45.2 | 55.9 |
| 4–5...... | 46.1 | 56.2 |
| 5–6...... | 46.4 | 56.4 |
| 6–7...... | 47.3 | 55.5 |
| 7–8...... | 47.4 | 54.8 |
| 8–9...... | 48.2 | 55.2 |
| 9–10..... | 47.1 | 54.1 |
| 10–11..... | 46.6 | 56.4 |
| 11–12..... | 48.9 | 53.2 |

in those with large farms. We also caution the reader, however, against the contrary conclusion he may deduce from a comparison of these series. The increased percentage of young children in groups that sow a small area, aside from the supposition that family size depends on farm size, depends at the same time not on area of sown but on the fact that, in the main, the classification by sown area is to a certain extent a classification by family age. In accordance with this, those that sow small areas consist of young families with a large number of young children, and those that sow more consist of older families in which small children do not play such a great part.

Thus, in Novgorod guberniya (according to budgets), for example, the percentage of young families—i.e. families consisting of a married couple and children not yet of working age—in categories sowing different areas amount to the following.

| Sown area (desyatinas) ......... | 0–2 | 2–4 | >4 |
|---|---|---|---|
| Percentage of young families .... | 42.9 | 20.8 | 0.0 |

Classification by sown area in Starobel'sk uezd, Khar'kov guberniya, (according to budgets) gives still more characteristic results.

| Sown area (desyatinas) ...... | 0.1–3.0 | 3.1–7.5 | 7.0*–15.0 | >15.0 |
|---|---|---|---|---|
| Percentage of young families .... | 76.4 | 38.5 | 4.0 | 0.0 |

In the main, this information is sufficient for some solution of the problem posed about the direction of dependence between family size and volume of economic activity, since *family age* can not, in any event, depend on the degree of material well-being. However, for a

---

* TRANSLATOR'S NOTE.—Thus in original; presumably a misprint for 7.6.

final explanation of this question, basic to our theme, we allow ourselves to focus the reader's attention, not on static data, but on data
of dynamic type, the elaboration of which is one of the brilliant
achievements in the recent history of Russian statistics.

In the course of the years before the war, in a whole series of guberniyas repeated statistical censuses were carried out in a technical manner that has allowed a genetic link to be established between the
farms described and the farms from which they came and which had
been statistically described 10, 15, or even 30 years before. These
investigations, started by the brilliant work of N. N. Chernenkov for
Saratov guberniya, completely overthrew many of our conceptions
about the peasant farm and provided a firm basis for a description
of its nature.

When we study the dynamics of these farms with the view that
family size is entirely determined by its economic situation, we might
expect that farms sowing small areas will in the course of 15 years
continue to sow the same small areas, and that farms well endowed
will, as before, sow large areas and retain a large family. The works
of Chernenkov, Khryashcheva, Vikhlyaev, Kushchenko, and others,
however, tell us something completely different, as may be seen from
Kushchenko's table (Table 1–10), which is analogous to all the others,
comparing the 1882 and 1911 censuses for Surazh uezd, Chernigov
guberniya.

TABLE 1–10
1911 Sown Area by 1882 Sown Area Groups (%)

| Desyatinas Sown in 1882 | Desyatinas Sown in 1911 | | | | | Total |
|---|---|---|---|---|---|---|
| | 0–3 | 3–6 | 6–9 | 9–12 | >12 | |
| 0–3....... | 28.2 | 47.0 | 20.0 | 2.4 | 2.4 | 100.0 |
| 3–6....... | 21.8 | 47.5 | 24.4 | 8.2 | 2.4 | 100.0 |
| 6–9....... | 16.2 | 37.0 | 26.8 | 11.3 | 2.4 | 100.0 |
| 9–12...... | 9.6 | 35.8 | 26.1 | 12.4 | 16.1 | 100.0 |
| >12...... | 3.5 | 30.5 | 28.5 | 15.6 | 21.9 | 100.0 |

We see that a considerable part of the farms that sowed small areas
gradually acquired a labor force as family age and size increased, and
by expanding their sown area passed into the higher groups, thus
also expanding the volume of their economic activity. Conversely,
former large farms passed into lower groups corresponding to the
small families created after division. This shows us that the demographic processes of growth and family distribution by size also determine to a considerable extent the distribution of farms by size of
sown area and numbers of livestock.

Therefore, since the work of Chernenkov, Khryashcheva, Vikhlyaev, and Kushchenko, when speaking of peasant farms that differ in sown area and in their distribution to sown area groups, those in statistical circles have begun to use the expression *demographic differentiation*, thus avoiding the social significance formerly ascribed to this difference. In saying this, of course, *we are not removing from our usage the concept of social differentiation*—something which is quite widespread in the countryside—but, as we will see from a subsequent chapter, this form of differentiation is not to be seen by simply grouping by sown areas; it has to be studied by other methods.

These materials do not give a final solution to the problem, which still calls for many painstaking studies extending over many years. Nevertheless, they give us some possibility of supposing within the limits of our statistical material—which, incidentally relates to repartitional commune areas—that the connection between family size and size of agricultural activity should be understood as a dependence of area of land for use on family size rather than conversely.

In all probability, in another agrarian regime less flexible than that of the repartitional commune the influence of the biological factor of family development on size of land for use would not stand out so prominently and be so evident as in our material. However, as, for example, analysis of the Starobel'sk budgets shows, the tendency of land for use to approach family size and composition may be achieved not only by communal repartitions but also with still greater success by short leases of land. The sale and purchase of land may also be the way in which land use is regulated in countries with private property in land.

In a number of countries where nonpartible inheritance is the rule—in southern Germany, for example—and equally where with its high degree of intensity the capitalist farm and all its lands forms a firmly welded production machine, the pressure of the biological development of the family undoubtedly can not influence the amount of land for use. This is expressed predominantly in changes in the relationship of own and hired labor serving the particular production machine and in the extent to which its own surplus labor goes off to work elsewhere. In this connection, the reflections of Professor A. Skalweit (Kiel) in his extended criticisms of the German edition of this book are very interesting.[4]

However, if the conditions of a somewhat inflexible agrarian regime also break the connection between family size and size of agri-

---

[4] A. Skalweit, "Die Familienwirtschaft als Grundlage für ein System der Sozial-ökonomie," *Weltwirt. Archiv*, April, 1924.

cultural activity—in this case, if the farm continues to use its own labor—this frequently means merely that the area of land for use has lost its ability to be a *measure* of the volume of economic activity and we ought to seek other measures. In the conditions in the U.S.S.R., however, and in those analogous to them, in the majority of cases we can confidently talk of this connection even within the limits of agriculture.

This circumstance ought to bring us to a characteristic conclusion. Any capitalist agricultural unit, its size being determined by a constant and unchanging amount of capital and land area, may in the course of an indeterminate lengthy period (within infinite limits) remain at one and the same volume; but the peasant farm in the course of decades, and in conditions analogous to those of Russian reality, constantly changes its volume, following the phases of family development, and its elements display a pulsating curve.

Although we have established by analysis of group averages that the volume of peasant farming depends on family size and composition (this dependence is clear, merely from the considerations, expressed at the start of the chapter, that the higher limit is determined by the maximum availability of the family labor force, and the lower by the minimum means of existence for the family), in order to avoid incorrect treatment of our conclusions we ought to stress that at any particular moment the family *is not the sole determinant of the size of a particular farm,* and determines its size only in a general way. The comparatively high correlation coefficients established between these figures are, nevertheless, far from 1.00. This alone indicates the existence of parallel factors which in their turn exert a pressure on the figure being studied.

In studying the road along which the peasant farm develops, we ought to notice that to convert the number of family working hands into farm size and income we must additionally determine: to what extent these hands may be utilized; what part of potential working time is actually expended; what is the intensity of their labor or its degree of self-exploitation; what are the available technical means of production with which labor enters the production process; how high, in the final result, will be the productivity of this labor, depending on natural conditions and the market situation. Only when we have compared the pressure of family size with the influence of these factors, establishing their interrelationships and the specific weight of each one in determining the structure and volume of the peasant family's economic activity, can we also approach a knowledge of the nature of the peasant farm.

CHAPTER 2

# Measure of Self-Exploitation of the
# Peasant Family Labor Force.
# The Concept of Advantage
# in the Labor Farm

In studying the annual productivity of peasant labor from various sources, we ought, in the first place, to distinguish between the concept of *gross product* of labor and its *net product*. By *gross product*, we understand all *income* the family receives in the course of a year, both from agriculture and from other applications of its labor in farming and in crafts and trades. By *net product*, we understand that part of gross product left after covering all annual overheads connected with capital renewal and annual expenditures on the farm. Thus, the net labor product is determined by the annual increment of material values becoming available to the farm and obtained as a result of its annual labor—in other words, the annual payment to the farm family for labor expended on it and in crafts and trades.

At the moment, we are not going into the national economic nature of this income and will not elucidate the elements of unearned income included in it. We limit ourselves to a private economic definition of this single peasant family income which becomes available in the course of the year.

In view of the numerous misunderstandings that largely obscure the essence of the matter, we ought to stress with particular insistence that by the product of peasant labor, peasant farm income, and so on we always understand the joint income of the peasant family both from agriculture and from crafts and trades, except, of course, in all those cases where a special note is made. This circumstance is exceedingly important for us, since our theory of the labor farm and of the

70

labor–consumer balance is *a theory of an economic unit or, what is the same thing, the economic activity of family labor* and not one of peasant agricultural production.

It is self-evident, as we will see from Chapter 4, that the peculiar features of the peasant family labor farm in many instances also considerably influence the organization of peasant agricultural production; but, in general, the peasant production is constructed, like any other, on the principle of the lowest production overheads and according to rules which follow from its technology. Since this production is carried on within the limits of the labor farm, its special features have decisive influence in determining the size of agricultural production, considerable influence on the degree of its labor and capital intensity and on its labor organization, and some influence on the assortment of produce grown on the farm in that on it these items are consumed in kind. For the rest, as will be seen from subsequent chapters, the market, conditions due to natural history, and technology are the determining factors.

You must have all this in mind when surveying our analysis of the economic conduct of the peasant family. You should also remember that by studying peasant farm productivity in the present chapter we are not solving the production problem of agricultural organization, but we are establishing the basis of the economic activity of family labor. This, *by the way*, together with the influence of the market, natural conditions, and technology, greatly influences the organization of peasant agricultural production.

Peasant labor productivity concerns us as a result of total family economic activity. In this respect, in Table 2–1 we compare some of

TABLE 2–1

| | Workers per Average Farm | Gross Product per Family | | |
|---|---|---|---|---|
| | | Average | Lowest | Highest |
| Novgorod Guberniya ........ | 3.84 | 618.5 | 169.0 (12) | 1981.0 (6) |
| Starobel'sk Uezd ............ | 3.57 | 918.9 | 195.9 (27) | 3393.0 (87) |
| Tot'ma Uezd .............. | 3.09 | 402.5 | 123.8 (8) | 1141.4 (69) |
| Volokolamsk Uezd .......... | 3.88 | 1070.0 | 373.0 (23) | 2172.4 (7) |

| | | Net Product per Family | | |
|---|---|---|---|---|
| | | Average | Lowest | Highest |
| Novgorod Guberniya ........ | 3.84 | 361.7 | 100.45 (12) | 923.08 (6) |
| Starobel'sk Uezd ............ | 3.57 | 529.1 | 91.0 (27) | 1554.0 (87) |
| Tot'ma Uezd .............. | 3.09 | 226.0 | 95.7 (8) | 663.3 (69) |
| Volokolamsk Uezd .......... | 3.88 | 512.0 | 271.7 (23) | 1428.6 (7) |

the materials at our disposal and obtain some output rates achieved by our Russian peasant families[1] (agriculture, crafts and trades).

Thus, in these four inquiries on Russian peasant families gross incomes—in terms of gold currency and prices of the year of the inquiry, including income in money and kind—fluctuate for individual farms from 123.5 to 3393.0 rubles, and on average from 402.8 to 1070.0 rubles. This is the basic figure for the national economy on which the economic system of the U.S.S.R. is being built. It is clear that the difference noted depends to a great extent on variations in family size. Therefore, in the interests of comparability it is essential to express these figures per full annual male worker, reducing female and child labor to these terms.

*Gross Income in Money and in Kind*
*from Agriculture, Crafts, and*
*Trades per Worker (Rubles)*

Novgorod budgets ................... 161.1
Starobel'sk budgets .................. 257.5
Tot'ma budgets ..................... 130.0
Volokolamsk budgets ............... 276.1

As is seen from the figures, even the average area gross product figures differ sharply from one another. In order to give our readers a fuller conception of these differences in peasant labor productivity, we allow ourselves to quote two tables showing the distribution of peasant farms within one and the same budget inquiry by different groups of annual budget net labor productivity per average worker (Table 2–2).

It is completely obvious that differences in the worker's annual

TABLE 2–2

| Starobel'sk Uezd | | | Volokolamsk Uezd | | |
|---|---|---|---|---|---|
| Annual Output per Worker (Rubles) | Number of Farms in Group | % | Annual Output per Worker (Rubles) | Number of Farms in Group | % |
| 0–50 ..... | 5 | 4.95 | 0–100 ..... | 2 | 8.0 |
| 50–70 ..... | 14 | 13.89 | 100–150 ..... | 9 | 36.0 |
| 70–90 ..... | 18 | 17.85 | 150–200 ..... | 7 | 28.0 |
| 90–110 .... | 18 | 17.85 | 200–300 ..... | 4 | 16.0 |
| 110–130 .... | 10 | 9.91 | 300–∞ ..... | 3 | 12.0 |
| 130–150 .... | 13 | 12.90 | | | |
| 150–170 .... | 9 | 8.91 | | | |
| 170–190 .... | 44 | 3.90 | | | |
| 190–∞ .... | 10 | 9.91 | | | |
| Total | 101 | 100.0 | Total | 25 | 100.0 |

---

[1] Numbers in parentheses indicate the farm number in the budget tables.

labor payment depend on two factors which determine his annual productivity. On the one hand is the *degree of intensity* of his annual work, the quantity of labor energy the peasant worker is able or wants to expend in the course of 12 months. On the other hand is the productivity of each labor unit expended, the economic and technical conditions that assure his labor of a particular productive effect. Often the most intensive daily labor gives insignificant annual income if it is applied to poor soils and in an unfavorable market situation for the produce grown. Conversely, working fertile soils with a rise in the market price of produce grown gives high income with comparatively little expenditure of energy.

In the present work, investigating the internal organization of the peasant farm, we cannot deal with the conditions that determine the level of labor productivity, since they depend not so much on on-farm factors as on general economic factors affecting the farm's existence. Soil fertility, advantageous location of farm in relation to market, current market situation, local land relations, organizational forms of the local market, and the character of trading and finance capitalism's penetration into the depths of the peasantry—these are the chief factors determining peasant labor productivity and pay. By their very nature, all these factors lie outside the field of our present investigation.

We will deal in this connection with the first of these two factors —the degree of intensity or measure of self-exploitation of peasant labor. Unfortunately, study of the organization of peasant labor was started by our statistics only in the last years before the war; due to this, we have very skimpy relevant material. Nevertheless, within the limits of this material we can draw a number of substantial conclusions by comparing the quantity of work time at the disposal of the peasant family in the course of the 365 days of the astronomical year with what it succeeds in spending on productive processes. Table 2–3 and Figures 2–1 and 2–2 give us some conception of the distribution of peasant family labor on different uses in the course of the year.

In Myshkino uezd, Yaroslavl' guberniya, unutilized labor force per peasant household amounted to the percentages in Table 2–4, according to estimates by zemstvo statisticians. In somewhat different forms, a description of a typical Tver guberniya farm, made in 1907 and accurate to one hour,[2] gives us a record of the same phenomenon (Table 2–5).

---

2 *Nuzhdy derevni* [Needs of the countryside], 1907 g. "Trudovoi krest'yanskii god v tsifrakh" ["The peasant labor year in figures"].

TABLE 2-3

| | Agricul-ture % | Crafts and Trades % | Total Produc-tive Labor % | House Work % | Unused Time % | Festi-vals % | Total % |
|---|---|---|---|---|---|---|---|
| Vologda Uezd, Vologda Guberniya | 24.7 | 18.1 | 42.8 | 4.4 | 33.8 | 19.8 | 100.0 |
| Volokolamsk Uezd, Moscow Guberniya | 28.6 | 8.2 | 36.8 | | 43.2 | 20.0 | 100.0 |
| Starobel'sk Uezd, Khar'kov Guberniya | 23.6 | 4.4 | 28.0 | 3.0 | 42.0 | 27.0 | 100.0 |

TABLE 2-4

| Group of Farms with Sown Area (Desyatinas) | Proportion of Annual Work | |
|---|---|---|
| | Male | Female |
| 0–5 ........ | 0.25 | 0.40 |
| 5–7 ........ | 0.20 | 0.30 |
| 7–10 ........ | 0.15 | 0.20 |
| 10–15 ........ | 0.10 | 0.13 |

TABLE 2-5

| | Men | Women |
|---|---|---|
| Number of hours spent awake ..................... | 5876 | 17876 |
| Number of hours spent working: on own farm ........ | 2206 | 2000 |
| in factory ........... | — | 1500 |
| Number of hours remaining unused for productive labor ........................... | 3670 | 14376 |

We see that of the total number of working days in the year, peasants spend a comparatively small proportion of their labor—in all, only 25–40 percent—on agriculture in the areas we have studied. Even if we add to this all work in crafts and trades, we still have to recognize that peasant labor is far from fully used and gives a use rate not exceeding 50 percent.

The main reason for this undoubtedly lies in the particular features of labor organization in agriculture. In contrast to the processing industry, in which labor processes are not connected with any time of the day or year, a great part of the agricultural process is exclusively seasonal in nature, and some demand particularly favorable weather conditions, which are not always present.

Because of this, the labor intensity curve in agriculture always shows extremely uneven development. Sowing, mowing, harvesting,

and some work on specialized crops sometimes demand the exceptional accumulation of a mass of labor in insignificant time periods,
while in other, sometimes very lengthy, periods of the farm year agriculture finds no objects on which to use its labor. Figure 2–1 for
Volokolamsk uezd clearly illustrates this idea.

FIGURE 2–1

INTENSITY OF LABOR EXPENDITURE ON
VOLOKOLAMSK FARM No. 11

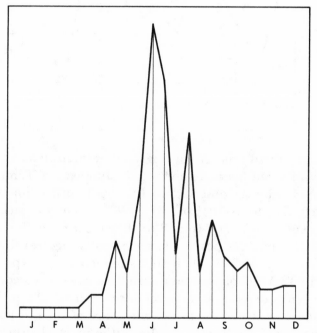

We must add that in different *farm periods* there are sharp changes
not only in the number of working days but also in the intensity of
each day's work. Thus, for example, in the already mentioned Tver
farm in 1907 the monthly average length of working day in hours of
actual work was:

| | | | |
|---|---|---|---|
| January | 6.3 | July | 9.1 |
| February | 2.8 | August | 7.8 |
| March | 4.5 | September | 7.8 |
| April | 6.3 | October | 2.1 |
| May | 6.3 | November | 3.8 |
| June | 9.3 | December | 6.1 |

The conclusion, in any event, remains the same: *in the labor farm,
rates of labor intensity are considerably lower than if labor were fully
utilized.* In all areas investigated, farm families possess considerable

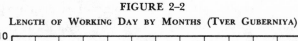

FIGURE 2–2

LENGTH OF WORKING DAY BY MONTHS (TVER GUBERNIYA)

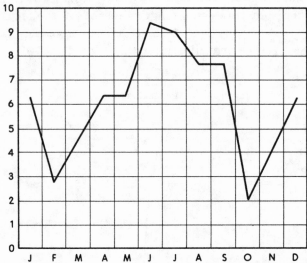

stocks of unutilized time. Accordingly, labor intensity rates, not being at their limits, can fluctuate one way or another. In Tambov guberniya, A. N. Chelintsev observed fluctuations in utilization of working time (excluding festivals) from 37 to 96 percent for men, from 15 to 55 percent women, and from 8 to 40 percent for half workers.

We can see how far peasant farms of the same area differ in this respect from Table 2–6 which shows annual labor expenditure by each of the 25 Volokolamsk uezd farms we have surveyed.

What factors determine the level of this intensity? For us, analysis of the influence of two factor categories are of the greatest interest. On the one hand are factors that lie in the internal structure of the family itself; chiefly significant is the pressure of family consumer demands on the workers. On the other hand are those production conditions which determine the level of labor productivity. Unfortunately, it is very difficult to record labor processes objectively, and we have almost no statistical materials of this sort at our disposal. Therefore, to measure labor intensity we have to make use not of a direct record of its expenditure in working days but of the results of this expenditure, recording the worker's annual earnings and, quite conventionally, assuming that each unit of value is obtained by approximately equal labor efforts. Furthermore, where our materials allow, we will also confirm our conclusions from the direct record of labor expenditure.

In 1912–13, we studied in detail the influence of the pressure of family consumer demands on the peasant worker's productivity, and

TABLE 2-6

| No. of Farm | Working Days per Year Spent Working per Worker (Volokolamsk Uezd) | | |
|---|---|---|---|
| | Farming | Crafts and Trades | Total |
| 1 ....... | 102.2 | 28.0 | 130.2 |
| 2 ....... | 99.0 | 0.0 | 99.0 |
| 3 ....... | 92.4 | 0.0 | 92.4 |
| 4 ....... | 104.1 | 50.1 | 151.0 |
| 5 ....... | 169.5 | 0.0 | 169.5 |
| 6 ....... | 85.6 | 0.0 | 85.6 |
| 7 ....... | 166.7 | 0.0 | 166.7 |
| 8 ....... | 176.0 | 0.0 | 176.0 |
| 9 ....... | 79.5 | 0.0 | 79.5 |
| 10 ....... | 71.9 | 50.0 | 121.9 |
| 11 ....... | 48.5 | 40.9 | 89.4 |
| 12 ....... | 73.8 | 58.8 | 132.6 |
| 13 ....... | 90.0 | 2.0 | 92.0 |
| 14 ....... | 125.8 | 0.0 | 125.8 |
| 15 ....... | 147.1 | 0.0 | 147.1 |
| 16 ....... | 174.0 | 42.0 | 216.0 |
| 17 ....... | 93.8 | 15.2 | 109.0 |
| 18 ....... | 168.4 | 35.2 | 203.6 |
| 19 ....... | 113.4 | 3.2 | 116.6 |
| 20 ....... | 68.8 | 10.0 | 78.8 |
| 21 ....... | 76.0 | 41.8 | 117.8 |
| 22 ....... | 117.0 | 31.8 | 148.8 |
| 23 ....... | 84.5 | 47.2 | 131.7 |
| 24 ....... | 89.6 | 23.6 | 113.2 |
| 25 ....... | 190.9 | 6.5 | 197.4 |
| Average | 118.1 | 13.7 | 131.8 |

our main conclusions have been confirmed by a number of recent investigations. To measure pressure of consumer demands, we made use of a coefficient relating number of farm consumer units to number of labor force—in other words, the relation of number of consumers to number of workers $(c/w)$. By grouping farms according to this relationship of budget surveys, we obtain the figures in Table 2–7 for annual (net) output per worker.[3]

[3] In relation to these Russian figures, it is interesting to note a corresponding calculation for Hamburg budgets which we have taken from *Erhebungen von Wirtschaftsrechnungen minderbemittelter Familien im Deutschen Reich* (Berlin, 1909), in which the increase in the burden of consumers on workers in the form of a limitation of the possible expansion of the worker's earnings was expressed not so much in the expansion of his output as in a reduction of the consumption level.

INFLUENCE OF $c/w$ RATIO ON BUDGETS OF HAMBURG WORKERS' FAMILIES

| $c/w$ ratio ......... | 1.01–1.15 | 1.16–1.30 | 1.31–1.45 | 1.46–1.60 | 1.61–1.75 | 1.76–1.90 | 1.91–∞ |
|---|---|---|---|---|---|---|---|
| No. of families ............... | 8 | 18 | 14 | 9 | 8 | 6 | 8 |
| Per worker from personal budget* ................... | 902 | 953 | 1020 | 986 | 1071 | 1063 | 1071 |
| Per consumer from personal budget* ................... | 854 | 802 | 764 | 662 | 652 | 590 | 494 |

* EDITORS' NOTE.—In marks, presumably. The Russian text does not specify.

TABLE 2–7

| | Number of Consumers per Worker | | | | |
|---|---|---|---|---|---|
| Starobel'sk uezd, Khar'kov gubalerniya c/w ratio ....... | 1.00–1.15 | 1.16–1.30 | 1.31–1.45 | 1.46–1.60 | 1.61–∞ |
| Workers "output" (rubles) ... | 68.1 | 99.0 | 118.3 | 128.9 | 156.4 |
| Novgorod guberniya c/w ratio ................ | 1.00–1.25 | 1.26–1.50 | 1.51–∞ | | |
| Workers "output" (rubles) ... | 91.56 | 106.95 | 122.64 | | |
| Vologda uezd, Vologda guberniya c/w ratio ....... | 1.01–1.15 | 1.16–1.30 | 1.31–1.45 | 1.46–1.60 | 1.61–∞ |
| Worker's "output" (rubles) ... | 63.9 | 79.1 | 84.4 | 91.7 | 117.9 |
| Vel'sk uezd, Volgoda guberniya c/w ratio ....... | 1.01–1.15 | 1.16–1.30 | 1.31–1.45 | 1.46–1.60 | 1.61–∞ |
| Worker's "output" (rubles) ... | 59.2 | 61.2 | 76.1 | 79.5 | 95.5 |

The materials collected in Volokolamsk uezd in 1910, where labor was recorded for each farm separately, enable us to directly measure the influence of an increase in the $c/w$ ratio on the intensity of peasant family labor (Table 2–8).

TABLE 2–8

| | Consumers per worker | | | |
|---|---|---|---|---|
| c/w ratio .......... | 1.01–1.20 | 1.21–1.40 | 1.41–1.60 | 1.61–∞ |
| Worker's "output" (rubles) .......... | 131.9 | 151.5 | 218.8 | 283.4 |
| Working days per worker .......... | 98.8 | 102.3 | 157.2 | 161.3 |

The table gives the same picture as does labor intensity expressed by the measure of annual earnings. Looking at the table, we see that, other things being equal, the peasant worker, stimulated to work by the demands of his family, develops *greater energy* as the pressure of these demands becomes stronger. The measure of self-exploitation depends to the highest degree on how heavily the worker is burdened by the consumer demands of his family. The force of the influence of consumer demands in this case is so great that for a whole series of areas the worker, under pressure from a growing consumer demand, develops his output in strict accordance with the growing number of consumers. The volume of the family's activity depends entirely on the number of consumers and not at all on the number of workers.

Thus, for example, we have the characteristic table (Table 2–9) for Starobel'sk uezd, Khar'kov guberniya.

However, such an exceptional determining influence of the demands of consumption takes place only when *other things are equal*.

TABLE 2–9

ANNUAL INCOME ("OUTPUT") OF FAMILY IN RUBLES

| Number of consumers in family | 0.0–4.0 | 4.1–6.0 | 6.1–∞ |
|---|---|---|---|
| Number of workers: | | | |
| 0.0–2.9 | 198.2 | 407.5 | 541.7 |
| 3.0–3.9 | 294.8 | 366.5 | 639.0 |
| 4.0–∞ | 238.7 | 427.0 | 531.7 |

More detailed analysis undoubtedly establishes that apart from consumption demands the conditions in which labor is applied also determine the worker's output to a considerable extent. Thus, if we compare the pressure on the worker's output from the increase in the $c/w$ ratio with the pressure from the amount of land the worker holds for this same Starobel'sk uezd, we get the very significant picture in Table 2–10.

TABLE 2–10

WORKER'S OUTPUT DEPENDING ON $c/w$ RATIO AND AMOUNT OF LAND HELD

| Arable per Worker (desyatinas) | Worker's Output c/w ratio | | | Consumer's Personal Budget c/w ratio | | |
|---|---|---|---|---|---|---|
| | 1.00–1.30 | 1.31–1.60 | 1.61–∞ | 1.00–1.30 | 1.31–1.60 | 1.61–∞ |
| 0.0–2.0 | 76.4 | 106.3 | 107.8 | 71.1 | 75.2 | 71.8 |
| 2.1–3.0 | 103.5 | 125.8 | 136.6 | 85.1 | 87.8 | 72.7 |
| 3.1–∞ | 105.1 | 128.6 | 175.8 | 86.3 | 85.9 | 88.7 |

As is seen from the increase in the series, better conditions for the application of labor gave the workers the opportunity to increase their output considerably, and this, with an unchanged $c/w$ ratio, inevitably brought about an increase in family and consumer well-being. Moreover, it is exceedingly significant and entirely of a pattern that an increase in worker's output caused by an increment in numbers of consumers does not cause a parallel increase in well-being, and in some budget inquiries (Novgorod) *even leads to a reduction in it.* An increase in annual productivity caused by improved production conditions, however, immediately increases well-being.

Quite clearly expressed series give us a whole number of direct classifications carried out on this principle. See, for example, Table 2–11.

This classification by amount of land held shows us the influence on the worker's output of availability of means of production and expanded opportunity for the application of his labor. According to materials collected by Professor E. Laur on the basis of Swiss peasant

TABLE 2–11

| | | | |
|---|---|---|---|
| Novgorod guberniya: | | | |
|     Sown area–consumer ratio ................. | 0–0.50 | 0.50–1.00 | 1.00–∞ |
|     Personal budget per individual, both sexes ... | 41.60 | 57.94 | 71.60 |
|     Worker's "output" ........................ | 77.60 | 105.67 | 132.10 |
| Starobel'sk uezd, Khar'kov guberniya: | | | |
|     Sown area–consumer ratio ................. | 0–1.50 | 1.50–2.50 | 2.51–∞ |
|     Personal budget per consumer ............. | 62.4 | 77.2 | 94.8 |
|     Worker's "output" ........................ | 80.6 | 115.8 | 151.4 |
| Starobel'sk uezd, Khar'kov guberniya: | | | |
|     Sown area–consumer ratio ................. | 0–1.50 | 1.51–2.50 | 2.51–∞ |
|     Personal budget per consumer ............. | 96.1 | 96.2 | 119.0 |
|     Worker's "output" ........................ | 186.2 | 148.4 | 253.4 |

farm accounts, we can also note the way in which the increase in productivity of each expended labor unit directly influences the well-being of peasant families[4] (Table 2–12).

TABLE 2–12

| | | | | | |
|---|---|---|---|---|---|
| Payment of working day on own farm (francs) ........... | 0–2 | 2–3 | 3–4 | 4–5 | 5–∞ |
| Personal budget per consumer (francs) ........... | 610 | 699 | 804 | 839 | 886 |

It follows from the table that incomes influenced by an increase in labor productivity grow considerably; yet, at the same time, the rate of increment of the budget considerably *lags behind* the rate of increment of labor productivity. The second circumstance undoubtedly indicates to us that *the annual intensity of labor declines under the influence of better pay,* because to remain the same it is absolutely essential that the productivity of the year's labor (and equally the standard of well-being) should grow in proportion to the increase in the pay of a unit of labor. As we will see below, this fact is very significant for theoretical analysis.

The Swiss budget materials, unfortunately, do not enable us to directly measure labor intensity at different productivity rates per unit. On the other hand, the only material suitable for such treatment showed this decline quite sharply. In this, a detailed record of labor was made for each farm from budget data for Volokolamsk uezd, Moscow guberniya (Table 2–13). Unfortunately, apart from the Volokolamsk budgets, we have no other materials which would allow us to make such a classification.

---

4 The data that form the basis for calculating this table were extracted by me personally in 1912 from tables of the Swiss Bauernsecretariat, put at my disposal by Professor E. Laur, and I take this opportunity of offering him my sincere thanks.

TABLE 2-13

| Payment per working day in agriculture (rubles) | 0–1.0 | 1.0–1.25 | 1.25–1.50 | 1.50–∞ |
|---|---|---|---|---|
| Number of days worked annually per worker per consumer | 114.3 | 100.2 | 93.1 | 90.1 |

Thus, the results of comparing the series lead us to the undoubted conclusion that the energy developed by a worker on a family farm is stimulated by the family consumer demands, and as they increase, the rate of self-exploitation of peasant labor is forced up. On the other hand, energy expenditure is inhibited by the drudgery of the labor itself.[5] The harder the labor is, compared with its pay, the lower the level of well-being at which the peasant family ceases to work, although frequently to achieve even this reduced level it has to make great exertions. In other words, we can state positively that the degree of self-exploitation of labor is established by some relationship between the measure of demand satisfaction and the measure of the burden of labor.

A simple consideration enables us to give a certain theoretical foundation to this empirical conclusion. As we know, the economic activity of labor differs from any other activity in that the quantity of values that become available to the person running the farm agrees with the quantity of physical labor he has expended. But the expenditure of physical energy is by no means without limit for the human organism. After a comparatively small expenditure essential to the organism and accompanied by a feeling of satisfaction, further expenditure of energy requires an effort of will. The greater the quantity of work carried out by a man in a definite time period, the greater and greater drudgery for the man are the last (marginal) units of labor expended.

On the other hand, the subjective evaluation of the values obtained by this marginal labor will depend on the extent of its marginal utility for the farm family. But since marginal utility falls with growth of the total sum of values that become available to the subject running the farm, there comes a moment at a certain level of rising labor income when the drudgery of the marginal labor expenditure will equal the subjective evaluation of the marginal utility of the sum obtained by this labor.

---

5 EDITORS' NOTE.—Chayanov introduces this term, *tyagostnost'*, to indicate labor inputs as subjectively assessed by the peasant. The term might be translated by "laboriousness" or "irksomeness," but "drudgery" seems preferable and has the advantage of being etymologically parallel to the Russian form. (Cf. DRUDGERY OF LABOR, in Glossary.)

The output of the worker on the labor farm will remain at this point of natural equilibrium, since any further increase in labor expenditure will be subjectively disadvantageous. Thus, any labor farm has a natural limit to its output, determined by the proportions between intensity of annual family labor and degree of satisfaction of its demands.

This statement may be graphically represented very clearly (Figure 2–3). We have a system of coordinates along the abscissa on which is

FIGURE 2–3

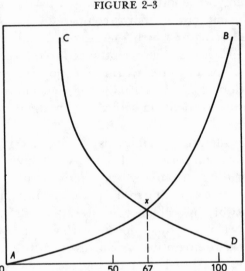

marked the sum of values (in rubles) earned in a year by the subject running the farm. The curve *AB* indicates the degree of drudgery attached to acquiring the marginal ruble marked along the abscissa. The drudgery of earning the tenth or twentieth ruble is insignificant, but the further he goes, the more difficult it is for the worker to earn each extra ruble.

The curve *CD* represents the marginal utility of these rubles for the farm family. The subjective evaluation of the twentieth and thirtieth ruble will be excessively high, since the family that has only these sums available will be able in the year to meet only its most elementary needs and despite great difficulty will, nevertheless, need to do without satisfying the rest. However, with each successive increase in the total sum of annual income the subjective evaluation of the marginal ruble will decline more and more, since it will satisfy the family's less important needs, as they see them.

The changes in this subjective evaluation of the marginal ruble are what give us the shape of the curve *CD*, which cuts the curve *AB* at point *x*, corresponding to a sum of 67 rubles received per year. At this output level, the subjective evaluation of the ruble obtained by marginal labor equals the subjective evaluation of the drudgery of this labor. As regards marginal utility, each succeeding ruble will be evaluated lower than the drudgery of winning it. Conversely, each preceding ruble would be evaluated higher than the efforts directed at winning it and would thus stimulate the continuation of work.

Thus, *in this case*, the sum of 67 rubles is the equilibrium point at which our worker's output naturally stops. It is self-evident that the shape of curves *AB* and *CD* are subjective in character and subject to change; and each change, in its turn, also changes the point of intersection, i.e., the output level at which equilibrium is achieved between drudgery of labor and measure of demand satisfaction.

Thus, for example, if we suppose that due to increased prices for agricultural produce labor productivity has doubled, each $n$th ruble will now be won by efforts which formerly were needed to obtain $n/2$ rubles. In accordance with this, the curve *AB* will fall to $A_1B_1$ (Figure 2–4), and equilibrium will be attained at the new point $x_1$, corre-

FIGURE 2–4

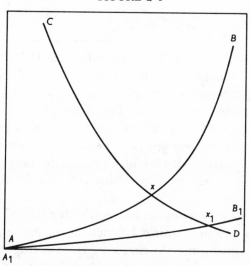

sponding to the increased output. However, output will not double but will increase to a much smaller extent. This is obvious from the drawing which shows that the quantity of labor expended in order to obtain this output (the distance of $x_1$ from the abscissa) will be less than was formerly expended (i.e., the distance of $x$ from the same abscissa). In other words, a rise in payment for a unit of labor on the labor farm leads to a rise in annual output and in family well-being with reduced intensity of annual labor. This completely corresponds to our empirical observations expounded above.

To the same extent, the effect of an increment in family consumer demands corresponds to the results of our classifications, i.e., change of curve $CD$ (Figure 2–5). In accordance with the increment in the

FIGURE 2–5

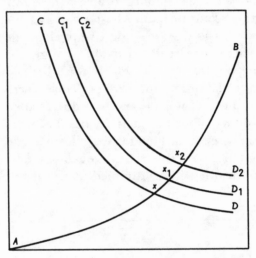

$c/w$ ratio, the curve $CD$ will rise to $C_1D_1$ and $C_2D_2$, since now the same degree of demand satisfaction will be attained with the output increase corresponding to the increase in the $c/w$ ratio. This, in its turn, will lead to new points of equilibrium $x_1$ and $x_2$, corresponding to the increased worker output obtained at the cost of raising labor intensity and increased drudgery. It is self-evident that such a rise in output can take place without any change in family composition simply by raising the demand level—for example, by the influence of urban culture.

Such are the simple considerations which theoretically assert the regular pattern of our empirical conclusions. All these theoretical considerations—downward shifting and intersecting curves and the equilibrium of subjective evaluations—have always evoked obdurate criticism from the late A. A. Kaufman and now from S. N. Prokopovich and many other economists, and have been a cause of their numbering me, without appeal, among the adherents of the Austrian school.

In the introduction to this book, we have already had occasion to touch on this misunderstanding and have observed that this accusation would be correct only if, like the Austrians, I were to deduce a complete system of the national economy from the equilibrium within the farm which has been noted; but this I do not do. Of course, I might, in expounding my views, avoid the curves and the Austrian terminology and say everything "in my own words"; but I think no one would gain from this manipulation, and my exposition would be more confused and less clear.

The objections of practicing agricultural officers are still more unfortunate; they are always inclined to assert that the labor–consumer balance theory tells them little about solving the problem of how to use chemical fertilizers or about the benefit of introducing early fallows. In this case, we must again observe that our theory is one of the economic activity of family labor and not a theory of production organization. The general conditions of production determine the composition and organization of separate production elements, and the farm principles we have studied are a criterion for the peasant family to include or not include these production elements in its farm composition. The materials we have collected in Chapter 4 indicate in detail the mechanics of this choice.

Summing up all we have said about the factors which establish the level of self-exploitation by the peasant worker, we can undoubtedly state that while the size of the capitalist farm is theoretically unlimited the scope of the labor farm is naturally determined by the relationship between family consumer demands and its work force. It is established at a level in accord with the production conditions in which the farm family finds itself.

According to Russian budget materials, we can establish average rates of net productivity per annual worker in labor agricultural economic units (Table 2–14).

TABLE 2–14

| | | | |
|---|---|---|---|
| Novgorod guberniya .... | 100.1 | Sychevka uezd .......... | 100.6 |
| Starobel'sk uezd ........ | 122.3 | Dorogobuzh uezd ....... | 97.2 |
| Volokolamsk uezd ....... | 140.1 | Porech'e uezd ........... | 115.6 |
| Gzhatsk uezd .......... | 110.9 | Voronezh guberniya .... | 68.8* |
| Vologda uezd .......... | 65.1 | Tomsk guberniya ....... | 66.5 |
| Vel'sk uezd ............ | 69.9 | Poltava guberniya ...... | 67.6 |
| Tot'ma uezd ........... | 82.2 | Kherson guberniya ...... | 86.0 |
| Tobol'sk guberniya ...... | 70.7 | Elizavetpol uezd ........ | 82.1 |

* The low figures for Voronezh and subsequent guberniyas and uezds may be explained to some extent by the fact that these budget studies were carried out before 1906 with a comparatively unfavorable market situation for farm produce. Taking them at prices of the 1910's, we would increase them by 10 percent or more.

Such is the basic economic balance which determines the structure of the whole peasant farm and its annual income. In such a general form, however, it still does not give us the opportunity to understand how a specific economic estimate is made on the peasant farm in each separate case, or how awareness of the basic equilibrium between measure of demand satisfaction and measure of the drudgery of labor reaches peasant consciousness. In other words, we ought to ask ourselves the basic question. Do not the characteristics of the peasant family farm we have disclosed influence the foundations of its economic calculations? Does the concept of advantage in the capitalist economic unit, which is fundamental to the views of A. Smith, D. Ricardo, and the whole of present-day political economy, correspond to the concept of advantage in the family farm?

An economic calculation of a capitalist economic unit may be entirely expressed by the following elementary formula:

$$GI - OM - W = NP,$$

where

$GI$ = gross income
$OM$ = outlays on materials
$W$ = wages
$NP$ = net profit.

All the elements of this formula are quantities easily expressible in one and the same units—say, rubles—and you need only simple arithmetic to determine precisely the net profit and, if it is higher than zero, to consider the farm is not operating at a loss. If the net profit in relation to capital invested in the farm gives a rate of interest higher than the usual discount rate in the country, it is also profitable.

Can this formula be applied to the family farm? It is not hard to be convinced that it cannot. In fact, it is applicable to the capitalist unit because all its four elements are expressed in like units. But for the peasant farm, only gross income and outlays on materials are expressed in objective units of value. Without wages, the peasant farm can express its labor expenditure *only* in physical units, which we have indicated by $L$. Since we cannot subtract days, as such, from rubles and kopeks, labor expenditures cannot be subtracted from the financial elements of the formula and can only be compared with them.

$(GI - OM)$, i.e., the net product of the particular labor expenditure, as defined at the beginning of this chapter may be subjectively recognized by our family as satisfactory or good compared with the subjective evaluation of the drudgery of this same labor,

$$(GI - OM) \geqq L,$$

or, on the contrary, the result obtained will be considered insufficient compared with the labor expenditure involved. If the subjective evaluation of the labor is higher than the evaluation of its results,

$$(GI - OM) < L,$$

then the particular expenditure will undoubtedly be recognized as disadvantageous.[6]

The most varied factors, both objective and subjective, will influence the results of this comparison. If we compare labor productivity with quantity of labor expended, we can express both by number of labor units and deduce the objective payment of, let us say, a working day,

$$(GI - OM) \begin{smallmatrix} \leq \\ = \\ > \end{smallmatrix} L$$

$$\frac{GI - OM}{L} \begin{smallmatrix} < \\ = \\ > \end{smallmatrix} x,$$

where

$x$ = the subjective evaluation of the drudgery of one working day.

Further, one and the same objectively expressed payment per labor unit, at one and the same level, will be considered now advantageous, now disadvantageous for the peasant family, primarily *depending on the state of the basic equilibrium between the measure of demand satisfaction and that of the drudgery of labor.* If in the farm's estimation the basic equilibrium has not yet been reached, then unsatisfied demands are still quite sharp, and the family running the farm is under a very strong stimulus to expand its work and to seek outlets for its labor while accepting a low level of payment. "Due to necessity," the peasant initiates what are, at first sight, the most disadvantageous undertakings.

Conversely, if the basic equilibrium is completely met in the farm's estimation, only very high labor payment will stimulate the peasant to new work. Thus, the marginal (the lowest of those allowed) pay-

---

[6] It may be said that in the reality around him the peasant can always evaluate his labor in accord with wages existing somewhere nearby. This is not correct, because hire is for the peasant only one of the possible instances of making use of his labor, and, moreover, in the majority of instances it is not an advantageous one. The subjective evaluation of the drudgery of winning the marginal ruble on his farm will always be almost less than when hiring himself out for work, since payment on his farm is higher than wages.

ment of a labor unit depends on the farm's general equilibrium and cannot be objectively determined a priori from outside.

The annual labor payment is the main thing for the family farm, but the payment per labor unit is derived according to how the farm's tasks are solved *as a whole.* Moreover, of course, the rate of payment per labor unit is taken into account in those subconscious, intuitive processes which establish, in their estimation, the moment that determines the annual equilibrium.

In order to make our argument obvious, let us introduce an example to make things clear. Let us suppose that a desyatina of oats gives, excluding seed, a harvest of 60 puds; the price of oats is 1 ruble a pud, the gross income is 60 rubles, outlays on materials for the crop 20 rubles; the number of working days necessary is 25, wages are 1 ruble. Then the elements of the calculation will be:

*For a Capitalist Farm*

Gross income .. $60 \times 1$ ruble = 60 rubles
Expenditure:
  Outlays on materials ...... 20
  Wages ................... 25
Net income ................ 15 rubles

*For a Family Farm\**

Gross income .. $60 \times 1$ ruble = 60 rubles
Expenditure:
  Outlays on materials ...... 20
Obtained for labor payment 40 rubles
Payment per
  working day .....$x = \frac{40}{25} = 1.60$ rubles

* EDITORS' NOTE.—See p. 273 for an explanation of Chayanov's terminology.

For the capitalist farm, the crop is evidently advantageous; for the peasant farm, it is advantageous if the consumer budget may not be met by other uses of labor that give a payment for the working day higher than 1.60 rubles.

Let us now suppose that the price of oats fell to 60 kopeks a pud.

*For a Capitalist Farm*

Gross income ...... $60 \times 0.6 = 36$ rubles
Expenditure:
  Outlays on materials ...... 20
  Wages ................... 25
Loss ...................... 9 rubles

*For a Family Farm*

Gross income ..... $60 \times 0.60 = 36$ rubles
Expenditure:
  Outlays on materials ...... 20
Obtained for labor payment .. 16
Payment per working day .. 0.64 rubles

As is seen from the table, the capitalist farm would have a net loss of 9 rubles a desyatina, and the cultivation of oats would become absolutely disadvantageous to it. For the peasant farm, however, labor payment would fall to 64 kopeks, and this figure would be completely acceptable if the basic economic equilibrium could not be met by directing its labor to occupations that gave a higher payment.

We will not give further examples, since even from these few calculations it can be established that given a deterioration in the market situation negative quantities (losses), thanks to the mechanism of the labor calculation, appear much later on the peasant farm than on the capitalist one (hence, the exceeding viability and stability of peasant farms). Frequently, the family farm's internal basic equilibrium makes acceptable very low payments per labor unit, and these enable it to exist in conditions that would doom a capitalist farm to undoubted ruin.

On the other hand, to a peasant farm in a situation of high rent in the economic sense some applications of labor are often unacceptable. These, although advantageous to a capitalist farm, give a lower labor payment than those by means of which the peasant farm meets its budget.

From what has been said, the particular features characteristic of the labor farm in the understanding of advantage are more or less clear. We consider it absolutely essential to note that this construction of the concept of advantage does not call for the peasant farm to behave in any economically extravagant way. In the majority of cases, the evaluation of comparative advantage based on the principle of net income gives the same result as an evaluation made without using the wage category based on the principle of reckoning the labor payment. And only in certain instances when the interests of the annual labor payment for the peasant farm begin to be particularly dominant over the interests in obtaining maximum payment per labor unit does the nature of the family farm stand out sharply, and then the peasant farm behaves in a way completely different from a capitalist farm in the same conditions. The conditions in which this takes place have been observed frequently enough in the epoch we are living through, and we will fully review them in subsequent chapters.

Professor Ernst Laur, in his review of the German edition of this book, points to the existence of certain peasant groups in Switzerland to which our principles of economic conduct might be extended. He notes that a colossal stimulus to accumulation and to acquisition is characteristic of the majority of the European peasantry, sometimes overcoming consumer demands. Undoubtedly, these same stimuli, though not in such an obvious way, are found in many strata of the Russian peasantry.

However, as we will see below in the chapter devoted to the circulation of capital in peasant farming, taking account of the processes of capital renewal and capital accumulation does not contradict our constructs but merely complicates them.

# CHAPTER 3

# The Basic Principles of
# Peasant Farm Organization

The basic principles of the family farm which we have stated do not belong merely to the peasant farm. They are present in any family labor economic unit in which work is connected with expenditure of physical effort, and earnings are proportional to this expenditure, whether the economic unit be artisan, cottage industry, or simply any economic activity of family labor. The peasant farm as such is a much narrower concept and includes, *as a family economic unit in agriculture*, a number of complications which follow from the nature of agricultural activity. They add to the appearance of its essentially family nature a series of peculiar features in the structure of crop and livestock farming.

In its organization, any agricultural undertaking is described by its system, by which, according to Lyudogovskii's classical definition, should be understood "the kind and manner of combining quantitatively and qualitatively land, labor and capital." By developing this definition, we can show a scheme of the basic elements that form any agricultural undertaking (Figure 3–1).

For any farming system, taking account of local conditions, we may, by a series of organizational calculations, determine both the technically most expedient relationship of its production factors and the absolute size of the farm itself to give the lowest cost for produce and, consequently, the highest income. By comparing elements of agricultural produce costs that declined as farm size increased (use of buildings and equipment, cost of general outgoings, etc.) with elements that increased with growth of farm area (on-farm transport, etc.), the author, with A. L. Vainshtein and I. D. Lopatin,[1] was able to establish

---

1 *Optimal'nye razmery sel'sko-khozyaistvennogo predpriyatiya*, Sbornik Nauchno-Issledovatel'skogo Instituta sel'skokhozyaistvennoi ekonomii [Optimal size of agricultural undertakings, a collection of the Agricultural Economics Scientific Research Institute], M., 1921 g.

FIGURE 3–1

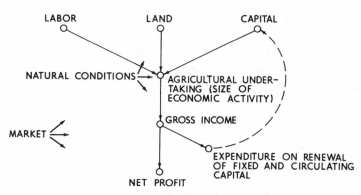

that optimal farm size for the long-fallow system varies from 1,500 to 2,000 desyatinas, for three-course with manuring about 400, and for a rotational system about 150 desyatinas.

It is self-evident that both size of farm area and proportions of production factors deployed on it are not limited to one optimal size and relationship. One can conceive of and observe in reality numerous farms where considerable deviation from these optimal norms sometimes takes place. However, the optimal combination gives the highest income, and any deviation from it gives the proprietor a reduced profit rate. Yet, it is also essential to note that this reduction of profit takes place most gradually, and it is this which explains the economic possibility for the existence of farms that greatly deviate from the optimal size and factor proportions.

If an organizer lacks sufficient land, capital, or work hands to develop his farm on the optimal scale, the undertaking will be built on a smaller scale in accordance with the minimum available factor. However, whatever the scale on which the farm is developed, there is always a proportion between its parts and a certain conformity in their relationships peculiar to each farming system. This is determined by *technical* expediency and necessity. Any violation of this harmony leads to an inevitable and perceptible reduction in the productivity of labor and capital expenditure, since it takes the farm away from the optimal combination of production factors. Thus, while preserving the proportionality of its parts and always striving for optimal size the farm can, in fact, be organized in the most varied sizes. This statement remains fully valid when dealing with the organization of an agricultural undertaking based on hired labor.

When approaching the organization of an undertaking based on the principles of the family labor farm, we first of all find that one of its elements—the labor force—is fixed by being present in the composition of the family. It cannot be increased or decreased at will, and since it is subject to the necessity of combining the factors expediently we naturally ought to put other factors of production in an optimal relationship to this fixed element. This puts the total volume of our activity within quite narrow limits. Hence, our diagram takes on a new form (Figure 3–2).

FIGURE 3–2

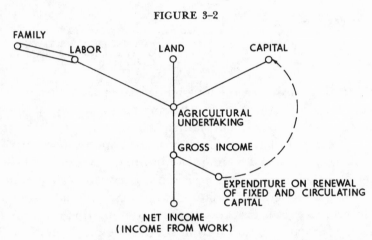

Thus, in the scheme of the harmoniously developed organic elements of the labor farm *undertaking* the labor force of the family is *something given*, and the farm's production elements are fixed in accordance with it in the technical harmony usual *among them*. Given freedom to acquire the necessary area of *land for use* and the possibility of having available the necessary means of production, peasant farms are structured to conform to the optimal degree of self-exploitation of the family labor force and in a technically optimal system of production factors as regards their size and relationship of the parts. Any excess of production means available to labor or of land above the technically optimal level will be an excessive burden on the undertaking. It will not lead to an increased volume of activity, since further intensity of labor beyond the level established for its self-exploitation is unacceptable to the family. Its productivity due to an increase in capital intensity naturally cannot be raised once the achieved rate of *provision* is itself optimal.

It does not follow from this, however, that family size also arithmetically determines farm size and the composition of all its elements. The literature of zemstvo statistics has more than once noted instances of clearly expressed overburdening of peasant farms—now with equipment (Volokolamsk uezd), now with buildings (Starobel'sk uezd), now with workstock.

Apart from this, it is essential to note that very frequently, due to constant or chance causes, land or means of production available is less than the optimum demanded and is insufficient for full use of the farm family's labor. Then, it is natural that the production element, the availability of which is less than the norm demanded by technical harmony, becomes to a considerable extent a determining factor for the agricultural undertaking. As long as the farm does not succeed in transferring this factor from the minimum to the optimum, the volume of activity will closely conform to its size.

Table 3–1, calculated by Professor L. N. Litoshenko in the collection, *On the Land* (M., 1922), quite clearly demonstrates this feature.

TABLE 3–1

| STAROBEL'SK UEZD, KHAR'KOV GUBERNIYA | | KOSTROMA GUBERNIYA | |
|---|---|---|---|
| Farm Sown Areas | Net Product per Worker in Farming | Farm Sown Areas | Net Product per Worker in Farming |
| <3 | 57 | <1 | 43 |
| 3–7.5 | 102 | 1–3 | 156 |
| 7.5–15.0 | 125 | 3–4 | 131 |
| >15 | 203 | 4–6 | 135 |
| | | >6 | 206 |

| VEL'SK UEZD, VOLOGDA GUBERNIYA | | TAMBOV GUBERNIYA | |
|---|---|---|---|
| Farm Sown Areas | Net Product per Worker in Farming | Farm Sown Areas | Net Farm Product per Consumer |
| <2 | 63 | <5 | 92 |
| 2–3 | 63 | 5–8 | 108 |
| 3–4 | 61 | 8–11.5 | 109 |
| 4–6 | 83 | 11.5–18.0 | 120 |
| >6 | 80 | >18 | 275 |

The table shows us clearly enough that farming incomes rise and fall in parallel with the increase and decrease in land held, and can be one of the measures of volume of farm activity. In looking at these tables, we consider it essential to note that L. N. Litoshenko classified the farms by size of sown area per family, while it would have been more correct to classify by sown area per worker[2] in order to elimi-

---

2 EDITORS' NOTE.—Sic. From Table 3–2, it will be seen that perhaps Chayanov meant to write "per consumer."

nate the influence of family size on the figures. However, in view of the more or less equal results from both ways of classifying we restrict ourselves to these inquiries, quoting, as an example of correct method, Table 3–2 for Novgorod guberniya.

Looking at this material we see that, proportionately, as land is insufficient and becomes a minimum factor the volume of agricultural activity for all farm elements is reduced at varying speeds, but unfail-

TABLE 3–2

NOVGOROD GUBERNIYA

| | Sown Area (Desyatinas) per Consumer | | |
|---|---|---|---|
| Per Worker | More than 1 | 0.50–1 | Less than 0.50 |
| Gross income from farming ........ | 176.95 | 125.34 | 71.33 |
| Farm expenditure .. | 111.64 | 67.82 | 44.25 |
| Annual labor payment from farming ........ | 65.31 | 57.52 | 26.58 |
| Fixed capital ...... | 622.32 | 418.52 | 283.61 |

ingly. But the work hands of the farm family, not finding a use in farming, turn, as we will see below, to crafts, trades, and other *non-agricultural* earnings to attain the economic equilibrium with family demands not fully met by farm income or by receipts from crafts and trades.

Yet, it is essential to note that the volume of agricultural activity is not a simple arithmetic *derivative* of the size of area used, and its growth rate considerably lags behind the development of the area. Thus, if we take as 100 the figures for sown area, farm expenditure, and income for farms with small sown area, the increment of these elements as the sown area increases will be as shown in Table 3–3.

TABLE 3–3

NOVGOROD GUBERNIYA

| | 0.0–0.50 | 0.51–1.00 | >1.00 |
|---|---|---|---|
| Sown area (desyatinas) per consumer .......... | | | |
| Sown area per worker .... | 100 | 184 | 340 |
| Farm expenditure per consumer ............. | 100 | 145 | 200 |
| Farm income per consumer ............. | 100 | 176 | 248 |

Incidentally, all these phenomena have long ago been disclosed by both Russian and European agricultural statisticians, who have adequately studied the influence of land use areas on the farm.

Data on the influence not of agricultural endowment but of the supply of capital on farm structure and income are much more novel for us; these we can obtain from new Russian budget inquiries. By studying the influence of amounts of capital available in the peasant farm, we will at the same time be studying the consequences for the farm which follow from a violation of the harmony of factors characteristic of the optimum. We have worked on the two most adequate budget investigations—for Novgorod and Tambov guberniyas—and in a system of combined tables have compared the influence of family size (number of workers) and availability of fixed capital (buildings, livestock, and equipment) with the volume of economic activity. In making use of this combined classification to study the influence of capital and family size, we must remember that in comparing these factors in absolute figures on the farm we inevitably come into conflict with the fact that the capital intensity of labor falls sharply with an increase in number of workers given the same amount of capital. Conversely, with increased capital, given unchanged family size, there will be an increase in this capital intensification. This is seen from the following tables.

TABLE 3–4

FIXED CAPITAL (RUBLES) PER WORKER

| Number of Workers in Family | Novgorod Guberniya Family Fixed Capital | | | | Tambov Guberniya Family Fixed Capital | | | |
|---|---|---|---|---|---|---|---|---|
| | *0–500* | *500– 1,000* | *1,000– 1,500* | *1,500– ∞* | *0–500* | *500– 1,000* | *1,000– 1,500* | *1,500– ∞* |
| 0–2 .... | 187 | 349 | — | — | 154 | 360 | — | — |
| 2–4 .... | 122 | 202 | 355 | 692 | 120 | 243 | 385 | 747 |
| 4–∞ ... | 71 | 146 | 213 | 309 | 86 | 139 | 208 | 368 |

Because of these differences in capital available, Table 3–4, while allowing us to analyze the influence of capital intensification with constant family size, does not allow us to trace the influence of family size on the farm, given the same rate of capital intensity. In carrying out our analysis in this form of comparison, this circumstance obliges us to repeat it subsequently in a somewhat changed form. Having made this reservation, we can now pass on to an analysis of the essence of our material. We will begin with an explanation of the influence of family size and amount of capital on the size of the family agricultural undertaking, for which sown area may be a measure.

Looking at Table 3–5, we see that the family holding a greater and greater quantity of capital naturally develops a greater and greater

TABLE 3–5

INFLUENCE OF CAPITAL AND FAMILY SIZE ON SOWN AREA

| Number of Workers in Family | Novgorod Guberniya Family Fixed Capital (Rubles) | | | | Tambov Guberniya Family Fixed Capital (Rubles) | | | |
|---|---|---|---|---|---|---|---|---|
| | 0–500 | 500–1,000 | 1,000–1,500 | 1,500–∞ | 0–500 | 500–1,000 | 1,000–1,500 | 1,500–2,000 |
| 0–2 .... | 1.7 | 2.1 | — | — | 3.4 | 3.6 | — | — |
| 2–4 .... | 2.3 | 3.3 | 4.5 | 5.1 | 3.1 | 4.6 | 7.7 | 8.1 |
| 4–∞ ... | 2.9 | 3.7 | 5.1 | 6.9 | 4.6 | 6.1 | 8.6 | 14.1 |

volume of agricultural activity. On the other hand, the table equally clearly shows that as the peasant family's work force increases it succeeds in developing a greater and greater volume of agricultural activity with the same amount of captial, covering its lack of capital by its labor intensity. In this instance, we clearly see that capital is not an arithmetic determinant of volume of activity but merely one of the conditions in which the family determines this.

As we know from the classification, with amount of capital remaining the same as the family increases, its workers are in a worsening situation as regards availability of fixed capital. Naturally, the equilibrium of the basic economic factors is attained at a lower level of the worker's economic activity, as is seen from Table 3–6.

TABLE 3–6

INFLUENCE OF FAMILY SIZE AND FIXED CAPITAL ON
SOWN AREA (DESYATINAS) PER WORKER

| Number of Workers in Family | Novgorod Guberniya Family Fixed Capital (Rubles) | | | | Tambov Guberniya Family Fixed Capital (Rubles) | | | |
|---|---|---|---|---|---|---|---|---|
| | 0–500 | 500–1,000 | 1,000–1,500 | 1,500–∞ | 0–500 | 500–1,000 | 1,000–1,500 | 1,500–∞ |
| 0–2 .... | 1.01 | 1.17 | — | — | 1.91 | 2.02 | — | — |
| 2–4 .... | 0.83 | 1.01 | 1.35 | 1.66 | 1.01 | 1.48 | 2.49 | 2.53 |
| 4–∞ ... | 0.56 | 0.75 | 0.89 | 0.98 | 0.94 | 1.23 | 1.56 | 2.38 |

As we see, the worker, falling into ever worse conditions, starts to reduce his output. By comparing this table with Table 3–7, which shows the fall in amount of means of production available to him, we can observe that the fall in sown area per worker takes place more slowly than the fall in capital available to him. This may be manifestly seen by comparing the course of these functions, for convenience, taking the first group as 100.

Here, too, we see that in agreement with our theory expounded in Chapter 2 the reduction of means of production influences the vol-

TABLE 3–7

CAPITAL AND SOWN AREA PER WORKER BY FAMILY SIZE

| Number of Workers per Family | Capital | Sown Area | Capital | Sown Area | Capital | Sown Area | Capital | Sown Area |
|---|---|---|---|---|---|---|---|---|
| | | NOVGOROD | GUBERNIYA | | | | | |
| 0–2 ....... | 100 | 100 | 100 | 100 | — | — | — | — |
| 2–4 ....... | 65 | 82 | 58 | 87 | 100 | 100 | 100 | 100 |
| 4–∞ ....... | 38 | 55 | 42 | 64 | 60 | 66 | 45 | 59 |
| | | TAMBOV | GUBERNIYA | | | | | |
| 0–2 ....... | — | — | 100 | 100 | — | — | — | — |
| 2–4 ....... | 100 | 100 | 53 | 73 | 100 | 100 | 100 | 100 |
| 4–∞ ....... | 72 | 93 | 30 | 61 | 54 | 63 | 50 | 94 |

ume of activity, not mechanically but by affecting the basic economic equilibrium, and makes the worker reduce his output due to the increasing drudgery of his work. And this ought to inevitably lead to a reduction in the family's well-being, i.e., lower the degree of satisfaction of its demands (consumer's budget), despite the possibility of making use of earnings from crafts and trades. We see this clearly from Table 3–8.

TABLE 3–8

SATISFACTION OF PERSONAL DEMANDS (CONSUMER'S BUDGET)
BY FAMILY SIZE AND AMOUNT OF FIXED CAPITAL (RUBLES)

| Number of Workers in Family | Novgorod Guberniya Family Fixed Capital | | | | Tambov Guberniya Family Fixed Capital | | | |
|---|---|---|---|---|---|---|---|---|
| | 0–500 | 500–1,000 | 1,000–1,500 | 1,500–∞ | 0–500 | 500–1,000 | 1,000–1,500 | 1,500–∞ |
| 0–2 .... | 93.5 | 143.0 | — | — | 90.0 | 100.1 | — | — |
| 2–4 .... | 67.8 | 74.9 | 104.1 | 152.9 | 85.8 | 97.2 | 113.9 | 129.2 |
| 4–∞ ... | 52.4 | 78.6 | 82.9 | 125.3 | 76.4 | 85.3 | 91.6 | 124.0 |

Thus, at the cost of reducing the labor productivity of the annual worker and the satisfaction of demands of the peasant family as it increases in size, it is possible with the same amount of capital to increase the volume of its agricultural undertaking.

Lowering the moment when economic equilibrium is attained, which we have pointed out, leads to the fact that despite the development of earnings from crafts and trades, given low agricultural incomes, the gross income of our family follows, in its general tendency, the sown area (Tables 3–9 and 3–10). We see that gross income reacts to the influence of family growth and increase in capital in the same way sown area does.

TABLE 3–9

FAMILY GROSS INCOME BY FAMILY SIZE AND AMOUNT OF FIXED CAPITAL (RUBLES)

| Number of Workers in Family | Novgorod Guberniya Family Fixed Capital | | | | Tambov Guberniya Family Fixed Capital | | | |
|---|---|---|---|---|---|---|---|---|
| | 0–500 | 500–1,000 | 1,000–1,500 | 1,500–∞ | 0–500 | 500–1,000 | 1,000–1,500 | 1,500–∞ |
| 0–2 .... | 373.5 | 528 | — | — | 347 | 551 | — | — |
| 2–4 .... | 434.5 | 542 | 810 | 1131 | 434 | 713 | 1295 | 1411 |
| 4–∞ ... | 524.0 | 710 | 999 | 1386 | 661 | 882 | 1229 | 2695 |

TABLE 3–10

GROSS INCOME PER FAMILY WORKER BY FAMILY SIZE AND
AMOUNT OF FIXED CAPITAL (RUBLES)

| Number of Workers in Family | Novgorod Guberniya Family Fixed Capital | | | | Tambov Guberniya Family Fixed Capital | | | |
|---|---|---|---|---|---|---|---|---|
| | 0–500 | 500–1,000 | 1,000–1,500 | 1,500–∞ | 0–500 | 500–1,000 | 1,000–1,500 | 1,500–∞ |
| 0–2 .... | 216 | 293 | — | — | 192 | 306 | — | — |
| 2–4 .... | 154 | 168 | 244 | 364 | 140 | 229 | 420 | 441 |
| 4–∞ ... | 102 | 142 | 176 | 194 | 135 | 177 | 223 | 454 |

As regards analysis of gross income, comparison of its amount with amounts of capital are particularly interesting (Table 3–11).

TABLE 3–11

GROSS INCOME PER ONE-HUNDRED RUBLES OF FIXED CAPITAL BY
FAMILY SIZE AND AMOUNT OF FIXED CAPITAL

| Number of Workers in Family | Novgorod Guberniya Family Fixed Capital | | | | Tambov Guberniya Family Fixed Capital | | | |
|---|---|---|---|---|---|---|---|---|
| | 0–500 | 500–1,000 | 1,000–1,500 | 1,500–∞ | 0–500 | 500–1,000 | 1,000–1,500 | 1,500–∞ |
| 0–2 .... | 116 | 84 | — | — | — | 65 | — | — |
| 2–4 .... | 126 | 83 | 69 | 53 | 117 | 94 | 107 | 59 |
| 4–∞ ... | 142 | 96 | 82 | 63 | 155 | 126 | 108 | 124 |

We see that as the family labor force and the relative labor intensification of the farm increases it becomes possible for the family to extract a greater and greater amount of gross income from each unit of capital. On the other hand, reading across, we see that as the capital intensification of the farm grows and its relative labor intensification falls the productivity of capital expenditure continually declines.

In order to dismiss the supposition that this increase and decline takes place because of earnings from crafts and trades, we have repeated this same analysis as regards size of sown areas per ruble of capital and have obtained the same tendencies, though less clearly marked (Table 3–12). We see that as in the case of gross income the size of sown area per 100 rubles fixed capital falls as the farm's capital intensity increases. By forcing up its labor intensification, the peasant family is in a position to make fuller use of the capital at its disposal the less it has.

TABLE 3–12

SOWN AREA (DESYATINAS) PER ONE-HUNDRED RUBLES OF CAPITAL

| Number of Workers in Family | *Novgorod Guberniya* Family Fixed Capital | | | | *Tambov Guberniya* Family Fixed Capital | | | |
|---|---|---|---|---|---|---|---|---|
| | 0–500 | 500–1,000 | 1,000–1,500 | 1,500–∞ | 0–500 | 500–1,000 | 1,000–1,500 | 1,500–∞ |
| 0–2 .... | 0.54 | 0.33 | — | — | — | 0.43 | — | — |
| 2–4 .... | 0.68 | 0.50 | 0.38 | 0.24 | 0.84 | 0.61 | 0.65 | 0.34 |
| 4–∞ ... | 0.78 | 0.51 | 0.42 | 0.31 | 1.08 | 0.87 | 0.75 | 0.65 |

As we have already noted, though enabling us to exhaustively analyze the influence of its capital intensity on the farm, the comparisons we have made give us little with which to make a comparative study of the influence of family growth and of increases in capital intensity. For an analysis of this comparison, we gave our combined tables a somewhat different form. We divided the whole of the material into groups by farm's capital intensity (the relationship of amount of fixed capital to number of workers) and broke it down within each group by family size (number of workers).

In this case, it became possible for us to trace, by reading across, the reaction of capital intensification given a constant composition of the family labor force and, reading down, the influence of family growth given a constant level of capital intensity. This comparison gave the results in Table 3–13.

TABLE 3–13

TOTAL FAMILY INCOME IN RELATION TO FIXED CAPITAL PER WORKER (RUBLES) AND FAMILY SIZE (NOVGOROD GUBERNIYA)

| Number of Workers in Family | *Fixed Capital per Worker* | | | |
|---|---|---|---|---|
| | 0–100 | 100–200 | 200–300 | >300 |
| 0–2 ......... | 169 | 352 | 426 | 528 |
| 2–4 ......... | 334 | 478 | 579 | 835 |
| >4 ......... | 523 | 749 | 923 | 1584 |

We can see that family growth gives a most clearly expressed reaction. Comparing it with the development of the factor, we ought to acknowledge, as we would theoretically expect, that the increase in the volume of activity proceeds almost in proportion to family growth and lags far behind the rapidity of the development of capital intensification, which we have already seen in analyzing the previous combination.

In concluding our analysis, we will look at the influence of number of family workers and capital intensity in providing the consumer with sown area (Table 3–14). It is clearly seen from the table that a

TABLE 3–14

SOWN AREA PER CONSUMER

| Number of Workers per Family | Fixed Capital per Worker (Rubles) | | | |
|---|---|---|---|---|
| | 0–100 | 100–200 | 200–300 | 300–∞ |
| 0–2 ......... | 0.43 | 0.64 | 0.72 | 0.99 |
| 2–4 ......... | 0.53 | 0.65 | 0.70 | 1.23 |
| 4–∞ ........ | 0.47 | 0.67 | 0.65 | 1.10 |

simple increase in the family, not affecting the conditions of economic equilibrium, has no specific influence in the provision of sown area for the consumer, while increase in capital intensity raises his annual earnings and, moreover, in accordance with the theory, at a rate less than the rate of increment of the factor. Thus, for example, for family size of 2–4 workers see Table 3–15.

TABLE 3–15

| Capital available per worker (rubles) .. | 0–100 | 100–200 | 200–300 | 300–∞ |
|---|---|---|---|---|
| Increase of capital available per worker .. | 100 | 200 | 325 | 525 |
| Increase of sown area per consumer ........ | 100 | 122 | 132 | 232 |

Such are the results of our empirical analysis. We will try to sum it up theoretically.

The empirical dependent relationships we have established show us that when, in a particular year, the farm does not have the land or capital needed to develop an agricultural undertaking optimal as to relationship between farm and family size it is obliged to make its volume of agricultural activity conform with these means of production in minimum supply. This volume is not established automatically by being arithmetically derived from the minimum element, but is set by a complex process of the influence of deteriorating conditions for agricultural production on the basic equilibrium of the economic factors. Moreover, the family throws its unutilized labor into crafts, trades, and other extra-agricultural livelihoods. The whole of its summed agricultural, crafts, and trades income is counterposed to its demands, and the drudgery of acquiring it leads to an equilibrium with the degree of satisfaction of these personal demands.

Therefore, all forms of the influence of family composition and size on the family worker's output, which we studied in Chapter 2, and the other consequences following from the on-farm equilibrium of production factors are naturally related to the summed family income and not to that part which its agricultural incomes constitute.

Our budget materials give us quite clear examples of how labor, lacking the necessary means of production for its full disposition in agriculture, pours into crafts and trades. Thus, for example, see Table 3–16 for Vologda uezd, where a detailed record of labor was made.

TABLE 3–16

PERCENTAGE WORKING TIME SPENT IN AGRICULTURE, CRAFTS, AND TRADES

| Sown Area in Each Field per Farm (Desyatinas) | Percentage of Working Year Spent on: | |
|---|---|---|
| | Agriculture | Crafts and Trades |
| 0.0–0.0 ....... | 10.3 | 41.9 |
| 0.1–1.0 ....... | 21.7 | 22.8 |
| 1.1–2.0 ....... | 23.0 | 21.9 |
| 2.1–3.0 ....... | 26.9 | 19.8 |
| 3.1–6.0 ....... | 28.1 | 13.7 |
| 6.1–10.0 ...... | 41.6 | 11.1 |

For a whole series of other investigations we unfortunately do not have a record of labor and can judge the relationship of crafts and trades and agricultural income by the results, i.e., by the production it brings to the farm. The result of this analysis, as has been established by Shcherbina for Voronezh guberniya, for example, is just the same.

Thus, the peasant family hastens to meet a shortfall in agriculture incomes by income from crafts and trades. However, in the majority of areas where budget inquiries have been made it does not fully succeed in doing this. This is particularly characteristic in Vologda uezd where, given the same labor expenditure, those engaging in crafts and trades are compelled to acquiesce in a lower standard of well-being, as can be seen from Table 3–17.

The cause of this is that incomes from crafts and trade in Vologda and, evidently, other uezds, too, result in a very low payment for labor. Consequently, earnings are won with great drudgery, and this in-

TABLE 3–17

|  | Annual Personal Budget per Consumer, Money and in Kind |
|---|---|
| Vologda Uezd | (Rubles) |
| 1. Purely agricultural labor families ................. | 78.3 |
| 2. Families with members hiring themselves out as workpeople or going into service ........... | 56.6 |
| 3. Families with members independently engaging in crafts or trades ...................... | 66.3 |
| 4. Families with members engaging in crafts and trades as entrepreneurs and using hired labor ..... | 148.9 |

evitably leads to the attainment of the basic economic equilibrium at a low level of well-being.[3]

All that has been said adequately shows us the complex processes of determining both the general and the particular agricultural volume of peasant family economic activity. Because the family's agricultural undertaking and crafts and trades activity are connected by a single system of the basic equilibrium of economic factors, they cannot be reviewed independently of one another. This compels us to change somewhat the morphological scheme of the peasant farm, which we gave at the start of this chapter, by including the process of work in crafts and trades.

By detailing the separate links, we obtain the scheme shown in Figure 3–3. We see that as a result of the mutual relationships of the factors we have studied the volume of agricultural, crafts, and trades

FIGURE 3–3

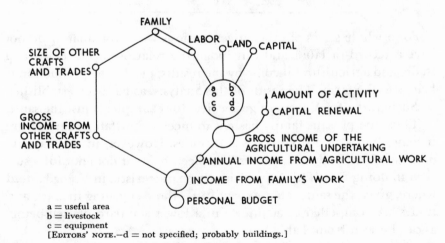

a = useful area
b = livestock
c = equipment
[EDITORS' NOTE.—d = not specified; probably buildings.]

---

[3] For Vologda uezd, earnings from crafts and trades, excluding income from commercial industrial undertakings, were 48.9 kopeks per working day, while from agriculture they were 59.4 kopeks, and even if all taxes and payments are excluded, 52.4 kopeks.

activity is established, the income from each of them is gathered in, and, combined, they give that synthetic single family labor income which, by comparison with its demands, also gives the basic economic equilibrium. For an exhaustive knowledge of the peasant farm's mechanism, it is of the greatest interest to quantitatively establish the force binding together all the elements of this system.

Thanks to the works of Professor S. N. Prokopovich, as well as of Kotov, Studenskii, Dzerzhanovska, Oparin, associates of the Post-graduate Seminar in Agricultural Economy and Policy, and others, we have some materials to judge the correlations between peasant farm elements. Thus, for example, the coefficients of correlation between incomes from farming and other elements of the economy, shown in Table 3–18, are known from S. N. Prokopovich's works.

TABLE 3–18

|  | Starobel'sk Uezd | Vologda Guberniya |
|---|---|---|
| Land use | 0.98 | 0.72 |
| Sown area | 0.93 | 0.77 |
| Mowing | 0.47 | 0.62 |
| Value of means of production | 0.82 | 0.68 |
| Value of buildings | 0.64 | 0.53 |
| Value of equipment | 0.84 | 0.66 |
| Number of head of livestock | 0.83 | 0.75 |
| Number of cows | 0.59 | 0.77 |
| Number of workstock | 0.76 | 0.46 |

As is seen from a comparison of the correlation coefficients, such elements as livestock, sown area, income from farming, and the value of means of production are most closely interconnected. That is, the elements of agricultural production depend on one another technically in the closest manner, and each is a gauge of that which is common to them all and which we call volume of economic activity. This connection between the elements of one and the same organizational plan—essentially a technical and not an economic connection —is so close that, as we pointed out at the start of the chapter, the agricultural officer Arnol'd, by processing a considerable mass of material, succeeded in even establishing functional formulas to connect their magnitudes in grouped averages.

Thus, for example, in his Kherson study[4] on the connection be-

---

4 *Osnovnye cherty agronomicheskoi tekhniki i sel'skokhozyaistvennoi ekonomii krest'yanskikh khozyaistv Khersonskogo uezda* [Basic features of agricultural technique and economy in Kherson uezd peasant farms], Kherson, 1902 g. Apart from the Kherson materials, Arnol'd subjected to mathematical processing a number of other

TABLE 3–19

| | | Groups by Size of Land for Use | | | | | |
| | | I | II | III | IV | V | VI |
|---|---|---|---|---|---|---|---|
| Myshkino uezd, | $y = 0.30 + 0.42x$ ... | 0.90 | 1.00 | 1.41 | 1.57 | 1.98 | 2.49 |
| Yaroslavl' guberniya | in reality ......... | 0.93 | 1.01 | 1.40 | 1.56 | 1.96 | 2.52 |
| Kozel'sk uezd, | $y = 0.60 + 0.15x$ ... | 0.89 | 1.21 | 1.60 | 2.01 | 2.74 | — |
| Kaluga guberniya | in reality ......... | 0.87 | 1.19 | 1.58 | 2.00 | 2.71 | — |
| Peremyshl' uezd, | $y = 0.63 + 0.12x$ ... | 0.81 | 1.10 | 1.43 | 1.79 | 2.46 | — |
| Kaluga guberniya | in reality ......... | 0.81 | 1.17 | 1.48 | 1.77 | 2.49 | — |
| Kuznetsk uezd, | $y = 0.60 + 0.56x$ ... | 0.72 | 0.79 | 0.90 | 1.14 | 1.50 | — |
| Saratov guberniya | in reality ......... | 0.76 | 0.76 | 0.93 | 1.22 | 1.50 | — |

SOURCE: A. Arnol'd, "Opyt primeneniya elementarnykh osnov analiticheskoi geometrii k issledovaniyu statisticheskikh zavisimostei" ["An attempt to apply elementary analytic geometry to research on statistical dependent variables"], *Trudy podsektsii statistiki XI s"ezda estestvoispytatelei i vrachei 1901 g.*

tween the quantity of usable land $(x)$ and quantity of workstock $(y)$ he found the formula $y = 1.65 + x/9$. The correspondence between the formula and reality is seen in Table 3–20. For the connection of the value of useful livestock and quantity of useful land we have the formula $y = (32 + 4.17x)$ (Table 3–21). The cost of large items of equipment is connected with the quantity of useful land per person by the formula $y = 100 + 68.2x$ (Table 3–22).

TABLE 3–20

| Groups | By Formula | In Reality |
|---|---|---|
| I..... | 6.64 rubles | 7.00 rubles |
| II..... | 4.34 | 4.29 |
| III..... | 3.33 | 3.27 |
| IV..... | 2.79 | 2.68 |
| V..... | 2.57 | 2.62 |
| VI..... | 2.07 | 2.15 |

TABLE 3–21

| Groups | By Formula | In Reality |
|---|---|---|
| I..... | 219.36 rubles | 219.22 rubles |
| II..... | 132.91 | 132.31 |
| III..... | 95.13 | 102.00 |
| IV..... | 74.83 | 92.80 |
| V..... | 66.36 | 63.09 |
| VI..... | 47.98 | 46.54 |

investigations and obtained a series of formulas, similar in general type, but differing sharply in their coefficients, depending on their area. Thus, for example, he established the formulas in Table 3–19 for the relationship of number of cows to sown area.

TABLE 3–22

| Groups | By Formula | In Reality |
|---|---|---|
| I..... | 593.81 rubles | 593.84 rubles |
| II..... | 349.64 | 359.69 |
| III..... | 273.23 | 266.18 |
| IV..... | 221.40 | 230.22 |
| V..... | 185.93 | 185.83 |
| VI..... | 147.74 | 154.33 |

As one should expect, all other connections, thanks to the multiplicity of factors influencing the farm's income, stand lower than the technical links noted for each of these factors. Thus, for example, from S. N. Prokopovich's same work were found correlation coefficients for farming income with the basic factors of the peasant undertaking's organization (Table 3–23).

TABLE 3–23

| | Starobel'sk Uezd | Vologda Guberniya |
|---|---|---|
| Landholding ........... | 0.78 | 0.71 |
| Number of workers ..... | 0.64 | 0.24 |
| Number of consumers ... | 0.61 | 0.41 |

The investigation of the peasant farm by correlation analysis of its elements is, unfortunately, in an embryonic state, despite a number of works already carried out. But, theoretically, we may foresee that we will have the following successive series of economic elements, the correlation coefficients of which will diminish as they become more distant from one another: *the family (workers and consumers); personal consumption; total family output in farming, crafts, and trades; annual income from farming; harvest, sown area, and other technical elements of the farm (livestock, equipment, and so on).*

The family, measured by number of consumers, and the size of the personal budget are so strongly correlated that first acquaintance with budget statistics consumption materials led investigators to the idea that the consumption standard was fixed. Only in subsequent work did they succeed in establishing that a certain similarity to an immobile consumption standard occurs only in those areas and periods when, because of the low productivity of peasant labor, incomes obtained barely meet the physiological minimum for existence (Voronezh and other budgets of the end of the nineteenth century).

Given a development of peasant labor productivity and an improvement in the market situation, the satisfaction of demands moves away from the physiological minimum. Under the influence of various factors, predominantly those present in the conditions of production, some considerable variation appears, but, all the same, the annual personal budget continues to be strongly correlated with family size. Passing from the personal budget to the size of the family's annual output from agriculture and from crafts and trades, we naturally get a weakening of the correlation with the family, since the sum of total output, apart from the personal consumption fund, includes income from which the family effects capital renewal and accumulation, i.e., processes not connected with family size to such a great extent.

The connection with family size of agricultural incomes taken separately is naturally still weaker, since the process of family division of labor between agriculture and crafts and trades depends not on absolute family size but on local general economic conditions. The technical items of production—sown area, (work) force, and equipment—ought to have a still lower correlation with the family, since, with the same volume of family economic activity determined by the basic on-farm equilibrium, according to differences in the production system they can combine in the most varied ways. At the same time, of course, given a uniform production system, the correlation of its separate technical elements ought to be close to 1.00.

Such is the basic mechanics by which the effective family work force establishes the volume of its agricultural undertaking, as well as the general level of its work intensity and the degree of its demand satisfaction in a particular market situation and taking account of the effective quantity of family consumers, land, and capital.

For a final clarification of this process, it is essential for us to answer the following three questions, which have not been sufficiently illuminated by earlier analysis.

1. We have pointed out that family labor, not finding occupation in its agricultural undertaking, turns to crafts and trades. It is exceedingly important to establish whether land hunger and shortage of capital are the sole factors which turn peasant labor to crafts and trades. In other words, we must explain: *What quantitatively determines the division of peasant labor between earnings from crafts and trades and from agricultural work?*

2. We have established that the effective size of peasant family landholding and capital, if they are at the minimum, are in many ways the determining factor in establishing the volume of the agricultural undertaking. It is essential to establish: *What determines the availability of land and capital itself in the peasant family, and does the family not try to develop it from the minimum to the optimum?*

3. We have noted that the agricultural ratio requires that any size of agricultural undertaking be organized in the most expedient relationship of its technical factors. It is essential to clarify the situation in which land and capital are at a minimum and the peasant family's agricultural undertaking is organized in accord with them. *Does not the mass of family labor remaining outside this undertaking and the mass of demands it has not satisfied have any influence on the economic and technical organization of the agricultural undertaking itself?*

We will try to answer each of these questions separately.

1. Our supposition that want of capital and, mainly, of land sometimes makes the peasant family throw a considerable part of its labor into crafts, trades, and other nonagricultural livelihoods is, in the majority of cases, perfectly correct. In accordance with it, departures for crafts and trades are particularly developed where there is considerable population density. However, we ought to make two provisos to this statement, and the second of these will be very significant for understanding the whole nature of the peasant farm.

First, very many crafts and trades depend in their development on the fact that the distribution of agricultural labor over time is very uneven, and whole seasons—for example, winter—are completely dead. At this time, peasant labor is free, and with very little intensity and, consequently, little drudgery, it is advantageous to use it in establishing the economic equilibrium by means of work in crafts and trades, thus easing the load of summer agricultural work. The figure of labor distribution over time for one of the Volokolamsk uezd peasant farms illustrates this idea quite clearly (Figure 3–4).

Second, and this is the main thing, in numerous situations it is not at all a lack of means of production which calls forth earnings from crafts and trades, but a more favorable market situation for such work in the sense of its payment for peasant labor compared with that in agriculture. Zemstvo statistics for Vladimir, Moscow, and other guberniyas give us much data to show that peasant farms of an area of seasonal distant work and of certain local crafts and trades make very little use of their effective agricultural means of production.

Thus, for example, in 1804, according to survey data for Shuya uezd, Vladimir guberniya, 44.8 percent of total area was arable, and according to the zemstvo registration of 1899, only 27.8 percent. (*Materialy dlya otsenki zemlei Vladimirskoi gubernii*) [Materials for evaluating the lands of Vladimir guberniya], I, X). Moreover, according to the investigator, this process has continued into our day. "The supplanting of agriculture by industry leads to a reduction

FIGURE 3–4
DISTRIBUTION OF WORK BY HALF-MONTHLY PERIODS

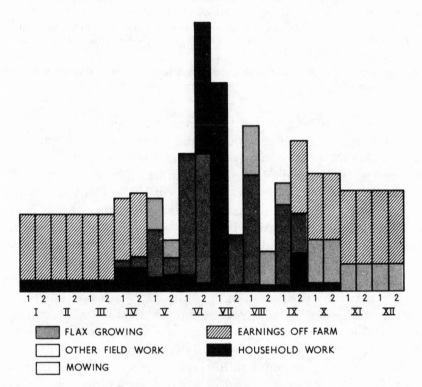

of arable and to its complete abandonment," the compiler of the collection writes, and he gives figures for the abandoned strips of the winter-sown area of from 3.7 percent (Shuya) to 7.1 percent (Vyazniki). This same picture has been noted in our period in Moscow guberniya, too.

In this case, evidently, the presence of crafts and trades is not explained by the absence of land, and you do not need second sight to understand the reason. It is entirely because here crafts and trades give a considerably higher payment per labor unit. With their help, one may obtain earnings with less drudgery, and the family prefers to square the basic economic equilibrium of consumption and labor expenditure predominantly by means of occupation in crafts and trades. In this case, the peasant family behaves with its labor just like a capitalist distributing his capital, so that it gives him the highest net income.

In meeting its demands, the peasant farm strives to do this most easily and, therefore, weighing up the effective means of production and all other objects to which its labor could be applied, distributes it in such a way that all opportunities that give a high payment may be used. Thanks to this, the peasant family, seeking the highest payment per labor unit, frequently leaves unused the land and means of production at its disposal, once other forms of labor provide it with more advantageous conditions.[5]

Below, we will see that the peasant family, given a lack of means of production, can, at the cost of reducing its labor payment, always expand the volume of its economic activity even within agricultural production. This forced agricultural work with its gradually declining rate of labor productivity is compared, in the peasant farm's estimation, with possible earnings from crafts and trades. These are also, of course, ranked in declining order of their labor payment. By comparing these two series, the peasant farm takes for the realization of its labor from both agriculture and crafts and trades those opportunities which guarantee it in total the highest payment per marginal labor unit.

In other words, we may theoretically assert that peasant family division of labor between earnings from agriculture and from crafts and trades is achieved by a comparison of the market situation in these two branches of the national economy. And since the relationship between these two market situations is inconstant, the relationship between labor expenditure on crafts and trades and on agriculture is also inconstant. In years of an unfavorable agricultural market situation—for example, given a harvest failure—the impossibility of attaining the economic equilibrium with the help of general agricultural occupations obliges the peasants to cast onto the labor market a huge quantity of peasant working hands who look for a livelihood from crafts and trades. As a result, we have the situation—normal for Russia, but paradoxical from a Western viewpoint—in which periods of high grain prices are, at the same time, periods of low wages.

In this respect, the work of N. P. Nikitin on Ryazan' guberniya is of very great interest. Its results, reported at Professor A. F. Fortunatov's seminar in Moscow, demonstrated with great clarity from the material of four decades the inverse proportion of the price of rye and the wages of agricultural workers. A curious comparison, made

---

[5] The sole feature in this case distinguishing the peasant family from the entrepreneur consists in the fact that the capitalist somehow or other always distributes all his capital entirely; but the peasant family never uses the whole of its labor completely and ceases to expend labor as it satisfies its demands and attains its economic equilibrium.

by K. K. Paas in his work on the fur trade, of the export of grain and furs from Siberia has the same significance[6] (Figure 3–5). This de-

FIGURE 3–5

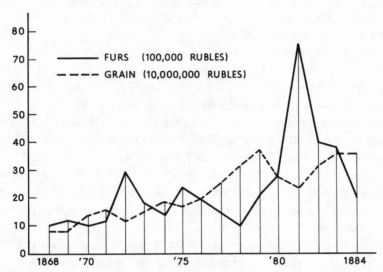

pendent relationship shows us that a deterioration in the market situation for agriculture pushes peasant labor out into hunting, which thus creates an increased supply and, hence, a fall in squirrel prices. Thus, here, too, the process is not a simple one but goes through an evaluation of two market situations[7] in the mechanism of the basic economic equilibrium.

2. The second of our questions, about the factors determining the availability of land and capital at the disposal of the family, is so significant in itself that it essentially requires an independent review. Below, we devote all of Chapter 5 to a review of the problem of capital. However, it is absolutely essential for us to pose this problem now in order that the reader should not think that size of land for use and of capital is a sort of deus ex machina in the form of a priori prerequisites of the peasant farm.

We know from Chapter 1 of our investigation that the size of the main factor for the construction of the labor farm—the family running the farm—depends chiefly on its age, and that its growth, being

---

6 K. Paas, *Kratkii obzor pushnogo dela v Rossii* [A brief survey of the fur trade in Russia], M., 1915 g., s.26. The diagram was drawn up by N. Turkin.

7 In essence, we may speak terminologically only of one single market situation of the entire national economy. If we conventionally talk of two market situations, we would need to speak more precisely of two portions of one system.

subject to biological laws, depends to a small extent on the family's economic state.

The size of area to be used is not so freely chosen and, as we see in Chapter 1 and the table of correlation coefficients, depends greatly on family size and general economic potential of the farm. In the case of communal land use, this correspondence is reached by means of general and particular repartition and, if this is insufficient, by renting land. We see from Table 3–24 how far the peasant farm tends,

TABLE 3–24
LAND RENTED (DESYATINAS) AND CONSUMER–WORKER RATIO

| Own Arable per Worker (Desyatinas) | Consumer per Worker | | |
|---|---|---|---|
| | 1.00–1.30 | 1.31–1.60 | 1.61–∞ |
| 0.1–2.0 ............... | 0.50 | 0.73 | 1.19 |
| 2.1–3.0 ............... | 0.08 | 0.56 | 0.50 |
| 3.1–∞ ............... | 0.10 | 0.41 | 0.65 |
| Average ......... | 0.23 | 0.57 | 0.79 |
| Average Consumer–Worker Ratio ......... | 1.15 | 1.45 | 1.75 |

by means of renting land, to bring the area it is exploiting agriculturally into optimal relationship with family size. This table is based on materials of the Starobel'sk budget inquiry, which notes the influence of family composition on size of rented area, given its own constant amount of land available.

However, the best proof of the constant tendency to bring size of agricultural area into an optimal relationship with family size are the dynamic investigations of Chernenkov, Kushchenko, Vikhlyaev, and Khryashcheva, which we quoted in Chapter 1. They show that as the family develops it moves over the years from one sown area category to another; although, of course, the general population density in a particular area, the conditions of the primary land allotment, and so on often provide insurmountable difficulties to the tendency to develop its land area to the optimum.

The expansion of land area encounters still greater difficulties in countries with a land regime of nonpartible inheritance, as well as in countries with an intensive capitalist farmer system of agriculture where each agricultural undertaking is firmly jointed together in all its parts by a production machine little subject to expansion and contraction. European critics of the present book—namely, Professor A. Skalweit, Professor M. Sering, and others—have noted this distinction of the European farm from that which I have described with particular insistence. With this, I cannot but agree, and ought to acknowledge that in cases where the land regime is not very flexible the relationship between land and family is regulated by a change in the amount of labor hired or hired out.

In particular, the peasant farm of Germany makes considerable use of hired labor for its work, and apart from that, thanks to a land regime of nonpartible inheritance, it is fixed as regards the land area given it and the firm economic organization constructed on it. Only in certain areas of southern Germany does Professor Skalweit note in peasant farms the same phenomena as those I have noted in the Russian materials (mobility of land for use under the influence of family growth, raising of land prices and rents above land rent in the economic sense, and so on).

This observation is completely justified and was made to me in private letters from Professors M. Sering, E. Laur, and others who have taken notice of my book. I was conscious of this circumstance even when I was working on this investigation. It was clear to me that in different countries economic organizations widely differing in nature are understood under the one term, the peasant farm. While with us in Russia 90 percent of the total mass of peasant farms are pure family farms, in Western Europe and America this group is insignificant socially, and the term peasant farm is applied to semi-capitalist farms. It was also clear to me that the land regime of nonpartible inheritance widespread in the West does not give even purely family farms a chance to disclose their characteristic features clearly enough.

However, I think that all this does not diminish my conclusions or make my book a narrowly Russian one. While in Western Europe the group of private family farms that work in a land regime where their characteristics may be particularly clearly expressed are a comparatively small part of the total mass of peasant farms, I have every reason to suppose that in a number of countries of Eastern Europe, and especially in non-European countries like India, China, and Japan, this group of farms forms a very considerable social sector. Its total proportion in the world economy is such that it fully deserves special attention and study.

Apart from that, as we will see in Switzerland and Czechoslovakia, i.e., in Western Europe itself, you may observe even in peasant farms squeezed by a regime of nonpartible inheritance some elements of the economic conduct we have established in the mode of determining the necessary degree of intensity.

Processes of capital accumulation are in this respect easier, but, as we will see in Chapter 5, they, too, demand some effort from the farm.

However, by taking in advance some of the conclusions of Chapter 5, we can still accept that the peasant farm with minimum land area and means of production has a real stimulus to develop them to the optimum, and in accord with its capability carries out this expansion if, of course, the agricultural market situation is not lower than the market situation for earnings from crafts and trades. Therefore, if in each particular year the volume of activity is determined by the means of production available in that year, the availability of means of production of itself, taken over long periods, is adjusted by the family or, more accurately, tends to be adjusted to the objective optimal volume of activity.

3. We have established that the peasant family without enough land and means of production at its disposal for the complete use of all its labor in the agricultural undertaking puts its surplus in another form of economic activity (crafts and trades). It frequently occurs, however, that the possibility of earnings from crafts and trades is also extremely limited or that payment for labor is very low.

In this case, it is sometimes advantageous for the peasant farm to violate the optimal combination of production elements for its activity and to force its labor intensity far beyond the optimal limits. Inevitably losing on unit labor payment, it nevertheless considerably expands the gross income of its agricultural undertaking and reaches a basic equilibrium between the drudgery of labor and consumption —within the limits of agricultural activity, of course—at a level of well-being lower than would occur given a farm optimal in size and proportions.

This forcing up of labor intensity, buying increased annual agricultural income at the price of reducing labor unit payment, is achieved either by an intensification of work methods or by using more labor-intensive crops and jobs. If we compare different crops from the viewpoint of labor quantity and gross income which each desyatina demands and gives, we will see a great difference between them. Note, for example, Table 3–25. We see that the replacement of oats by flax, for example, as it were increases four times the area of the spring-sown field, making it possible to dispose of four times the quantity of labor on the same area. In exactly the same way, we can increase the labor

TABLE 3-25

LABOR EXPENDITURE PER DESYATINA OF OATS, POTATOES, AND FLAX

| | Working Days per Desyatina | Outlays on Materials per Desyatina | Gross Income (Rubles per Desyatina) | Gross Income less Outlays on Materials | Payment per Working Day |
|---|---|---|---|---|---|
| OATS | | | | | |
| Moscow uezd ........ | 24.7 | 14.90 | 66.35 | 51.41 | 2.08 |
| Volokolamsk uezd ... | 22.5 | 16.94 | 46.44 | 29.50 | 1.31 |
| Vologda uezd ........ | 32.2 | 12.99 | 39.71 | 26.72 | 0.83 |
| Bronnitsy uezd ...... | 20.0 | 14.45 | 44.97 | 30.52 | 1.52 |
| POTATOES | | | | | |
| Moscow uezd ........ | 48.9 | 51.00 | 137.20 | 86.20 | 1.76 |
| Volokolamsk uezd ... | 47.2 | 21.37 | 63.75 | 42.38 | 0.90 |
| Vologda uezd ........ | 56.9 | 26.79 | 121.90 | 95.11 | 1.67 |
| Bronnitsy uezd ...... | 47.9 | 21.72 | 94.50 | 72.78 | 1.62 |
| FLAX | | | | | |
| Volokolamsk uezd ... | 83.0 | 15.95 | 90.66 | 74.71 | 0.90 |
| Vologda uezd ........ | 88.2 | 13.32 | 93.33 | 80.01 | 0.91 |

intensity of our farms by introducing root crops and potatoes into their fields.

Taking one of the Volokolamsk farms we described in 1910 and making an extract for it from the 1898 census, we have the comparison in Table 3–26. In the twelve years that separate the two periods

TABLE 3-26

CHANGE OF A THREE-COURSE GRAIN FARM TO CLOVER- AND FLAX-GROWING

| | Rye | Oats | Potatoes | Flax | Clover | Fallow |
|---|---|---|---|---|---|---|
| 1898: 1.8 workers, 3.9 desyatinas of arable | | | | | | |
| Desyatinas of sown ..... | 1.33 | 1.00 | 0.20 | 0.17 | 0.00 | 1.20 |
| Working days .......... | 40.7 | 22.5 | 9.1 | 14.1 | 0.0 | 0.0 |
| Labor payment ......... | 26.80 | 29.50 | 8.11 | 12.10 | 0.00 | 0.00 |
| 1910: 2.4 workers, 3.9 desyatinas of arable | | | | | | |
| Desyatinas of sown ..... | 1.00 | 0.00 | 0.15 | 0.83 | 1.00 | 0.92 |
| Working days .......... | 30.6 | 0.0 | 7.1 | 68.3 | 20.0 | 0.0 |
| Labor payment ......... | 20.18 | 0.00 | 6.35 | 62.00 | 40.00 | 0.00 |

taken, the farm underwent a fundamental break: sowing of forage was introduced, and commercial flax-growing reduced the growing of oats. In total, the 1898 farm, with 86.6 working days, obtained 77 rubles, 47 kopeks, giving a payment per day of 89.5 kopeks; the 1910 farm, with 126.0 working days, obtained 128 rubles, 50 kopeks, or 102.0 kopeks per working day. But it is still more important that even though one worker in 1910 had a total of 1.63 desyatinas of sown instead of the 2.17 in 1898 he could dispose of 52.5 working days on the farm instead of the 48.2 in 1898; i.e., despite the pressure on land, he was able to increase the labor energy used.

Excluding years of favorable market situation, high labor intensive crops usually give a smaller labor payment than do more extensive crops. Therefore, peasant farms turn to intensive crops only when, due to land pressure, they cannot meet their demands to the necessary extent with an optimal labor payment and do not have advantageous crafts or trades. Thus, for example, N. P. Makarov observed the influence of land pressure, shown in Table 3–27, on the development

TABLE 3–27

| Areas | Desyatinas of Sown per Worker | Percentage of Arable under: | |
| --- | --- | --- | --- |
| | | Flax | Potatoes |
| Oats and flax ...... | 2.6 | 14.0 | 3.9 |
| Potatoes and flax ... | 2.2 | 16.6 | 27.4 |
| Potatoes .......... | 0.9 | 3.5 | 77.9 |

of labor intensive crops of flax and the almost kitchen garden growing of potatoes (101 working days per desyatina) for three districts of Kostroma uezd.

However, the deepest and most interesting investigations in this respect are not Russian but western ones, carried out by E. Laur in Switzerland and K. Brdlik in Czechoslovakia. They disclosed the sharp deviation of small-scale farms from the optimum due to the impossibility of achieving the basic economic equilibrium at the optimum. The results of these investigations are summarized briefly in Table 3–28, for Switzerland, and in Table 3–29, in a different form, for the Czechoslovak farms.

In studying both these tables, we can come to a single conclusion which is most clearly expressed in the Swiss work. The peasant farm, restrained by its land area, forces up its labor intensity more than three times as against the optimal intensity for the capitalist farm. It also somewhat increases its capital intensity and thus almost doubles its gross income; however, this is achieved at the cost of reducing the payment per labor unit, which requires that the farm's equilibrium be established at a lower level of well-being. Similar forcing up of intensity is quite unacceptable to the capitalist farm, since in this event the land rent, in the economic sense, per hectare falls almost

TABLE 3-28

SWITZERLAND, 1910

| Farm Size (Hectares) | Hectares per Consumer | Percentage Hired Labor | Working Days | Outlays on Materials | Outlays on Materials per Working Day | Gross Income (Francs) | Payment per Labor Day (Francs) | Economic Rent per Hectare (Francs) | Consumer's Budget |
|---|---|---|---|---|---|---|---|---|---|
| 0–5 ... | 1.2 | 7.4 | 147 | 304.9 | 2.07 | 902.0 | 2.90 | 68.0 | 609.9 |
| 5–10 ... | 2.1 | 19.4 | 115 | 212.8 | 1.85 | 777.7 | 3.36 | 77.2 | 638.1 |
| 10–15 ... | 3.2 | 30.1 | 89 | 214.9 | 2.51 | 728.1 | 3.62 | 85.4 | 706.3 |
| 15–30 ... | 4.8 | 47.5 | 76 | 183.5 | 2.42 | 610.0 | 3.87 | 85.9 | 779.6 |
| 30–∞ ... | 7.9 | 57.3 | 56 | 170.6 | 3.04 | 501.0 | 3.70 | 86.9 | 802.4 |

TABLE 3-29

CZECHOSLOVAKIA

| Farm Size (Hectares) | Labor in Terms of Annual Workers | Cost of Work (Crowns) | Gross Income (Crowns) | Payment of Labor (Crowns) | Net Profit on Capital (Crowns) | Gross Payment of Labor per Annual Worker (Crowns) |
|---|---|---|---|---|---|---|
| 2–5 ... | 0.57 | 329 | 532 | 420 | 12 | 737 |
| 5–20 ... | 0.27 | 221 | 451 | 333 | 59 | 1675 |
| 20–100 ... | 0.22 | 170 | 416 | 305 | 88 | 1890 |
| >100 ... | 0.17 | 138 | 408 | 265 | 78 | 2401 |

one and a half times. We consider it absolutely essential to stress that these conclusions have not been reached on the basis of Russian budgets but on European material.

Given the low degree of mobility of land areas we have already noted in Western Europe, the pressure of demographic elements leads, not to fluctuations in the area under agricultural exploitation, but to combinations with the degree of agricultural intensity. For our conception of the family farm, both methods are equivalent, and this we would particularly like to stress for our West European critics who are inclined to recognize our constructs as applicable only to the Russian and, in general, to the Eastern peasant farm.

Apart from the described pressure of surplus labor on farm organization, displacing intensity from its optimum, it is essential to note that the family character of the undertaking affects a whole series of other technical changes, as we will review in the following chapter.

Such are the particular features introduced into the family labor farm by the technical conditions of agricultural production. In their basic features, the mechanics of combining the economic factors peculiar to this form of economic activity may be considered to have been established.

Kurt Ritter,[8] noting in his review of my book the same factors as does Professor Skalweit,[9] points to the incorrect nature of my terminology and says *that even purely family farms*, insofar as they become commodity producers and dispose of their produce on the capitalist market and are subject to the influence of its prices, should be called capitalist farms, since they form part of the capitalist system of the national economy.

In some respects, this may be correct, since the term capitalism is exceedingly overloaded with meaning and may cover the most disparate phenomena. However, it is essential to remember that the main part of our analysis is not national economic but private economic in character, and we needed an organization to separate family undertakings from those constructed on the basis of hired labor. The hired we have called capitalist, since in their private economic organization they have elements of capitalist relations. If Dr. Kurt Ritter finds it possible within capitalism as a national economic system to give two different terminologies for hiring and nonhiring farms in the private economic sense, we will merely welcome it. We note only that the family farm is also conceivable outside the capitalist system of national economy.

For many of our readers, however, the concrete features of the living peasant farm are not yet depicted beyond our graphs, comparison of figures, Arnol'd formulas, and correlation coefficients. For a whole series of our further theoretical constructs, too, it is absolutely essential to make our abstract schemes concrete and to descend from the study of the statistician and economist, working with his volumes of statistical tables, closer to the concrete life and work of the organizing agricultural officer. In accordance with this, we devote our next chapter to a more or less detailed analysis of the concrete questions of individual peasant farm organization.

---

8 (Conrad's) *Jahrbücher für Nationalökonomie und Statistik*, Vol. 122, Book 5, p. 680, Jena, 1924.

9 A. Skalweit, "Die Familienwirtschaft als Grundlage für ein System der Sozialökonomie," *Weltwirtschaftliches Archiv*, Vol. 20, Book 2 (1924), p. 232.

# CHAPTER 4

## *The Organizational Plan of the Peasant Farm*

One of the commonest and most unfortunate difficulties in understanding the peasant farm is our characteristic statistical method of perceiving and thinking about it. Concepts of 1.78 horses compared with 8.34 persons of both sexes, 26.15 percent without horses, a decline in the average number of livestock held (in terms of large ones), depending on a rise in the percentage of literacy—these are the images and conceptions in which Russian economists are accustomed to think about the subject of our inquiry. Nevertheless, we can surely suppose that to think in this way about the peasant farm production machine is the same as to describe the structure of a modern steam engine as consisting of 39 percent Fe, 31 percent Cu, 16 percent $H_2O$ and 14 percent various organic substances.

To pass, even for a short time, from figures of the "Collection of statistical and economic information on agriculture in ——— guberniya" to concrete, practical work among living peasant farms is enough to doubtlessly convince oneself that one must master more than the totals of classifications by sown area and the correlation coefficients of its elements to understand the peasant farm; such data mainly describe, not the structure of the peasant undertaking as such, but a broad collection of peasant farms. One must seize hold of its living organizational ideas, the machinery of its individual economic organism which is "the subjective teleological unity of rational economic activity, i.e., running the farm." In brief, we will fully understand the basis and nature of the peasant farm only when in our constructs we turn it from an object of observation to a subject creating its own existence, and attempt to make clear to ourselves the internal considerations and causes by which it forms its organizational production plan and carries it into effect.

With particular insistence, Russian critics of our early works usually call our theory a *consumer* theory of the peasant farm and contrast it with the acquisitive concept of the farm. In this, there is either a great misunderstanding or a wish, for the sake of polemics, to give our views an obviously distorted image.

Any economic unit, including the peasant farm, is acquisitive—an undertaking aiming at maximum income. In an economic unit based on hired labor, this tendency to boundless expansion is limited by capital availability and, if this increases, is practically boundless. But in the family farm, apart from capital available expressed in means of production, this tendency is limited by the family labor force and the increasing drudgery of work if its intensity is forced up. The labor–consumer balance we have analyzed is the expression of the mechanism for limiting the peasant family's consumer tendencies. Given high labor productivity, the peasant family will naturally tend not only to meet its personal demands but also to expand the farm's capital renewal and in general to accumulate capital.

Of course, in speaking of the peasant farm we still do not need to conceive of its organizational plan in nature as a conscious structure, written out with all its tables and maps into a large in-folio volume. It is equally undoubted, however, that like Molière's Jourdain who had talked prose for 40 years without suspecting it, our peasant for hundreds of years has been carrying on his farm according to definite, objectively existing plans, without, perhaps, fully recognizing them subjectively.

The very advantage or disadvantage of any particular economic initiative on the peasant farm is decided, not by an arithmetic calculation of income and expenditure, but most frequently by intuitively perceiving whether this initiative is economically acceptable or not. In the same way, the peasant farm's organizational plan is constructed at the present time, not by a system of connected logical structures and reckonings, but by the force of succession and imitation of the experience and *selection*, over many years and often subconsciously, of successful methods of economic work. Therefore, we do not aim at issuing our further logical constructs as a priori deliberations of the peasant organizing his farm. Rather, we conceive them as a method for the a posteriori organized recognition of our subject, and merely hope that in time, given the development of our social agricultural science, some of our a posteriori considerations may also become practical methods which our peasants may use for the practical arrangement of their farms.

The tentative nature of our further considerations frees us from a full and exhaustive calculation of the entire farm structure and allows us to limit ourselves to certain organizational considerations of a general character. These are essential to us either for a deeper understanding of what has been expounded in the preceding chapters or for subsequent chapters. We will, therefore, not aim at giving guidance for the practical composition of organizational plans but propose mainly to stress those predominantly technical connections and norms which bind the separate elements of the farm together and will be essential for our understanding of the economic phenomena which arise on the basis of them.

From what we have said in preceding chapters, it is clear that the family of the peasant-run farm, beginning to organize production, tends in the final result to satisfy its demands to the fullest extent possible and to ensure the further stability of the farm by a process of capital renewal with the least expenditure of energy. For this purpose, it aims at ensuring such applications for its labor as would ensure the highest of all possible payments per, labor unit.

Each peasant farm is a constituent part of the general system of the national economy and is determined by those static and dynamic factors peculiar to its current phase of development. Undoubtedly, outside general national economy analysis we cannot fully understand the nature of a single private economic undertaking. However, to understand the foundations of any private undertaking and to make clear the general economic processes themselves we must fully elucidate to ourselves the work mechanism of the economic machine which, subject to the pressure of national economic factors, organizes a productive process within itself and, in its turn, with others like it, influences the national economy as a whole. Our task is to study the structure of this machine and its mechanism for work performed within the limits of the organizational plan.

Without deep acquaintance with this apparatus, we will never fully understand how the peasant farm feels the pressure of national economic factors and how it reacts to the pressure. In this respect, the farm family uses, within its power, all the opportunities of its natural and historical position and of the market situation in which it exists. But since the combination of natural and market conditions is extremely varied in different areas, in studying peasant farm organizational structure we will naturally come up against a still greater variety of types and forms of structure. Natural and national economic area differences are also complicated for individual farms by differences in family composition, landholding, and availability of capital. Among these differences in the farm's organizational plan, the most basic one which determines the whole character of the farm's structure is the degree to which the farm is linked with the market—the development of commodity production in it.

In this chapter, we are not setting ourselves the task of making clear the causes which oblige peasant farms to expand or contract commodity production elements. The development of the market in a seminatural agricultural country is one of the most complex problems in the theory of the evolution of the national economy and thus is beyond the limits of our study. So, in the meantime, we limit ourselves to organizational analysis of the private economy. Therefore, in studying the peasant farm in this chapter from a private economic viewpoint we take the particular degree to which it is money based as *something given*, supposing that circumstances do not give it the opportunity to develop commodity production with advantage more extensively than has been done.

The budget materials at our disposal enable us to establish the levels of money (commodity) nature shown in Table 4–1 for various areas of Russia.

TABLE 4–1

PEASANT FARM INCOMINGS AND OUTGOINGS IN MONEY AND IN KIND

| | Incomings | | | | Outgoings | | | |
|---|---|---|---|---|---|---|---|---|
| Uezds | In Kind | In Money | Total | Percent in Money | In Kind | In Money | Total | Percent in Money |
| Volokolamsk ...... | 670.0 | 528.1 | 1198.1 | 44.2 | 554.9 | 500.1 | 1055.0 | 47.3 |
| Gzhatsk .......... | 451.9 | 247.0 | 713.9 | 34.4 | 463.2 | 251.1 | 714.3 | 35.2 |
| Porech'e ........ | 621.0 | 198.6 | 819.7 | 24.2 | 628.0 | 198.6 | 826.7 | 24.0 |
| Sychevka ........ | 485.5 | 288.2 | 773.7 | 37.3 | 488.0 | 284.1 | 767.1 | 37.0 |
| Dorogubuzh ...... | 650.1 | 180.3 | 830.4 | 21.7 | 640.2 | 213.4 | 853.6 | 25.0 |
| Starobel'sk ....... | 568.1 | 442.0 | 1010.1 | 43.7 | 499.0 | 436.5 | 934.5 | 47.7 |
| Vologda .......... | 238.5 | 209.6 | 548.1 | 38.3 | 238.7 | 217.7 | 556.4 | 39.1 |
| Vel'sk ........... | 361.2 | 121.9 | 438.1 | 27.8 | 317.0 | 123.5 | 440.5 | 58.0 |

In order to understand from an organizational point of view the meanings of differences in the extent to which money and commodity elements are developed, we allow ourselves to compare two farms which are characteristic in this respect—an almost natural-economy Tot'ma farm and a largely money-based, flax-growing Volokolamsk farm. From the zemstvo statistical handbook for Tot'ma uezd, Vologda guberniya—one of the most obscure, nonmonetary corners of the country—let us extract the summary graphs of the budget tables relating to the farm group that sows the largest area. Then let us compare the average figures obtained with an ordinary Volokolamsk farm which we have picked at random from the 25 budget monographs for 1910 (Table 4–2).

TABLE 4–2

CONSUMER'S BUDGET ON A NONMONETARY AND A MONETARY FARM: EXPENDITURE IN KIND AND IN MONEY (RUBLES)

| | Tot'ma Uezd | | Volokolamsk Uezd | |
| --- | --- | --- | --- | --- |
| | In Kind | In Money | In Kind | In Money |
| Rye ..................... | 58.5 | — | 26.0 | 40.0 |
| Barley ................. | 13.3 | — | — | — |
| Wheat .................. | 9.5 | 0.6 | — | 7.5 |
| Oats .................... | 4.4 | 0.1 | 5.0 | — |
| Malt .................... | 3.9 | — | — | — |
| Groats ................. | 7.8 | — | — | 13.5 |
| Peas .................... | 3.8 | — | — | — |
| Potatoes ............... | 5.8 | — | 12.0 | — |
| Cabbage ............... | 0.3 | 0.0 | — | — |
| Cucumbers ............ | 0.1 | — | — | 11.0 |
| Onions ................. | 1.3 | 0.0 | 1.0 | — |
| Other vegetables ....... | 1.7 | — | — | — |
| Vegetable oil .......... | 2.2 | 1.0 | 18.8 | — |
| Fungi .................. | 4.1 | — | — | — |
| Berries ................ | 2.3 | — | — | — |
| Payment for milling .... | — | 3.6 | — | 4.5 |
| Beef ................... | 3.9 | 1.2 | — | 6.0 |
| Veal ................... | 1.8 | — | 20.0 | — |
| Mutton ................ | 3.9 | — | — | — |
| Pork ................... | 6.8 | 1.4 | — | 5.0 |
| Eggs ................... | 5.2 | 0.0 | 0.5 | — |
| Milk and milk products .... | 51.3 | — | 150.0 | — |
| Poultry ................ | 0.2 | — | 0.5 | — |
| Fish ................... | 2.1 | 4.5 | — | 10.0 |
| Salt ................... | — | 1.8 | — | 2.0 |
| Condiments ........... | — | 0.6 | — | 16.8 |
| Tea and sugar ......... | — | 11.8 | — | 50.0 |
| Tobacco ............... | — | 0.3 | — | — |
| Alcohol ............... | 3.5 | 6.1 | — | 21.0 |
| Hops .................. | 0.1 | 0.5 | — | — |
| Clothing ............... | 4.3 | 10.8 | — | 145.0 |
| Games ................. | 0.0 | 0.3 | — | 3.0 |
| Flax spinning .......... | 4.0 | — | — | — |
| Wool .................. | 2.5 | — | — | — |
| Sheepskin ............. | 1.2 | — | — | — |
| Soap .................. | — | 1.1 | — | 12.0 |
| Lighting .............. | — | 1.9 | — | 4.0 |
| Firewood ............. | 8.6 | 3.6 | 20.0 | 50.0 |
| Utensils ............... | 0.0 | 1.8 | — | 2.0 |
| Spiritual needs ......... | — | 4.8 | — | 4.5 |
| Total ............. | 218.4 | 57.8 | 253.0 | 497.8 |
| | 276.2 | | 750.8 | |
| Percentage ......... | 70.1 | 20.9 | 33.7 | 66.3 |
| | 100.0 | | 100.0 | |

The table allows us to see real differences at first glance. In looking at the table, we see that the money expenditure of the consumer's budget in Tot'ma farms comes to only 22.0 percent of the total, while in the Volokolamsk farm it reaches 61.1 percent. In other words, the almost natural economy of the Tot'ma peasant farm is an isolated economic machine with few social and economic links with the outside world. Conversely, the Volokolamsk peasant farm has been drawn into the world's economic circulation and lives, not merely by its own home produce, but by a share of the general national income, and fulfills part of the work of the common national machine of the economy. Naturally, such a structure of a money-based farm could not but affect its production organization. Numerous items of the consumer budget met in kind in Tot'ma uezd demand of the farm a complex organization, giving 32 forms of produce. In Volokolamsk uezd, however, the 10 items of the budget met in kind allow a great simplification of economic organization. We can, in part, judge the comparative complexity of the arrangements in both these farms from Table 4–3.

Thus, in the Tot'ma farm, 87 percent of the total income is consumed on the farm in kind, and its production is determined qualita-

TABLE 4–3

INCOME IN KIND AND IN MONEY, TOT'MA AND VOLOKOLAMSK FARMS (RUBLES)

|  | Tot'ma Uezd | | Volokolamsk Uezd | |
|---|---|---|---|---|
|  | In Kind | In Money | In Kind | In Money |
| Rye ..................... | 74.4 | 6.5 | 27.0 | — |
| Barley ................... | 21.7 | — | — | — |
| Wheat .................. | 12.5 | 0.7 | — | — |
| Oats .................... | 59.5 | 19.4 | 55.0 | — |
| Potatoes ................ | 7.5 | — | 18.0 | — |
| Flax seed ............... | 2.1 | 0.8 | 25.0 | 140.0 |
| Flax fiber .............. | 5.6 | 3.3 | — | 306.0 |
| Peas .................... | 4.3 | — | — | — |
| Cabbage ................ | 0.3 | — | — | — |
| Cucumbers .............. | 0.1 | — | — | — |
| Onions ................. | 1.2 | — | 1.0 | — |
| Other vegetables .......... | 1.7 | — | — | — |
| Beef .................... | 4.0 | — | — | — |
| Veal .................... | 2.1 | — | 20.0 | — |
| Mutton ................. | 3.9 | — | — | — |
| Pork .................... | 6.8 | — | — | — |
| Milk and milk products .... | 52.1 | 7.6 | 150.0 | — |
| Hides and wool ........... | 5.8 | 0.5 | 1.0 | 7.5 |
| Poultry products ......... | 0.6 | 0.6 | 1.0 | — |
| Total .............. | 266.1 | 39.4 | 298.0 | 453.5 |
| Crafts and trades .......... | — | 48.9 | — | 85.0 |

tively and quantitatively by consumer demands. In the Volokolamsk farm, though, only 39.6 percent of what is produced is prepared for direct family consumption; the remaining 60.4 percent is thrown onto the market and serves family consumption only in the sense that necessary objects may be acquired for the money received. Farms from other areas give us various rates of commodity production intermediate to the extreme types we have looked at.

Commodity type farms are distinguished from nonmonetary farms by other real differences in the character of their economic calculations, apart from the considerable simplification of their organizational plan which we have already looked at. In the nonmonetary farm, the activity of the man that ran it was directed to a whole series of separate consumer demands and in many ways had a *qualitative* hue. It was necessary to obtain for family consumption such and such products, precisely those and no others. The *quantity* could be measured only for each demand separately: "there's enough," or "there's not enough," and is there much "not enough"? Thanks to the elasticity of consumer demand itself, such a measurement could not be very exact.

Therefore, in the nonmonetary farm the question of whether it is more advantageous to sow rye or mow hay, for example, could not arise, since they could not replace each other and thus had no common scale for comparison. The value of the hay obtained was measured in terms of the need for fodder, and the value of the rye in terms of feeding the family. You could even assert that meadows increased in value the poorer they were and the more labor they required to obtain each pud of hay.

The farm's tasks take on quite another character as soon as it enters into the sphere of monetary and commodity circulation. Economic activity loses its qualitative hue. Demands may now be satisfied by purchases; concern with "quantity"—*obtaining the greatest quantity* which, being exchanged, may take any "qualitative" form needed to meet family demands—now steps into the foreground. As its monetary nature develops, the "quantity" obtained more and more frees itself from "quality," and starts to have the abstract character of "value."

Given widely developed commodity exchange, what its labor is expended on makes no difference to the farm family, provided only that it is utilized as fully as possible and well paid by the market at the value of the produce obtained. And since the level of payment for labor invested in various products is finally determined by the state of the market, it is self-evident that as the commodity nature of the farm develops the farm's organization in a nonmonetary system, totally established by family consumer demands, begins to be more and more influenced by the market situation[1] as regards farm *composition*, retaining the pressure of consumer demands only in determining the total *volume* of activity. Such is the internal organizational and economic meaning of a transition from a nonmonetary farm structure to a monetary and commodity one.

The farm is freed from the "qualitative" effect of consumer demands, and in commodity production, by constantly adapting to a changing market situation it is able to increase considerably the quantity of values acquired and its labor payment. Thus, for example, I. N. Zhirkovich,[2] on the basis of Volokolamsk budget materials, established the effect of the development of a farm's marketability shown in Table 4–4.

TABLE 4–4*

| Money Receipt from Agriculture per Worker (Rubles) | Assumed Net Income (6 Rubles per Worker in Groups of Farms by Desyatinas of Land Used per Worker) | | |
|---|---|---|---|
| | *0.0–2.5* | *2.5–5.0* | *over 5.0* |
| 0–60 ........ | 50 | 69 | — |
| 60–120 ........ | 144 | 134 | 110 |
| >120 ........ | — | 204 | 154 |

\* Editors' note.—The meaning of this table is not entirely clear in the Russian original.

The reader who has attentively studied the first chapters of our inquiry can clearly see that the subject of our analysis is precisely such a farm which has been drawn into commodity circulation. If we speak of its consumer character, we understand by this the consumer demand influence in establishing the basic economic equilibrium of the labor farm and not the qualitative influence of consumption on farm structure. This qualitative influence takes place in the nonmonetary farm and is retained to a very small extent in the farms we have studied which have passed over to monetary and commodity production. Only that which is advantageous to have in kind is retained. Usually, depending on area and type of farm, this is vegetables, potatoes, milk, meat, oats, and some other grains. (See Table 4–5.)

---

1 Editor's note.—Reading *kon"yunktury*, instead of *kul'tury*.

2 *Sel'skoe i Lesnoe khozyaistvo* [Farming and Forestry], Nos. 5–6 (1922), p. 21. See there, too, tables for Vologda budgets for the dependence of conventional net income on amount of money received per desyatina of land for use.

TABLE 4–5

PERCENTAGE MARKETED OF CERTAIN ITEMS

| | | Volokolamsk | Gzhatsk | Porech'e | Sychevka | Dorogobuzh |
|---|---|---|---|---|---|---|
| Rye | grain)..... | 4.1 | 0.0 | 0.0 | 0.0 | 0.0 |
| | straw)..... | 0.0 | 0.0 | 6.0 | 0.7 | 2.4 |
| Oats | straw)..... | 10.5 | 0.0 | 3.8 | 0.0 | 0.0 |
| | grain)..... | 1.2 | 0.0 | 7.2 | 0.0 | 0.9 |
| Potatoes ........ | | 1.2 | 0.0 | 1.2 | 0.2 | 3.8 |
| Flax | fiber)..... | 99.5 | 100.0 | 85.3 | 97.2 | 79.5 |
| | seed)..... | 51.7 | 64.8 | 58.9 | 62.4 | 56.6 |
| Vegetables ...... | | 10.0 | 0.0 | 0.9 | 0.0 | 1.1 |
| Clover hay ..... | | 1.9 | – | – | 3.7 | 0.0 |
| Meadow hay .... | | 1.3 | 0.2 | 4.1 | 6.7 | 0.1 |
| Milk .......... | | 0.4 | 0.0 | 0.0 | 0.0 | 0.0 |
| Meat .......... | | 0.0 | 0.0 | 0.0 | 0.0 | 0.0 |

Thanks to its contact with the market, the farm is able to throw out of its organizational plan all production sectors which give little income and in which the product is obtained on the farm with greater effort than that required to obtain its market equivalent by other forms of economic activity which give greater income. Only that which *either gives a high labor payment or is an irreplaceable production element for technical reasons* remains in the organizational plan.

In differing soil and climatic production conditions and in different states of the local market situation, the combination of production elements will vary widely. In direct proximity to large industrial centers, we will encounter farms forcing up fresh milk or vegetable production; farther off on sands we will see farms with extensive potato crops, and on clayey loams, flax. In northern areas with abundant fodder, we will come on dairying for export, and, within the sphere of influence of ports, on the deep black earth soils we will find extensive grain production.

Given an unmodified type of peasant *farm*, the basis of which we have analyzed in preceding chapters, we will always encounter in it the most varied systems of agricultural *production*. Wishing to recognize a pattern in the way these economic structures are formed, we can follow, link by link, all of their organizational plan, using the usual methods of organizational calculation elaborated by the German schools of Goltz and Aereboe, and introducing certain additions and alterations due to the peculiarities of the labor farm. The classical method for drawing up an organizational plan is to establish a sequence of organizational considerations and calculations such that each subsequent stage could be rather fully constructed on the data and figures obtained as a result of work on preceding stages.

In order to look at the peasant farm's organizational plan in all its detail, it is essential for us to review the following sequence of organizational considerations, which we have adjusted to the peculiar features of the family farm.

1. Choosing the farm's trend on the basis of available information on income from individual crops, methods of raising crops, and livestock accepted or capable of being adopted in the particular area.

2. Organizing individual sectors of the peasant farm and making subsidiary estimates.

*a*) Account of the family labor force and its consumer demands.

*b*) Account of land held and possible land for use.

*c*) Organization of field-cropping.

*d*) Organization of draft (workhorses).

*e*) Organization of feed-getting.

*f*) Organization of commercial livestock.

*g*) Organization of manure.

*h*) Organization of the kitchen garden, orchard, and other sectors.

*i*) Physical organization of the area.

*j*) Account of all work in agriculture.

*k*) Organization of equipment.

*l*) Organization of technical production, cottage industry, and crafts and trades away from home.

*m*) Organization of buildings.

*n*) Organization of capital and money circulation.

3. Verifying the balances.

*a*) The balance and organization of labor.

*b*) The estimate and calculation of income.

As will be seen subsequently, the organizational problems we have listed are given in an order more or less corresponding to the sequence of organizational considerations. Another sequence, of course, might also be proposed. However, practical experience shows, whatever the sequence adopted, that in working out any of the organizational sections we would always have to take account more or less hypothetically of all the others, and frequently, in going through a whole series of the first sections, we would have to encounter difficulties and to return again to the first section, starting the work afresh. Only by means of gradual and repeated amendment of the calculations can one finally balance up all the farm sectors into an entire system.

Readers acquainted with the methods for drawing up organizational plans in capitalist agriculture can observe that our system is quite close to that of, say, Goltz, and at first glance will not find in it anything specifically peculiar to the labor farm. Therefore, in approaching an item-by-item survey of the organizational plan, we draw the reader's attention with particular insistence to the nature of our further considerations, since the peculiar features of peasant farm organization do not consist in the sequence of these considerations, but in the criteria with the help of which they are effected.

### Account of the Family Labor Force and Its Consumer Demands

For us, the farm family is the primary initial quantity in constructing the farm unit, the customer whose demands it must answer and the work machine by whose strength it is built. To avoid misunderstandings, we consider it essential to repeatedly state that the forms of farm and production created by the family are largely preordained by the objective general economic and natural conditions in which the peasant farm exists. But the volume of economic work itself and the mechanism for constituting the farm derive predominantly from the family, taking into account all other elements of the economic circumstances.

We have reviewed in detail family composition and the work force structure at different phases of its development in Chapter 1, and there is no point in repeating them here. Therefore, we limit ourselves to a brief inquiry into the quantitative expression of the consumer demands, which are the basic stimulus in the labor family's economic activity, and into their elasticity. Table 4–6, which we have taken from S. A. Klepikov's work, gives us a conception of the basic item of the peasant's personal budget—the actual consumption rates for various forms of food.

As is seen from the table, peasant diet is fairly stable and varies sharply only in produce, which to some extent is a "luxury." Consumption rates for clothing and other items in the personal budget vary much more, as may be seen from Table 4–7.

The elasticities we have shown by comparing individual items of the personal budget by areas appear with still greater prominence by comparing farms that differ in wealth. Thus, for example, we have the instances in Table 4–8 where consumption is constricted by a reduced level of well-being.

TABLE 4-6

PEASANT FAMILY CONSUMPTION IN TERMS OF AN ANNUAL MALE CONSUMER (PUDS)

| Guberniyas | Grain Products: Flour, Groats, Legumes | Potatoes | Vegetables and Fruit | Vegetable Oil | Sugar | Meat and Fish | Milk, Sour Cream, Curds | Butter | Eggs |
|---|---|---|---|---|---|---|---|---|---|
| Vyatka ......... | 28.5 | 4.7 | 4.5 | 0.06 | 0.13 | 1.08 | 17.6 | — | 0.16 |
| Vologda ........ | 20.3 | 7.4 | 2.0 | 0.08 | 0.38 | 1.29 | 13.8 | 0.09 | 0.06 |
| Olonets ........ | 29.0 | 10.3 | 3.0 | 0.24 | 0.40 | 7.74 | 16.0 | 0.34 | 0.05 |
| Novgorod ...... | 26.8 | 10.5 | 4.2 | 0.14 | 0.45 | 1.39 | 15.5 | 0.11 | 0.11 |
| Kostroma ...... | 19.3 | 6.0 | 4.6 | 0.23 | 0.42 | 0.84 | 10.1 | 0.12 | 0.14 |
| Moscow ....... | 17.1 | 15.5 | 3.7 | 0.40 | 0.44 | 1.91 | 18.1 | 0.21 | 0.04 |
| Kaluga ......... | 17.7 | 11.3 | 5.9 | 0.25 | 0.34 | 2.00 | — | 0.01 | 0.00 |
| Tula .......... | 21.3 | 27.8 | 7.0 | 0.23 | 0.34 | 2.19 | 11.6 | 0.06 | 0.15 |
| Penza ......... | 21.1 | 15.0 | 3.4 | 0.19 | 0.20 | 2.01 | 10.0 | 0.10 | 0.14 |
| Tambov ....... | 21.1 | 15.7 | 6.9 | — | — | 1.74 | 17.3 | 0.02 | — |
| Khar'kov ...... | 23.7 | 7.2 | 3.2 | 0.26 | 0.12 | 3.14 | 3.5 | 0.10 | 0.16 |
| Poltava ....... | 19.7 | 14.3 | 8.4 | 0.19 | 0.20 | 3.24 | 7.4 | — | 0.09 |
| Kherson ....... | 34.5 | 10.8 | 3.2 | 0.27 | 0.18 | 2.84 | 0.1 | — | 0.10 |
| Average .. | 23.14 | 12.1 | 4.6 | 0.19 | 0.28 | 2.45 | 13.7 | 0.10 | 0.09 |

TABLE 4–7

AVERAGE ANNUAL EXPENDITURE PER CONSUMER

|  | Clothing (Rubles) | Soap (Russian Pounds) | Lighting (Rubles) |
|---|---|---|---|
| Novgorod guberniya ....... | 10.5 | 3.3 | 0.60 |
| Starobel'sk uezd .......... | 21.15 | — | 0.60 |
| Volokolamsk uezd ......... | 24.94 | 9.8 | 1.12 |
| Gzhatsk uezd ............. | 9.99 | 6.5 | 1.36 |
| Porech'e uezd ............. | 6.40 | 2.8 | 0.67 |
| Sychevka uezd ............ | 7.78 | 3.8 | 1.01 |
| Dorogobuzh uezd .......... | 5.61 | 2.5 | 0.55 |
| Vologda uezd ............. | 12.73 | 3.9 | 1.04 |
| Tot'ma uezd .............. | 4.74 | 2.1 | 0.57 |

TABLE 4–8

| Total Annual Expenditure per Consumer on Personal Needs (Rubles) | Including (in Rubles) | | |
|---|---|---|---|
|  | Food of Vegetable Origin | Vodka, Tea, Sugar, Tobacco, Etc. | Clothing |
| More than 90 .............. | 34.60 | 18.00 | 88.35 |
| 70–90 ..................... | 31.20 | 10.64 | 66.42 |
| 50–70 ..................... | 25.10 | 7.81 | 50.97 |
| Less than 50 ............... | 20.60 | 5.05 | 35.37 |

Summarizing all expenditures on personal needs and expressing them in terms of one consumer, we have the rates in Table 4–9, which are the basic figures in organizing the farm.

TABLE 4–9

ANNUAL EXPENDITURE IN KIND AND IN MONEY
PER CONSUMER (RUBLES)

| | |
|---|---|
| Volokolamsk uezd, Moscow guberniya ...... | 100.1 |
| Novgorod guberniya ...................... | 76.6 |
| Starobel'sk uezd, Khar'kov guberniya ....... | 87.3 |
| Gzhatsk uezd, Smolensk guberniya ......... | 75.4 |
| Porech'e uezd, Smolensk guberniya ........ | 72.9 |
| Sychevka uezd, Smolensk guberniya ........ | 72.9 |
| Dorogobuzh uezd, Smolensk guberniya ..... | 72.0 |
| Vologda uezd, Vologda guberniya .......... | 64.1 |
| Tot'ma uezd, Vologda guberniya .......... | 51.8 |

In using these figures, we must not forget that they are not something fixed but can, as we see, fluctuate within very wide limits. An increase in these rates depends not only on increased incomes and the larger budget which follows but also on an expansion of the demands themselves due to elements of higher urban culture that penetrate into the countryside. In this case, apart from the quantitative increase in the budget, its structure also changes, as is seen from the following analysis of the influence of an increase in the extent to which the farm is money based, and in having crafts and trades. Thus, for Starobel'sk uezd, Khar'kov guberniya, see Table 4–10.

TABLE 4–10
EXPENDITURE PER CONSUMER (RUBLES)

| | Percentage Gross Income in Money | | |
|---|---|---|---|
| | *0–50* | *50–75* | *>75* |
| Grain ......... | 25.9 | 23.3 | 20.3 |
| Clothing ...... | 20.4 | 20.80 | 26.0 |
| Vodka ........ | 0.71 | 0.77 | 1.27 |
| Tea, sugar .... | 0.85 | 0.84 | 1.82 |

The influence of the extent to which the farm is money based may be noted still more sharply in the type of consumption in the northern countryside where there are crafts and trades. Thus, for example, for the Moscow and Smolensk guberniya flax area we have the rates in Table 4–11 for expenditure per consumer on clothing (rubles).

TABLE 4–11

| | Percentage of Personal Budget in Money | | |
|---|---|---|---|
| *Consumer Budget* | *1–40* | *40–50* | *50–100* |
| 0–70.0 rubles ......... | 5.60 | 5.80 | 6.04 |
| 70.1–80.0 rubles ...... | 5.85 | 9.65 | 18.81 |
| 80.1–90.0 rubles ...... | 6.85 | 11.12 | 22.50 |
| >90.0 rubles ...... | 8.77 | 19.40 | 34.75 |

As we see, in areas of commodity farming, and especially in areas of crafts and trades, under pressure of new urban habits and a range of new urban demands that penetrate the foundations of country life the structure of consumption and its level are subject to very considerable changes.

It is essential to remember that the consumption rates we have quoted are precisely rates of real consumption and by no means a quantitative expression of demands themselves as such. Speaking generally, the demand for any product for personal consumption cannot be expressed by any one figure; and if, generally speaking, it can be expressed in figures, then it is in the form of a whole scale of consumption rates which corresponds to the gradual satiation of demand and its extinction.

In accordance with what has been said, the rates we have quoted are not a quantitative expression of any "consumption living standard," with which we are constantly reproached, but are degrees of satiation of demand corresponding to the on-farm equilibrium factors we have studied in earlier chapters. Hence, it is clear that the consumption levels we have quoted depend not only on the demand pattern of the families studied but also on the pattern and conditions of their productive work.

Thus, to sum up, we can establish that personal budget size per consumer fluctuates around 70–100 rubles, giving an average family an annual budget of 500–800 rubles. This is approximately the sum which the peasant family's economic activity should give to achieve the basic economic equilibrium, apart from income needed to renew capital circulating in the production process. Moreover, as we will see below, the family's level of well-being depends not so much on development of demands as on the production conditions available to peasant family labor.

### Account of Land Held and Possible Land for Use

The organizational plan of an agricultural unit based on hired labor takes the organization of its area as the initial determinant in constructing its economy; and although it finally completes this section of the organizational plan corresponding to the situation in other sections, it may freely take the plan as the starting point for its considerations. But in the family farm where it is not land but the family labor and consumer elements which are given, the problems of organizing the area naturally cannot be so significant.

In countries where, by the law or custom of nonpartible inheritance or because the economic machinery for production has become set in its routine, the land regime makes land use somewhat immobile, we encounter the land area as a determinant, even in family farms. Disharmony between family labor force and area worked is regulated either by hiring a work force and going to work on the side, or by combining the farm's intensity in such a way as to displace it from the optimal level as regards the market. But in countries where the land regime makes the land area extremely mobile, the determining significance of "available" area falls to zero.

Communal repartitions, long-term and short-term rentings, and (for countries where private property in land still exists) purchases and sales permit adequate adjustment of size of land for use to the farm's requirements. A good illustration of this is the influence of family composition on size of land rented which we have established for Starobel'sk uezd: this can be seen from the table we have already quoted (Table 4–12). Looking at the table, we see that under pressure from the increasing burden of consumers on workers the amount of land rented obediently increases.

TABLE 4–12

RENTED ARABLE PER WORKER (DESYATINAS)

| Own Arable per Worker (Desyatinas) | Consumers per Worker | | |
|---|---|---|---|
| | 1.00–1.30 | 1.31–1.60 | >1.60 |
| 0.1–2.0 .... | 0.63 | 1.16 | 1.45 |
| 2.1–3.0 .... | 0.19 | 1.45 | 1.27 |
| 3.0–7.0 .... | 0.41 | 1.51 | 2.99 |
| Average ... | 0.41 | 1.37 | 1.60 |

EDITORS' NOTE.—This table purports to be the same as Table 3–24, but the data are different.

The best confirmation, however, of the instability of peasant farm land areas is the results we have already quoted from the works of N. N. Chernenkov, P. Vikhlyaev, A. Khryashcheva, and K. Kushchenko on peasant farm dynamics. These are constructed by comparing repeated censuses and show most clearly the small degree to which peasant farms retain their old land areas, even for comparatively short periods of 10–15 years (see p. 67).

Therefore, if we do consider it essential for the peasant farm organizer also to begin his considerations with the land, we take it, not as a "given" initial determinant, but as very important initial material which we should inevitably take into account in our further deliberations. In approaching farm organization, we naturally should take account of how much land is available to the farm, its disposition, quality of soils, relief, and presence of exclusively meadow and exclusively pasture areas, i.e., those which, due to moisture or relief, cannot be used in any other way. Apart from this, it is essential to disclose the land rental opportunities which the farm may have. All this information is absolutely essential in order to construct the further sections of the farm's organizational plan, even though we did not take land as the initial material for our economic development.

Having finished the farm organization in its main sections, we will return again in the section to organization of the area in the land use measures meaning of the word. Prior to reviewing this section, we postpone all questions about the technical organization of the area.

*Organization of Field Cultivation*

In making a record of the basic elements that comprise the labor farm—the family and land—we can also pass on to the organization of the farm itself, the cultivation of its fields, meadows, livestock, and other sectors. The organizer ought naturally to begin his work by arranging that sector which is the dominant item in his income. For a suburban dairying area, this will be cattle; for market garden areas, it will be vegetable raising. Since for the overwhelming majority of Russian farms field crops are the most important sector, we put that at the basis of our considerations.

In order to organize cultivation of the fields, it is essential for us to find the best system, i.e.:

1. To select crops and forms of exploiting them which will give the highest and most stable payment for labor. Moreover, not only commodity crops have to be selected but also crops to meet the family's needs in kind, if this is more advantageous than acquiring the produce on the market by expanding the commodity area. In taking account of the advantageousness of commodity crops, one should, as Filippovskii rightly points out, also pay attention to commodity circulation costs, i.e., the overheads and outlays in kind and in money connected with the sale and purchase of goods.

2. To combine them with other auxiliary crops in a relationship and crop rotation which would not exhaust the soil but would restore its fertility.

3. To establish a rotation and relationship of crops that would give the most convenient distribution of labor throughout the year, i.e., a smooth distribution without excessive bunching in critical periods and without obligatory unemployment in other seasons.

4. Having established the best system of field cultivation in accordance with the tasks mentioned above, we must determine the desired *size* (volume) of field cultivation (arable) applicable to our farm family and its work force.

Having information at our disposal on the yields of individual crops, the labor and capital expenditure they need, as well as data on the state of the market situation in the area of our farm and the means of communication, it is not difficult to make clear which crop and what form of exploitation give the highest labor payment and are thus the most desirable for the farm. Our budget literature enables us to establish the rates of such payment for certain areas, as is seen from Table 4–13.

The rates of labor payment we have quoted vary extremely by crops and by areas, and no less over time. It is not difficult to trace the factors that cause this variation. First of all, there is the soil and the

TABLE 4–13

PAYMENT BY COST OF PRODUCE EXCLUDING OUTLAYS ON MATERIALS PER
WORKING DAY (KOPEKS)

| Uezd | Rye | Oats | Flax | Clover | Average Payment per Working Day |
|---|---|---|---|---|---|
| Starobel'sk ......... | — | — | — | — | 133.0 |
| Volokolamsk ....... | 84.6 | 109.6 | 157.1 | 256.0 | 138.0 |
| Gzhatsk ........... | 45.1 | — | 110.1 | — | 137.0 |
| Porech'e ........... | 54.3 | 63.7 | 115.7 | — | 123.0 |
| Sychevka .......... | 63.8 | 94.3 | 115.2 | 672.0 | 156.0 |
| Dorogobuzh ....... | 71.0 | 106.9 | 97.0 | 507.5 | 147.0 |
| Vologda ........... | 87.0 | 83.0 | 91.0 | — | 86.0 |

climatic conditions which influence the harvest and work forms. It is sufficient to trace the influence of categories of soil, even if only by the inquiries on Saratov guberniya, to become convinced of this factor's significance. The location of the farm in relation to the market, i.e., the means of communication which connect them, has no less, if not greater, significance.

Thus, for example, in his work *Die Rentabilität der Wirtschafts-system nach Thünens isolirtem Staat und in unserer Zeit* (Berlin, 1909), which is based on concrete material, Professor F. Waterstradt calculates the influence of distance from the market (by railway) for four farms, each of 250 hectares with the following systems:

1. A farm with alternate husbandry, sugar beet, and cattle-raising (80 cows).
2. A fodder farm with increased cattle-raising (160 cows).
3. A farm with permanent natural pasture.
4. A sugar beet farm (26 percent of the area under sugar beet).

According to Professor F. Waterstradt's calculations, the net income of these farms, depending on degree of fertility, will *change in the way shown in Table 4–14 with distance from sales point.*

TABLE 4–14

NET INCOME OF TWO-HUNDRED-FIFTY HECTARE FARM (THOUSAND MARKS)

| Distance from Market by Railway (Kilometers) | First Category of Fertility | | | | Third Category of Fertility | | | |
|---|---|---|---|---|---|---|---|---|
| | Farm System | | | | Farm System | | | |
| | I | II | III | IV | I | II | III | IV |
| 0 .......... | 45.7 | 42.4 | 42.7 | 50.1 | 20.6 | 20.9 | 24.9 | 20.6 |
| 25 .......... | 41.3 | 39.2 | 39.7 | 44.5 | 17.3 | 18.2 | 22.4 | 16.1 |
| 50 .......... | 39.3 | 37.1 | 37.8 | 41.5 | 15.4 | 16.5 | 20.8 | 13.6 |
| 75 .......... | 36.2 | 34.8 | 35.7 | 37.3 | 13.0 | 14.6 | 19.1 | 10.3 |
| 100 .......... | 34.2 | 32.8 | 33.8 | 34.6 | 11.5 | 13.0 | 17.6 | 8.2 |
| 300 .......... | 23.6 | 21.1 | 22.6 | 21.6 | 6.2 | 9.9 | 14.9 | 2.1 |
| 200 .......... | 18.0 | 18.9 | 21.2 | 13.8 | 1.4 | 7.4 | 12.9 | 4.5 |
| 400 .......... | 12.5 | 17.1 | 19.9 | 6.3 | 3.3 | 5.1 | 11.1 | 10.8 |

Looking at the table relating to the first, *highest*, category of fertility, we see that with distance from the market not exceeding 100 kilometers the farm of type IV is first in income. At a greater distance, up to 250 kilometers, first place passes to farms of type I, and at a distance of 300 kilometers or more type III begins to take the lead. At a lower level of fertility (third category), the picture changes and the type III farm predominates all the time. According to F. Waterstradt's calculations, the farm's distance from the railway station is of still greater significance.

No less interesting are the results of an investigation by one of the most outstanding Russian statisticians, G. I. Baskin, on the influence of distance from produce sales point on peasant farms in the south of Samara guberniya (in A. N. Chelintsev's version) (Table 4–15). Such

TABLE 4–15

| Distance to Sales Point | Long-Fallow as Percentage of Area Sown | Fallow | Pigs per 100 Desyatinas Sown |
|---|---|---|---|
| 0 . . . . . . . . . . | 24.0 | 1.0 | 2.7 |
| 0–25 . . . . . . . . | 27.4 | 3.6 | 4.2 |
| 25–50 } 50–100 } . . . . . . . . | 39.7 | 0.3 | 2.8 |
| >100 . . . . . . . . | 283.5 | 0.0 | 0.5 |

are the factors on which spatial differences depend; differences over time, however, depend on yield and price levels. We can see from the following calculations how great are fluctuations of this type.

A desyatina of flax in 1900–1910 in Volokolamsk uezd, depending on these factors, gave the rates of labor payment shown in Table 4–16.

TABLE 4–16

| | 1901 | 1902 | 1903 | 1904 | 1905 | 1906 | 1907 | 1908 | 1909 | 1910 | Average |
|---|---|---|---|---|---|---|---|---|---|---|---|
| Yield per desyatina (puds) . | 18.9 | 25.8 | 18.1 | 20.0 | 20.3 | 32.2 | 25.8 | 14.9 | 17.5 | 14.2 | **20.8** |
| Price (kopeks per pud) . . . . . . . . | 400 | 295 | 491 | 418 | 405 | 420 | 302 | 328 | 415 | 460 | **393** |
| Gross income per desyatina (rubles) | 75.6 | 76.1 | 88.7 | 83.5 | 82.1 | 135.0 | 77.9 | 48.9 | 72.5 | 65.3 | **80.6** |
| Gross income per desyatina with constant yield of 20 puds . . . . . . . . | 89.0 | 59.0 | 98.2 | 83.6 | 81.0 | 84.0 | 60.4 | 65.6 | 83.0 | 92.0 | **78.7** |
| Gross income per desyatina with constant price of 4 rubles a pud . . | 75.6 | 103.2 | 72.4 | 80.0 | 81.2 | 128.8 | 103.2 | 59.6 | 70.0 | 56.8 | **83.6** |

If the yield had remained the same for this period, let us say 20 puds of flax per desyatina, under the influence of price changes alone we would get gross income fluctuations as shown in row 4. If the price always remained at 4 rubles a pud, gross income depending on harvest fluctuations would be as in row 5.

Calculating for each of the series quoted the average arithmetic deviation from the general average of the figures for individual years, we obtain the following coefficients for each series.

Instability of harvest per desyatina ......... 20.6%
Instability of price per pud of flax ......... 13.0%
Instability of gross income per desyatina .... 16.6%

We see that prices are the most stable; the explanation is that for flax they are not determined by any one uezd and its harvest but by the whole world total flax production. In view of prewar Russia's almost monopolistic situation on the world market, however, these prices were somewhat inversely proportional to the Russian harvest, and thanks to this they smoothed out fluctuations in gross income compared with harvest per desyatina. In this case, the flax market, despite its world significance for Russian flax-growing, might be considered a local market, since it was almost entirely determined by the Russian harvest.

In all local market produce, where price fluctuations are connected with and counterposed to harvest ones, fluctuations in labor payment and income will, in general, be less sharp than those in prices and harvest taken separately. For produce with a wider (world) market, for which local prices determined by the world harvest are completely unconnected with local harvests, these fluctuations do not correspond, and income is frequently more unstable than prices or harvests.

Thus, for example, if we take the average fluctuations in Poltava guberniya in harvest, prices and gross incomes for rye, as local market produce, and for spring wheat, as world market produce, we obtain the measurement of instability shown in Table 4–17.

Looking at these figures, we see that, despite great fluctuations in

TABLE 4–17

|  | Instability (Average Deviation from the Average) of | | |
|---|---|---|---|
|  | Harvest per Desyatina | Price | Gross Income |
| Rye .............. | 33.4% | 26.0% | 15.4% |
| Spring wheat ...... | 31.1% | 19.1% | 32.6% |

rye harvests and prices, gross income from rye is more stable than the gross income from the world market crop, wheat. All the phenomena of these annual fluctuations which have been noted must undoubtedly be taken into account in estimating the advantageousness of individual crops. However, not the annual but the longer term fluctuations in the market situation are of still greater interest to us.

The chief importance for us is that long-term changes in the market situation completely alter the comparative advantageousness of crops, and frequently one which paid very well subsequently falls out of the rotation as a completely disadvantageous crop. Our institutes concerned with market forecasting, observing the state of the market and frequently foreseeing its fluctuations, ought in future to be responsible for a constant watch on the probable profitability of different crops, and by this comparative analysis give a pointer to the practical workers in agriculture as to the selection of the annual direction of their economic work.

Information on the comparative expected income from various spring grains is for us practical workers in agriculture immeasurably more important than any sort of barometer and index of the market situation for 20 or 60 commodities, which, unfortunately, the workers in these market forecasting institutes have not yet mastered. These are the conditions in which our farm, according to its soil, climatic, and market data, may select its most advantageous crops. To cultivate them as field crops, it is essential to analyze them from the viewpoint of agricultural science, putting them into a particular system of crop rotation and restoration of soil fertility.

For our part, it would be naive to attempt in these pages to expound the basic laws of contemporary agricultural science. It is enough for us to know that with a very small number of exceptions the repeated cultivation of one plant from year to year on one spot is impossible, since it causes so-called soil "exhaustion" for this crop, drains away the nutrient juices specifically essential for this crop, fills the soil with toxins, i.e., with plant secretions harmful to its cultivation, and so on. Therefore, from the viewpoint of agricultural science it is absolutely essential to alternate crops; moreover, numerous agricultural experiments have established the most favorable crop sequence. Thus, we know that in the northern area flax does very well after clover, that root crops provide for a following crop of grains, and so on. All these observations and scientific rules lead to a system of well-known crop rotations which guarantee the most stable and highest soil fertility.

Having determined what are, from an economic viewpoint, our most advantageous crops and those required to meet certain farm needs in kind (fodder, etc.), we should connect them in a particular crop rotation, often adding auxiliary crops, not very advantageous in payment for labor but essential for reasons of agricultural technique. The combinations of different crops are extremely varied. Some theoreticians of farm organization usually treat them as a series of typical *field-cropping systems*, distinguishing them mainly by the methods they use to restore soil fertility.

In one of our early works (1911), we investigated the various forms of field-cropping systems encountered in Russia. Making use of Professor A. F. Fortunatov's enormous library, we were able to reduce all the local statistical and agricultural studies to six types: (1) three-course, (2) two-course, (3) irregular cropping, (4) the Perm' system of irregular cropping, (5) the long-fallow system, and (6) various systems with manuring by grazing the stubble. The map in Figure 4–1 gives us an idea of the distribution of these systems, according to our summary, for the area of former European Russia toward the start of the twentieth century. In working out this map, all the field-cropping systems were divided into the following basic types listed above.

1. Three-course.  In this case, three-course means not so much the classical *rotation* of fallow, winter sown, and spring sown, as the economic system of three-course cropping in Russia, i.e., the division of the arable into transferable areas common to all proprietors, with obligatory common grazing after harvest—in a word, the *communal* three-field system of cropping. On the basis of painstaking investigations, we have succeeded in establishing the southern boundary of the area where the three-course system in this sense predominates; this is shown on the map in Figure 4–2.

Thus, here are included three-field farms with a rotation of fallow, spring sown, and partial leys, and, on the other hand, cases of three-course rotation—fallow, winter sown, spring sown—on one or two fields, or on several independent of one another and not connected with neighboring ones by a common and obligatory crop (the Perm' system of irregular cropping). I have also considered it not possible to include in this section three-field and abandonment rotations of the Siberian type—i.e., a long-fallow system in which a three-course rotation is worked three or four times and the area then abandoned for a long period.

2. Two-course.  A crop rotation of fallow, winter sown, or fallow, spring sown on two fields, with obligatory common grazing after har-

FIGURE 4–1

PEASANT FIELD SYSTEMS IN RUSSIA AT THE END OF THE NINETEENTH CENTURY

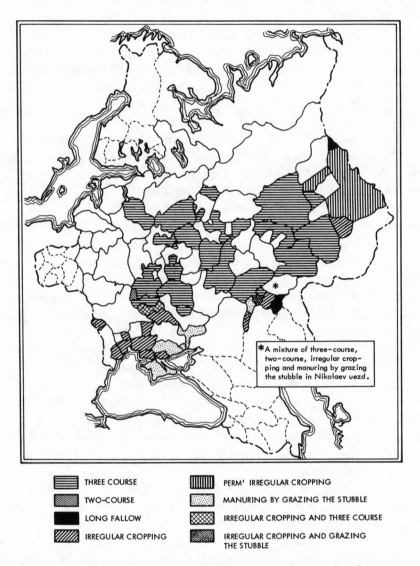

*A mixture of three-course,
two-course, irregular cropping and manuring by grazing
the stubble in Nikolaev uezd.

| | | |
|---|---|---|
| ▤ THREE COURSE | ▥ PERM' IRREGULAR CROPPING | |
| ▨ TWO-COURSE | ⣿ MANURING BY GRAZING THE STUBBLE | |
| ■ LONG FALLOW | ▦ IRREGULAR CROPPING AND THREE COURSE | |
| ▧ IRREGULAR CROPPING | ▩ IRREGULAR CROPPING AND GRAZING THE STUBBLE | |

vest, this system is in its general arrangement close to the three-course
rotation.

3. Irregular cropping. Included in this section are all "systems"
characterized by the fact that the individual farm fields have no
connection with one another and their cycle of sowings is carried out
completely independently, sometimes by the irregular sowing of grain
following grain, but sometimes having a certain periodicity, including common grazing on the stubble after a certain interval of years.

FIGURE 4–2

PROBABLE SOUTHERN LIMIT OF AREA WITH PEASANT THREE-COURSE SYSTEM IN
THE LATE NINETEENTH CENTURY

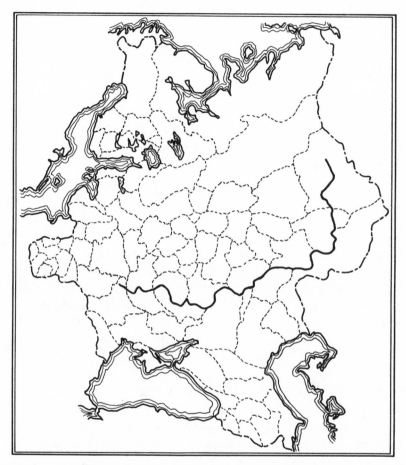

We have considered it convenient to separate from this group the
Perm' system of irregular cropping, as it is called, in which the periodicity is definitely sustained and amounts to a usual three- or four-
course rotation. It differs from the other systems only in that each
piece of land proceeds quite independently without any dependence
on the others. Thus, there is no spatial system, and only the temporal
one is observed.

4. The long-fallow system.   This section consists of systems in
which the exclusive use of abandonment as a method for restoring fertility makes it necessary for land used as arable *to pass to other categories*—steppe, forest, and so on. Here the period of abandonment
much exceeds the period as arable. One of the determinants of this
system is that the time to plow up the abandoned land is not deter-

mined by the time spent without sowing but by the land's "ripeness";
this is judged by the vegetational cover. Strictly speaking, this system
is close to the irregular cropping system we have established, since
while having a sequence (system) in time, it has no spatial one. However, the fact of transition from one land category into another obliges
us to treat it as an independent section.

5. The system of grazing the stubble.    This group is very broad
and includes a number of varied forms; it is purely artificial in character. Its determining characteristics are the presence of two or more
annual grazings on the stubble and, chiefly, together with a sequence
in time, the presence of some elements of a spatial system which con-
nects the separate farm fields.

In the two decades that have passed, certain changes have naturally
been noted in the geography of field-cropping systems. First of all, the
so-called ley systems have developed and continue to develop with exceptional rapidity in the Moscow area and in all western guberniyas.
In these systems, in which fallows are retained as a method for restoring soil fertility, sowings of annual or perennial grasses are introduced
and make the crop rotation into a system of semialternate husbandry,
restore the structure of the field, and, if legumes are included in the
grass mixture, directly enrich the soil with nitrogen. In many areas,
particularly in the sugar beet-sowing areas of the Ukraine and in
patches in other guberniyas, genuine alternate husbandry systems
without fallow have also been included in our systems of field cropping and have acquainted us with the sowing of root crops.

Such a subdivision is somewhat different from the usual one, and
so we consider we may say a few words about the classification system
as a whole and its themes. We dare suppose that every system—and, in
general, any theory—is something artificial, and its significance is always only temporary and pedagogic. It aims to enable the thinking
mind to perceive with as little effort as possible the whole mass of factual material and to grasp it as clearly as possible. In view of this,
there may be a great number of classification systems; they are all
"correct," and the whole question is which is simplest and most convenient. We personally ascribe great significance to the *purposive*
evaluation of the systems—i.e., evaluation of any system according to
how convenient it is for a particular purpose—supposing that for different purposes the material we have may be grouped into different
systems.

Taking this into account, to classify raw material *still not fully
studied* we ought to dwell on a system that rests on concrete, easily

established features (of a morphological character). Mainly, we should try to avoid introducing into the structure of the system any trace of a theory or hypothesis with historical, geographical, or any other content, i.e., of the sort that should, in any event, appear as the last stage of the work, the last conditional feature, but by no means be posed a priori.

In grouping the raw material, I have not considered that I had the right to use so-called "historical" systems which are so widespread among us. First, this would introduce an a priori premise about the specific historical sequence of systems. Second, the existing "historical" systems are, *from a historical point of view*, the crudest simplification of the development process of field-cropping systems and are also essentially morphological systems, and ones with poor morphological features, moreover.

Let us take for analysis the usual series (Ludogovskii): (1) long-fallow, (2) grain, (3) improved grain, (4) alternate husbandry, (5) free. For Russia, it has no *historical* significance. Thus, our southern irregular cropping with plant following plant, frequently according to the demands of the market, should, strictly speaking, be put in system 5. But at the same time, in the reality of Russia—in Saratov guberniya, for example—irregular cropping follows immediately after a long-fallow; in Poltava it precedes three-course; and, finally, in Kursk it arises on the ruins of three-course system. Systems involving abandonment, which evidently should be put in the long-fallow section, both precede irregular cropping and also follow it, and in many cases they arise on the ruins of a three-course system (Chernigov and Vladimir guberniyas).

Within the limits of the field-cropping systems we have reviewed, various forms of sequence of crops or crop rotations are possible. Their variety is so great that the painstaking researchers could write a large, multivolume study on them. Unfortunately, such a work was written by Ermolov in his day only as regards the advantages of the large-scale landlord farms. Peasant crop rotations are still waiting to be studied. Of course, within the limits of this book we cannot make such a summary. Therefore, in speaking of crop rotations and wishing to explain the peculiar features of rural activities, we limit ourselves merely to a review of our northern ley rotations.

The first form of clover-sowing on the peasant farm is the so-called partial ley. In its most widespread type, one or two zones in the winter field are allocated, and the rye is undersown with clover. The following year, now the spring-sown field, the first year's mowing of clover will be on these sections. In the third year, the clover sections are in the fallow field and are fenced off from the livestock. In the fourth year, the clover is usually left, in the winter-sown field the third year's mowing of clover is taken, and the rye in the other part of the same field is undersown with clover. In the fifth year, the sections where the clover has been are under flax. Since with this form of ley the clover is sown annually in the winter field, the rotation is as shown in Table 4–18.

TABLE 4–18

PARTIAL LEY ROTATION

| | Year | | | | | |
|---|---|---|---|---|---|---|
| Field | 1st | 2nd | 3rd | 4th | 5th | 6th |
| I ....... | $WC_w$ | $SC_1$ | $FC_2$ | $WC_3C_w$ | $SFlC_1$ | $FC_2$ |
| II ....... | S | F | $WC_w$ | $SC_1$ | $FC_2$ | $WC_3C_w$ |
| III ....... | F | $WC_w$ | $SC_1$ | $FC_2$ | $WC_3C_w$ | $SFlC_1$ |

W—winter-sown field.
S—spring sown.
F—fallow.
Fl—Flax.
$C_w$—undersown clover.
$C_1$—first year's mowing of clover, and so on.

We see that from the fifth and sixth years, when the rotation has been established, clover is mown each year on part of each of the three fields, and flax following on clover occupies part of the spring-sown field. We should recognize that this rotation is very flexible and convenient; though it lacks regularity, the proprietor is always able, without violating the sequence of crops, to adapt the fodder area according to his wishes. It is easy to pass from this crop rotation to a correct six-course rotation: it requires only the annual sowing of the winter course with clover—*not an arbitrary part* but *half* of it. Then each of the three fields is split into two, and we will have a six-field rotation with a six-year sequence of crops.

*Six-field Crop Rotation, Type I*

$WC_w - C_1 - C_2 - C_3 - S - F/WC_w$, and so on

This rotation is found very rarely, since it reduces the grain area too much and, by bringing the clover area up to 50 percent, causes clover to be sown too frequently on the same ground, which leads to clover sickness. Therefore, the third clover crop ($C_3$) is retained in the rotation only where there is a large market demand for timothy.

Usually, however, flax is put in place of the third clover crop, and this gives the favorite Volokolamsk rotation.

*Six-field Crop Rotation, Type II*
$WC_w - C_1 - C_2 - Fl - S - F/WC_w$, and so on

This rotation, which gives a considerable fodder area (33 percent), allows an equally considerable area of spring-sown grains to be grown. Flax following after clover is one-sixth of the whole rotation. At the same time, the fallow and winter sown is reduced, but the farm is not much concerned with the winter sown, since in any event its grain is enough for only six months, and the labor used in growing rye achieves a minimal payment compared with that for other crops, as we saw in Chapter 1. Therefore, this rotation is very popular and is rarely rejected, which cannot be said of the Yaroslavl' rotation favored by agricultural officers.

The *Yaroslavl' rotation*, as is well known, is an eight-course rotation on four fields, so that each year one field is under rye, one under clover, one is spring sown, and one fallow. Table 4–19 shows the crop sequence in this quite complicated rotation.

TABLE 4–19
YAROSLAVL' FOUR-FIELD CROP ROTATION

| | Year | | | | | | | |
|---|---|---|---|---|---|---|---|---|
| Field | 1st | 2nd | 3rd | 4th | 5th | 6th | 7th | 8th |
| I ...... | $WC_w$ | $C_1$ | $C_2$ | S | F | W | S | F |
| II ...... | S | F | $WC_w$ | $C_1$ | $C_2$ | S | F | W |
| III ...... | F | W | S | F | $WC_w$ | $C_1$ | $C_2$ | S |
| IV ...... | $C_2$ | S | F | W | S | F | $WC_w$ | $C_1$ |

We see that clover in this rotation is sown alternate years and cropped for two years, so that the clover field, too, is not sown to spring grains annually but in alternate years. This is very inconvenient on a flax-growing farm, since in years when the spring sown follows winter sown the flax does badly, and in years when clover is being grown part of its area should be devoted to oats and potatoes, thus causing a loss for flax-growing. Because of this, despite its advantages (the harmonious combination of winter and spring sown and fallow approximating to a three-course rotation, small number of fields, and so on), this rotation is inconvenient for flax-growing areas.

Moreover, the rotation is so complicated that the slightest deviation causes terrible confusion which is difficult to correct, and deviations occur very frequently. Sometimes, they forget to undersow the clover and sow the first spring grain in place of the clover; more frequently, they simply long for a third year's clover crop. The result is complete confusion. In Volokolamsk uezd, this rotation is most frequently rejected, and in 1910 two-thirds of the settlements with Yaroslavl' rotations had finally abandoned them.

The eight-year sequence on eight fields, called the Shipovo Volokolamsk eight-field rotation, is in somewhat better condition.

### The Volokolamsk Eight-field Rotation
$$WC_w - C_1 - C_2 - S - F - W - S - F$$

Despite its title, this crop rotation is not very widespread in Volokolamsk uezd, although it enables flax to follow after clover each year.

I shall not deal with the peasant farm seven-field, nine-field, and five-field rotations with a ten-year sequence, since they differ from those treated only in that clover is cropped not two but three years. In conclusion, I shall describe one curious rotation created by the peasants of Kholmets, a hamlet in Volokolamsk uezd. This rotation is an eight-field one, and each fallow is linked with a particular cycle of crops (Table 4–20). A new item here, as compared with the preceding rotations, is *pasture,* which we have indicated with a P.

TABLE 4–20

| Field | 1st | 2nd | 3rd | 4th | 5th | 6th | 7th | 8th | 9th |
|---|---|---|---|---|---|---|---|---|---|
| | | | | | | | | | *Year* |
| I ....$WC_w$ | $C_1$ | $C_2$ | P | W | S | F | P | $WC_w$ |
| II ....W | S | F | P | $WC_w$ | $C_1$ | $C_2$ | P | W |
| III ...P | $WC_w$ | $C_1$ | $C_2$ | P | W | S | F | P |
| IV ...P | W | S | F | P | $WC_w$ | $C_1$ | $C_2$ | P |
| V ....F | P | $WC_w$ | $C_1$ | $C_2$ | P | W | S | F |
| VI ....$C_2$ | P | W | S | F | P | $WC_w$ | $C_1$ | $C_2$ |
| VII ....S | F | P | $WC_w$ | $C_1$ | $C_2$ | P | W | S |
| VIII ....$C_1$ | $C_2$ | P | W | S | F | P | $WC_w$ | $C_1$ |

From this, it can be seen that each year a quarter of the area is under winter sown, a quarter is pasture, and an eighth is under spring-sown grain. This rotation is a complete contrast to the typical spring-sown Volokolamsk six-field, type II. It is an excellent cattle-farming rotation, since the three-year clover and the two-year fallow give ideal abundant pasture, and after this the livestock go over to the first-year fallow, which is then producing abundant grass. Unfortunately, according to the Kholmets peasants, sowings of flax do badly, and this rotation is hardly likely to become widespread in flax areas.

As regards pasture, peasant crop rotations proposed recently by A. G. Doyarenko at the Timiryazev Agricultural Academy Experimental Station are still more interesting and are based on an entirely new principle. The academy's experimental station has tenaciously and successfully worked on the problem of early fallows that give an appreciable increase in yields. Despite the obvious income to be gained from this, early fallows have not become accepted on the peasant farm because of the lack of pasture to which the livestock can be transferred from the fallow tilled in May or April. The task for the experimental station, then, was to find pasture. The answer was found by forming an abundant area of special fallows sown with pasture mixtures and especially of quick pasture crops between harvest and sowing which, undersown to rye along the boundaries, at harvest give a dense, low growth used for grazing throughout the autumn and in spring until the late potatoes are sown.[3] These are the methods for creating a fodder area and its ensiling, with other elements of field husbandry.

Crop rotations, as we have seen, provide a very flexible technical solution to the tasks that natural conditions, market situation, and internal economic factors set before the family farm. In addition, the *intensity of the factors of cultivation* which constitute the content of man's agricultural activity is important in describing the field-cropping system adopted.

Tillage, cultivation, and even harvest methods may be changed in their labor and capital intensity. For example, the same potato crop can be grown by using 40 or 120 workdays, with a corresponding harvest; a desyatina of fallow may have 1,000 or 3,000 puds of dung spread on it, and so on. The intensity of cultivation factors on each farm depends on price levels and local natural conditions. As we saw at the end of Chapter 3, the on-farm factors of the family undertaking determine this intensity to a considerable degree, sometimes making it rise above the optimal level for farms based on hired labor. Unfortunately, empirical studies of agricultural production technique are so insignificant that we are not in a position even to fully illustrate these statements.

After determining the most advantageous crops and linking them in a rational crop rotation from the viewpoint of agricultural science, we ought to check this rotation from the aspect of labor organization

---

3 EDITOR'S NOTE.—The meaning of this sentence is not entirely clear in the Russian version.

in time. Each crop has its own individual features as regards labor organization, and their labor intensive periods occur at different times. Table 4–21 and Figure 4–3, which we have calculated for Volokolamsk uezd, give quite a clear picture of this. As is seen from the work

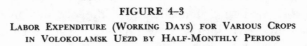

FIGURE 4–3

LABOR EXPENDITURE (WORKING DAYS) FOR VARIOUS CROPS
IN VOLOKOLAMSK UEZD BY HALF-MONTHLY PERIODS

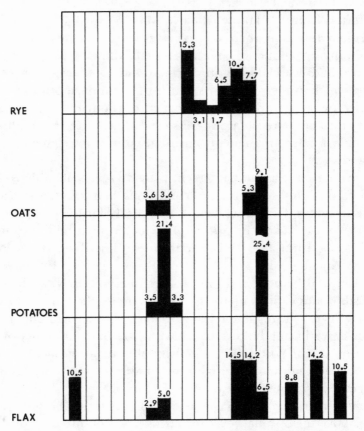

distribution over time, rye is predominantly a summer crop, potatoes and especially spring-sown grains are spring and autumn crops, while flax, unlike the others, involves expending energy in winter on the primary processing of the fiber.

For the peasant farm, the task is to compose its field cultivation of such crops and proportions that the critical moments characteristic of their labor organization do not coincide, and the general labor intensity on the farm should be more or less uniform. In this respect, the labor farm's tasks differ sharply from those of the capitalist farm, which solves the critical moments of its labor organization with the help of temporary labor, frequently from outside. The capitalist farm is, therefore, not merely unconcerned about distributing work as evenly as possible over the year, but even aims at making it uneven in principle and at timing the greatest blocs of labor for the cheap wage periods. Studies of a number of Austrian farms give us characteristic examples of labor distribution over time and we show one of these (Figure 4–4).

FIGURE 4–4

NUMBER OF WORKERS PER 100 HECTARES ON A BEET FARM IN LOWER AUSTRIA

(The two peaks indicate the planting and harvesting periods)

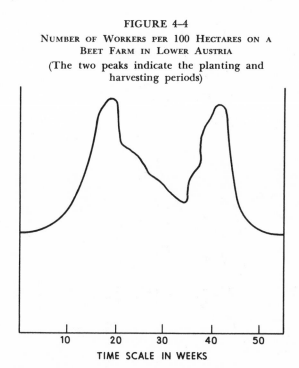

TIME SCALE IN WEEKS

It is clear that such a development curve for peasant farm labor intensity is quite senseless, since at critical periods the farm family would be worn out and for the rest of the year would be unemployed. Hence, on peasant farms there is a more uniform distribution of labor, as is seen from the diagram of a Volokolamsk farm (Figure 4–5).

Thus, by means of a series of repeated estimates we establish the field-cropping system best for the particular area and market situation; we introduce the necessary corrections if required for the specific features of this particular farm. We should then proceed to establish the volume of field-cropping activities, starting from the family labor force and the conditions present for land use. As we

## TABLE 4-21

### Labor Expenditure (Working Days) for Certain Crops in Volokolamsk Uezd by Half-Monthly Periods

| 1 Desyatina of | Jan. | Feb. | Mar. | Apr. 1 | Apr. 2 | May 1 | May 2 | June 1 | June 2 | July 1 | July 2 | Aug. 1 | Aug. 2 | Sep. 1 | Sep. 2 | Oct. | Nov. | Dec. | Total |
|---|---|---|---|---|---|---|---|---|---|---|---|---|---|---|---|---|---|---|---|
| Rye .......... | — | — | — | — | — | — | — | 15.3 | 3.1 | 1.7 | 6.5 | 10.4 | 7.7 | — | — | — | — | — | 45.0 |
| Oats .......... | — | — | — | — | 3.6 | 3.6 | — | — | — | — | — | — | 5.3 | 9.1 | — | — | — | — | 21.6 |
| Potatoes ......... | — | — | — | — | 3.5 | 21.4 | 3.3 | — | — | — | — | — | — | 25.4 | — | — | — | — | 58.2 |
| Flax .......... | 10.5 | — | — | — | 2.9 | 5.0 | — | — | — | — | — | 14.5 | 14.2 | 6.5 | — | 8.8 | 14.2 | 10.5 | 87.2 |

FIGURE 4–5

DISTRIBUTION OF WORK BY HALF-MONTHLY PERIODS

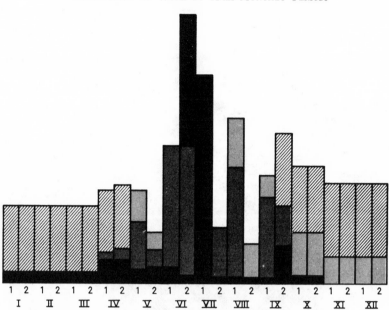

FLAX GROWING          EARNINGS OFF FARM

OTHER FIELD WORK      HOUSEHOLD WORK

MOWING

EDITORS' NOTE.—This figure appears to be the same as Fig. 3–4.

know, this question is finally solved by the equilibrium of the on-farm factors we have studied; yet we can give its objective maximum and minimum limits, called the labor and consumer rates.

At one time, much attention was devoted to both these rates in our agrarian literature. From the extensive literature of the question, most interesting are the works of N. P. Makarov, who summed up all preceding work in his report to the Second Congress of the Agrarian Reform League in 1917. In this case, the amount of arable which uses the family's whole labor force with normal intensity is taken as the labor rate. To determine this, it is necessary to take the labor intensity curve for the chosen crop rotation and analyze the number of desyatinas that our family can cope with in the period of greatest labor intensity.

If harvesting is taken as this period, the map (Figure 4–6), drawn up by N. P. Makarov, gives an approximation of the labor rate for bread grains. The considerable difference between north and south is

FIGURE 4–6

LABOR RATES FOR SOWING GRAINS

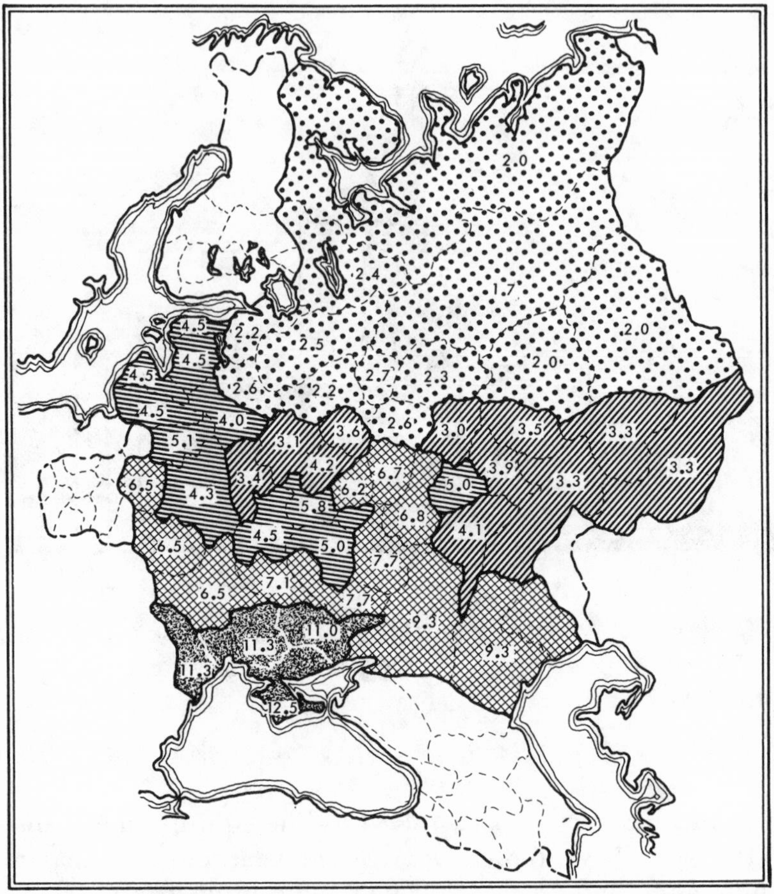

explained by differences in technology (sickle, scythe, reaper, etc.). In the chosen crop rotation, the secondary crops which give a maximum labor intensity in other periods have to be added to the grain-sown area; thus, we obtain in sum the sown area, which determines the size of the field cultivation.

If the area so calculated cannot be fully developed because of the conditions of land use, it then must be determined taking them into account. By means of reviewing the crop structure and the work methods, the farm must be somewhat intensified so that at the cost of a reduction in labor payment the family labor force can be rather fully deployed on the reduced area.

The consumer rate, of great significance in agrarian problems, has no particular value for us in view of the considerable development of crafts and trades in Russian peasant activity. However, if we understand it as the area of field cultivation with which the peasant family will be able to meet its needs at the lowest observed household consumption level or other levels of well-being, according to Makarov's works, for a medium-sized farm of the central Tambov guberniya zone we will have:

| | |
|---|---|
| Actual land use by family .................... | 9.8 |
| Consumer rate for: medium consumption ...... | 9.8 |
| highest consumption ....... | 12.8 |
| Labor rate using in agriculture the time of those going to work in crafts and trades, total ..................................... | 15.7 |
| One-Half ................................. | 12.8 |
| One-Fourth ............................... | 11.3 |

For Vologda uezd we have:

| | |
|---|---|
| Actual land use ............................ | 7.8 |
| Consumer rate: medium consumption .......... | 6.0 |
| increased consumption ......... | 7.9 |
| highest consumption .......... | 10.6 |
| Labor rate with full use on agriculture and all time on crafts and trades ............... | 10.0 |

Makarov's comparisons are particularly interesting in that they clearly show that the marginal labor rate cannot give the peasant the high level of consumption observed in the wealthiest village strata and founded on skilled crafts and trades or nonlabor income.

*Draft*

The account we have finished of field crops gives us a basis for calculating the draft power required on the farm, since nine-tenths of it is needed in field-cropping. Thus, for Starobel'sk uezd we have:

| *Horse Workdays Expended on* | *Percentage* |
|---|---|
| Fields ......................... | 92.7 |
| Meadows ...................... | 2.3 |
| Forest ......................... | 1.0 |
| Vegetable garden ............... | 4.0 |
| Total for farm ........... | 100.0 |

In the north, a somewhat greater amount of horse work is spent on meadows and forest, but we have no more precise estimates.

Since we do not aim at giving practical guidance on organizing peasant farms, we will not discuss here all possible forms of draft but will limit ourselves to an estimate of horse draft as the most widespread form. The number of horses required is reckoned in the same way the labor rates of land use are determined, according to the critical period for labor organization. But here, our deliberations proceed in the opposite direction. In calculating the labor rate, we took possible family labor intensity throughout the whole critical period and calculated the area with which this labor could cope. In calculating draft power, however, the area is given, and we must say how many horses are needed to cope with a particular sown area in the critically intensive period of horse work. Dividing the total horse work required by the horse's labor productivity rate, we obtain the figure we are seeking, which we round to a whole number. Thus, for Volokolamsk uezd see Table 4–22.

TABLE 4–22

HORSE WORKDAYS PER DESYATINA SOWN

|  | Apr. | May | June | July | Aug. | Sep. | Nov. Dec. | Total |
|---|---|---|---|---|---|---|---|---|
| Rye ....... | 0.2 | 0.4 | 11.9 | 2.6 | 10.5 | 0.3 | 0.9 | 26.8 |
| Oats ....... | 2.2 | 7.5 | — | — | 1.0 | 2.0 | 0.3 | 13.0 |
| Flax ....... | 5.4 | 7.8 | — | — | 3.1 | 1.8 | 2.6 | 20.7 |
| Potatoes ... | 2.6 | 13.4 | 2.6 | — | — | 6.1 | — | 24.7 |
| Clover ..... | — | — | 1.0 | 3.4 | 0.1 | 0.3 | — | 4.8 |

FIGURE 4–7

HORSE WORKDAYS PER DESYATINA SOWN

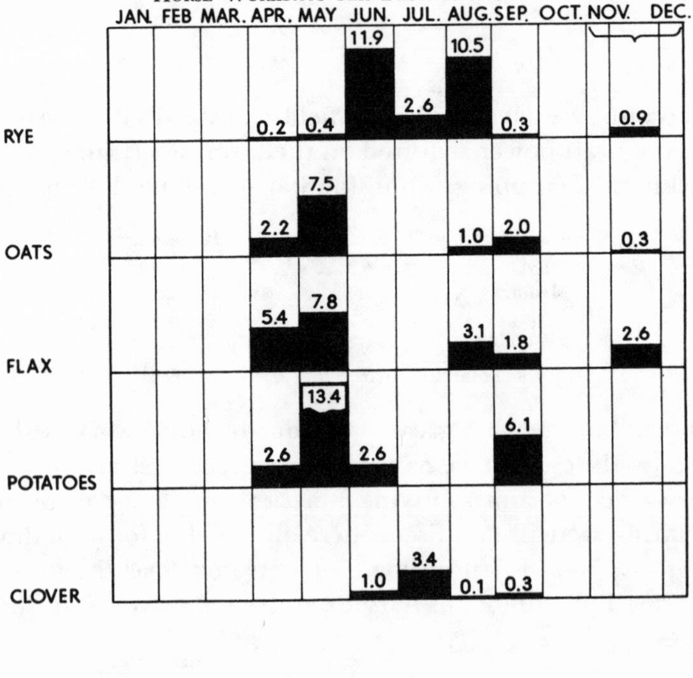

Quite naturally, given such a method for establishing the amount of draft power required, the number of horses on the farm should be more or less proportional to its sown area. Thus, for Starobel'sk uezd see Table 4–23.

TABLE 4–23
SOWN AREA AND WORKSTOCK (ITEM 59)
(per Farm)

| Sown Area | Desyatinas Sown | Workstock in Terms of Working Horses | Number per Desyatina |
|---|---|---|---|
| 0.01–3.0 ......... | 1.76 | 0.59 | 0.33 |
| 3.01–7.50 ........ | 5.56 | 1.80 | 0.34 |
| 7.5–15.00 ....... | 11.60 | 4.32 | 0.37 |
| >15.00 ....... | 23.09 | 7.08 | 0.31 |
| Average ....... | 9.62 | 3.18 | 0.33 |

In Starobel'sk uezd, there are 3.00 desyatinas of sown per horse. For other areas, we have: Volokolamsk uezd, 2.6 desyatinas; Gzhatsk uezd, 2.6; Porech'e uezd, 3.2; Sychevka uezd, 3.3; Dorogobuzh, 2.4 desyatinas. Because the number of horses depends on the critical period in their labor organization, which is extremely unevenly distributed through time, for the greater part of the year the peasant farm horse has no work and is, in general, little used. Table 4–24, showing how horse work is distributed on the flax and clover farm of Ivan Kokushkin in Novoselki, Sereda volost, Volokolamsk uezd, gives us a clear picture of how the farm's two horses are used.

It is obvious from the table that although the horses are used little, Ivan Kokushkin cannot manage with one horse, since in the second half of July and the first half of August his needs for draft power exceed that of one horse if we suppose that the demands amount to 12 workdays in the half-month. A comparison of these figures with data from other areas is shown in Table 4–25.

The fact that the Russian peasant horse is not used much explains why, although it is fed on hay, it endures much, serves long, and, in general, is little subject to disease. The horse's low utilization coefficient means that draft power is not cheap for our peasant farm. Table 4–26 gives a workhorse account for an average Volokolamsk uezd peasant farm with 2.52 horses.

Consequently, one working day cost 68.5 kopeks. It is self-evident that with the horse being used even less the cost of its upkeep divided by a smaller and smaller number of working days means such a high

## TABLE 4-24
### Horse Workdays per Farm

| | Jan. | Feb. | Mar. | Apr. 1 | Apr. 2 | May 1 | May 2 | June 1 | June 2 | July 1 | July 2 | Aug. 1 | Aug. 2 | Sep. 1 | Sep. 2 | Oct. | Nov. | Dec. | Total |
|---|---|---|---|---|---|---|---|---|---|---|---|---|---|---|---|---|---|---|---|
| Rye | — | — | — | — | — | — | — | — | 22 | — | — | 16 | — | — | — | — | — | — | 38 |
| Oats | — | — | — | — | — | — | — | — | — | — | — | — | — | — | — | — | — | — | — |
| Flax | — | — | — | — | 8 | 8 | — | — | — | — | — | — | 6 | — | — | 1 | — | — | 23 |
| Potatoes | — | — | — | — | ½ | 2 | — | ½ | ½ | — | — | — | — | 1 | — | — | — | — | 4½ |
| Clover | — | — | — | — | — | — | — | — | — | — | 2 | — | — | — | — | — | — | — | 2 |
| Hay meadows | — | — | — | — | — | — | — | — | — | — | 4 | — | — | — | — | — | — | — | 4 |
| Carting firewood | — | — | — | — | — | — | — | — | — | — | — | — | — | — | — | — | — | 12 | 12 |
| Other work | — | — | — | — | — | — | 3 | — | — | — | — | — | — | — | — | — | — | — | 3 |
| Hire to other farms | 20 | — | — | — | — | — | — | — | 2 | 6 | — | — | 1 | — | — | — | — | 8 | 37 |
| Family trips | 6 | 6 | 6 | 6 | 2 | 2 | 2 | 4 | — | 2 | 2 | 1 | 2 | 2 | 6 | 6 | 6 | 8 | 69 |
| Total | 26 | 6 | 6 | 6 | 10½ | 12 | 5 | 4½ | 24½ | 8 | 8 | 17 | 9 | 3 | 6 | 7 | 6 | 28 | 192½ |

FIGURE 4–8

HORSE WORKDAYS

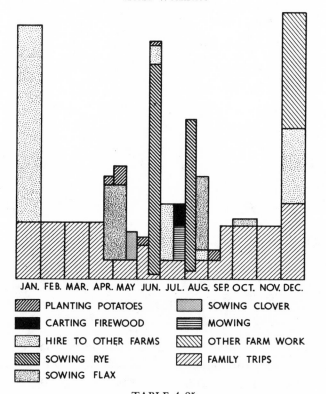

JAN. FEB. MAR. APR. MAY JUN. JUL. AUG. SEP. OCT. NOV. DEC.

▨ PLANTING POTATOES     ▨ SOWING CLOVER

■ CARTING FIREWOOD     ▤ MOWING

▦ HIRE TO OTHER FARMS     ▨ OTHER FARM WORK

▨ SOWING RYE     ▨ FAMILY TRIPS

▨ SOWING FLAX

TABLE 4–25

WORK PER HORSE FOR THE FARM

| Uezd | Total Work-days per Year | Percentage Use | Horse Work-days per Desyatina of Arable | Horse Work-days per 100 Human Workdays |
|---|---|---|---|---|
| Volokolamsk ....... | 48.6 | 16.6 | 12.3 | 29.3 |
| Gzhatsk ........... | 48.6 | 13.3 | 14.8 | 27.1 |
| Porech'e ........... | 79.6 | 21.8 | 12.6 | 31.2 |
| Sychevka .......... | 67.6 | 18.5 | 7.8 | 32.2 |
| Dorogobuzh ........ | 68.5 | 18.8 | 12.5 | 25.2 |

cost for draft power that the peasant cannot keep a horse. It is more advantageous to hire one, even though at a very high price. Thus, the cost of a horse's working day, assuming 30 days per desyatina and 50 rubles as the cost of maintenance, is as seen in Table 4–27 and Figure 4–9. These figures give us the economic basis for a more or less rational lack of horses.

Undoubtedly, in many cases the peasant whose horse has died or

TABLE 4–26

| Debit | | Credit | |
|---|---|---|---|
| Cost of horses at start of year ... | 113.10 | Cost of horses at end of year ... | 125.75 |
| Horses purchased during year .. | 6.70 | Manure (1818.6 puds) ......... | 12.76 |
| Share in general expenses ...... | 18.89 | Received for manure .......... | 15.93 |
| Care of horses ............... | 11.94 | Work on own farm: | |
| Feed ...................... | 120.67 | 104.6 days on field work | |
| Other expenditure .......... | 7.45 | 5.1 on meadows | |
| | | 19.7 on general work | |
| | | 52.0 on services to family ... | 124.34 |
| Total ................. | 278.75 | | 278.75 |

TABLE 4–27

| Farm Size (Desyatinas) | Horses Required | Cost of Horse Workday (Kopeks) | Loss or Profit Compared with Hire at 80 Kopeks a Day |
|---|---|---|---|
| 1 .......... | 1 | 160 | −80 |
| 2 .......... | 1 | 83 | − 3 |
| 3 .......... | 1 | 50 | +30 |
| 4 .......... | 1 | 42 | +38 |
| 5 .......... | 2 | 67 | +13 |
| 6 .......... | 2 | 56 | +24 |
| 7 .......... | 2 | 47 | +33 |
| 8 .......... | 2 | 42 | +38 |
| 9 .......... | 3 | 56 | +24 |

has been stolen is without a horse because he is unable to allocate from his miserly income the money necessary to get a new one. But on farms without many resources, it is simply not an advantage to the

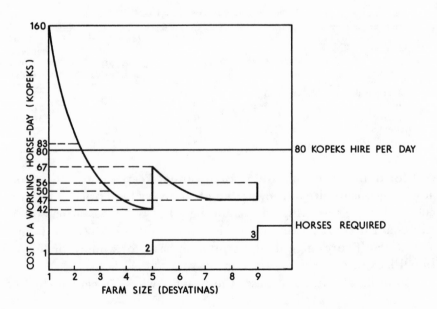

peasant family to have a horse, and they prefer to hire one, frequently with a man. On these grounds, curious cases sometimes occur, as in Vologda guberniya, when a semiproletarianized family hired a rich peasant who, in this case, was a worker not only receiving full payment for his labor but also taking a share from the labor payment of his master.

## Feed-getting

Having finished the account of the workstock, we cannot pass on to the organization of commercial livestock raising without a preliminary calculation of the farm's fodder resources. However strange it may seem to the reader who is not an agricultural officer, the organization of feed-getting is almost the center pin in farm organization.

All sectors of the farm are connected in one way or another with fodder organization, some as suppliers (meadow, pasture, field-cropping, housekeeping), others as consumers of the fodder stocks. Therefore, every change in the organization of any farm sector also reflects, to some extent, on the organization of feed-getting and, frequently, through it on other sectors of the organizational plan. Thus, for example, the literature has noted more than once the disintegrating effect of flax cultivation in the three-field peasant farm. When flax is introduced where feed-getting is overwhelmingly based on the straw from spring-sown grains, this stock of fodder is reduced. This, in turn, reduces the livestock sector, the amount of dung produced, and thus leads to soil exhaustion.

In practice, on the Russian peasant farm feed-getting is based on two different types of reckoning: (1) with a surplus of natural feed stocks, (2) with a distinctly marked lack of stocks.

In the first type, when there are huge amounts of straw from the spring grains (the southeastern extensive grain farm), many natural pastures (Siberia and the northeast of European Russia), or abundant supplies of offals from industrial production (sugar beet and distilling areas), the feed problem amounts to the fullest use of some form of commercial livestock farming. Here, feed-getting is not arranged according to the livestock required but, on the contrary, the stock are arranged according to the feed naturally obtained. One way to use the mass of heavy threshing-floor feeds and industrial offals is to transfer from horse to ox draft and to organize meat and draft production.

However, in the majority of Russia's guberniyas we meet with the directly contrary type of reckoning caused by a deficiency of feed, when the absolutely essential number of stock, sometimes required only for draft and dung, cannot be supplied with feed from the farm's resources.

A rough estimate, which apart from everything else is a check for all the sections of the organizational plan reviewed earlier, will easily show us the situation on most peasant farms in European Russia.

### The Organizational Plan of a Consumer Three-field Farm

1. The usual peasant family consists of 6 persons, equal to 3.5 full adult consumers, if we take the children's consumption in terms of that of adults.

2. For 3.5 consumers, 20 puds of grain a year per consumer are needed, which makes 20 × 3.5 = 70 puds per family.

3. With a harvest of 50 puds a desyatina (excluding seed), this requires 1.4 desyatinas of (winter) rye sown.

4. With a three-field system, this will mean 1.4 desyatinas of winter sown + 1.4 desyatinas of spring sown + 1.4 desyatinas of fallow, or 4.2 of arable in all.

4. To work 2.8 desyatinas of sown, the farm ought to have one horse (a horse can work up to 4 desyatinas of sown).

6. For 1.4 desyatinas of fallow at the usual peasant rate of 1,500 puds of dung per desyatina, 1,500 × 1.4 = 2,100 puds of dung are required.

7. One average head of cattle with normal peasant feeding provides about 500 puds of dung. Thus, to obtain 2,100 puds, 4.2 head of cattle are required, corresponding to the following composition of the herd—for example, 1 horse, 2 cows, 2 small stock.

8. To overwinter this stock, with 180 days in stall, 125 puds of hay a head are needed, that is, 4.2 × 125 = 525 puds of hay.

9. With an average hay harvest for Russia of 100 puds, 525 × 100 = 5.25 desyatinas of meadow are required, amounting to 1.24 desyatinas per desyatina of arable. The total farm area (arable and meadow) will equal 9.45 desyatinas or 10 desyatinas with the homestead.

10. If, however, we take the hay harvest at 90 puds—and this agrees better with our dry valley meadows—the meadow to arable ratio will be 1.4

However, it is by no means everywhere that peasant farms can have such an abundance of meadow. In the north of Russia, only in Vologda guberniya are there settlements where there is more than a desyatina of meadow to each desyatina of arable. In other places, due to the pressure on the land, meadows have to be plowed and feed-getting transferred to the arable. In accordance with this, we must alter the final section of our reckoning. Let us suppose that of our 1.4 desyatinas in the spring-sown field a whole desyatina is sown to oats, which gives 70 puds of fodder. Supposing that 10 puds of oats straw replaces 6 puds of hay, we can replace hay with the straw, and we will manage, not with 525 puds of hay, but with 466 puds, which requires

4.66 desyatinas of meadow. Then the meadow–arable ratio will be such that in our settlements there will be 11 desyatinas of meadow to 10 of arable, and the total area of the two on the farm will be not 9.45 but 8.86 desyatinas. If lack of land does not allow the farm to have this amount, the number of livestock must be reduced and manuring of the fields cut back, or, better, the peasant must sow part of the fields to grass.

Such are the serious difficulties we meet with in feed-getting in the organization of the consumer unit. It is self-evident that these difficulties increase many times if we try to develop livestock-raising as a commercial commodity sector of the farm and attempt to raise peasant family well-being by intensification.

The three tables given below (Tables 4–28, 4–29, 4–30) show us rather clearly the variety and intensity with which the peasant farm manages to obtain fodder in different circumstances. First, we will look at the way fodder is obtained on a three-field farm abundantly supplied with meadow. We can consider an average farm of Vologda uezd as such an example (Table 4–28).

TABLE 4–28

| | |
|---|---|
| Arable ...................... | 3.7 desyatinas |
| Meadow .................... | 6.1 |
| | 9.8 |
| Livestock: | |
| Horses .................... | 0.9 head |
| Cows ..................... | 2.1 |
| Small livestock ............ | 2.4 |
| Poultry ................... | 3 |
| Total in terms of cattle ...... | 3.6 |
| Expended on feed: | |
| Meadow hay .............. | 499.0 puds |
| Straw (from spring and winter grains) ............ | 93.0 |
| Chaff ..................... | 26.2 |
| Additives ................. | 6.1 |
| Grain .................... | 24.0 |
| Total ............... | 648.3 puds |

Although the farm has more than one and a half desyatinas of meadow to each desyatina of arable, it can maintain less than four head of cattle. This is explained by the poor hay harvests obtained from northern dry valley meadows and the very lengthy stalled period during the long northern winter. Nevertheless, although the amount of fodder gathered in by the Vologda farm is not great its quality is very high; so coarse, straw-type fodder is less than a fifth of the total.

The stock of fodder in a southern three-field farm in Voronezh guberniya is made up quite differently (Table 4–29). Here, almost all

TABLE 4–29

| | |
|---|---|
| Arable ...................... | 10.1 desyatinas |
| Meadow  ..................... | 1.2 |
| | 11.3 |
| **Livestock:** | |
| Horses ..................... | 1.6 |
| Oxen  ...................... | 1.0 |
| Cows  ...................... | 1.2 |
| Small  livestock  ............ | 16.0 |
| Total livestock in terms of cattle ................. | 7.8 |
| **Expended on feed:** | |
| Meadow hay  .............. | 108.8 puds |
| Straw (from spring and winter grains) ........... | 594.0 |
| Chaff  ..................... | 143.0 |
| Additives  ................. | 34.4 |
| Grain ...................... | 40.0 |
| Total  ................. | 920.2* |

\* Editors' note.—The total given in the Russian
original is 921.1. We have assumed the error to be in
the addition, but it may be in the constituent items.

the land is arable. With the short period of winter stalling (140 days
as against the 180 days in Vologda), these fodder stocks, which are one
and a half times those in Vologda, enable twice as many livestock
to be kept. On the other hand, the quality of the feed cannot be called
good, since three-fourths of it is coarse fodder, which explains the
high death rate among stock in the south and the great quantity of
small livestock. Here, feed-getting is almost entirely transferred to the
arable and based on using the wastes from the field crops.

We have quite a different picture (Table 4–30) on the clover farms
of Volokolamsk[4] uezd where, thanks to the clover, the farm creates exceedingly abundant feed stocks for itself. Looking at the table, we see
that because clover was introduced the Volokolamsk farm, without
increasing the meadow area, created abundant feed stocks of fine
quality. We can judge how beneficial are the results of introducing
sown grasses from Table 4–31, drawn up by Moscow statisticians,
which describes the changes that take place in livestock farming after
a more or less lengthy period of sowing grasses. We see that as grass-
sowing and the accompanying improvement in fodder stocks become

---

4 Editor's note.—Reading *Volokolamskogo* instead of *Vologodskogo*.

TABLE 4–30

| Arable | 7.1 desyatinas |
|---|---|
| Meadow | 2.2 |
| | 9.3 |

Livestock:

| Horses | 2.5 |
|---|---|
| Cows | 2.4 |
| Small livestock | 3.5 |
| Total livestock in terms of cattle | 6.1 |

Expended on feed:

| Meadow hay | 298.4 puds |
|---|---|
| Clover hay | 429.0 |
| Straw from winter grain | 271.0 |
| Straw from spring grains | 92.0 |
| Grain | 56.6 |
| Cake | 6.2 |
| Total | 1,153.2 |

FIGURE 4–10

ORGANIZATION OF FEED-GETTING

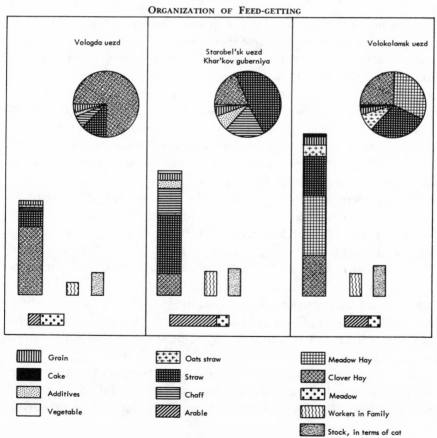

Vologda uezd

Starobel'sk uezd
Khar'kov guberniya

Volokolamsk uezd

| | | |
|---|---|---|
| Grain | Oats straw | Meadow Hay |
| Cake | Straw | Clover Hay |
| Additives | Chaff | Meadow |
| Vegetable | Arable | Workers in Family |
| | | Stock, in terms of cat |

TABLE 4–31

GRASS SOWING AND THE PEASANT FARM

| | Horses per 100 Households | Average Weight of Live Cow | | Average Annual Milk Yield |
|---|---|---|---|---|
| Settlements without sown grasses ................. | 115 | 16 puds | 24 Russian pounds | 98 vedros |
| Settlements sowing grasses for 1–3 years ........... | 115 | 17 | 16 | 111 |
| Settlements sowing grasses for 3–13 years .......... | 126 | 19 | 32 | 113 |
| Settlements sowing grasses for more than 13 years .. | 129 | 19 | 12 | 123 |

established the number of horses considerably increases. On the farms of peasants who start sowing grasses, the average weight of cows increases and the milk yield goes up rapidly, increasing by 30 percent in 13 years of clover-sowing. Such are the abundant fruits of introducing sown grasses. However, the proprietor who wishes to reconstruct his farm cannot stop at increasing the quantity of feed on the farm; it is also quite important to improve its quality.

As is seen from the tables, the farm feed resources are extremely limited and give very little opportunity to develop commercial livestock raising; this requires special measures. In our example, the effect of sown grasses on the feed situation is especially obvious. In areas where local conditions make the development of dairying or pig farming particularly advantageous, feed stocks may be increased either by introducing into the rotation roots and tubers for feed or by purchasing concentrates (cake and offals).

The problem of summer grazing is still more difficult in Russia. The lack of dry feed, apart from all other considerations, makes improbable the transfer of our livestock farming to a stalled system; the absence of good pasture obliges us to use for the stock all types of land which give any sort of feed at all. Peasant stock cause much harm to the farm by being pastured on the land, in the meadows until forbidden, in the forest, in the fallow field, in the meadow after mowing, and on the stubble. Their trampling destroys the soil structure and causes unbelievable losses to forestry. Some statistical information we have collected gives the following disquieting picture.

For Vologda guberniya, Tot'ma uezd, we have an average for several years where they start to pasture the animals on fallow, two of the three meadows, on arable, on meadow until forbidden, and on spring grain field until sowing (a typical Russian use), 24 days, which amounts to 17 percent of the total time. They are grazed on special pasture in the forest for the following 60 days, 41 percent of the total time; for a further 19 days, 13 percent of the time, they are pastured on fields of winter-sown stubble and on the aftermath (of meadows). For a further 42 days, until stalled, i.e., 29 percent of the total time, they are pastured on wastes, the stubble of the spring grains, and the forest. In all, this is 100 percent and 145 days.

The whole is estimated at 64 puds of hay per head. Thus, we see that special pasture serves for grazing only 40 percent of the total time, and half of that is forest grazing. These are the data for the north of Vologda guberniya. We quote the data for Vologda uezd in Table 4–32.

TABLE 4–32

AVERAGE FOR FIVE YEARS

| | | |
|---|---|---|
| Spring field before sowing ...... | 10.9 days | The type is the same, pasture figures as pasture for a very small part of the time. |
| Hayfields until forbidden ........ | 18.0 | |
| Fallow and two of the three meadows .............. | 22.1 | |
| Forest and pasture .............. | 47.5 | |
| Stubble ...................... | 43.8 | |
| | 142.3* | |

\* EDITORS' NOTE.—The total given in the Russian original is 152.2

Moscow guberniya data for 1912 is as follows.

Period 1. The livestock were driven out on April 18; the first bite appeared on May 2. Consequently, 14 days were dead. The stock had to be fed at home; they moved over the field but did not feed from it. Till May 20, they fed off the water meadows until it was forbidden.

TABLE 4–33

| | Percentage of Settlements |
|---|---|
| Fallow ........................... | 50.4 |
| Fallow and pasture ................. | 14.0 |
| Fallow and forest .................. | 7.5 |
| Fallow and part of the meadow in sequence ..................... | 2.1 |
| Fallow and rented pasture .......... | 2.9 |
| Pasture .......................... | 10.0 |
| Forest ........................... | 2.9 |
| Allocated meadow ................. | 1.0 |
| Rented areas ..................... | 3.0 |
| All types ........................ | 4.0 |

Period 2. Different villages use different grazing areas as pasture (730 villages in all) (Table 4–33).

Now let us turn to the extreme south, to Taurida guberniya, where pasture used is as shown in Table 4–34. Even if we take virgin land

### TABLE 4–34

Virgin land and forest .............. 60 days
Virgin land, forest, and fallow ....... 30
Virgin land, forest, and aftermath
    of meadows ..................... 50
Virgin land, forest, aftermath, and
    winter-sown stubble ............. 30
Virgin land and forest ............. 30
Forest ........................... 90

as pasture, here, too, forest, fallow, aftermath, and stubble are used as pasture. As is seen, everything is made to contribute to pasture, and this makes the fodder question still more basic and the sharpest problem in our agricultural thinking.

### FIGURE 4–11
#### ANNUAL GRAZING BY LAND TYPE

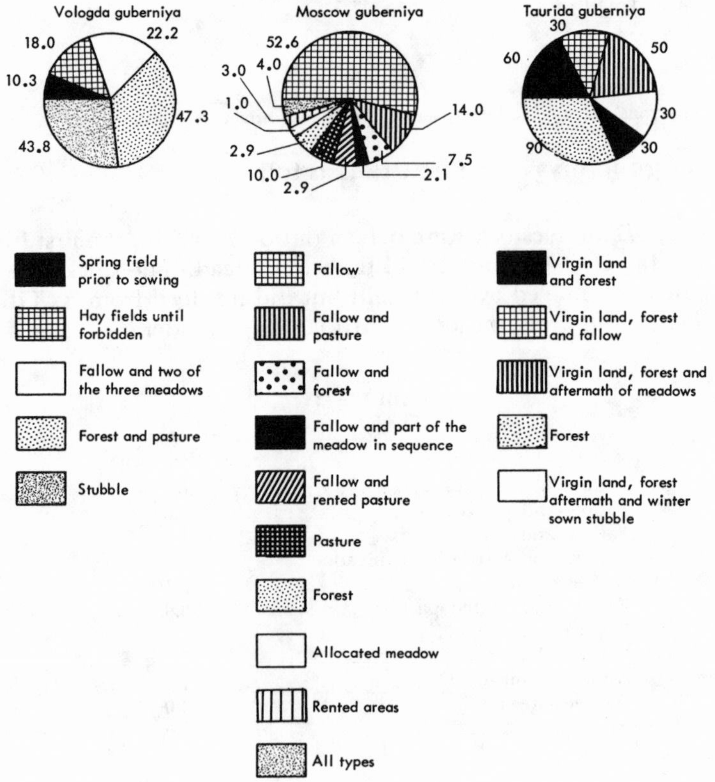

Vologda guberniya
18.0    22.2
10.3
43.8    47.3

Moscow guberniya
52.6
3.0  4.0
1.0
14.0
2.9
7.5
10.0    2.1
2.9

Taurida guberniya
30
60    50
30
90    30

Spring field prior to sowing

Hay fields until forbidden

Fallow and two of the three meadows

Forest and pasture

Stubble

Fallow

Fallow and pasture

Fallow and forest

Fallow and part of the meadow in sequence

Fallow and rented pasture

Pasture

Forest

Allocated meadow

Rented areas

All types

Virgin land and forest

Virgin land, forest and fallow

Virgin land, forest and aftermath of meadows

Forest

Virgin land, forest aftermath and winter sown stubble

## Commercial Livestock Farming

The fodder estimate example we made in the preceding section also determines the possible amount of commercial livestock. The type of feed stocks on the farm, market conditions, and, finally, work force available and demand for draft force and dung are the factors that determine the type of livestock farming.

Professor A. N. Chelintsev, who has devoted much study to livestock farming, has noted that pig farming is quite developed in intensive farming areas. Conversely, in extensive farms with poor quality fodder stocks sheep farming is common. Because of this, the intensity of livestock farming may be fully indicated by the number of pigs to that of sheep.

Of the three possible forms of cattle, the *draft and meat* one, based on using a great quantity of residues from threshing floors or industrial offals, naturally has a high percentage of oxen. Of the two others, the most intensive *dairying* form depends on a high percentage of cows in the herd (up to 75 percent, according to Chelintsev), while the *meat* form—animals being fattened for meat—naturally gives a much lower percentage of cows.

It is self-evident that in each of these types the organizational basis for commercial livestock farming is quite different in character. To review them in all their variety of possible forms would require dozens, if not hundreds, of pages. Therefore, in approaching their organization solely to throw light on the general economic problems before us we will deal with only two factors.

1. Study of herd composition and changes in composition over time in order, by means of this example, to trace how technical and economic factors mutually determine the forms of capital of the agricultural undertaking.
2. Study of the general annual turnover of livestock farming in order to acquaint the reader with the peasant farm's production machine in the livestock farming sphere.

To answer the first problem, we should first of all deal with the theoretical analysis of the herd's development. Let us take a 1925 herd of 100 cows, each weighing 20 puds, and 50 yearling calves, each weighing 10 puds. In the course of the year, 10 cows are culled because of old age, and 80 cows have a calf each.

Obviously, to retain the herd's composition at the end of the year 10 heifers in the course of the year must be reclassed as cows to replace those culled, and 50 of the newborn calves should be taken as future yearlings. These 60 head are *replacements* needed to maintain the same composition of the herd. The rest of the young animals—40 heifers and bullocks, and 30 calves—are surplus to replacement requirements and without harming the herd may be slaughtered or sold, together with the 10 culled cows, to provide the farm with income. Expressing cows and young animals, not in numbers of head, but puds of liveweight, we can represent the herd's development by Figure 4–12.

FIGURE 4–12

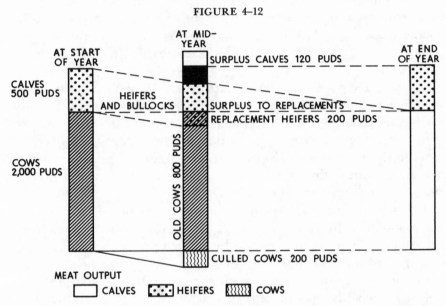

Having looked at the machinery for the development of the herd, we can also see the means of controlling it. It is obvious that to increase the herd organically one need only allocate a greater share than usual as replacements and, by reducing the amount of meat for market, obtain the next year an increase in the basic number of the herd. This method can be applied unless the young animals are so deficient that there are not enough even for the usual number of replacements. It is clear that in this case building up the numbers of young animals should precede an increase in the adult numbers.

Undoubtedly, on a single farm possessing not 100 but 23 cows these processes will not be so obvious, but their character and content will be the same. Tables 4–35 and 4–36 enable us to compare our theoretical estimates with real facts.

Careful study of Table 4–35 shows us that this year was very unfavorable for the Starobel'sk farms' livestock holdings and led to a no-

## TABLE 4-35

### Composition and Movement of Capital Devoted to Livestock
#### (Rubles)

| Sown Area per Farm (Desyatinas*) | Value of Stock at Start of Year | Sales | Lost and Carried Off | Slaughtered | Purchases | Increase in Value During Year† | From Offspring | Obtained in Kind from Outside | Value of Livestock at End of Year |
|---|---|---|---|---|---|---|---|---|---|
| 0.00 ............ | 19.9 | 10.4 | 0.7 | 4.3 | 12.2 | 1.5 | 1.7 | – | 19.9 |
| 0.01–3.00 ...... | 50.2 | 40.1 | 0.7 | 2.7 | 42.2 | 3.2 | 1.6 | 0.5 | 54.2 |
| 3.01–7.50 ...... | 228.8 | 71.7 | 22.6 | 22.4 | 68.1 | 28.4 | 17.4 | 0.3 | 226.9 |
| 7.51–15.00 ..... | 539.0 | 138.1 | 31.8 | 49.0 | 123.7 | 31.2 | 33.9 | 0.1 | 519.0 |
| >15.00 ......... | 961.0 | 184.6 | 59.5 | 79.2 | 145.9 | 69.3 | 69.9 | 14.2 | 937.0 |
| Average ........ | 412.4 | 100.7 | 26.8 | 36.1 | 88.9 | 32.4 | 28.6 | 3.3 | 402.0 |

* Editors' note.—Russian text reads "rubles."

† Includes increase in value of animals reclassified as adult as well as all other changes in value of animals evident on comparing valuations at start and end of year.

ticeable reduction in the value of the herd. This reduction may be explained by both the high percentage of losses and the considerable surplus of sales over purchases. By expressing the averages for all farms as a percentage of the value at the start of the year, we obtain the account in Table 4–36 of the movement of capital in livestock for

TABLE 4–36

VALUE OF THE HERD AND CHANGES DURING
THE YEAR PER AVERAGE FARM*
(percentages)

| | |
|---|---|
| Value of herd at start of year ............. | 100.0 |
| Purchases .............................. | 21.6 |
| Received in kind from outside ........... | 0.8 |
| From offspring ......................... | 6.9 |
| Increase in value of animals ............. | 7.9 |
| Sales .................................. | 24.4 |
| Lost and carried off ..................... | 6.5 |
| Slaughtered ............................ | 8.8 |
| Value at end of year .................... | 97.5 |

* Includes increase in value of animals reclassified as adult as well as all other changes in value of animals evident on comparing valuations at start and end of year.

the year. In comparing these data with studies of other areas, we may note the high percentage of losses and the low percentage of increase from offspring.

FIGURE 4–13

VALUE OF HERD AND CHANGES DURING THE YEAR PER AVERAGE FARM
(% of Herd's Value at Start of Year)

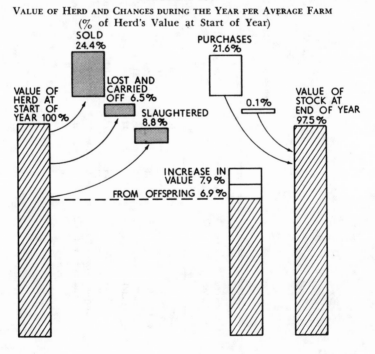

The greatest difference between the table and our scheme is that apart from organic growth there are purchases. These are on a scale that indicates the considerable mobility of this form of peasant farm capital. In reality, as we will see below, livestock is one of the most mobile of the peasant farm elements that comprise its fixed capital, for it can easily be sold on the market and without great loss in price. Because of this, livestock often acquires the features of reserve capital, and in good harvest years the peasants let a great number of young animals into their herds so that in poor years they may begin to sell this reserve fund.

In studying the relationship between prices of meat and fodder, Professor A. N. Chelintsev drew what is at first sight a completely paradoxical conclusion and asserted that these prices are inversely proportional, i.e., the dearer fodder, the cheaper meat. The significance of livestock as a peculiar sort of reserve capital, which we have noted, can completely dispose of this seeming incongruity. In years of good harvests and comparative well-being, peasant farms have, first, no stimulus to get rid of their young animals. Second, they use their savings to begin to increase the numbers of livestock, which may be easily kept on cheap feed. Conversely, in years when there is a dearth of fodder, and grain and hay prices are high, the farms need to sell this reserve capital, which is no longer paying for itself and which they are no longer able to maintain in such numbers. Frenzied mass selling sets in, reducing prices to an incredible level. It is well known, for example, that in the famine year of 1921 in the lower Volga area meat was cheaper than bread.

The picture of the influence of harvests on livestock sales in a meat area, such as the former Don Forces Oblast as analyzed by Professor A. N. Chelintsev in his *Theoretical Basis of Peasant Farm Organization,* is very interesting. We have condensed it into Table 4–37.

TABLE 4–37

| Years with Harvest of | Average Annual Off-Farm Movement for Observed and Following Year |
|---|---|
| 0–30 puds .......... | 114.1 thousand head |
| 30–60 .......... | 70.1 |
| >60 .......... | 61.7 |

Having thus noted the composition of the herd we can pass on to the economic turnover of livestock farming. Cattle farming can naturally pursue six aims.

1. Selling surplus young animals as bloodstock.
2. Selling replacements and young animals for meat.

3. Selling for meat after preliminary fattening and when the young are somewhat older.
4. Working oxen and cows as draft.
5. Producing dung for manuring.
6. Dairying and selling milk.

For north Russia, a combination of aims 2, 5, and 6 is the most widespread type, with the last item mainly dominant and giving the whole activity a commodity dairying bias. More frequently, however, we have livestock farming for dung with noncommodity milk consumption and incidental sales of young animals that are surplus to replacement requirements. This widespread type, combined with pig and sheep farming for own consumption, is very clearly seen from the account in Table 4–38 of an average Volokolamsk farm's commercial livestock work.

Reviewing the account gives us a clear conception of the pitiful state of livestock farming and the paltry subsistence effort, which in bookkeeping terms shows the considerable loss of 8.3 percent of turnover. Livestock farming not only brings in almost no money income, but also requires a fair amount of additional outgoings from the farm. The labor used in this activity receives no payment.

Developed dairying in Vologda and other areas presents quite a different picture; here, it occupies a more noticeable place in both quality and quantity. It is self-evident that to achieve good results in livestock farming, one must have good techniques and be well-organized, but it is also at least as important to have a market situation favorable to this sector. For example, for dairying to become profitable in the same Volokolamsk farm it would be sufficient for the price of a vedro of milk to go up from 50 kopeks to 1 ruble. It would expand and improve its techniques, as has happened in a number of villages close to the railway line, where butter-making cooperatives have developed.

The last question about stock farming, and the most important one to us, is the relationship of its size to that of field cropping. We have so far determined that stock farming starts from available feeding stuffs. But this assumption, required by our argument, is not correct or, more precisely, is a very conventional one, since on any farm the amount of feed available may be reduced or considerably forced up, given the same area. The same peasant farm may have one, two, or three head of cattle, depending on circumstances.

Since on any farm there are threshing-floor residues, kitchen waste, and hay from land that can be used only as meadow, each one has a

## TABLE 4-38
### COMMERCIAL LIVESTOCK ACCOUNT

| From Credit Account | Debit | Rubles | Rubles | Credit | Rubles | Rubles | To Debit Account |
|---|---|---|---|---|---|---|---|
| Capital | Value of stock at start of year | 155.40 | | Value of stock at end of year | 144.15 | | Capital |
| Cash | Stock purchased during year | 12.09 | | Stock sold during year | 32.70 | 176.85 | Cash |
| Buildings | Use of buildings | 7.54 | | Home produced: | | | |
| General | Proportion of general expenses | 6.77 | | Milk, 178.9 vedros | 89.60 | | |
| Workers | For labor | 23.79 | | Meat, 6.2 puds | 35.74 | | |
| Stocks | Homegrown feeds and litter | 126.16 | | Hides | 0.48 | | Stocks |
| | Purchased feeds | 10.83 | | Wool, 9.9 Russian pounds | 3.36 | | |
| Cash | Herdsman and veterinary services | 8.16 | | Dung, 1808.6 puds | 12.73 | 141.91 | |
| | | | 350.74 | Produce sold: | | | |
| | | | 350.74 | Milk, 0.4 vedros | 0.80 | | |
| | | | | Hides | 0.84 | | Cash |
| | | | | Wool | 1.00 | 2.4* | |
| | | | | Loss | | 321.40 | Balance |
| | | | | | | 29.34 | |
| | | | | | | 350.74 | |

* EDITORS' NOTE.—Sic. Presumably this figure should be 2.64.

certain amount of fodder obtained incidentally and consisting of items hard to sell on the market. This is enough to keep, apart from draft stock, at least one cow producing essential manure. In this way, incidental produce is most advantageously converted into milk, even if only for the family's own use.

This stock and produce (dung and milk) is obtained almost free, with minimal effort, by the farm family. However, with a somewhat greater intensity the farm's resources allow enough fodder for another animal; this means looking after the mown areas, more careful harvesting of feeding stuffs, and perhaps hiring a meadow or buying some hay. In this case, of course, the feeding stuffs will not be free, but their price cannot be very high.

The farm can, of course, still further increase the amount of feeding stuffs available by further developing its resources, introducing a fodder course by sowing grasses or roots, creating artificial meadows or pastures, and by buying in concentrates and stalling the stock. These efforts will enable it to keep a third, fourth, or perhaps even a fifth cow, provided, of course, that there are enough family workhands to look after and milk them. This intensified feed-getting is possible if the market situation pays for the increased cost of seed for the feeding stuffs.

### Subsequent Sections of the Organizational Plan

In reviewing the organization of field-cropping, draft, and commercial livestock farming, we have dealt rather fully with almost all the basic organizational problems of the farm's production sectors. Since it is not our task to compile a guide on farm organization, we will limit ourselves to these and will not deal with the organization of manure, the vegetable garden, orchards, incidental sectors, and so on. We will focus all our attention on those aspects in which the peculiar peasant farm features which we have established are clearly expressed. To this end, we will discuss: (a) organization of the area, (b) organization of labor, (c) organization of equipment, (d) organization of buildings, (e) organization of capital and money circulation. These will enable us to easily substantiate our conclusions from preceding chapters and to collect material for the subsequent ones.

#### ORGANIZATION OF THE AREA

In organizing peasant farms, one must almost always take account of their exceedingly poor layout. The excessive intermingling of the peasant household's strips, their length, and the fragmentation of arable and meadow frequently attain quite Homeric proportions. The fault for this lies partly with the excessively intermingled allocations made to peasant communes in the 1861 reform, and mainly with the communal egalitarian methods of repartitioning. The land was broken up into sections of equivalent quality, and a strip from each section was allocated to almost every member of the commune. We can judge what sort of land allocation was made to the communes when the peasants were liberated if only from the plan (Figures 4–14 and 4–15) of the lands held by the settlements of Kon'kovo and Nikulin, described by P. A. Vikhlyaev in his book on Moscow guberniya agriculture. Of course, this plan shows a somewhat hypertrophied

FIGURE 4–14

PLAN OF KON'KOVO VILLAGE, MOSCOW UEZD

| FAMILIES HOLDING LAND | 55 |
|---|---|
| TOTAL LAND | 214.7 DESYATINAS |
| OF WHICH | |
| HOMESTEAD | 28.0 |
| ARABLE | 103.7 |
| HAYFIELD | 22.2 |
| FOREST | 37.5 |
| PASTURE | 12.0 |
| UNSUITABLE FOR USE | 11.3 |

FIGURE 4–15

PLAN OF NIKULIN VILLAGE, BRONNITSY UEZD

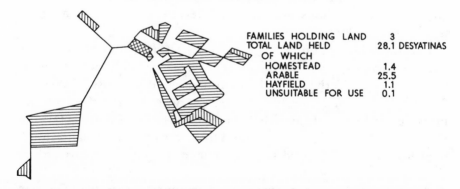

| FAMILIES HOLDING LAND | 3 |
|---|---|
| TOTAL LAND HELD | 28.1 DESYATINAS |
| OF WHICH | |
| HOMESTEAD | 1.4 |
| ARABLE | 25.5 |
| HAYFIELD | 1.1 |
| UNSUITABLE FOR USE | 0.1 |

land disorganization. However, even with quite a good layout of communal lands on the whole, the organization of the individual peasant household area is scarcely satisfactory in the overwhelming majority of cases.

The map (Figure 4–16) showing the land of a Volokolamsk uezd peasant may be taken as a typical example of arable strip layout where

FIGURE 4–16

LAND OF A VOLOKOLAMSK UEZD PEASANT

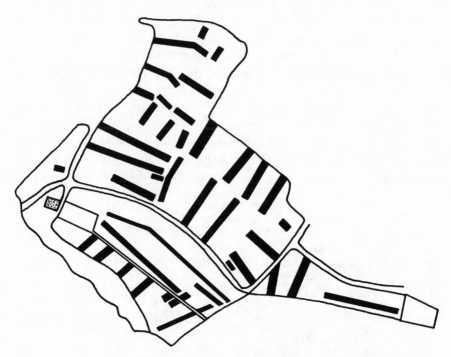

there is repartitional communal land use. In a considerable number of instances, the organization of the peasant farm area is still less satisfactory. For example, there is in zemstvo statistics the case of a Ryazan' guberniya peasant household with a 4-desyatina holding fragmented into more than 200 strips.

It is essential to note, though, that such fragmentation is not restricted solely to communal land use; to a very considerable extent it is also met with in the old individual household land use of Western Europe. Thus, for example, Dr. Herbst,[4] who studied the land use measures of 19 run-of-the-mill German farms of 50 to 60 hectares in the neighborhood of Weimar, found that only one had its land in less than five pieces. The aspects of their land use may be expressed by Table 4–39.

As the table shows, the level of land arrangement in these German farms could not be taken as a model. Such fragmentation of the land and the enormous average distance of fields from the house leave the

---

[4] Dr. Herbst, "Guts-und Betriebsverhältnisse bauerlichen Güter," *Thiel's Landwirts. Jahrbuch*, 1908, No. 381.

TABLE 4–39

| Number of Pieces | Number of Farms | Average Distance of Field from House | | Distance from House to Most Distant Piece | |
|---|---|---|---|---|---|
| | | (Kms.) | Number of Farms | Maximum Distance (Kms.) | Number of Farms |
| 1–4 ........ | 1 | | | | |
| 5–9 ........ | 9 | 0.5–1.0 | 4 | 0.5–5.0 | 13 |
| 10–14 ........ | 7 | 1.1–2.0 | 9 | 5.1–10.0 | 4 |
| 15–19 ........ | — | 2.1–3.0 | 4 | >10.0 | 2 |
| >19 ........ | 2 | >3.0 | 2 | | |

peasant farm with all the disadvantages of a small farm as regards use of means of production, draft, and so on. At the same time, they also give it all the disadvantages of the largest farms by contributing to exceedingly high on-farm transport overheads. What this means economically may be judged from Table 4–40, which shows the increase in overheads per desyatina of oats, depending on distance from the house and the corresponding increase in journeys and repartitions.

TABLE 4–40

COST OF WORK ON A DESYATINA OF OATS BY DISTANCE

| Distance of Field from House | Work by People | | Work by Horses | | Total Cost (Rubles) |
|---|---|---|---|---|---|
| | Working Days | Cost (Rubles) | Working Days | Cost (Rubles) | |
| 0 ............ | 13.5 | 16.2 | 8.5 | 6.8 | 23.0 |
| 100 sazhens ...... | 13.7 | 16.4 | 8.8 | 7.1 | 23.5 |
| 1 versta ....... | 15.8 | 18.9 | 10.1 | 8.1 | 27.0 |
| 2 ............ | 18.6 | 22.3 | 11.9 | 9.5 | 31.8 |
| 3 ............ | 21.9 | 26.3 | 13.9 | 11.1 | 37.4 |
| 4 ............ | 26.1 | 31.3 | 16.1 | 12.8 | 44.1 |
| 5 ............ | 33.0 | 39.6 | 19.7 | 15.8 | 55.9 |
| 6 ............ | 42.3 | 50.0 | 22.3 | 17.9 | 68.7 |

These figures are still further increased for crops requiring much manure or many cultivations, or for produce not easily transported, like roots, tubers, and fruits.

From what has been said, improved organization of the area is nearly the most essential and important agricultural measure, and land measures are one of the basic sectors of economic policy in all agrarian countries. Nevertheless, methods of land use measures and the effects resulting from them cannot concern us in this book; this is a subject for treatises on agrarian policy. On the other hand, some of the methods employed in running fragmented and distantly scattered

FIGURE 4–17

Cost of Work per Desyatina of Oats
According to Distance

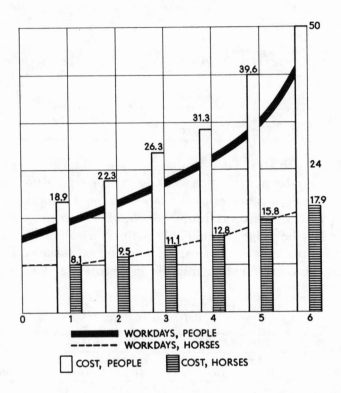

WORKDAYS, PEOPLE
------- WORKDAYS, HORSES

☐ COST, PEOPLE    ▤ COST, HORSES

bits of land are of exceptional interest in learning about the nature of the labor farm.

First of all, the peasant farm establishes various methods for dealing with the zones which vary by distance. Frequently, they simply abandon the most distant pieces, while very distant ones are dealt with in overnight trips of a few days' duration for sowing and harvesting. Those slightly less remote are worked with a particular extensive, often plunderous, "outfield" rotation, and on the more accessible ones there is a correct and comparatively intensive form. However, even within the limits of the nearest areas field cultivation often shows differences both in tillage and cultivation of the plants, and mainly in the rate at which manure is applied.

This spectrum of tillage intensity determined by distance from the house makes the exploitation of any one holding extremely elastic. With the same intensity and drudgery of peasant family work, the holding will give the most varied amounts of produce. Under pressure from on-farm factors, the family may extend the more intensive forms ever farther and farther from the home. We have no doubt that work in progress on outfield rotations and the methods of running them will enrich our knowledge of the peasant farm.

THE ORGANIZATION OF LABOR

Having outlined the agricultural sectors and the needs for on-farm transport, we can sum up all labor expenditure on our peasant farm and review its organization. We already know that the peasant family makes far from full use of the available work time. In part this is due to the seasonal nature of agricultural work and its absence in the dead periods of the year; in part it is because when it has met its demands with a certain part of its labor effort and has reached its internal economic equilibrium, the peasant family has no further stimulus to work.

Figure 4–18 gives a very clear conception of how annual labor is distributed on a flax farm. We see that only a quarter of working days

FIGURE 4–18
ANNUAL WORK BY FARM SECTORS, VOLOKOLAMSK AND VOLOGDA UEZDS

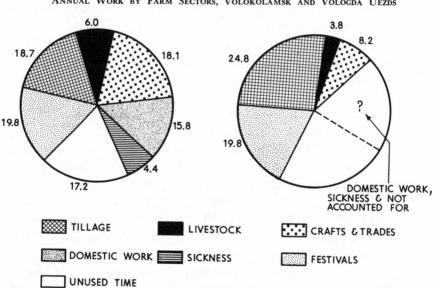

are spent on agriculture, including mowing and all field work as well as scutching and dressing the flax. A very considerable amount of working time goes on crafts, trades, and domestic work. Time devoted to festivals is indicated in the figure by stippling; and we see that it is almost the same amount as the time spent on agriculture.

Data from Vologda allow us not only to note general work distribution, but also to see separately how men and women, boys and girls work. From Figure 4–19 we see that a great part of a man's work is in

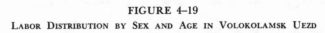

FIGURE 4–19

Labor Distribution by Sex and Age in Volokolamsk Uezd

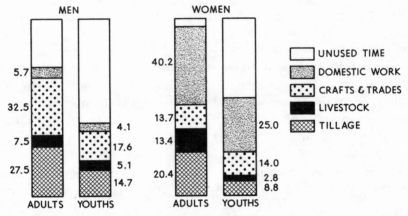

crafts, trades, and agriculture. The woman's labor is used predominantly in domestic work. In general, the woman works more than the man, but her work is not so hard.

Adolescents work fewer days than adults. The distribution of their labor by farm sectors is according to their sex; in general, boys are engaged more in agriculture and girls spend many days on domestic work.

The distribution of labor by size of holding is interesting. From the data of a Vologda study, we can construct Figure 4–20. It is interesting to observe that labor intensity remains the same in all groups, and an increase in land used merely causes an increase in work on the farm at the expense of crafts and trades, which are noticeably cut back. We hasten to remind the reader again that the amount of land held does not always cause such a distribution; in frequent instances, it is due to a combination of advantages derived from agricultural crops and from work in crafts and trades.

Such are the most general data from our statistics on labor organization. Let us now turn to a more detailed study on our Volokolamsk farm. Here, the peasant family, together with short-term workers, has 384.53 working days on the farm, or 111.8 per worker per year, and 144.5 days if crafts, trades, and hire for agricultural work are taken into account. 27.3 working days are spent per desyatina of suitable land, and 28.2 days per 100 rubles of capital (Table 4–41). In Table

FIGURE 4–20

LABOR COMPOSITION ON FARMS WITH DIFFERENT SOWN AREAS

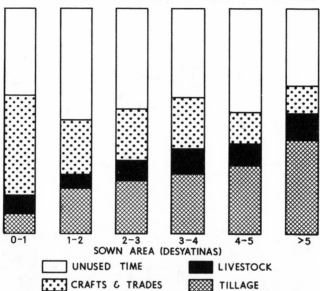

SOWN AREA (DESYATINAS)

☐ UNUSED TIME     ■ LIVESTOCK

▨ CRAFTS & TRADES     ▨ TILLAGE

EDITORS' NOTE.—Chayanov gave no legend, but it should presumably be the same as for Fig. 4–18.

TABLE 4–41

WORK BY FARM SECTORS IN VOLOKOLAMSK UEZD
(Working Days of One Full Worker)

| | Own and Short-Term Workers | Day Laborers | Total | Percentage of Farm Activity |
|---|---|---|---|---|
| Field-cropping, including: ..... | 301.25 | 30.97 | 332.22 | 79.7 |
|    Rye ..................... | 75.56 | 4.49 | 80.05 | 19.1 |
|    Oats ................... | 24.08 | 1.60 | 25.68 | 6.2 |
|    Flax ................... | 155.99 | 13.94 | 179.93 | 43.0 |
|    Potatoes ................. | 16.57 | 0.50 | 16.97 | 4.3 |
|    Clover .................. | 29.05 | 0.54 | 29.59 | 7.1 |
| Meadows ..................... | 30.70 | — | 30.70 | 7.4 |
| Vegetable gardening .......... | 6.00 | — | 6.00 | 1.4 |
| Horses ...................... | 13.30 | 0.40 | 13.70 | 3.3 |
| Production cattle ............ | 26.50 | 1.00 | 27.60 | 6.6 |
| Social work ................. | 6.78 | — | 6.78 | 1.6* |
| Total for farm .......... | 384.53 | 32.37 | 416.90 | 100.0 |
| In addition, hired out for agricultural work .............. | 21.52 | — | 21.52 | — |
| Crafts and trades ............ | 87.56 | — | 87.56 | — |
| Total ................. | 493.61 | 32.37 | 525.98 | — |
| Work days in year ...... | 1255.0 | — | — | — |

* EDITORS' NOTE.—Russian text has 1.69. The total then does not sum to 100.0.

4-42, we compare the Volokolamsk figures with those from other flax-growing areas (see Figure 4-21 also).

TABLE 4-42

|  | Workdays of One Worker | | Workdays per Desyatina of Arable on Field Cropping |
|  | Spent on Own Farm | On Own Farm and on Side |  |
| --- | --- | --- | --- |
| Volokolamsk .......... | 111.8 | 144.6 | 36.6 |
| Gzhatsk .............. | 70.7 | 35.9 | 43.2 |
| Porech'e ............. | 120.1 | 122.2 | 38.8 |
| Sychevka ............ | 80.1 | 103.8 | 24.8 |
| Dorogobuzh .......... | 94.7 | 130.8 | 39.5 |

FIGURE 4-21

WORKDAYS EXPENDED BY WORKER ON OWN FARM AND ON SIDE

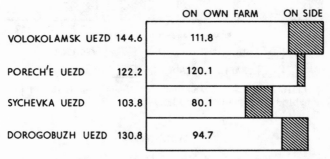

Such is the organization of labor on peasant farms in the U.S.S.R.

ORGANIZATION OF EQUIPMENT

Leaving aside the transport equipment absolutely essential for the farm—the cart and sleigh—all other agricultural implements and machines now widely used in agriculture could be replaced by manual work with simple implements such as mattocks and spades. Therefore, in speaking of agricultural machines and implements we should primarily establish why and in what circumstances they are advantageous and are used.

As is well known, there are two reasons for using machines: (1) they greatly economize on labor and thereby reduce the cost of work; (2) they permit a better quality of work and thereby increase farm income. Let us look at both of these aspects.

The following account of labor expenditure for extensive winter sowing without dunging, made by Ivan Lopatin, can very clearly demonstrate how much labor expenditure is reduced by using machines.

*Manual Work*

|  |  | Days |
|---|---|---|
| 1. | Tillage to a depth of about 4 inches with *sokha* or one-horse plow | 2 |
| 2. | Harrowing arable 3 times after tillage | ⅓ |
| 3. | Second tillage to the former depth with same implements | 2 |
| 4. | Harrowing twice after second tillage | ⅓ |
| 5. | Sowing seed by hand | 2 |
| 6. | Working in seed with *sokha* | |
| 7. | Harrowing 3 times after working in | ⅓ |
| 8. | Harvesting the grain with sickle, binding sheaves, and stacking | 6 |
| 9. | Carting 10 stacks from field to threshing floor and ricking with an average distance of 1 versta or 10 runs per stack | 1 |
| 10. | Threshing 10 stacks with flails | 6 |
| 11. | Winnowing 50 puds of grain with spades | 2 |
| 12. | Sorting 10 puds of seed on the riddle | 1 |
| | Total | 23 |

*Machine*

|  |  | |
|---|---|---|
| 1. | Tillage to a depth of about 7 inches with a two-horse plow | 2 |
| 2. | Harrowing after tillage | 0.5 |
| 3. | Second tillage to a depth of not more than 4 inches with a multifurrow or horse cultivator | 0.7 |
| 4. | Harrowing after good cultivation not required | |
| 5. | Supposed cultivation of arable by cultivator and light harrow | 0.7 |
| 6. | Drilling in seed | 0.3 |
| 7. | Harrowing not required | |
| 8. | Harvesting with reaper-binder | 0.3 |
| 9. | Carting 20 stacks with a cart carrying 4 at a time, 5 journeys | 0.5 |
| 10. | Threshing 20 stacks with a steam thresher | 2.0 |
| 11. | Separation of the grain is carried out by the same machine | |
| 12. | Sorting out seed | |
| | Total | 7.0 |

In making this comparison, however, it is essential to bear in mind that the economy in labor expenditure is not of itself the decisive factor, since it is accompanied by an increased amount spent on amortization and upkeep of the machines. In determining the cost of machine work, we ought to take both elements into account. (See Figure 4–22.)

In agricultural economics courses and in specialized works, various authors have given different formulas for estimating this cost. For example, Professor V. G. Bazhaev, in his agricultural economics course,[5] gives this formula to calculate the cost of a working day for an agricultural machine:

$$x = a + b + c + d + \frac{e + B}{m},$$

where $x$ is the cost of the working day for the machine; $a$, the daily

---

[5] Summary of the agricultural economics course given by Professor V. G. Bazhaev in 1903–4 in the Kiev Polytechnical Institute (3d ed.; Kiev, 1913), p. 128.

FIGURE 4–22

LABOR EXPENDITURE WITH
MANUAL WORK AND MACHINE WORK

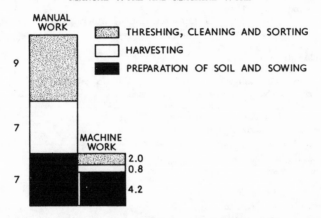

cost of workers on foot, tending the machine; *b*, the daily cost of mounted workers attending machine; *c*, the cost of grease; *d*, the cost of fuel (if the machine has an engine); *e*, the annual deduction for repairs and amortization; *B*, interest on the capital spent in purchasing the machine; *m*, the number of machine workdays in the year.

Other authors also give similar formulas, but in a somewhat different form. For example, in his course[6] one of my predecessors in the department, K. A. Werner, professor of the Petrovskii Academy, devised the following formula to calculate the cost of one machine working day:

$$w = \frac{p}{m} + (x + y + z),$$

where *p* = 4.5 percent of the annual payments of capital spent on the machine + interest to cover repairs and insurance in the year; *m* = days of actual work by the machine; *x* = the cost of a day's fuel and grease; *y* = the cost of manual labor with the machine for a day; *z* = the cost of a day's draft work with the machine, moving it or bringing supplies.

The formula we have proposed on the basis of work by the French economist Fr. Beçu has a somewhat different content. As distinct from the formulas of V. Bazhaev and K. Werner, it is primarily based, not on the machine workday, but on the unit of machine production (desyatina of land, 100 puds of threshed grain, etc.). Afterward, figures

---

[6] K. A. Werner, *Sel'skokhozyaistvennaya ekonomiya* [The Agricultural Economy], M., 1901 g.

are added to express the improvement or deterioration resulting from machine work compared with manual work.

*A* represents annual expenditure on the machine, whether it works or not, i.e., outlays on amortization, interest on capital invested in the machine, and insurance premiums. *B* represents the expenses of running the machine per machine workday, i.e., wages of workers on the machine, cost of draft, grease, and repair. Then, the cost of one machine workday may be expressed:

$$x = \frac{A}{n} + B,$$

where *n* is the number of days in the year on which the machine worked. It is clear from the formula that the cost of one machine workday should decrease as *n* increases—in other words, the more the machine is used.

In order to learn the cost of machine work per desyatina, one must divide the day's work figure by the number of desyatinas with which the machine deals in a day. If the machine's daily productivity is *k* desyatinas, the cost of machine work per desyatina will be:

$$y = \frac{A}{n \cdot k} + \frac{B}{k}.$$

Since the machine frequently carries out only part of the work, leaving the rest to hand labor (for instance, reapers require hand binding of the sheaves), if the cost of this handwork per desyatina is *C* we obtain the final expression of the cost of machine work per desyatina:

$$y = \frac{A}{n \cdot k} + \frac{B}{k} + C.$$

If we now indicate the cost of manual work per desyatina as *R*, we can say that it is advantageous to replace manual work by the machine if

$$R \gtreqless \frac{A}{n \cdot k} + \frac{B}{k} + C.$$

Let us try to fathom out the conditions needed for such an inequality. On the left hand side of the inequality, *A*, *B*, *C*, and *k* depend on the cost and quality of the machine and on the wage level; they are fairly stable and constant. The figure most liable to fluctuate is *n*, i.e., the number of days on which the machine can be used. This figure depends on the area the farm has, and in our formula $n \cdot k = S$ is the direct expression of this determining area. With a decline in the area used (*S*), outlays on amortization and interest on capital (*A*) fall on a smaller number of desyatinas; thus the cost of machine work can rise considerably and exceed the usual cost of manual work.

In order to determine the marginal size of area at which machine work is possible—i.e., when cost of machine work equals that of manual work—we should put the figure we seek in our formula as $S$ and write the following equation:

$$R = \frac{A}{S} + \frac{B}{k} + C.$$

Hence:

$$S = \frac{A}{R - \left(\dfrac{B}{k} + C\right)}.$$

Obviously, if the area actually exploited is greater than this, machine costs less than manual work; if lower than this, it costs more.

We will explain our theoretical reckoning with a specific example—the work of a mowing machine. Let us suppose that its output is 3.5 desyatinas a day and cost is 200 rubles; then the basic elements of our formula are compounded as follows:

*A*

| | |
|---|---|
| 4% on capital ................ | 8 rubles |
| Amortization (over 10 years) ... | 20 |
| Total *A* ............... | 28 rubles |

*B*

| | | |
|---|---|---|
| Worker's wages .............. | 1 ruble | |
| Cost of draft (2 horses) ........ | 1 | 50 kopeks |
| Grease and repairs ........... | 1 | |
| Total *B* ............... | 3 rubles | 50 kopeks |

$C$ is zero, since the mowing is entirely carried out by machine. Three mowers are required for hand mowing a desyatina a day. If we pay them a ruble a day, the cost of hand mowing is three rubles.

Let us suppose that our farm has 70 desyatinas of meadow. Then, according to our formula, the cost of machine harvesting one desyatina is:

$$\frac{28}{70} + \frac{3.50}{3.5} = 1 \text{ ruble } 40 \text{ kopeks.}$$

Thus, with 70 desyatinas of meadow mechanical harvesting is more than twice as advantageous as manual.

Let us try to determine in accordance with our formula the minimal area at which the mowing machine can be economically used. We have:

$$\frac{28}{3.00 - \dfrac{3.50}{3.5}} = 14 \text{ desyatinas.}$$

Thus, mechanized mowing is possible only on farms with not less than 14 desyatinas of meadow. For example, let us take a farm with 7 desyatinas of meadow. The cost of mechanized mowing for a desyatina of meadow will be:

$$\frac{28}{7} + \frac{3.50}{3.5} = 5 \text{ rubles,}$$

i.e., two rubles dearer than harvesting by hand.

In all our preceding constructs and reckonings, we have assumed that the quality of the work carried out by machine remains the same as that done by hand. However, this is not so in reality. We know that, apart from saving labor, by using a seed drill we economize seed, saving 6–8 puds per desyatina. In addition, sowing in rows increases the yield of grains. We also know that when threshing is speeded by using a machine a smaller amount of grain is eaten by mice, but the straw from the threshing machine is poorer than that from the flail. We also know that using Walcour and Randell harrows not only speeds the work but also raises yields, and so on.

Obviously, we should introduce into our formula a factor for qualitative effect, expressing it, of course, in rubles. Taking the improvement (or deterioration) of work with mechanization as $M$ rubles a desyatina, the cost of machine compared with manual work will be expressed as

$$R = \frac{A}{S} + \frac{B}{k} + C - M;$$

hence the marginal area that justifies the use of machinery is

$$S = \frac{A}{(R + M) - \left(\dfrac{B}{k} + C\right)}.$$

For a number of machines (seed drills, Randell harrows, etc.), the area calculated in this way will be smaller than that when quality is not taken into account.

Such is the theory of machine use in agriculture. The well-known fact that machines are used less as farm size decreases is explained by these circumstances. Reckoning for his three-field farm, Ivan Lopatin gives the sequence in Table 4–43 for the rational introduction of individual agricultural machines and implements as size of arable increases.

TABLE 4–43

| Size of Arable | Put to Use |
|---|---|
| 2 desyatinas ...... | Plow |
| 10   .............. | Hand-operated winnowing machine |
| 15   .............. | Threshing machine, horse rake |
| 20   .............. | Harvesting machine |
| 22   .............. | Drill, sorter |
| 30   .............. | Surface plow |
| 50   .............. | One-horse thresher |
| 70   .............. | Two-horse thresher |
| 400   .............. | Steam thresher |

Since machines are thus gradually put to use, the cost of machines per desyatina and, consequently, their amortization will be insignificant on small farms. (See Figure 4–23.) It will increase as they do more and reach a maximum at 50 desyatinas, when drills are put to use.[7] After this, as machines are increasingly used, it will fall, and when they are fully used it will thereafter remain constant.

In fact, agricultural machines are distributed among farms, just as our theory has indicated. For example, in Germany the percentage of all farms using machines, according to the 1907 census, was as shown in Table 4–44.

However, it is essential to point out that the formula given above is a law that applies only to capitalistically organized undertakings. The ideas at the basis of labor farm organization very frequently introduce substantial corrections. Thus, at the present time in southern Russia reapers, and even reaper-binders, have become widespread

FIGURE 4–23

MACHINES PUT TO USE BY SIZE OF ARABLE

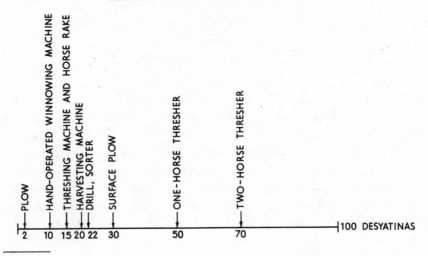

---

7 EDITORS' NOTE.—According to Figure 4–23, drills are put to use at 22 desyatinas.

TABLE 4–44

FARM SIZE AND AGRICULTURAL MACHINES

| Farm Size | Percentage of Farms Using Machines |
|---|---|
| 0–  0.5 hectares . . . . . . . . . . | 0.9 |
| 0.5–  2.0 . . . . . . . . . . . . . . . . . | 8.9 |
| 2.0–  5.0 . . . . . . . . . . . . . . . . . | 32.4 |
| 5.0– 20.0 . . . . . . . . . . . . . . . . . | 72.5 |
| 20.0–100.0 . . . . . . . . . . . . . . . . . | 92.0 |
| >100.0 . . . . . . . . . . . . . . . . . | 97.5 |

on the peasant farm, and are used on areas so small that, according to our formula, their work cannot be advantageous. We must in this instance, therefore, seek the cause for their being widely used, not in the advantage to be derived from them, but in the peculiar features of the labor farm.

One task that distinguishes the labor farm from the capitalistically organized farm is its attempt to distribute its labor as equally as possible over time. Therefore, peasant farms usually suffer excessively from the irregularities in labor organization over time that are characteristic for many crops. The harvest period, with its maximum labor intensity, thus determines the area to be exploited. If the ripe wheat can stand without shedding, let us say one and a half weeks, obviously the size of the peasant farm's sown area will be what the family can harvest in the course of this week and a half.

This constraint on the area to be exploited has a very bad effect on other periods of the year when the family cannot use its full labor force on the restricted area and suffers from a surplus of free labor without work. Aiming to expand the worked area, the peasants of southern Russia sometimes sow wheat varieties that can stand for a long time without shedding (Beloturka, for instance). By sowing Beloturka instead of other, more advantageous varieties, the peasant farm reduces its net rate of income per desyatina, but it can expand its land use and thus increase its gross income.

The use of harvesting machines on small areas where they cannot pay for themselves means the same thing. For example, according to zemstvo statistical data for Starobel'sk uezd, Khar'kov guberniya,[8] 4.3 working days are spent in harvesting one desyatina.

Let us suppose that we have a family with two workers and that the possible harvesting period is 10 days; then the maximum area the

---

[8] *Materialy dlya otsenki zemel' Khar'kovskoi gubernii, vyp. III* [Materials for evaluating the lands of Khar'kov guberniya, fasc. III], Khar'kov, 1907 g.

family can harvest with its own resources will be 20/4.3, that is, 4.65 desyatinas. And since a desyatina requires a total of 21.4 workdays and gives a gross income of 29 rubles, 10 kopeks, excluding seed, our farm family will be able to work 94.8 days (47.4 working days per worker a year) and to increase its means of subsistence by 139.3 rubles. But by using a harvesting machine, the family can more than double the worked area, and by sowing, let us say, 10 desyatinas, it will be able to use about 200 working days a year and obtain 291.6 rubles gross income. Deducting 30 rubles from this for amortization and repairs, we have 261.6 rubles, i.e., over 100 rubles more than with manual work. Such a considerable increase in means of subsistence is a tremendous advantage to the labor farm even though, in bookkeeping terms, to use a reaper on 10 desyatinas is surely unprofitable.

TABLE 4-45

WORKDAYS SPENT ON ONE DESYATINA OF WHEAT

| | |
|---|---|
| Tillage | 3.6 |
| Sowing and drilling in | 1.7 |
| Weeding | 4.4 |
| Harvesting | 4.3 |
| Carting | 1.9 |
| Threshing | 3.6 |
| Winnowing | 1.9 |
| Total | 21.4 |

Thus, we see that the peculiar features of the labor farm, given abundant land, increase the opportunities to use machines. Such is the significance of the machine on the labor farm in resolving the periods of critical labor intensity; but the mechanization of labor has quite different characteristics in periods of weak labor intensity.

Thus, for example, the agricultural officer D. I. Kirsanov said at the 1900 Perm' meeting:

If there is an advantageous use for peasant family labor in wintertime, the agricultural officer will do a great service by spreading threshers and freeing a considerable part of peasant labor for other productive work. But if the peasant has nothing to do in wintertime except thresh his grain, the spread of the threshing machine can only be seen as unproductive expenditure of the peasant's already scanty capital.

Kirsanov very aptly points out a situation in which the labor farm's tasks clash with labor mechanization, despite the perhaps great advantage, by bookkeeping standards, of machine work. Such in their most general outlines are the limits and significance of machine use in capitalist and labor farms.

BUILDINGS

It is exceedingly easy to make an estimate for buildings on any farm. Taking account of livestock numbers, the amount of equipment, and the produce obtained with large harvests, it is not hard to determine the area or even the volume of covered space required to maintain the means of production and the produce obtained on the farm.

According to our calculations made on materials from Starobel'sk uezd, 3.1 square sazhens of agricultural buildings are required per desyatina of arable, excluding the hut in which the farm family lives. This figure changes according to farm size; larger farms, which use their buildings more and build them higher, manage at a lower rate. Figures for Starobel'sk uezd are shown in Table 4–46. The cost per

TABLE 4–46

| Sown Area (Desyatinas) | Square Sazhens of Agricultural Buildings per Desyatina of Field |
|---|---|
| 0.01– 3.0 | 5.2 |
| 3.01– 7.50 | 4.4 |
| 7.51–15.00 | 2.7 |
| >15.00 | 2.5 |

desyatina of using buildings (amortization and repairs) in Volokolamsk uezd, for example, amounted to 4.32 rubles.

The chief feature in the organization of peasant farm buildings is that buildings, as the most lasting means of production, more often do not correspond to the general volume of activity, which changes as the family grows, as there are repartitions among family members, and so on. The building "overload" on young farms that have just become separately established and have received a shed or a barn designed for the much larger area of the father's farm is largely explained by this.

THE ORGANIZATION OF CAPITAL

By putting a value on buildings, livestock, and equipment and by summing these valuations, we obtain the size and composition of fixed capital for Russian peasant farms (Table 4–47).

Thus, the fixed capital of an average peasant family fluctuates between 500 and 1,500 rubles, depending on the area. By comparing these figures with number of workers and area sown, we obtain the totals in Table 4–48.

TABLE 4–47

VALUE OF PEASANT FARM MEANS OF PRODUCTION

| | Buildings | Livestock | Equipment | Total |
|---|---|---|---|---|
| Starobel'sk uezd, | | | | |
| Khar'kov guberniya ....... | 420.5 | 471.2 | 100.4 | 993.6 |
| Volokolamsk uezd, | | | | |
| Moscow guberniya ........ | 909.0 | 268.0 | 189.0 | 1365.6 |
| Vologda uezd, | | | | |
| Vologda guberniya ....... | 453.0 | 137.0 | 82.3 | 672.3 |
| Tot'ma uezd, | | | | |
| Vologda guberniya ....... | 313.9 | 108.9 | 44.1 | 466.9 |
| Gzhatsk uezd, | | | | |
| Smolensk guberniya ....... | 1123.6 | 212.7 | 83.2 | 1419.5 |
| Sychevka uezd, | | | | |
| Smolensk guberniya ...... | 1262.0 | 174.0 | 100.2 | 1536.2 |
| Porech'e uezd, | | | | |
| Smolensk guberniya ...... | 1309.0 | 267.0 | 74.0 | 1650.6 |
| Dorogobuzh uezd, | | | | |
| Smolensk guberniya ...... | 717.0 | 271.5 | 82.0 | 1070.6 |
| Voronezh guberniya ........ | 341.0 | 130.2 | 79.1 | 652.2 |
| Tambov guberniya ........ | 550.5 | 316.5 | 98.1 | 965.1 |
| Chernigov guberniya ....... | 504.5 | 512.5 | 238.8 | 1255.8 |
| Novgorod guberniya ....... | 489.0 | 173.3 | 82.0 | 500.3 |

In order to move from general rates of available fixed capital to its circulation, and to compare its annual movement with the amount of circulating capital, we must make clear how much the peasant farm should spend on replacement of worn-out fixed capital and on its upkeep and repair. Budget works give these rates:

|  | Percentage | i.e., about |
|---|---|---|
| On buildings ............ | 5– 6 | 50 rubles |
| Equipment .............. | 18–25 | 30 |
| Livestock, we assume, can renew itself. | | |

We can judge the amount of circulating capital required according to the composition of expenditure on seed, fodder, rent, and so on. In Starobel'sk uezd, this amounts to 359.44 rubles for the average farm, and in Volokolamsk to 536.36 rubles. Then we may put forward the scheme in Table 4–49 for the process of capital circulation and renewal for the average peasant farm.

The 520 rubles annual net earnings of the family amounts to about 150 rubles per worker, or about 1.30 rubles per workday. Comparing the figures from our scheme with actual payment in agriculture in different areas, we have the figures in Table 4–50. The unexpected approximation of the Swiss peasant's labor payment to the Russian

FIGURE 4-24

VALUE OF PEASANT FARM MEANS OF PRODUCTION

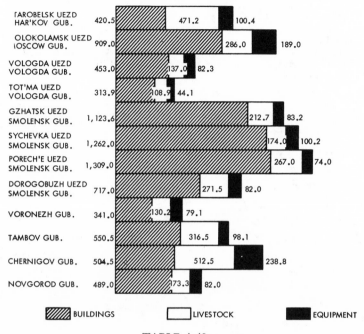

TABLE 4-48

| | Total Value per | |
|---|---|---|
| | Desyatina Sown | Worker |
| Starobel'sk uezd, Khar'kov guberniya ...... | 103.4 | 278.1 |
| Volokolamsk uezd, Moscow guberniya ....... | 229.7 | 352.0 |
| Vologda uezd, Vologda guberniya ....... | 257.8 | 221.6 |
| Tot'ma uezd, Vologda guberniya ....... | 126.3 | 148.5 |
| Gzhatsk uezd, Smolensk guberniya ...... | 330.1 | 327.5 |
| Sychevka uezd, Smolensk guberniya ...... | 256.3 | 420.6 |
| Porech'e uezd, Smolensk guberniya ...... | 275.0 | 429.9 |
| Dorogobuzh uezd, Smolensk guberniya ...... | 237.8 | 278.2 |
| Voronezh guberniya ........ | 68.2 | 164.5 |
| Tambov guberniya ........ | 148.3 | 243.8 |
| Chernigov guberniya ....... | 153.2 | 452.5 |
| Novgorod guberniya ....... | 148.4 | 198.9 |

TABLE 4–49

| Initial Factors | Gross Income | Distribution | |
|---|---|---|---|
| Labor of 3.5 workers | | Renewal of fixed capital | 80 |
| Fixed capital, 1,200 rubles | 1,100 | Renewal of circulating capital | 500 |
| Circulating capital, 500 rubles | | Payment for family labor | 520 |

data cannot confuse us and does not contradict the Swiss peasant family's higher standard of well-being. This is derived, not from a high payment per labor unit, but from the ability and skill to make more use of the working year in the sense of working more days, and mainly from capitalist profit on the hired labor employed on the majority of Swiss farms.

With these organizational considerations, we end this long-drawn-out chapter; we suppose they are enough to substantiate our somewhat abstract theoretical conclusions and to select problems for further chapters.

TABLE 4–50

| | |
|---|---|
| Starobel'sk uezd | 1.33 |
| Volokolamsk uezd | 1.38 |
| Gzhatsk uezd | 1.37 |
| Porech'e uezd | 1.23 |
| Sychevka uezd | 1.56 |
| Dorogobuzh uezd | 1.47 |
| Laur's Swiss budgets | 1.52 |

# CHAPTER 5

# *Capital on the Labor Farm*

The basic rules we have shown for drawing up a peasant farm's organizational plan give us considerable material to judge how means of production are organized in the farms we have studied. We now know the technically necessary supply rates for various forms of means of production, the rates at which they wear out and are replaced, and the relationships between value of buildings, equipment, livestock, and so on. It must be acknowledged, however, that in establishing these relationships we have until now not gone beyond the limits of technical analysis. We have studied buildings, livestock, and agricultural machines simply as such. Even when speaking of their *value*, we were essentially speaking of their value as current equipment, and not of capital as an *abstract* sum of values in production circulation on the farm. Now that we know the technical work conditions and value of means of production, we can pass on to the most important problem in our study—how peasant farm capital is formed and renewed as a sum of values that the family allocates from its personal consumption for productive ends.

The problem of capital on the labor farm is the most important in our whole study because in developing the theory of the peasant farm as a farm that fundamentally differs from the capitalist farm we can consider our task done only when we can undoubtedly establish that on the labor farm capital as such is subject to other circulation laws and plays a different part in its composition than it does in capitalist undertakings. Several statements that certainly indicate a role for capital on the labor farm somewhat different from that which it plays in capitalist undertakings have been established by the materials we dealt with in Chapters 3 and 4.

Thus, we know that economic activity and the quantity of labor used on the peasant farm are determined not so much by the amount of the proprietor's capital as by family size and the equilibrium achieved between its demand satisfaction and the drudgery of labor.

195

It is true that the availability of a particular amount of capital, by changing the conditions for labor use, greatly influences the achievement of this equilibrium, but it does so as one of the conditions, *indirectly*, and not as the main factor.

We also know that the relationship of the elements of production —in particular, land and capital—on the peasant farm where there is relative shortage or abundance of land does not correspond to the capitalist optimal which would give the highest return on the capital invested in the undertaking. In attempting to increase its total annual income, the peasant farm often increases outlays of labor *and capital* per unit area far above the optimum rate which, in bookkeeping terms, gives a small percentage profit or none at all. Finally, we see that by increasing the farm's labor intensity the peasant family may, with the same capital, considerably raise the volume of activity and also its gross income, again at the cost of reducing payment per labor unit and the net bookkeeping profit.

These observations are, substantially, enough to answer the negative part of our question and to recognize that capital does not always play the same part on the peasant as on the capitalist farm. It may be arranged to pursue other aims and originate in other forms. We will try to explain what these aims are and what are the particular forms of capital use.

First, we will try to pose the question as accurately as possible so that the answers will not be misinterpreted. To this end, we will go into the morphology of capital circulation on labor and capitalist undertakings, and will construct a schematic model of this circulation.

The scheme of capital circulation in a capitalist undertaking was established in K. Marx's well-known formula:

$$M-C-M+m$$

and may be graphically shown (Figure 5–1).

FIGURE 5–1

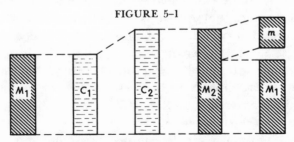

EDITORS' NOTE.—Chayanov supplied no legend; the formula $M - C - M^1$ comes from Vol. I of Marx's *Capital*, Part II, Ch. IV. $M$ = Money, $C$ = Commodities, and $M^1$ = the original sum advanced, plus an increment.

We see that the capital advanced is invested in elements of production (land, equipment, labor, and so on); when these have gone through their production cycle they are *sold* for money and give gross income. From gross income, first, the advanced capital is renewed; then, all that remains is the undertaking's net profit. The profit is the farm's target, and, therefore, the elements of production are compounded in a way that, at the particular price levels, is optimal and gives the greatest excess of gross income over capital advanced.

In analyzing the nature of the labor farm, we can easily establish that its characteristics scheme of capital circulation will be somewhat

FIGURE 5-2

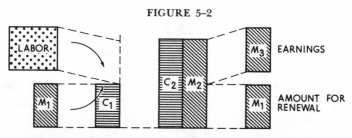

EDITORS' NOTE.—Chayanov supplied no legend; the formula $M - C - M^1$ comes from Vol. I of Marx's *Capital*, Part II, Ch. IV. $M$ = Money, $C$ = Commodities, and $M^1$ = the original sum advanced, plus an increment.

different, since in addition to capital the family contributes its own labor in production. We see in the scheme that the labor and capital contributed by the peasant family combine the production factors (labor, land, equipment, and so on). As a result of the production process, these give gross income. From this gross income, part should be devoted to renewal of capital advanced to its former level in order to keep activity at the former volume, and part to expanded reproduction if the family is expanding its economic activity. All the remainder is available to satisfy the usual family demands, or otherwise for reproduction of the work force.

Comparing both schemes, we see that for the capitalist entrepreneur the sum of values that serves to renew the work force is, from his private economic viewpoint, indistinguishable from other parts of the capital advanced to the undertaking, and is determined by the objective national economic category of wages and number of workers required for the particular volume of activity. This, in its turn, is determined by the total size of the entrepreneur's capital.

However, on the labor farm, so far as it remains such, the sum of values that serves to renew the work force is the cultivating peasant's personal budget. This budget is determined by family size and the extent to which their demands are satiated, and this depends on a whole series of effective conditions synthesized in the on-farm equilibrium, which, as we know, determines the total volume of the family's economic activity. Hence, it would seem that the amount of capital and, consequently, the amount annually allocated for capital renewal should be composed according to the technical requirements, depending on the volume of economic activity established by this equilibrium. At the same time, however, we know that the basic equilibrium itself, which determines the volume of family economic activity, largely depends on the availability of capital to labor—in other words, on the amount of capital advanced with the labor. We have at first sight a logical vicious circle.

In resolving it, we also come near to posing our central problem: *What sort of link or, more accurately, interrelationships are there between the capital advanced or, similarly, annually renewed and the basic economic equilibrium between the drudgery of labor and family demands, which establishes the amount of annual earnings?*

It would be naïve to consider their link a one-sided dependence of one on the other. We have before us two interconnected groups of phenomena which form a single system by establishing an equilibrium between the components of both groups. The task of this chapter is to disclose the mechanism for establishing this equilibrium. Yet, while in the past we have rather fully established how capital, according to its *intensity*, influences production and the basic economic equilibrium, now we will focus our attention mainly on the *origin* of this capital, on the factors that determine its amount, and on the processes of capital renewal and formation.

Putting it more simply, we ought to determine the conditions in which, while setting its economic equilibrium for the particular year, the peasant family will, at the same time, be able to completely renew the physical capital used on production. We should also determine the conditions in which it will be unable to do this, and how in setting its on-farm equilibrium it will be able to achieve expanded reproduction of its physical capital. In other words, which factors determine, in each particular year, the division of the peasant family's gross income into expenditure on capital formation and renewal of the labor force, taking into account that the expenditures are not controlled by wage rates?

Let us first sum up the empirical material we have and the empirical conclusions to which elaboration of this material may lead. Since study of capital circulation is the most important thing for us, especially the processes of capital renewal and formation, we will turn our attention to them first, and will try to analyze, in the budget materials we have collected, the composition and movement of the "economic expenditures," as they are called, which reflect these processes.

By "economic expenditures" we mean all expenditure in the current year, in money and kind, intended for production, not consumption. Quite consciously, we include in their total both expenditure connected with circulation (for seed, fodder, and so on) and expenditure on renewing and forming fixed capital (erection and repair of buildings, and even purchases of land), since both equally are capital advanced for production purposes. Table 5–1 acquaints us with the prewar composition of these expenditures for more or less typical farms in northern and southern European Russia.

TABLE 5–1

|  | Starobel'sk Uezd | | Novgorod Guberniya | |
| --- | --- | --- | --- | --- |
|  | Per Farm (Rubles) | Percentage | Per Farm (Rubles) | Percentage |
| Rent for land ............... | 30.92 | 5.7 | 3.84 | 1.6 |
| Erection and repair of buildings ............... | 21.97 | 4.1 | 5.25 | 2.0 |
| Acquision and repair of equipment ............ | 26.39 | 4.9 | 10.86 | 4.3 |
| Purchases of land and livestock .................. | 111.79 | 20.6 | 7.25 | 3.0 |
| Wages of hired workers ...... | 5.43 | 1.0 | 5.81 | 2.3 |
| Taxes and payments ......... | 12.54 | 2.3 | 11.89 | 4.8 |
| Maintenance of stock and poultry ............... | 135.46 | 43.4 | 134.10 | 53.3 |
| Seed ....................... | 50.40 | 9.3 | 36.20 | 14.6 |
| Manure ................... | 0.00 | 0.0 | 13.70 | 5.5 |
| Miscellaneous .............. | 47.34 | 8.7 | 21.80 | 8.6 |
| Total ................ | 542.24 | 100.0 | 250.70 | 100.0 |

Table 5–2 is a characteristic comparison of economic expenditure with expenditure on personal consumption. In it, we have added certain other material to the data from Starobel'sk uezd and Novgorod guberniya.

The variations in personal and economic expenditure observed between areas are explained by differing forms of economic activity. In northern areas, crafts and trades play almost the most important part in peasant economic activity; therefore, the volume of agricultural activity, both absolutely and relative to personal budgets, will

TABLE 5–2

EXPENDITURE ON PERSONAL AND ECONOMIC DEMANDS

| | on | | | Expenditure on Economic Needs | |
|---|---|---|---|---|---|
| | Personal Expenditure | Economic Needs | Total | | Per 100 Rubles on Personal Consumption |
| Budgets | Per Farm | | | Percentage | Rubles |
| Novgorod .......... | 375.11 | 250.70 | 625.81 | 40.0 | 66.9 |
| Starobel'sk ......... | 470.78 | 542.24 | 1013.02 | 53.5 | 115.1 |
| Volokolamsk ....... | 497.20 | 557.50 | 1054.70 | 52.8 | 112.0 |
| Tot'ma ............ | 201.50 | 176.30 | 377.80 | 46.8 | 87.6 |

be much less than in the south. Moreover, the capital intensity of the particular system may introduce considerable modifications. By attentively studying budget materials from other areas, one might in all probability notice many other territorial variations.

Such is the general information on expenditure on personal and economic ends. Now, let us try to analyze their interrelationship. First, we will try to follow the changes in each one as income increases.

TABLE 5–3

NOVGOROD BUDGETS
(rubles)

| | | Economic Expenditure | | |
|---|---|---|---|---|
| Personal Budget per Consumer | Consumer's Budget | Per Consumer | Per 100 Rubles Personal Expenditure | Fixed Capital per Consumer |
| 0.0– 49.0 ...... | 44.5 | 27.0 | 60.8 | 58.3 |
| 50.0– 59.9 ...... | 55.2 | 31.9 | 57.8 | 72.9 |
| 60.0– 69.9 ...... | 64.7 | 40.2 | 64.7 | 114.8 |
| 70.0– 79.9 ...... | 73.3 | 53.7 | 73.3 | 132.1 |
| 80.0– 89.9 ...... | 84.5 | 49.3 | — | 153.0 |
| 90.0– 99.9 ...... | 95.6 | 79.2 | 82.8 | 242.4 |
| 100.0–109.9 ...... | 105.9 | 85.0 | 80.3 | 257.0 |
| 110.0–119.9 ...... | 113.9 | 81.6 | 71.7 | 227.3 |
| 120.0–129.9 ...... | 126.0 | 88.9 | 70.5 | 335.0 |
| 130.0–∞ ........ | 172.4 | 86.6 | 50.2 | 361.0 |

The Novgorod guberniya budget materials in Table 5–3, ranked by level of consumer's personal budget, give us a particularly clear picture of the relationship between income level and its distribution between personal and economic expenditure.

Let us trace the course of the figures we have analyzed in Figure 5–3.

FIGURE 5–3

ECONOMIC EXPENDITURE PER CONSUMER
AND PERSONAL BUDGET NOVGOROD GUBERNIYA

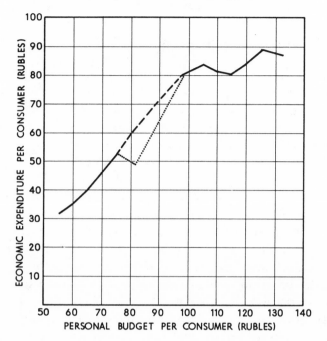

In following the curve, we see that as its well-being grows the Novgorod peasant farm increases its capital intensity more and more until it reaches a level of about 80 rubles economic expenditure per consumer. After this, the advances for capital formation increase no further, but fluctuate about this sum, and the proportion of economic expenditure falls.

This observation has recently been made by other economists (A. L. Vainshtein, G. A. Studenskii, and others) as well as by us; it permits us to suppose that in peasant farm organization there exists a certain limit to rational equipping of the work force with means of production. Any increase in capital available to the worker up to this limit obviously helps to raise labor productivity. At this limit, the maximum is reached and the available capital enables the work force to develop its full production potential. No further increase in the farm's capital intensity (unless accompanied by a change in technique, of course) can increase labor productivity and alter the basic equilibrium of on-farm factors.

Such is the first empirical conclusion we can make from looking at the process of capital formation. By studying the table, however, we can draw a further, more important conclusion. We see in the table and graph that economic expenditures, i.e., the amount spent from annual earnings on renewing capital, run parallel to the personal budget. At the same time, while the farm's capital intensity has not yet reached its optimum, the growth rate for capital renewal in most cases exceeds that for personal budgets.

Noting this link, we may suppose that determining expenditures on capital renewal is inseparably linked with that of personal budgets. One way or another, these expenditures *are included in our system of the basic economic equilibrium between drudgery of labor and the farm family's demand satisfaction.*

We see that at a low level of personal budget the process of capital formation, or even only of capital renewal, cannot take place to any considerable extent. So far are elementary needs from being satisfied that there can be no thought of limiting consumption and devoting any considerable amount to capital formation. Only gradually, as labor productivity increases and the personal budget can be expanded to meet the chief family needs one after another, is the head of the farm able to direct an ever-increasing part of income to capital renewal and formation. In other words, we can say that on the family farm advances to renew and to form capital carried out from the same budget are linked to the process of satisfying personal demands, and in every case their amount depends on the degree to which these demands are satisfied.

The last formulation is, of course, an oversimplified scheme necessary to underline our thought; but, as we will see below, deeper analysis indicates that it is in a certain sense quite correct.

As long ago as 1913, we were able to observe that the farm's capital intensity depended on family well-being. At that time, while working on budget materials from peasant farms of Starobel'sk uezd, Khar'kov guberniya, we unexpectedly came on a certain connection between capital and the factors comprising the personal budget of the farm family, which is shown in Table 5–4. This table has undoubtedly stressed the peculiarity we have noted in the composition of the labor farm's capital.

Strict critics who look at the statistical series we have compared and recognize the connection between family's personal budget and economic expenditure as established may entirely reject our conception of this connection. They may simply suppose that in renewing itself the capital circulating on the peasant farm automatically gives for each unit a corresponding level of family well-being, and that

TABLE 5–4

NUMBER OF COWS AND HORSES PER CONSUMER BY
ARABLE AND PERSONAL BUDGET

| Arable (Desyatinas) Per Consumer | Personal Budget | | | |
|---|---|---|---|---|
| | 0–70.0 | 70.1–90.0 | 90.1–∞ | Average |
| | Cows | | | |
| 0–2.0 ......... | 0.11 | 0.17 | 0.13 | 0.14 |
| 2.1–3.0 ......... | 0.20 | 0.26 | 0.44 | 0.30 |
| 3.1–∞ ......... | 0.11 | 0.30 | 0.26 | 0.22 |
| Average .. | 0.14 | 0.24 | 0.28 | — |
| | Horses | | | |
| 0–2.0 ......... | 0.14 | 0.17 | 0.26 | 0.19 |
| 2.1–3.0 ......... | 0.26 | 0.20 | 0.22 | 0.22 |
| 3.1–∞ ......... | 0.11 | 0.20 | 0.29 | 0.30 |
| Average .. | 0.17 | 0.19 | 0.24 | — |

there is no on-farm equilibrium concerned at all. Despite the naïveté of this sort of remark, it has very frequently been made to us. Essentially, we can answer with a simple question. If the personal budget is subordinate, why does the farm family, having received a certain gross income as a result of the year's work, not try to take the process of capital formation to the optimum that would insure it the highest income? Why is it sometimes obliged to limit itself to merely renewing clearly insufficient capital, and sometimes forced to restrict even the process of renewal? Once the extent to which demands are met is a derived figure, what then insures that the money in the personal budget is not allocated to expand renewed capital?

To us, the answer to this question is clear. If the year's income level depended more on the capital advanced during the year, then its distribution, and primarily its distribution between personal and economic demands, would, in turn, depend on the present and intended basic equilibrium of on-farm factors.

Not a single element in the family farm is free; they all interact and determine one another's size. No other explanation can be given for that fading and recovery in capital formation which we clearly see in the countryside during favorable and unfavorable harvest and market situations.

Undoubtedly, however, as we make our analysis more precise and clearly establish the direction of the connection we should do it so that the results may not be interpreted ambiguously. First, once we assert that capital formation depends on the on-farm equilibrium we ought to show how it depends on the mechanism of this equilibrium.

For example, since capital formation is affected by the general equilibrium of on-farm factors, conditions influencing this equilibrium cannot but affect the factors. As we know, one such factor is the numerical relationship of family consumers to workers. Let us see how capital formation reacts to this factor. To do this, we divide family farms into two subgroups; the first has a lower-than-average consumer–worker ratio, and the second has a higher-than-average one. In Table 5–5, we reckon the totals by half-groups. For almost all

TABLE 5–5
NOVGOROD GUBERNIYA

| | Expenditure on Economic Requirements per Consumer | |
| Personal Expenditure per Consumer | Consumer–Worker Ratio | |
| | Less Than Average | Above Average |
|---|---|---|
| 0.0– 49.9 ...... | 28.5 | 25.1 |
| 50.0– 59.9 ...... | 35.5 | 27.8 |
| 60.0– 69.9 ...... | 42.5 | 37.4 |
| 70.0– 79.9 ...... | 59.4 | 48.7 |
| 80.0– 89.9 ...... | (48.0) | 50.6 |
| 90.0– 99.9 ...... | 84.6 | 74.3 |
| 100.0–119.9 ...... | (64.0) | 98.2 |
| 120.0–∞ ........ | 89.7 | 86.7 |

groups, the consumption significance of a ruble of income grows as the family is increasingly burdened with consumers and the farm can advance a relatively smaller amount of capital.

It is necessary to note that other budget materials do not show such a clear reaction as the Novgorod ones, nor do they as regards the influence of the consumer–worker ratio on the consumer's budget. In 1912, I noted this in essays on the theory of the labor farm, and the late V. K. Dmitriev paid particular attention to it. On the other hand, economic expenditure per worker will always give us a sharply expressed series (Table 5–6).

Other studies give a reaction of similar type, as may be seen from Table 5–7. These series leave us in no doubt that advances for the

TABLE 5–6
NOVGOROD GUBERNIYA

| Consumer–Worker Ratio | Economic Expenditure per Worker |
|---|---|
| 1.0 –1.25 .............. | 59.61 |
| 1.26–1.50 .............. | 73.85 |
| 1.51–∞ ................ | 82.55 |

TABLE 5–7

CONSUMER–WORKER RATIO AND CAPITAL RENEWAL

| | Consumer–Worker Ratio | | | | |
|---|---|---|---|---|---|
| | 1.01–1.15 | 1.16–1.30 | 1.31–1.45 | 1.46–1.60 | 1.61–∞ |
| | Economic Expenditure per Worker | | | | |
| Khar'kov guberniya ....... | 110.6 | 207.9 | 286.5 | 318.6 | 348.0 |
| Tambov guberniya ....... | 93.1 | 155.4 | 165.0 | 136.3 | 215.3 |
| Smolensk guberniya ...... | 148.9 | 154.4 | 197.4 | 194.5 | 237.0 |
| Vologda uezd ........... | 56.1 | 59.2 | 91.5 | 81.5 | 104.0 |

reproduction of physical capital are subject to pressure from family composition, and it is clear that in this case there cannot be any reverse influence by capital advanced on family composition. The dependence of capital formation on the on-farm equilibrium is clearer in this example than anywhere else.

However, despite the entirely convincing nature of these comparisons it was of considerable interest to us to compare groups in which the direct influence of personal budget on economic expenditure would be stressed, while at the same time the reverse influence of agricultural income on personal expenditure would be excluded. Such a comparison was essential for us to finally dispense with the supposition we have noted: the personal budget crudely and directly depends on volume of economic activity determined by *available* means of production. This view is, unfortunately, quite widespread in some circles.

We found such a comparison for the Novgorod farms, with their considerable activity in crafts and trades, by constructing a combined table showing agricultural income per consumer and personal budget. These did not correspond in Novgorod because of receipts from crafts and trades. This comparison gave the result in Table 5–8.

The table very clearly shows that at the same level of agricultural income the amount of capital advanced for production purposes

TABLE 5–8

EXPENDITURE ON ECONOMIC REQUIREMENTS BY
PERSONAL BUDGET AND AGRICULTURAL INCOME
(Novgorod Budgets)

| Farms by Consumer's Personal Budget | Agricultural Income per Consumer | | |
|---|---|---|---|
| | 0–69.9 | 70–99.9 | 100–∞ rubles |
| | Economic Expenditure per Consumer | | |
| High ......... | 27.1 | 41.2 | 60.8 |
| Average ........ | 31.8 | 47.4 | 77.2 |
| Low .......... | 43.6 | 53.5 | 94.5 |

changes very greatly, depending on personal budget. Since personal budget differences at the same level of agricultural income might be solely due to greater or smaller receipts from crafts and trades, we have directly classified farms according to their amount of craft and trade activity. Table 5–9, which is very characteristic, resulted.

TABLE 5–9

FARM'S CRAFTS AND TRADES ACTIVITY, AGRICULTURAL INCOME, AND ECONOMIC EXPENDITURE
(Novgorod Budgets)   (Rubles per Consumer)

| Agricultural Income | Economic Expenditure | | Fixed Capital | |
|---|---|---|---|---|
| | Farms with Little Crafts and Trades Activity | Farms with Much Crafts and Trades Activity | Farms with Little Crafts and Trades Activity | Farms with Much Crafts and Trades Activity |
| 30.0– 39.9 . . . . . . | 25.8 | 20.7 | 30.5 | 42.9 |
| 40.0– 49.9 . . . . . . | 20.6 | 30.9 | 59.3 | 74.7 |
| 50.0– 59.9 . . . . . . | 27.6 | 34.1 | 112.4 | 94.3 |
| 60.0– 69.9 . . . . . . | 40.0 | 42.6 | 84.1 | 130.2 |
| 70.0– 79.9 . . . . . . | 41.0 | 40.3 | 107.2 | 148.8 |
| 80.0– 89.9 . . . . . . | 43.8 | 48.3 | 114.2 | 195.3 |
| 90.0– 99.9 . . . . . . | 55.6 | 56.4 | 183.8 | 182.1 |
| 100.0–109.9 . . . . . . | 53.1 | 63.5 | 111.7 | 173.7 |
| 110.0–129.9 . . . . . . | 47.8 | 78.3 | 116.8 | 355.9 |
| 130.0–139.9 . . . . . . | 81.7 | 84.6 | 195.0 | 235.0 |
| 140.0–∞ . . . . . . . . | 104.2 | 100.7 | 380.5 | 311.5 |

As the table shows, in eight out of the eleven categories crafts and trades activity led to an increase in economic expenditure per consumer. This conclusion, at first sight paradoxical, is explained by the fact that in this classification such activity means a higher personal budget rate, which leads to an inevitable increase in capital advanced.

Because these empirical conclusions show that capital formation and renewal undoubtedly depend on the basic equilibrium of the family undertaking's on-farm factors, we are obliged to provide a theoretical justification. As we will see below, a very simple range of considerations will be enough to incorporate the capital renewal process into the system of equilibrium between drudgery of labor and demand satisfaction we have several times analyzed.

The problem we wish to analyze may be divided into two independent questions: (1) What influence does farm capital and varying capital intensity have on achieving the equilibrium on the family farm? (2) What influence does the basic equilibrium of on-farm factors in the family farm have on advancing means (capital) to the farm's production cycle? We will first deal with question 1.

FIGURE 5–4

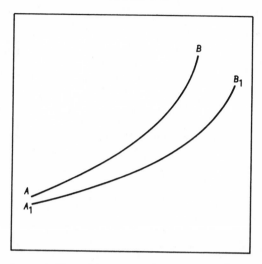

Let us take the usual graph we use for our analysis of this equilibrium. It is determined by the intersection of the curve for increasing
drudgery of labor, *AB*, and the demand satisfaction curve, *CD*. To
explain how the farm's capital intensity is connected with the equilibrium, we should explain how the presence and varying intensity of
capital formation influences each of these curves separately.

Any increase in capital intensity or, what is the same thing, in
availability to the family of means of production—if it is rational, of
course—increases the family labor force's productivity. Moreover, this
increase can be of two types. (1) Increased farm capital may raise the
productivity of all labor expenditure on the farm. In terms of our
graph, this will mean that thanks to increased capital intensity the
family will obtain each unit of farm gross income with less than previous labor intensity. In the graph, this means a downward shift in
the curve *AB*, as shown in Figure 5–4, where $A_1B_1$ corresponds to the
increased capital intensity. (2) Without leading to a general rise in
labor productivity, increased farm capital can have a positive effect
on a particular farm sector. In this case, obviously, the farm will obtain the greater part of its gross income with the same degree of
drudgery as formerly, and only part of the annual income will be
obtained with reduced labor intensity. In the graph, this will mean
that for a considerable length the curve *AB* will run as before, and
only at a certain moment, corresponding to the introduction of the
new capital, will it be shifted downward, as shown in Figure 5–5.

Thus, a rational increase in farm capital intensity causes the curve

FIGURE 5–5

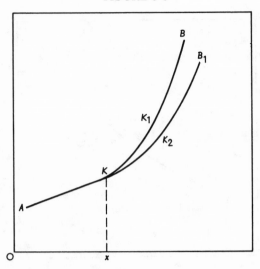

of increasing drudgery of labor to be shifted downward for the whole or part of its length.

However, observing the increase in gross labor productivity is not enough to judge the effect of varying capital intensity in achieving on-farm equilibrium. We must find the effect of increased capital intensity on the demand satisfaction curve (*CD*).

Any capital advanced means directing resources available to the cultivating peasant into production instead of into personal consumption, i.e., the reduction of consumption. Even if—and for sim-

FIGURE 5–6

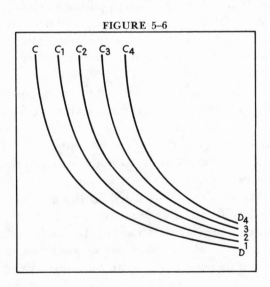

plicity in our analysis we accept this hypothesis—the capital advance is made with *loan* capital, paying off the debt at the end of the year means a deduction from gross income for nonconsumption ends. Therefore, any increase in farm capital intensity means that a smaller part of each unit of gross income will be directed to satisfy personal demands. In other words, with increasing capital intensity each unit of gross income will give less demand satisfaction. In the graph, this leads to an upward shift of the curve *CD* as shown in Figure 5–6. This will give us a series of new curves, $C_1D_1$, $C_2D_2$, $C_3D_3$, and $C_4D_4$.

If we now compare the old curves *AB* and *CD*, prior to spending the new material values on production, with the new curves $A_1B_1$ and $C_1D_1$, we naturally see that this leads to a new point of equilibrium ($x_1$) (Figure 5–7). It is clear that the application of capital which we have analyzed will be acceptable to our farm only when the new equilibrium is established (1) *with less drudgery of marginal labor*

FIGURE 5–7

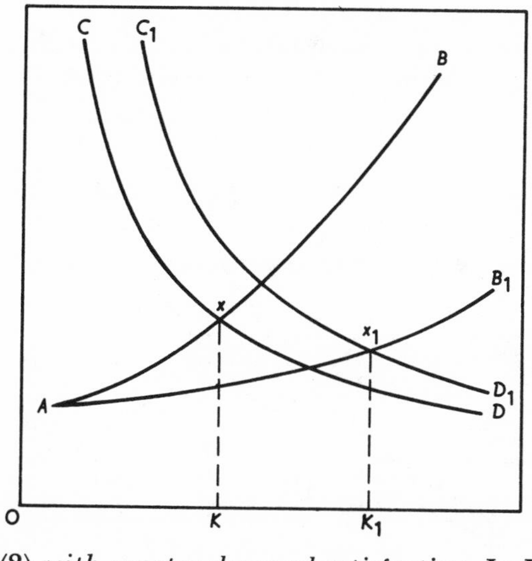

*expenditure*, (2) *with greater demand satisfaction*. In Figure 5–8, this condition is fulfilled. Conversely, the new capital expenditure will *not be advantageous* from the labor farm's point of view as soon as, despite the increased net income, it leads to (1) *increased drudgery of marginal labor expenditure*, (2) *a reduction in demand satisfaction*.

Figures 5–8 and 5–9 show the advantageous and disadvantageous application of the same capital sum. In the second application, the growth in labor productivity was so insignificant that it could not cover the large deduction from the farm's income.

FIGURE 5–8
ADVANTAGEOUS

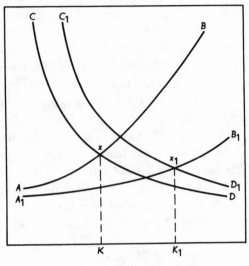

FIGURE 5–9
DISADVANTAGEOUS

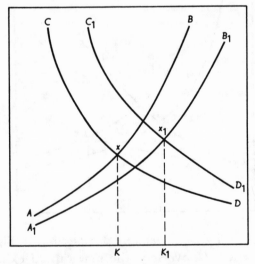

Such is the part played by capital renewal in the general system of establishing the labor farm's basic economic equilibrium. But since not a single peasant farm exists without some capital expenditure, the graphs we gave in Chapter 2 are simplified ones. They start from the proposition that the family's economic expenditure is zero, and to avoid misunderstandings we consider it necessary to qualify this now.

To show as clearly as possible how much capital renewal on labor farms differs from that on the capitalist farm, we will analyze two examples long known in agricultural literature but not yet theoretically treated.

A. F. Fortunatov and other authors have often quoted the report on the work of agricultural bodies in popularizing machines, which D. G. Kirsanov, a Perm' agricultural officer, presented at the Perm' Agricultural Congress. Kirsanov notes the great difficulties in popularizing threshing machines in areas where there are no crafts and trades in winter and, apart from threshing, nothing else with which the population can occupy itself. It is true that the introduction of the threshing machine eases the work and frees many hands, says Kirsanov; but since these hands can find no other work to do, this does not increase peasant family income by a kopek. The cost of the thresher, though, is a considerable deduction from the meager peasant budget.

By using our graphical analysis method, we can construct the effect of Kirsanov's thresher, starting from the proposition that it has no effect on reducing the drudgery of marginal labor expenditure, but reduces that of certain expenditures of average drudgery which do not affect the equilibrium of the economic factors. Then, acquiring a threshing machine gives us the effect shown by *AB* and *CD* in Figure 5–10.

The threshing machine shifts curve $AM_1B$ to $AM_2B$, but this change has no further influence on the curve *AB*. The change in *CD*

FIGURE 5–10

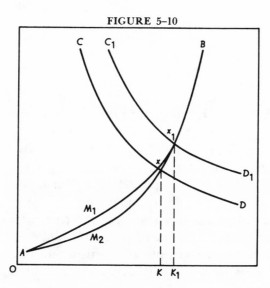

to $C_1D_1$ gives a new equilibrium position, aggravating the drudgery of labor and reducing the farm family's demand satisfaction.

The second example is still more interesting. It comes from our observations in the Southeast, where small farms on the Don and Kuban often use harvesting machines on areas where they cannot be made to pay for themselves. The cause of this is that the ripe grain remains in the ear only four or five days, and without the machine the family could harvest only a much smaller field area than it could sow and cultivate. Since harvesting, like Kirsanov's thresher, is not in a marginal situation as regards drudgery of labor, the reduction of labor payment due to the machine's being unprofitable is recouped by an increased volume of activity. This results in a more favorable position of the equilibrium, as is seen in Figure 5–11.

FIGURE 5–11

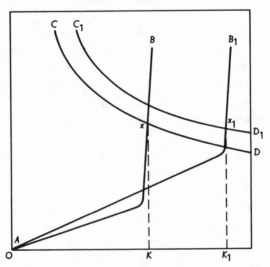

The sharp turns in curves $AB$ and $A_1B_1$ result because apart from spring-sown grains all other agricultural activities give a much smaller labor payment. Therefore, acquiring a harvesting machine and slightly reducing labor payment for wheat harvesting permits this work, much more advantageous than the rest but formerly constrained by the critical harvest period, to be expanded.

Quite enough has been said to understand the mechanism that determines the advantages or disadvantages of a particular use of capital on the labor farm. It is self-evident that given the possibility—which, it is true, is hardly ever encountered—of using unlimited credit free of interest, the peasant family will increase its capital to a stage where all its work force is optimally equipped with means of production. This will correspond economically and technically to family composition, and will give maximum annual labor payment with minimum intensity.

In order to have a clearer conception of how this optimal farm capital intensity is established, we will again make use of our graphic method and see how equilibriums are established with varying farm capital intensities. Let us take the economic work of a family without any capital. In Figure 5–12, this is represented by the *AB* curve of drudgery of labor. *CD* shows demand satisfaction and four possible degrees of capital intensity for the farm as a whole (I is $C_1D_1$ and $A_1B_1$, II is $C_2D_2$ and $A_2B_2$, III is $C_3D_3$ and $A_3B_3$, IV is $C_4D_4$ and $A_4B_4$). We see in Figure 5–12 that by increasing the farm's capital intensity from zero to the first degree and from the first to the second we raise the farm's well-being, since the effect of intensity, in the sense of a

FIGURE 5–12

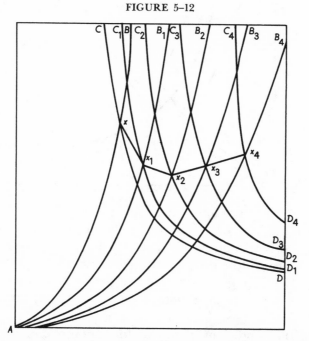

reduction of the drudgery of labor, exceeds the cost of the expenditure. However, this third degree is the optimum, since with further intensification deductions from personal budget to be spent on intensification become so perceptible that they cannot be compensated by a continuing reduction in the drudgery of labor.

The graph we have analyzed is constructed on the assumption that there is no return to credit. If the credit granted our farm becomes subject to interest, the scheme for determining the optimum remains basically the same; $C_1D_1$ will merely shift to $C_2D_2$, and so on. They will all shift upward, since it will be necessary to deduct from income not only the renewal of capital already advanced but also the interest on it. In this case, many applications of capital can become disadvantageous, as can be seen from the example shown in Figure 5–13. Therefore, any return on the use of capital will also lower the farm's optimal capital intensity. The higher the interest rates the farm has to pay on loans, the further it will reduce it.

FIGURE 5–13

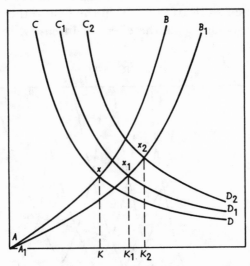

In any event, the peasant farm's capital intensity will always tend toward an optimum corresponding to the objective situation. And however speedily this optimum is achieved, any further increase in capital intensity will be disadvantageous to the farm family. Its free resources will either go to increase the personal budget or be put aside as savings and become, not a labor farm, but a capitalist category.

Such are the conditions of capital formation and renewal, given credits subject to interest or not. Some of our critics have argued against the need to make use of the labor–consumer hypothesis in interpreting family farm phenomena. They have pointed out to us that in this particular case whether a specific capital expenditure can or cannot be made may be expressed very simply and objectively. "If the use of capital gives an increase in net annual earnings per peasant family worker, the expenditure will be considered advantageous and, if resources are available, will be made."

In reply, we have every ground for saying that it is just this pseudo-objectively posed question which the peasant cannot answer without subjectively balancing those on-farm equilibrium factors which so irritate our critics. We will try to explain what has been said with two examples, making a comparison with the possible behavior of a capitalist farm. Let us suppose that in the area where the farm is situated there is a large rentable area very suitable for exploitation. The capitalist farm that has resources will exploit this area as much as possible, until either it comes up against technical difficulties, or the expansion of the rented area becomes objectively disadvantageous because of distance and growing transport costs.

Obviously, the labor farm, despite the objective advantage of renting 50 or 100 desyatinas, will limit the area rented to a few desyatinas —to the quantity that will square the labor–consumer balance. For each desyatina, without losing its objective advantage, subjectively means an increase in the drudgery of labor due simply to the increase in the annual amount. I venture to assure my critics that it is impossible to establish by any objective estimates or factors the point to which possible renting will take place and to which capital for rent and running the farm will be carried.

In exactly the same way, when stalling cattle the number of cows and, consequently, the amount of capital spent on them and on the means of production serving them will be established on the capitalist farm by the objective disadvantage of further expanding the herd. On the *family farm*, the amount will be set by the number of cows, where looking after the last one involves no more drudgery than not satisfying those demands that the income from this "marginal" cow might meet.

The only time an objective estimate might give some result is when some means of production are replaced by others, improved and more expensive and, consequently, requiring increased farm capital intensity. However, even in this case the new use of capital will be inevitably reflected in the general balance and will be able to expand or contract the volume of the family's farm work in sectors other than those to which capital is directed. As we saw in the examples of the Perm' thresher and the Kuban' reaper, frequently the basic equilibrium becomes complicated, as also does the question of advantage, applicability, and partial expenditure of capital on farm improvement. The moment of equilibrium, however, is decisive for determining the total absolute amount of capital, depending in general on the volume of activity.

Our analysis completely answers the first of the questions we posed on the influence of capital intensity in establishing the on-farm equilibrium. It has shown us the theoretical meaning of the optimal equipping of the farm family with capital, which we had empirically established.

Now we can pass to the second question we posed—how the state of the on-farm equilibrium influences capital formation and renewal. As we see from empirical analysis, farms are not always able to carry capital formation to a level that would guarantee them an optimal degree of capital intensity, have to work with their labor insufficiently supplied with means of production, and must square the on-farm equilibrium at a reduced level of well-being.

Moreover, empirical materials indicate, as we know, that the average peasant family on its farm is able to increase capital formation only in parallel with an increase in the personal budget, i.e., only if, due to some cause or other (a more favorable market situation or advantageous earnings from crafts and trades), the farm gross income increases.

Let us try to enter into the theoretical motives for such economic conduct. The peasant family as a result of its year's work receives, let us say, 1,000 rubles gross income in kind and money. What part of this will be directed to consumption needs and what will go on economic expenditure? This is one of the most complex problems in peasant farm organization. Every ruble of this thousand may be intended both for consumption and for the economy. It is quite clear that in order to exist the family should spend a considerable part of this income on its consumer needs. As needs are satisfied, the consumer evaluation of each ruble to be spent will fall, but however small it is, in all probability in any year the peasant family would be able to find a consumption purpose for all its annual income.

An obstacle to this is the insistent need, for the sake of the farm's future existence, to advance part of gross income to renew circulating capital and the exhausted part of fixed capital. Every farm family understands precisely what these economic expenditures mean. From its many years of experience, the family knows that to reduce its economic resources will mean a greater intensity of labor effort in the following year and, despite this, will result in a reduced level of well-being. In just the same way, it clearly understands that its future position may improve if capital formation is increased. In other words, the production purpose of every ruble can be evaluated from the viewpoint of the level of well-being in a future year, which is supposed to be linked to a particular amount of capital renewal in the current year. Based on our earlier analysis, we can also graphically express this form of evaluating rubles directed to productive purposes.

To show the effect on the on-farm equilibrium of varying amounts of loan capital advanced, which was returnable after use, we put in Figure 5–12 the demand satisfaction established by the on-farm equilibrium corresponding to each unit of capital advanced. If we now mark off the total amount of capital to be advanced against the subjective evaluation of that demand satisfaction which corresponds to each amount advanced, we obtain a curve of the subjective evaluation of rubles successively directed to capital accumulation from the point of view of their future consumption effect (*KM* in Figure 5–14). By this, we find a measure to evaluate the production purpose of rubles comparable with that usual for evaluating their consumption purpose (*CD*).

FIGURE 5–14

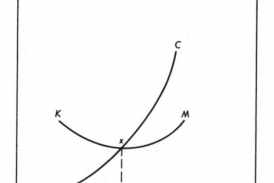

Let us compare both curves in order to divide the gross income of 1,000 rubles which we have taken; the function of the consumption value of successive expenditures will run from right to left (*CD*). Then, we have the following system of curves which intersect at *x*, corresponding to 600 rubles on personal consumption and 400 on economic purposes. By comparing both curves we can trace peasant family psychology as it decides the basic question of its economic conduct: *at what level should it call a halt to consumption in order to assure a sufficient level of well-being in future years?*

If the family wishes to fix its well-being in future years at the same level at which it halts its consumption in the particular year—this should be taken as usual—obviously, it has to allocate to economic needs an amount which corresponds to the point of intersection or, similarly, to the equilibrium. In our graph, this takes place at an economic expenditure of 400 rubles. With any smaller expenditure, it is clear that the family, having improved its consumption in the current year, will in the next year strike an economic balance with much more drudgery and less demand satisfaction, as is clear from the curves for any sum less than 400 rubles.

If, however, the family wishes to raise its well-being in future years above the level at which it can stabilize itself from this year, it must undertake a certain reduction of its well-being in this year, and at this price, having increased the amount of capital available to its labor, provide for increasing its well-being in the future. We do not have empirical material with which to judge capital accumulation over a number of years on the same farm, and we therefore refrain from making any deeper analysis. It will be more prudent to accept—though this does not always correspond with everyday reality—that available income is divided according to the equilibrium of production and consumption evaluations or, more accurately, a desire to maintain a constant level of well-being. Accepting this conventional proposition, we will easily be able to theoretically explain the phenomenon we have observed of the growth of capital formation as gross incomes rise and its parallelism with increases in personal budget.

In fact, our analysis of the mechanism for dividing gross income between economic and consumption purposes was adapted in the graph to a gross income of 1,000 rubles. With a smaller sum—for example, 700 rubles—the course of the curves naturally changes somewhat. The curve *DC*, showing consumption evaluations, does not start at 1,000 but at 700 rubles and will take a higher course relative to the production evaluation curve, and equilibrium will be reached with a much smaller allocation to consumption needs, as is seen from Figure 5–15. The two graphs show us how, by making graphs of evaluations for consumption purposes (*DC*) separately for each amount of gross income, we can divide gross income between con-

FIGURE 5–15

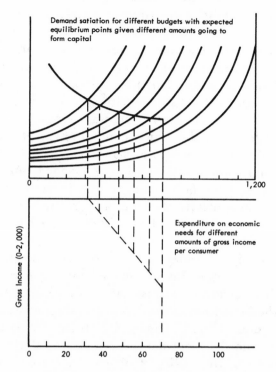

sumption and economic expenditure for any amount, and express it graphically.

Such is the mechanism for splitting off capital formation from the food consumption of gross income. Our theoretical analysis discloses it only in its most general features, but the results obtained are enough to show how the process differs considerably from the usual type of capitalist circulation of capital according to the formula, $M-C-M+m$.

Here, in the Russian edition of my study, I must make a certain digression and focus the reader's attention on some consideration of what has just been said. I have expressed the whole theoretical analysis of the basis on which capital renewal and accumulation takes place in the family farm as an equilibrium between subjective evaluations of different on-farm phenomena. I have used demand satisfaction, marginal expenditure of work force, equilibrium graphs, and displacement of curves showing data in conventional terms, not subject to precise measurement. These and other concepts and methods are so unusual that by making use of them in expounding my theory I run the great risk of not finding a common language with the Russian reader. When I had written out a fair copy of my study and read it through, I even thought, at one time, of entirely omitting this complex and difficult part. I tried to deal with it without making use of complex curves and conventional figures. These attempts, however, did not succeed, since the fundamental subject of my analysis—the family farm's labor–consumer balance—cannot be expressed in any objectively final figures. To dispense with analyzing the relationship of this balance with capital formation was completely impossible, since without it the whole theoretical content of Chapter 2 would be not only incomplete but even quite incorrect.

Therefore, after basic reorganization, I decided not to exclude the theoretical sections of the German edition from the Russian one, especially since they merely develop and refine what analytical method there was in Chapter 2. I merely considered it necessary to justify my arguments.

Due to the use of similar terms, many readers who skim through my theoretical formulas might include me in the Austrian school and thus pay less attention to this study. I have already protested about this in the introduction, but consider it appropriate to dwell on this question once more. The marginal utility school, whose many services to economics I do not deny, attempted to derive from subjective evaluations of the utility of objects *an entire* system of the national economy. This was its main error.

I do not do this. My whole analysis up to the present has been one of *on-farm processes*. I have striven to make clear to myself how *from a private economic viewpoint* the family farm's producing machine is organized, how it reacts to the particular effect of general economic factors pressing on it, how its volume is determined, and how capital formation takes place on it. It seems to me I have succeeded in showing that in its economic behavior the family farm, lacking the category of wages, differs from the economic unit based on hired labor both in making its estimates and in labor motivation, and that capital circulation takes place on it in a somewhat different fashion from that on the usual capitalist unit, which has been analyzed with such brilliance in Volume II of *Capital*.

Since without wages I could not give an objective estimate in value terms of on-farm phenomena as regards determining net profit as the difference between gross income and expenses, I had to introduce the hypothesis of the labor–consumer balance as a model which replaces the labor family's economic consciousness, or rather that of its head. I succeeded in showing that with the help of such an artificial machine the peasant farm can determine the volume of its economic work and react to all general economic factors, to price fluctuations, improvements in production techniques, to increased fertility, and to other factors generating rent in the economic sense. Finally, it can in a regular fashion carry out capital renewal and accumulation and circulate loan capital internally. In brief, it can exist in the present-day commodity structure of the economy as a whole.

We saw that the economic behavior of a machine thus constructed was in many cases identical with that of mechanisms based on hired labor, but in some cases—predominantly in instances of agrarian overpopulation—they differed sharply. In our view, the value of our constructs lies in the possibility they give for understanding these differences in economic behavior. Therefore, Professor Karl Diehl, of Freiburg, was quite right when, in reviewing the German edition of my book, he wrote that neglecting these distinguishing features of the family farm and extrapolating the economics of Smith and Ricardo onto it led the British to make a number of bad mistakes in their Indian economic policy.

Now, since we have theoretically constructed the family farm's economic machine, we must introduce it into the system of the present-day national economy, dominated by capitalist relations. We must explain to what extent various factors in this system will have an effect on our machine, and to what extent mass processes taking place in the farm sector—the elements of which are constructed like our machine—will themselves affect the existing system of the national economy. In both cases, of course, the connection between the family farm's machine and the national economy will be maintained, not by subjective evaluations, but by completely objective figures in value terms. These are obtained as a result of the family production we have analyzed, or they serve as its preconditions. In other words, any sort of subjective evaluation and equilibrium, which we have analyzed *as such*, does not appear from the depths of the family farm and show itself on the surface. Externally, it will be represented by the same objective figures as any other.

The peasant farm may refrain from buying an object it has subjectively valued at less than the market price, but if it does buy it will pay the same rubles for it as would a neighboring purely capitalist undertaking. However, as we will try to show in subsequent chapters, the family farm, due to the peculiar internal structure of its economic machine, has a number of objective features in respect of the national economy, both within the family farm sector and as it affects other components of the general economic system. Below, we try to show the general economic consequences that follow from the nature of the family farm's internal organization. It is in these parts of our work, and *only* in these, that our conclusions on the theory of the national economy may agree with or differ from those of the marginal utility school, the orthodox Marxists, Marxist–revisionists, neo-classicists, Anglo-Americans, and others.

Essentially speaking, for any of these theories to be universal its constructs should deal with all those peculiar features of family farm economic behavior we have shown empirically, and perhaps even with our conception of on-farm organization. In any event, our view on the family farm machine structure does not of itself contradict a single theory of national economy; it merely requires them to make some active effort in order to perceive it.

Thus, our farm, with all its peculiar features—and perhaps precisely because of these features—becomes subject to the most unrestrained capitalist exploitation and becomes an inseparable part of the capitalist system, so far as the family farm exists within an economy dominated by capitalist relations; so far as it is drawn into commodity production and is a petty commodity producer, selling and buying at prices laid down by commodity capitalism; and so far as its circulating capital is, in the end, bank loan capital. A Marxist author, for example, in order to explain the peculiar features of this form of exploitation, will have to take into account the peasant farm peculiarities we have established, the more so since Karl Marx himself had noted many of our propositions when he spoke of rent on the peasant parcellated farm.[1] Our digression from the direct development of our theme has gone on too long; we will end it and return again to the question of capital circulation on the peasant farm.

It seems to us that our analysis of the on-farm equilibrium's influence on capital circulation on the family farm enables us to formulate the following propositions.

1. At any particular level of technology and in a particular market situation, any labor family able to control the amount of land for use can increase its labor productivity by increasing the farm capital intensity to a certain level optimal for this family. Any forcing up of capital intensity

---

[1] K. Marx, "Sharecropping and peasant parcellated property," *Capital*, Vol. III, part 2, chap. 47, section v., pp. 339–50. On p. 347, for example, we read the following: ". . . with parcellated farming and small scale landed property . . . production to a very great extent satisfies own needs and is carried out independently of control by the general rate of profit." [Translated from Russian. The Kerr ed. (1909), p. 943, differs.]

beyond the optimum increases labor drudgery and even reduces its payment, since, on the one hand, increased expenditure to replace exhausted capital will counteract the useful effect of further capital intensification, while on the other, the economic realization of this capital requires the farm family to intensify its labor more than is permitted by the equilibrium of on-farm factors.

2. Far from all family farms work at optimal capital intensity. Many of them run their farms without adequate capital and receive a reduced payment for their labor. Often, these farms, despite every effort to bring farm capital to optimal size, cannot do this, since capital renewal, linked through our equilibrium with the satisfaction of personal demands, cannot reach an amount that would insure expanded capital reproduction.

3. In general, the processes of capital formation and renewal are tied into a certain equilibrium with other family farm processes (labor intensity, satisfaction of personal demands, and so on), and their force depends on these others. In poor farming years, capital renewal dies down, together with the fall in the personal budget and the rise in self-exploitation of the family labor force. In good years, it results in expanded capital reproduction, together with a rise in personal consumption and a fall in labor intensity.

Such are the fundamentals of capital structure and circulation on the family farm. In view of the exceptional significance of capital formation in peasant agrarian countries for the economy as a whole, we have no doubt that further study of these processes is the next thing and should start with the collection of empirical material.

In concluding the chapter on capital on the labor farm, we are also concluding the first part of our study, which has been devoted to the composition of the individual agricultural labor farm. All that has been said is the result of almost twenty years of work by a number of Russian economists who had before them the exceptionally rich material collected by Russian zemstvo statistics over half a century. In its present systematic form, this gives a more or less finished outline of peasant farm theory. In evaluating what has already been done, however, we again repeat that we have merely laid the basis for further, more detailed work; we have put forward ideas for a whole series of empirical studies. We must hope that the next generation of economists will succeed in developing the study of individual peasant farm organization fully and on the basis of a much greater quantity of material.

CHAPTER 6

# Consequences for the Economy
# Following from the Family Farm's
# Organizational Features

In the course of the preceding five chapters, we have very carefully —and perhaps even somewhat wearisomely for the reader—tried to stress that we are making our analysis at the private economic level, i.e., at the level of studying the internal workings of the peasant family economic machine. It is obvious that our theoretical construct of the labor farm machine cannot be conceived as hanging in a vacuum. We took our farm to be a commodity one and, consequently, one entering into a certain system of the economy which coexists with it, through credit and commodity circulation.

Dr. Kurt Ritter,[1] one of the critics of the German edition of this book, recognized the family undertaking's internal organizational features, which we have noted. But, at the same time, he considered it essential to retain for it the term "capitalist farm," because as it enters into the capitalist system of the present-day national economy, the family farm forms but a part of it. Selling and buying commodities at capitalist market prices, paying for its loan capital at the usual bank rate, and shaken by every crisis and depression of the capitalist system, it is thus merely a variant or phase of contemporary capitalism from the viewpoint of the economy as a whole.

The Kiel professor, A. Skalweit,[2] adopts almost the same attitude. We have nothing against such a conception, and, in substance, the whole content of the five preceding chapters could be fully accommodated within it, with certain terminological corrections. If, with par-

---

[1] *Jahrbücher für Nationalökonomie und Statistik*, Vol. 122 (June, 1924), p. 681.

[2] August Skalweit, "Die Familienwirtschaft, als Grundlage für ein System der Sozialökonomie," *Weltwirtschaftliches Archiv*, Vol. 20, part 2 (1924), pp. 231–46.

ticular insistence, we have counterposed, and continue to counterpose, the family to the capitalist farm, we have done so at the organization and production level—the labor farm contrasted to the farm based on hired labor. In this respect, these are two completely different economic machines which react differently to the same economic factors.

However, as regards the national economy, at the present time they are both elements in the same economic system whose pulse is felt, though differently, by both. The whole question consists simply in how this single economic system is formed—this system which we agree to call capitalist in view of the hegemony of capitalist relations. Or, more accurately, is there a difference in structure and functioning of the national economy's machine when machines of family type are only units in it, and when the overwhelming proportion of agricultural output is produced by such machines?

To avoid the accusation of being static, I am even prepared to rephrase this question. In the composition and functioning of the national economy's machine (as regards pricing, income distribution, location of production, etc.), is there a difference between the phase of capitalist development in which the number of family undertakings comprise a substantial part of production and the phase in which they have lost any significance?

In our opinion, there are such differences. Great family farm sectors of the national economy, in general always passive, are drawn into the capitalist system of the economy and subordinated to the organizing centers of capitalism. They themselves then begin to influence these centers with the peculiar features of their economic behavior, and immediately in some sectors this influence starts to act as a determinant. In other words, the present-day phase of capitalism, in which most industry and commerce is based on machines that exploit hired labor and a considerable part of agriculture is based on the family farm machine, should inevitably reflect the influence of both types of economic activity.

In theory, studies of the national economy from Ricardo to our day have been constructed deductively on the motivation and economic estimates of homo economicus, who works as a capitalist entrepreneur and builds his undertaking on the basis of hired labor. It turns out, in reality, that this classical homo economicus often does not sit in the entrepreneur's chair, but is the organizer of family production. Therefore, the system of theoretical economics constructed on the entrepreneurial activity of homo economicus as a capitalist is clearly one-sided and is inadequate for learning about economic reality in all its actual complexity.

What refinements can the partial transfer of homo economicus from one category to another introduce into the theory of the national economy? To answer this question and clearly detail possible deviations, it would be best to repeat the theoretical mistake of present-day economists, but in reverse. That is, we would assume that every homo economicus without exception is an organizer of a family economic unit, that hired labor and employers do not naturally exist, and that the national economy is formed from the interrelationships of these family units. In present conditions, such a hypothesis seems a little strange, but for a whole series of past epochs prior to the birth and development of capitalism such a construction might be closer to reality than the conception of, let us say, Adam Smith.[3] For us, such a system would be of great analytic interest. It would have the same relation to present-day theoretical economics as Lobachevskii's geometry has to that of Euclid. Lobachevskii forewent parallel lines; we have dropped wages.

However, we do not think we are able or have the right to occupy the reader by expounding the economics of a pure labor unit culture.[4] We will only analyze some general economic consequences which follow from family farm organizational features and are very significant at this moment in real life.

Thus, merely having an understanding of the general economic categories of the family labor farm, which in theory have been fully and clearly established, we can begin to throw light on such confused and complex problems as land prices, formation of the agricultural produce market, development of industrial crises in agrarian countries, and, finally, location of agriculture. The inability of the usual capitalist interpretation to deal with these has already been shown by Kossinskii, Chelintsev, Pervushin, Makarov, and other recent economists.

The problem of rent in the economic sense on the labor farm is the first of these questions. This was posed by A. N. Chelintsev in his economic study answering the question of his title, *Does economic*

---

3 It is no chance that we encounter the first formulation of labor–consumer balance in Proverbs, chap. 16, v. 26: "He that laboreth, laboreth for himself; for his mouth craveth it of him."

4 We made some attempt to do so in an article, "Zur Frage einer Theorie der nicht-kapitalistischen Wirtschaftssysteme," *Archiv für Socialwissenschaft und Sozialpolitik*, Book 3, Vol. 51 (1924). [EDITORS' NOTE.—An English translation of this article is given above, pp. 1–28.]

*rent exist in the labor farm?* and still earlier by Professor Bulgakov and the Marxist–revisionists, and partly even by Marx himself. It is well known that A. N. Chelintsev's work concludes that the peasant farm receives no rent in the economic sense, and the degree of rent due to a particular location or the quality of its land has the effect only of raising or lowering the farm family's consumption level.

In our opinion, full understanding of the rent factor, which according to A. N. Chelintsev is expressed on the peasant farm only by a rise in consumption level, requires a much deeper theoretical explanation than a simple reference to increased consumption. According to our earlier analysis, the very fact of increasing the consumption level is also a lowering of labor intensity and an increase in the farm's power to form capital; i.e., it is a much more complex phenomenon.

First, what is *rent* as a general economic phenomenon? According to the usual school definition, *"rent is the part of income which the entrepreneur pays to the landowner for using the land."* In other words, we have before us a real social and economic phenomenon that exists in a specific setting of social relations, arising on the basis of agricultural production and controlled by these relations. Precisely this phenomenon and nothing more was the subject of analysis by Ricardo and other Englishmen.

This notion was frequently carried over into the analysis of farm income on the entrepreneur's land in the sense that part of the net income was separated out on the books, always by extremely notional methods. This part was what the farm might or ought to pay for the land if it were owned by someone else. In this sense, the "rent" was an accounting, "valuation" concept, depending on the bookkeeper's arithmetic, and not at all a real social and economic phenomenon dependent on the movement of social relationships. Professor Fr. Aereboe has given the most brilliant demonstration of this in his latest work on land valuation, in which he proved that it is impossible to value plots of land from bookkeepers' calculations of net profit and "rent."[5] Only the net income of the undertaking, as expressed in the annual increment of values on the farm, is the sole reality of such a unit.

The calculation of "rent," which is often very necessary and useful, bears to the *social and economic phenomenon of rent* as much relation as the valuation of produce circulating in kind on the farm bears to the phenomenon of market price. In exactly the same fashion for

---

[5] Fr. Aereboe, *Die Beurteilung von Landgütern und Grundstücken*, Berlin, 1921.

the family farm, the rents the peasant farm pays for hired land are the only complete social and economic reality. However, as many empirical studies have shown, neither the origin of these prices nor their level will correspond to the rent paid by farms organized on hired labor.[6] This we shall see below. But since the family farm in its pure form has no wage category as something objectively given, it is absolutely impossible to deduce this "rent payment," even by calculation from the family farm income.

The sole general economic realities in the family farm system are: (1) the farm's gross income, (2) sums spent from it on capital renewal, (3) the family personal budget, and (4) savings not invested in own farm. All these four figures are quite real, and in that they are in value terms, they are social and economic phenomena, dependent on a complex system of social relations and frequently determined to a great extent by quotations on the London stock exchange rather than by the local rainfall.

In making a general economic analysis of the peasant farm, our task should be to study the influence of various general economic factors on these processes of capital renewal and accumulation and the level of the farm's well-being. Since the subject of our analysis is not its rent payments, the question of economic rent on the peasant farm should not amount to calculating some rate per desyatina of "unearned income" called the economic rent of the land. It should be a careful study of the influence that rent-forming factors on the peasant farm have on the three real categories noted above—capital formation, level of labor intensity, and peasant family personal budget. In other words, if we have any plot of land that because of its fertility and proximity to the market is in a favorable rent situation, we will have before us the following four approaches to analyzing its economic rent.

|  | Social and Economic Analysis | Valuation and Bookkeeping Analysis |
|---|---|---|
| 1. An entrepreneur capitalist works the land, renting it from a landowner. | Explanation of mechanism with the help of which market prices, land fertility, and other rent-forming factors influence the level of rents paid. |  |

---

6 Noting this, K. Marx wrote ". . . this is rent only nominally, not rent as an independent category opposed to wages and profits."

|  | *Social and Economic Analysis* | *Valuation and Bookkeeping Analysis* |
|---|---|---|
| 2. An entrepreneur capitalist works the land he owns. | Explanation of the influence of rent-forming factors on net income size. | Calculation of economic rent is made by deducting capital interest from net income; the remainder is taken as economic rent and, as a rule, rarely coincides with the real rents paid and the bank rate on land price. |
| 3. A family farm works the land, renting it from a landowner. | Explanation of the mechanism with the help of which, on the one hand, the rent-forming factors listed above and, on the other, population density and income structure influence the levels of rents paid. In this case, the level of rents may not coincide with those paid in the first case. | |
| 4. A family farm works the land it owns. | Explanation of the influence of rent-forming factors on capital formation, labor intensity, and increasing the well-being of family farms with differing family composition and amounts of land available. The difference between the incomes of two farms in different situations as regards economic rent per desyatina will not necessarily coincide with high payment of rents for these lands by family and capitalist farms, and with the calculated valuation rent of a capitalist farm. | From the materials of type 4 farms, it is impossible to put forward any valuation methods to calculate payment of rents which in analogous circumstances would be paid by farms of type 3. By means of a series of conventional methods, pricing family labor at wage rates and so on, you can, of course, calculate "capitalist rent" in the economic sense, as is done for type 2. But these exercises, often very useful, for example, to allocate taxes, etc.— purposes for which you can work with relatively inaccurate figures—*will have no social and economic content.* |

To construct a theory of economic rent elements on the labor farm, it seems to us necessary to trace the effect on it of the usual rent-forming factors that create and quantitatively determine the differential rent of capitalist agriculture. It is clear that for the peasant farm both better quality of fields and more favorable situation of the farm as regards the market leads either to a fall in material expenditure and labor effort to obtain the same gross income, or to a rise in this income given the same expenditure and labor effect.

In both cases, this will mean for the labor farm an increased payment per labor unit in more favorable conditions as regards economic rent. It will lead to establishing a new equilibrium between drudgery of labor and demand satisfaction, as is shown on a graph of the type we already know (Figure 6–1), where $A_1B_1$ indicates the drudgery of labor in a situation of more favorable economic rent.

FIGURE 6–1

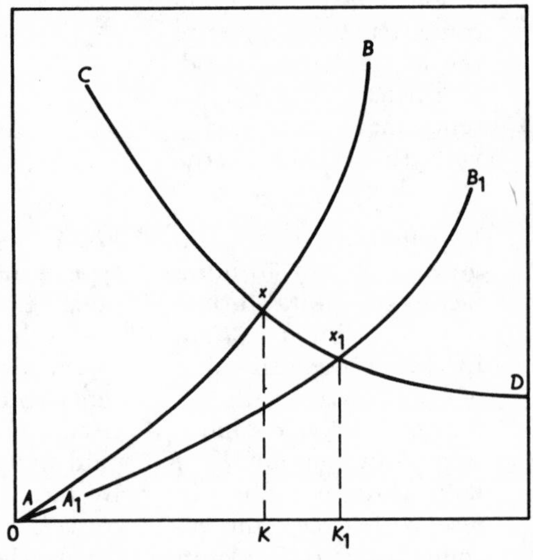

We have before us the picture usual for a labor farm with rising productivity per labor unit, in this case due to a transfer from a plot of land with a low economic rent to one with higher rent. It is the same picture as that we noted in cases of the use of new machines, a more favorable market situation, and other examples in Chapter 2. In other words, transferring our family to work on land where expenditures of labor and capital have greater rentability does not bring it any new *unearned* source of income, but simply creates better conditions for labor use. In similar fashion, a transfer to lands that, given capitalist exploitation, have a negative economic rent does not mean a loss for the labor farm in the capitalist sense of the word—i.e., a reduction in the values circulating on the farm—but will only make the conditions for labor use worse and may correspondingly change the equilibrium of the farm's basic on-farm factors.

Moreover, according to what has been said in Chapter 2, the increment in consumption and in overall family income that accompanies transfer to lands with high economic rent will not correspond even quantitatively to the increment of capitalist economic rent with the same transfer. We know (p. 80) that with a rise in labor productivity the new on-farm equilibrium is established at an output level which in its rate of increase lags behind that of productivity. The farm, having met its demands by increased receipts from a high rent use of labor, will be able to reduce the total amount of labor effort and reject from its organizational plan occupations which give comparatively low labor payments.

As we know, a good example of this is the increase in worker's output on Swiss peasant farms under the influence of increasing rentability for labor use. Table 6–1 gives these figures again in a somewhat changed form.

TABLE 6–1
INCREASING RETURNS AND WELL-BEING OF PEASANT FAMILIES

|  | Payment per Working Day on Own Farm (francs) | | | | |
|---|---|---|---|---|---|
|  | 0–2 | 2–3 | 3–4 | 4–5 | 5 and over |
| Expenditure on personal consumption per consumer . | 610 | 699 | 804 | 839 | 886 |
| Same, as percentage of group 1 ................. | 100 | 114 | 132 | 137 | 145 |
| Increase in payment, as percentage of group 1 .. | 100 | 166 | 233 | 300 | 366 |

Therefore, if we even purely arithmetically and in bookkeeping fashion deduct the old from the new income and divide the remainder by the number of desyatinas, the answer will not correspond to the difference in the capitalist economic rent of these lands. Furthermore, if, completely contrary to the labor farm's organizational principles, we withdraw one desyatina from the whole farm, value the farm's labor according to wage rates, and check the balance of this isolated desyatina according to capitalist bookkeeping methods, the increase in the bookkeeping "net income" from it will be different from that on the capitalist farm. This is because in the majority of cases the labor farm will, in accord with its estimate of advantage, take the intensity of its cultivation to a level other than that of the capitalist farm.

The accounts of Swiss farms made by Professor E. Laur by all the rules of capitalist bookeeping, which we know well, are a particularly interesting example of this. In his summary table, we find the figures in Table 6–2.

TABLE 6–2

INTENSITY AND ECONOMIC LAND RENT ON SWISS PEASANT FARMS, ACCORDING TO E. LAUR'S STUDY, 1910

| Land for Use (Hectares) | Intensity per Hectare | | Economic Land Rent per Hectare (francs) | Hectare per Consumer |
| | Working Days | Gross Income | | |
| --- | --- | --- | --- | --- |
| 0– 5 . . . . . . . . . . . | 147 | 902.04 | 68.0 | 1.21 |
| 5–10 . . . . . . . . . . | 115 | 777.70 | 77.2 | 2.06 |
| 10–15 . . . . . . . . . | 89 | 728.10 | 85.4 | 3.21 |
| 15–30 . . . . . . . . . | 76 | 610.03 | 85.4 | 4.82 |
| 30 and over . . . . . | 56 | 500.99 | 86.9 | 7.86 |

We see that rent based on hired labor in each of the three classes sowing much land is almost the same amount—about 85 francs a hectare. Farms of labor type with little land cannot achieve a balance at the optimal level of intensity and are obliged to force up their intensity, thus increasing their gross income but losing their economic "rent" calculated in bookkeeping terms. Their technical weakness also has some effect on reducing rent in small parcellated farms.

Thus, rent-forming factors have quite different quantitative effects on the labor and the capitalist farm. For our theoretical analysis, however, it is not this lack of quantitative coincidence but the very deep differences in the nature of the two phenomena springing from the rent-forming factors which are much more important. These are capitalist rent on the one hand, and increasing labor productivity on the other.

We must not forget, as we have already noted, that David Ricardo, in working out his theory of rent, had as the subject of his analysis a quite specific social and economic phenomenon, that is, the share of unearned income which the farmer-entrepreneur, working with hired labor, paid to the landowner. This phenomenon was quite clearly determined by general economic categories (wages, interest on capital, and market prices) and was completely unthinkable outside that economy, as any capitalist economic unit is, in general, inconceivable in isolation.

However, apart from the technical conditions of production, raising labor productivity on the peasant farm and the resulting consequences, such as raising the consumption level and the ability to form capital, depend on one general economic category alone—market prices. These consequences do not and cannot react to other factors—wages, interest on capital, and so on. Other than this, we may consider labor farms as being perfectly natural economic units. Then, all the same, a difference in quality of fields retains its power as a rent-forming factor. This leads to the fact that aside from the influence of any general economic categories farms in favorable situations as regards economic rent will have, according to their particular on-farm labor composition, a higher consumption level, greater ability to form capital, and less labor intensity.

In other words, the rent element in the labor farm may be thought of outside any general economic categories that are *conditio sine qua non* to understand capitalist rent and for the very existence of the capitalist farm.

Thus, summarizing all that has been said, we may recognize that those rent-forming factors which on the capitalist farm give rise to economic land rent phenomena as a particular form of unearned income cause on family and labor farms a rise in consumption level, an increase in the ability to form capital, and a slackening of labor intensity. Moreover, the amount of increased consumption and capital accumulation will not coincide with the size of capitalist economic rent of these lands, and will depend to a considerable extent on subjective peculiarities in the composition of each farm and the total population density of the area.

The problem of *land price* is directly *connected with* the problem of economic rent, which on the capitalist farm is linked to it. This problem is particularly important for us. Where there is a land market, the general economic category of land price that is characteristic of the labor farm clashes on a *single* land market with the corresponding category of the capitalist farm. Here, for the first time we will see a collision between two systems of national economy, and we will be able to analyze the mechanism for establishing the resultant.

For the capitalist farm, the question of land price is resolved with great clarity by a formula, according to which the land price is the rent of the land capitalized at the usual market interest rate on capital. For the labor farm, this sort of construction is quite impossible due to the absence of economic rent as a particularized income which really exists. Therefore, as regards the peasant farm we may pose the problem only in its primary form as a question: What is the price the peasant family can and will pay for land?

To answer this question, we will start our analysis by explaining the mechanism for the formation of rents. We will try to use the same process we used in the preceding chapter in studying the part played by capital in family production.

It is clear that the peasant labor farm will consider worthwhile the rent paid for any plot of land that enables it to achieve its internal balance at a more favorable point of equilibrium between drudgery of labor and demand satisfaction than it would have without it. To do this, it is necessary that other than the deduction for rent the labor used on the rented land should receive from income a payment higher than the marginal payment obtainable if the equilibrium of on-farm factors were established without the rent payment.

FIGURE 6–2

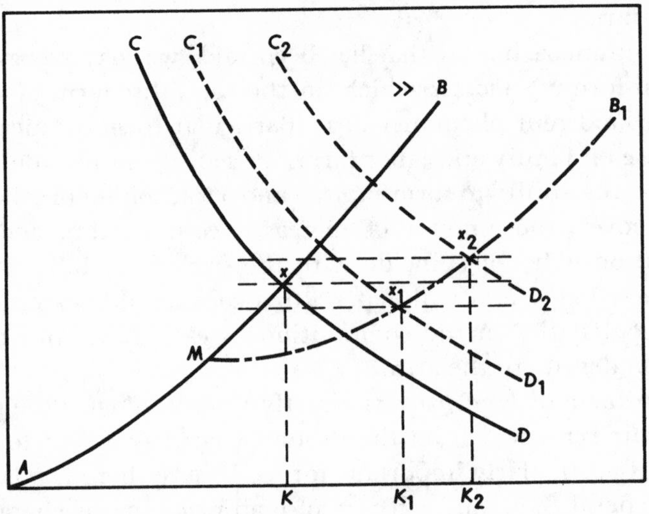

We shall use a graph, the same as those we used to establish the profitability of a particular use for capital. In Figure 6–2, $AB$ and $CD$ and point $x$ indicate the equilibrium established without rent payment. $AMB_1$ indicates the change in labor productivity brought about by the introduction of the rent. $C_1D_1$ and $C_2D_2$ indicate the subjective evaluation of the marginal ruble of income, the first deducting 20 rubles for the rent, the second deducting 40 rubles for the rent of the same land. As the graph shows, the rent of 20 rubles for this plot will be worthwhile, since this equilibrium point is reached at a higher level of demand satisfaction $(x_1 k_1 < xk)$; but 40 rubles of rent will be unacceptable to the family, since in this case the balance is achieved at a more unfavorable equilibrium point $(x_2 k_2 > xk)$. In other words, our farm will be able to pay 20 rubles rent, but there will be no sense in its paying 40.

In accordance with this, in areas where there is a vast amount of land, where net labor payment on peasant farms is no lower than wages, and where farms operate at optimal intensity, the peasant farm will, if it has to pay rent, pay no more than capitalist farms, and more probably will take land only at lower amounts. In overpopulated areas, however, in order to establish its internal equilibrium the peasant farm is obliged to force up intensification far above the optimum. Where payment per labor unit in the peasant farm's usual sectors is lower than the capitalist farm's wages, the peasant farm will consider it worthwhile to pay a much higher rent than the capitalist rent. This will leave it a labor payment below capitalist farm wages. Nevertheless, given a severe pressure on the land, these "hunger rents," as P. P. Maslov has called them, can improve the peasant farm's internal equilibrium point.

Numerous studies of Russian rents and land prices have illustrated for a great many areas the case we have theoretically explained. They have indicated clearly and without doubt that the Russian peasant in overpopulated guberniyas before the war paid rents higher than the agricultural undertaking's total net income. Table 6–3 shows figures for Voronezh guberniya (*Sel'skokhozyaistvennyi obzor po Voronezhskoi gubernii za 1903–04g.* [Agricultural survey of Voronezh guberniya for 1903–4], vyp. III, s.77) (rubles).

In a completely analogous way, the evaluation process also determines the amount the peasant farm can pay for purchased land. The only difference is that in view of the considerable sums involved payment extends over several years and is often accompanied by a conscious reduction in the consumption level.

The nature of evaluation of hired and purchased lands which we have established for the peasant farm is based on the marginal labor payment and its increase from the new equilibrium of on-farm factors resulting from these new lands. This brings us to a paradoxical conclusion: in overpopulated areas, the poorest peasant families will pay the highest prices for land and in rent. Incidentally, this entirely agrees with reality and was noted in his time by K. Marx[7] in Volume

---

[7] K. Marx, *Capital*, trans. V. Bazarov and I. Stepanov (2d ed.; M., 1908), Vol. III, part 2, p. 339f.

TABLE 6–3

| Uezds | Average Rent Paid per Desyantina of Winter Sown | Average net Income per Desyatina of Winter Sown with Economical Sowing | Difference |
|---|---|---|---|
| Voronezh .......... | 19.97 | 8.26 | 11.71 |
| Trans-Don ........ | 16.20 | 5.03 | 11.17 |
| Zemlyanka ....... | 20.59 | 8.27 | 12.32 |
| Nizhnedevitsk ...... | 20.75 | 6.32 | 14.43 |
| Korotoyak ........ | 19.41 | 2.72 | 16.63 |
| Bobrov ........... | 18.87 | 7.67 | 11.20 |
| Novokhopersk ..... | 19.25 | 6.51 | 12.74 |
| Boguchar ........ | 8.88 | 3.85 | 5.03 |
| Pavlovsk .......... | 13.20 | 6.27 | 6.93 |
| Ostrogozhsk ....... | 14.70 | 2.49 | 12.21 |
| Biryuchevo ........ | 17.72 | 2.54 | 15.18 |
| Valuiki ........... | 12.79 | 3.74 | 9.05 |
| Average ..... | 16.80 | 5.30 | 11.30 |

TABLE 6–4

| Land Use (Hectares) | Farm Intensity (per Hectare) | | Capitalized "Rent" per Hectare (francs) | Purchase Prices per Hectare of Land According to Valuation Lists |
|---|---|---|---|---|
| | Workdays | Gross Income | | |
| I.   <5 ...... | 147 | 902.0 | 1,697 | 2,988 |
| II.   5–10 ...... | 115 | 777.7 | 1,930 | 2,458 |
| III. 10–15 ...... | 89 | 728.1 | 2,134 | 2,216 |
| IV. 15–30 ...... | 76 | 610.0 | 2,144 | 2,145 |
| V.   >30 ...... | 56 | 500.1 | 2,171 | 1,541 |

III of *Capital*. His views on land rent in the parcellated peasant farm and on the rents it pays are very close to our theories.

Professor E. Laur's table on Swiss farms (Table 6–4) is a good illustration of this proposition. As is seen from these figures, labor farms of classes I and II are obliged, due to the relative shortage of land, to intensify their activity above the optimum and thus considerably to reduce the "rent" in bookkeeping terms. At the same time, in complete accord with our theory, they also pay the highest prices for land. Such is the nature of land valuation characteristic of the labor farm.

We will try to establish the character and results of the collision that takes place on the unified land market between this valuation principle and the usual capitalist land price which arises on the basis of capitalized rent.

In areas where there is an absolute surplus of land, and even where population density corresponds to optimal intensity for agriculture, there is and can be essentially no basis for a collision. But in areas of overpopulation, as farms increase and there is a relative shortage of land, ever-growing numbers of buyers and hirers appear able to pay prices higher than capitalist ones. At first, this has no effect on the single price of the capitalist market, and labor farm purchases take place as chance, sporadic deals. But gradually they become more and more significant, and finally the labor farm valuation becomes decisive for the market and puts aside the capitalist-based price. Moreover, the labor farms, of course, are victorious not only in establishing the market price but also in the struggle for land; a clearly marked transfer of lands from capitalist to labor farming takes place.

The sale of private landowners' holdings to peasants in Russia at the end of the nineteenth and start of the twentieth centuries is a fine illustration of this transfer. This has been brilliantly analyzed by V. Kossinskii in his study, *The Agrarian Question.* Of the lands obtained by private owners in 1861, in 1877 they owned 87 percent; in 1887, 76 percent; in 1897, 65 percent; in 1905, 52 percent; and in 1916, 41 percent. Moreover, of this amount two-thirds was rented by peasants.

Conversely, the economic history of Britain gives us examples of times when the large-scale capitalist farm, by making use of movements in the market situation, was able to pay excessive rents. It could pay more for its land than could the labor farm, and it broke down and destroyed the labor farm. The spread of wool farming in eighteenth-century Britain is a good example of this.

In completing the description of how the labor farm's nature influences the general economic category of land prices and the land market, we can notice the very interesting instance when the farm's peculiar features are shown estimating the advantage of any sort of land improvement. For the agricultural undertaking organized on capitalist lines, adoption of a particular possible land improvement measure depends on whether the increase in *economic rent*, resulting from the improvement of the plot, is greater than, or at least equal to, the capital interest rate usual in the country in relation to the capital involved. Obviously, the capitalist farm will never carry out improvements that give an increase of rent in the economic sense less than the usual capitalist income on the capital required for the improvement. It is equally obvious that all these considerations are quite inapplicable to improvement on the labor farm, if only because it has no category of capitalist economic rent.

Exactly as with rents and land purchase, the family farm's decision on the question of the advantage from improvement will depend on

the effect this improvement will have on the on-farm equilibrium between drudgery of labor and demand satisfaction. In a situation of
relative land shortage, the family, needing to expand its economic
activity, will carry out many improvements disadvantageous and not
available to the capitalist farm, just as it pays land rents and prices
considerably exceeding the *capitalist* economic rent of these lands.

In other words, on labor farms in overpopulated areas the limits to
improvement are much broader than those on capitalistically organized farms. It would, of course, be exceedingly difficult to quantitatively express these broader limits characteristic of the labor farm. We
are inclined to suppose that, in general, it is impossible to establish
this, like much else in the labor farm, a priori by any objective estimate. It depends on the degree to which the farm family is supplied
with means of existence, on the amount of surplus labor, on the possibility or impossibility of other means of extending the use of its labor,
and on other conditions which are, difficult or impossible to record
a priori.

The sole objective figure on which our estimates may be based, in
our opinion, is local land price,[8] and, in particular, prices of lands
formed by improvements that are carried out. For carrying out fundamental improvements, like the acquisition of new land, is an extension of the sphere available to labor by increasing the area of suitable
land. Undoubtedly, for example, the labor farm will not drain a
marshy meadow if the cost is higher than the purchase price of
meadows in the locality. On the other hand, if the labor farm, seeking
to increase uses for its labor, buys new land at prices higher than the
capitalized economic rent, it is also undoubted that any expansion of
workable area by fundamentally improving its own land is an advantage to it. This is so once the cost of the improvements is less than the
selling price of the land, even though the expected increase in economic rent calculated in bookkeeping terms might be less than the
normal interest rate on the capital laid out.

Moreover, as we have already noted in Chapter 5, the peasant farm
pays little heed to the market interest rate on capital, not only as regards capital for improvements but also in general for all capital uses.
Therefore, you may frequently meet much greater capital intensification on peasant farms than on optimally arranged capitalist undertakings. At the same time, however, this capital intensification is
usually accompanied by and causes an even greater labor intensification in agriculture.

---

8 In countries where there is a land market.

Another feature of the peasant farm which follows from the nature of its capital circulation is its ability to pay very high interest on sums borrowed. However, unlike the land market, this has no consequences for the economy as a whole and does not affect the world discount rate, since the volume of peasant farm credit in circulation is microscopically small compared with bank and other credits. Therefore, the sole general economic consequence of this pitiful capacity is rural usury, which once ran wild in all peasant countries and is still far from extinct.

The student of market prices for raw material and foodstuffs of agricultural origin should pay more attention to the peasant labor farm than does the financier. In volume, a considerable part of this produce comes from labor farms, and, what is more important, so do the price-determining marginal units of many forms of produce. This appears most clearly with specific produce from overpopulated areas (flax, hemp, sunflower, tobacco, etc.) in which, as we know from what has gone before, the labor intensity and high gross income so attract peasant farms that they agree to very low payment per labor unit for these crops. As a result, such a low-price market situation is created for this produce that it becomes completely disadvantageous for the capitalist farm and disappears from its organization plan. Fiber flax cultivation is particularly characteristic in this respect; before the war more than 90 percent was sown on peasant fields.

Apart from the produce of labor-intensive crops which has been mentioned, many others reflect the peculiar nature of the labor farm. We have already mentioned that Siberian squirrel prices are inversely proportional to grain prices. Equally peculiar, as A. N. Chelintsev succeeded in showing in his work on trends in cattle farming, are meat prices, which in many areas are often inversely proportional to their cost. Professor Chelintsev succeeded in showing that in good feed harvest years the peasants put a very large number of livestock for overwintering. Because of this, the supply of livestock, especially of young, for slaughter falls; this causes a rise in meat prices. Conversely, in years when there is lack of fodder and hay is expensive, the peasants, with no chance of feeding their livestock, try to get rid of it at any price. As a result, meat prices sometimes fall below bread prices, as we were able to note in Russian famine districts in 1921.

Speaking generally, the influence of peasant labor farm peculiarities on the *process of price formation and commodity market structure,* as well as on the nature and course of *general economic crises,* as they are called, is an exceptionally interesting theme for independent study. In this entirely unstudied field there may be unexpected discoveries awaiting the student, which may force a revision of the fundamentals of existing theory. Such, as far as one can say from the present state of our young science, are the general economic consequences of the peculiar notion of advantage and of other features of the private economic basis in the peasant labor farm.

At the end of the nineteenth century, when analyzing the origins of capitalist land rent, K. Marx noted the considerable differences between parcellated peasant farming and capitalist agriculture. He asserted that in this parcellated farming "production . . . to a very great extent satisfies own needs and is completely independent of control by the general rate of profit."[9] He came to a number of conclusions close to our observations; however, neither he nor subsequent economists have developed these observations adequately.

As we have seen from the content of this chapter, these general economic consequences involve considerable theoretical conclusions. As regards the peasant labor farm, they make it necessary to review such theoretical fundamentals as the theory of rent, views on land prices, calculations for land improvements, and views on capital interest and the forms its circulation takes. With further and deeper investigation, they promise a considerable refinement in the study of rent-forming factors.

Yet, it is also necessary to note that in real life where the labor farm system coexists with the general economic system of capitalism it also has an immense effect on the wage category of the capitalist system. In peasant agrarian countries, where the complete crystallizing of a professionally pure proletariat has not fully developed, the peasantry is an inexhaustible source from which urban industry draws its labor force.

The supply of labor from the countryside, however, as we have seen from N. P. Nikitin's work, directly depends on how well peasant families are able to establish their internal balances from agricultural income alone. In years of high agricultural income, the countryside has no stimulus to cast its labor onto the market; conversely, it loads the market in years of agricultural depression. It reduces and raises wages according to the peasant farm's internal processes. In other words, *in this case* the labor farm system is not only free of control by wages, but, on the contrary, precisely through this category it also subordinates the whole system of the capitalist economy to its internal equilibrium between demand satisfaction and the drudgery of labor.

---

[9] K. Marx, *Capital* [trans. from Russian, Vol. III, Book 2, p. 347. Cf. Kerr ed., p. 943].

To a still greater extent, of course, the peculiar features of the family farm are evident in determining the economic content of peasant farms themselves, and thus the location of farming. The question of the location of agriculture is such a big theme in itself that we refrain from dealing with it here. We merely observe that in areas of agrarian overpopulation, as may be seen from the preceding chapters, we must inevitably come up against labor intensive crops, the labor intensification of farms, high prices for land and rents, low wages, and the development of crafts and trades outside agriculture.

As we have already indicated, all the general economic observations we have made are static in content and fragmentary. It is undoubted, however, that every student of the peasant farm as a general economic and historical phenomenon ought to pay them the most serious attention and use them frequently to understand the dynamic phenomena he is studying.

## CHAPTER 7

# The Family Farm as a Component of the National Economy and Its Possible Forms of Development

Our study approaches its end. We have reviewed in great detail the economic activity of the individual peasant family; we have analyzed the mechanism of the internal equilibrium of on-farm factors which gives a "teleological unity" to its activity. Finally, we have explained those features in the composition of rent, capital interest, and price formation which follow from the particular economic behavior of the peasant labor family.

Now we must review the last question—the question of the family farm's place in the present-day national economy, its features as a social and economic whole, its links with the capitalist economy, and the forms of their relationship to one another. Finally, we must try to make clear to ourselves possible forms of the peasant farm's further development.

This group of questions, as might be expected today, always evokes the keenest interest and the sharpest polemics. Therefore, in this concluding chapter we have allowed ourselves to cast our net much more widely than we did in the German edition; and we have focused particular attention on possible future forms—something we did not do at all in the German edition.

The usual accusation is that all our constructs are static, and that we are inclined to idealize the petty bourgeois spirit of the present-day peasantry and to consider it in its present form almost an ideal agricultural economic organization. I must hope that this chapter will be able to rout both these accusations. Our analysis in all six preceding chapters was static because they were dealing with static problems. Now, after we describe the place of the family farm in the general economic system—also, if you like, statically—we will try to show the forms of its dynamic development in all the complexity of their contemporary economic setting.

Further, the conclusions in our analysis of the labor farms' great resistance and their historical stability have been taken as idealized. When we were speaking of what existed, they took us to be speaking of what should be. This requires us to pay particular attention to analyzing possible forms of future peasant farm development which, in our opinion, should be considered progressive and in the direction of which we ought to develop our economic policy. Yet, here again, we will *start* by describing what exists, again with a static analysis.

We must begin with a review of how a peasant farm social sector is formed from individual farms at different ages of family development, and also a review of what social links unite the individual farms into a certain social whole. In other words, we start with a study of peasant farm morphology as a social sector.

Statistical studies of Russian peasant farms, started more than half a century ago, at their first steps stumbled on the very great heterogeneity in peasant farm composition. Everywhere, they noted the presence not only of small but also of medium and even comparatively large peasant agricultural undertakings. In B. N. Knipovich's consolidated work, which we have already had occasion to quote, the results of a considerable number of relevant zemstvo statistical censuses are summarized. Table 7–1 may acquaint us, in fairly detailed fashion, with the distribution of peasant farm composition by sown area classes, a variable which may be taken as an indicator of farm size.[1]

We can very clearly see from the table that in the mass the peasant farm is a quite variegated mixture of small-, medium-, and large-scale agricultural undertakings. Comparing different areas, we should note that this heterogeneity is more marked in some than in others. Nevertheless, whatever group of peasant farms we take, their distribution curve will, in general, be similar.

When we compare our figures with handed-down estimates of peasant farms in the eighteenth and seventeenth centuries, we are convinced that the heterogeneity we have found is not a characteristic merely of the current historical period; it was just as clearly seen in very distant periods. Thus, in Table 7–2 we have compared data from

---

[1] Essentially, sown area is an indicator of *agricultural production*. It would be better to take gross income or amount of capital to describe the *farm*, but we have no materials for this.

TABLE 7-1

| Percentage of Farms | | Percentage of Farms | | Percentage of Farms | |
|---|---|---|---|---|---|
| *Ekaterinoslav Uezd* | | *Samara Uezd* | | *Poltava Guberniya* | |
| Landless | 4.9 | Without sown | 11.8 | Without sown | 3.1 |
| Desyatinas: | | Desyatinas: | | Desyatinas: | |
| <1 | 3.2 | <1 | 17.9 | <1 | 8.5 |
| 1– 3 | 11.2 | 3– 6 | 21.1 | 1– 2 | 13.1 |
| 3– 5 | 19.5 | 6– 9 | 14.6 | 2– 3 | 12.3 |
| 5–10 | 35.2 | 9–12 | 10.2 | 3– 6 | 29.4 |
| 10–15 | 15.3 | 12–15 | 6.8 | 6– 9 | 15.7 |
| 15–20 | 5.1 | 15–20 | 6.8 | 9–15 | 11.6 |
| 20–25 | 1.5 | 20–30 | 6.0 | 15–25 | 4.4 |
| 25 and over | 4.1 | 30–40 | 2.2 | 25–50 | 1.6 |
| | | 40 and over | 2.6 | 50 and over | 0.3 |
| | 100.0 | | 100.0 | | 100.0 |

| *Voronezh Guberniya* | | *Tula Guberniya* | | *Kaluga Guberniya* | |
|---|---|---|---|---|---|
| Without sown | 7.60 | Without sown | 15.7 | Without sown | 4.5 |
| Desyatinas: | | Desyatinas: | | Desyatinas: | |
| <1 | 2.27 | <1 | 9.1 | <3 | 27.6 |
| 1– 5 | 43.33 | 1– 2 | 15.5 | 3– 6 | 42.1 |
| 5–10 | 30.98 | 2– 5 | 32.4 | 6– 9 | 16.8 |
| 10–20 | 13.58 | 5–10 | 21.4 | 9–12 | 5.6 |
| 20–40 | 1.92 | 10–15 | 4.4 | 12 and over | 3.4 |
| 40 and over | 0.32 | 15–25 | 1.3 | | |
| | | 25 and over | 0.2 | | |
| | 100.00 | | 100.0 | | 100.0 |

| *Vladimir Guberniya* | | *Vologda Guberniya* | | *Perm' Guberniya* | |
|---|---|---|---|---|---|
| Without sown | 26.6 | Without sown | 6.2 | Without sown | 2.6 |
| Desyatinas: | | Desyatinas: | | Desyatinas: | |
| <3 | 27.5 | <2 | 36.9 | <5 | 75.7 |
| 3– 6 | 36.2 | 2– 3 | 28.4 | 5–10 | 17.7 |
| 6– 9 | 8.0 | 3– 6 | 26.9 | 10–15 | 3.3 |
| 9 and over | 1.7 | 6 and over | 1.6 | 15 and over | 0.7 |
| | 100.0 | | 100.0 | | 100.0 |

the 1767 Rumyantsev census of Chernigov guberniya and the 1883 zemstvo statistical census.

No so long ago, the inclination was to ascribe the heterogeneity we have noted in peasant farm size entirely to dynamic social disintegra-

TABLE 7–2

PERCENTAGE OF PEASANT FARMS WITH GIVEN NUMBER OF WORKERS
(FAMILY MEMBERS)

| | Number of Workers | | | | | Total Families |
|---|---|---|---|---|---|---|
| | 0 | 1 | 2 | 3 | 4 | |
| 1767 | 7.8% | 55.1% | 24.4% | 8.0% | 4.7% | 100.0% |
| 1883 | 8.2% | 61.1% | 24.1% | 6.2% | 1.1% | 100.0% |

tion among the peasantry, i.e., to the gradual concentration of production in the hands of large peasant farms, which prepared the soil for a further, purely capitalist concentration taking place in parallel with the proletarianization of small and medium peasants. There is no doubt that some such social differentiation does take place in the countryside, but more careful analysis of peasant farm composition shows that the heterogeneity cannot be fully explained by social differentiation. It depends not only on dynamic development but also considerably on the effect of demographic factors which follow from the nature of the peasant farm.

In short, we are right in supposing that the heterogeneity we have shown in peasant farm composition is not a phenomenon of the recent historical process but, in many respects, is a derivative from the very nature of the peasant farm. It is easy to illustrate this theoretically. In Chapter 1, we looked in great detail at individual peasant family development. Now let us take as our basis the theoretical scheme of family development that we gave. Let us accept that due to increase in population and to deaths the number of families of each older age group will differ from the number in the preceding group, and that the family, maturing after twenty-five years, remains undivided for eight years, having two young families within it. Given all this, we obtain the following theoretical composition for a mass classification of peasant families by size:

| Family size (persons) | 0–3 | 4–6 | 7–9 | 10 and over |
|---|---|---|---|---|
| Families in group | 20.5% | 35.5% | 29.8% | 14.2% |

According to our preceding chapters, such demographic composition is quite enough to cause considerable differentiation in sizes of agricultural undertakings, even with other things being equal. To compare our theoretical composition with family composition found in reality, we can quote the figures of a Starobel'sk study.

| Family size | 0–3 | 4–6 | 7–9 | 10 and over |
|---|---|---|---|---|
| Families in group | 16.8% | 22.8% | 32.7% | 27.7% |

Some differences occur between our theoretical curve for farm distribution by sown areas and those observed in reality because, first, as we know, farm sown areas are not determined by demographic factors alone, and, second, apart from social differentiation caused by differences in family age, there are some elements of economic differentiation. In addition, the demographic process of family growth itself, which we have taken as the basis for our calculation, in reality takes place in a much more complex way than that adopted in our simplified scheme.

Fortunately for us, several outstanding Russian statisticians, headed by N. N. Chernenkov, A. I. Khryashcheva, and P. A. Vikhlyaev, have exhaustively studied, in a number of areas in European Russia, the phenomenon in which we are interested. We can study the problem posed not merely by means of a priori constructs, but also by means of a posteriori analysis of empirical material.

The works of N. N. Chernenkov, P. A. Vikhlyaev, A. I. Khryashcheva, and G. I. Kushchenko, which we have quoted several times, compare the data of repeated peasant farm censuses. Methodologically, they differ from all analogous comparisons in Russian and West European statistics. This is because in comparing two different years they did not work on the totals for each year taken wholesale, but traced the fate of each category of farms individually and, in recent work, even of each farm for the period between the censuses. The results of this sort of comparison have shown that in the depths of the peasantry there primarily takes place a series of very complex and tangled demographic processes.

Returning to the site of their first study after 15–30 years, the statisticians first had to state that a certain part of the farms had simply ceased to exist; they died out. Another section had migrated from the area being studied. Finally, a considerable part had, through the dividing of families, broken down into two or three independent farms, and only a part remained complete from the preceding census. These processes may be very clearly traced in Table 7–3, taken from Kushchenko's work on Surazh uezd, Chernigov guberniya. We will also make use of this material in our subsequent analysis, since, though it coincides with other work, Kushchenko's study gives more salient results as it compares censuses separated by 30 years.

We see from the table that during 30 years the farms studied suffered the most diverse fates; only three quarters of them retained

TABLE 7–3

SURAZH UEZD 1911 FARMS AS PERCENTAGE OF THOSE OF 1882

| 1882 Sown Area (Desyatinas) | Died out | Migrated | Divided | Undivided | Farms that Disappeared |
|---|---|---|---|---|---|
| 0– 3 ......... | 32.5 | 19.4 | 6.2 | 41.9 | 51.9 |
| 3– 6 ......... | 10.4 | 22.2 | 15.4 | 52.0 | 32.6 |
| 6– 9 ......... | 4.2 | 19.9 | 26.1 | 49.8 | 24.1 |
| 9–12 ......... | 3.5 | 15.6 | 35.1 | 45.8 | 19.1 |
| 12 and over .... | 1.7 | 7.1 | 57.6 | 33.6 | 8.8 |

their individual existence within the area. To a considerable extent, small farms migrated, broke down, and in part left agriculture. Large and older farms appeared to be more settled, but, on the other hand, more than half of them reached full maturity and broke down into a number of new farms.

Aside from farms that migrated and ceased to exist, we should note in making a deeper analysis that farms which in whole or in part lived through a 30-year period underwent many economic changes. Some predominantly young ones strengthened their economic position and expanded; others, mainly the large old farms, declined and passed into lower economic classes. For example, Table 7–4 shows percentages for farms that did not divide for all the 30 years from 1882 to 1911. In the table, "increasing their sown area" means farms passing during the period into higher sown area classes; "reducing their sown area" means farms falling during the 30 years into lower sown area classes.

Table 7–5 is a still more characteristic picture of the fate of farms

TABLE 7–4

SURAZH UEZD FARMS 1911 AS PERCENTAGE OF
THOSE UNDIVIDED SINCE 1882*

| Sown Area (Desyatinas) | Retaining Same Sown Area | Increasing Their Sown Area | Reducing Their Sown Area | Total |
|---|---|---|---|---|
| 0– 3 ...... | 28.4 | 71.6 | — | 100.0 |
| 3– 6 ...... | 50.0 | 39.0 | 11.0 | 100.0 |
| 6– 9 ...... | 33.4 | 30.7 | 36.9 | 100.0 |
| 9–12 ...... | 22.0 | 34.0 | 44.9 | 100.0 |
| 12 and over . | 41.4 | — | 58.0 | 100.0 |

* EDITORS' NOTE.—The figures are as given in the Russian text. They do not in all cases sum to 100.0.

FIGURE 7–5

SURAZH UEZD FARMS 1911 AS PERCENTAGE OF
THOSE DIVIDED SINCE 1882*

| Sown Area (Desyatinas) | Retaining Same Sown Area | Increasing Their Sown Area | Reducing Their Sown Area | Total |
|---|---|---|---|---|
| 0– 3 ...... | 27.8 | 72.8 | — | 100.0 |
| 3– 6 ...... | 43.6 | 18.0 | 38.4 | 100.0 |
| 6– 9 ...... | 21.5 | 11.2 | 67.3 | 100.0 |
| 9–12 ...... | 7.0 | 5.7 | 87.3 | 100.0 |
| 12 and over . | 17.4 | — | 84.6 | 100.0 |

* EDITORS' NOTE.—The figures are as given in the Russian text. They do not in all cases sum to 100.0.

that divided. It shows into what class farms go as a result of family division.

Looking at both tables, we first see sharply marked economic growth in the farms with small sown areas, especially among the undivided farms. Conversely, among farms that in 1882 were large we see still more clearly a breakdown and economic decline, particularly among farms that divided. We see both currents, the rising and the falling, quite clearly from the summary table from G. A. Kushchenko's study (Table 7–6).

TABLE 7–6
SOWN AREAS 1911 AS PERCENTAGE OF FARMS IN 1882*

| 1882 | 0–3 | 3–6 | 6–9 | 9–12 | 12– | Total |
|---|---|---|---|---|---|---|
| 0– 3 ....... | 28.2 | 47.0 | 20.0 | 2.4 | 2.4 | 100.0 |
| 3– 6 ....... | 21.8 | 47.5 | 20.4 | 8.2 | 2.4 | 100.0 |
| 6– 9 ....... | 16.2 | 37.0 | 26.8 | 11.3 | 8.7 | 100.0 |
| 9–12 ....... | 9.3 | 35.8 | 26.1 | 12.4 | 16.1 | 100.0 |
| 12 and over . | 3.5 | 30.5 | 28.5 | 15.6 | 21.9 | 100.0 |

* EDITORS' NOTE.—The figures are as given in the Russian text. They do not in all cases sum to 100.0.

We have before us a complex picture of the dynamics of peasant farm composition. The class with small sown area shows great growing power, and almost three-fourths of its farms in the 30 years pass into higher sown area classes. On the other hand, both classes with large sown area in 1882 give a clear picture of decline and breakdown.

Before us are two powerful currents. One, in which the young, undivided farms with small sown area mainly participate, is rising, expanding the volume of its farms under pressure of family growth. The other is declining, largely due to the dividing of old, complex families.

What we have shown for Surazh uezd is not chance, as may be confirmed by analogous *summary* tables for other areas where the fate of individual farms has been traced by repeated censuses. Thus, we have the following works by P. A. Vikhlyaev on Moscow guberniya and A. I. Khrashcheva on Tula guberniya.

P. A. Vikhlyaev, *Vliyanie travoseyaniya na nekotorye storony krest'yanskogo khozyaistva* [The effect of leys on certain aspects of the peasant farm], M., 1913, s. 15.

A. I. Khryashcheva, *Sbornik statistiko-ekonomicheskikh svedenii po Epifanskomu uezdu, Tul'skoi gubernii* [Collection of statistical and economic information on Epifan' uezd, Tula guberniya], Tula, 1913.

In the tables for both Moscow and Tula guberniya, we see the same two social currents, one rising and the other declining. They are expressed more weakly than in Surazh uezd, since the interval between censuses in Moscow and Tula was much shorter.

In thinking about these processes, of course, we ought to acknowledge that these currents are determined not only by the demographic processes of family growth and division. Farms may increase and decline with unchanged family composition due to *purely economic causes*. Apart from this, favorable and unfavorable market situations as regards the general economy can make it considerably easier or more difficult for the family to develop its activity in accordance with its own growth. There is, nevertheless, no doubt at all that demographic causes play the leading part in these movements.

As a result of the interrelationship of these two counterposed social currents, present peasant farm composition is established at any particular moment and gives a distribution by sown area classes which we have already looked at from B. N. Knipovich's materials. If both currents are mutually balanced, despite the fact that individual farms will pass in great numbers from class to class, the numerical relationship of the classes will remain unchanged. If we merely make a wholesale comparison of the totals of the two censuses separated by a long time interval, we get a picture of complete static calm. Even though completely different farms form them, the classes as such remain the same, and their heterogeneity or, as was formerly said, peasant farm differentiation, will be the same with a repeated as with the initial registration.

However, more frequently an area's general economic market situation, its price levels, land pressure, and so on make the social currents we have studied depart from a state of mutual equilibrium. Then, one of them begins to temporarily predominate over the other, and after a few years a noticeable change occurs in the relationship between the classes. For example, if due to adverse economic circumstances the growth of young family farms is restrained and their breakdown increased we see, as shown in Figure 7–1, the increase in farms in the lower classes. This is the "general downward movement," according to N. P. Oganovskii's definition, i.e., a reduction of the general level of well-being. The results of Kushchenko's study of the distribution of Surazh farms by sown area may serve as an example of this (Table 7–7).

Conversely, while a favorable economic market situation helps the rapid growth of young, developing farms and permits this process to

## FIGURE 7–1
### DOWNWARD MOVEMENT

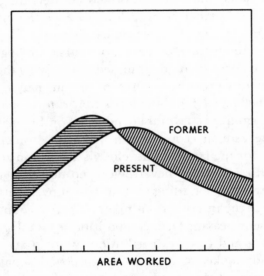

FORMER

PRESENT

AREA WORKED

### TABLE 7–7
PERCENTAGE OF SURAZH FARMS BY SOWN AREA

| | Desyatinas | | | | | |
|---|---|---|---|---|---|---|
| | *0–3* | *3.1–6.0* | *6.1–9.0* | *9.1–12.0* | *>12* | *Total* |
| 1882 .......... | 10.8 | 34.5 | 25.9 | 13.5 | 15.3 | 100.0 |
| 1911 .......... | 13.2 | 38.6 | 25.0 | 11.2 | 11.0 | 100.0 |
| Change, as percentage of 1882 ...... | +31.5 | +12.0 | − 3.5 | −17.0 | −28.0 | — |

predominate over decay, after a short period the growth of higher classes at the expense of the medium ones will be clearly noticed. In this case, expressed graphically, we will have a "general upward movement," to use N. P. Oganovskii's term (Figure 7–2).

From time to time, comparison of two registrations discloses a cycle of phenomena more complex than a simple predominance of one social current over another. For example, growth may predominate among young families passing from lower economic to medium classes, but at the same time this may be accompanied by intensive division and decline of large, old families. Then, comparing the two registrations, we will have a reduction of the extreme classes and a considerable increase in medium ones, as seen in the "leveling" graph and Kushchenko's table on horses on the same Surazh farms (Figure 7–3 and Table 7–8).

FIGURE 7–2
UPWARD MOVEMENT

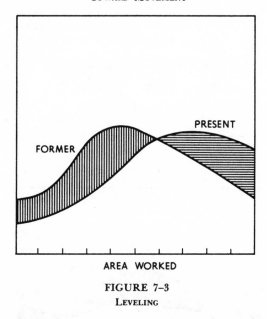

AREA WORKED

FIGURE 7–3
LEVELING

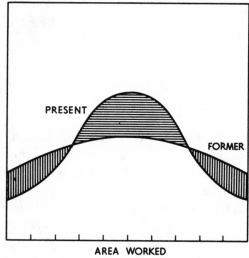

AREA WORKED

Conversely, an intense economic crisis may greatly weaken the growth of young, developing farms and at the same time show the great stability of old households with many workers and large sown area. As a result, we have, by comparing the two censuses, a development of the highest and lowest classes at the expense of the middle ones. This is shown in Figure 7–4, and there are many examples of it

TABLE 7–8
SURAZH UEZD (PERCENTAGE OF FARMS)

| | *Without Work-stock* | *With Workstock (Head)* | | | | |
|---|---|---|---|---|---|---|
| | | *1* | *2* | *3* | *4* | *5* |
| 1882 ............ | 10.6 | 27.7 | 29.8 | 14.2 | 9.1 | 8.6 |
| 1911 ............ | 9.6 | 24.6 | 40.1 | 15.9 | 6.6 | 3.2 |
| Change, as percentage of 1882 ....... | −9.5 | −11.0 | +34.6 | +12.0 | −27.9 | −62.8 |

FIGURE 7–4
DIFFERENTIATION

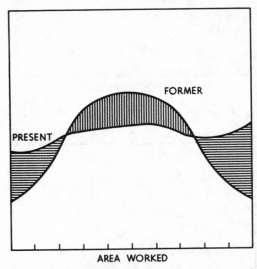

AREA WORKED

from the pitiful memory of the Russian peasantry's history at the end of the nineteenth century. N. P. Oganovskii calls this process "differentiation." Table 7–9, for Ekaterinoslav guberniya, gives a good example of this type of movement in peasant farm composition.

Finally, we can have still more complicated systems of development in social composition, and as a result of the interrelationship of both

TABLE 7–9
EKATERINOSLAV GUBERNIYA (PERCENTAGE OF HOUSEHOLDS)

| | *Without Sown Area* | *Sown Area (Desyatinas)* | | | | |
|---|---|---|---|---|---|---|
| | | *<5* | *5–10* | *10–20* | *20–50* | *>50* |
| 1886 ......... | 4.6 | 19.3 | 28.7 | 35.1 | 11.6 | 0.7 |
| 1901 ......... | 6.8 | 15.7 | 28.0 | 29.8 | 17.6 | 2.1 |
| + or − ...... | +47.8 | −18.7 | − 2.5 | −15.2 | +51.7 | +200.0 |

currents we can, as shown in Figure 7–5, have an upward movement accompanied by leveling and a downward movement together with differentiation, and others.

FIGURE 7–5
UPWARD MOVEMENT WITH LEVELING

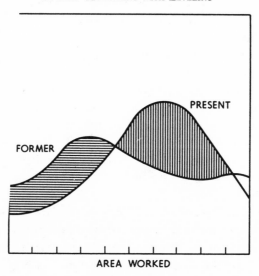

According to A. I. Khryashcheva's study, the development of the Russian peasant farm during the period of the war and the revolution, which we have now lived through, is a good example of sharply expressed leveling accompanied by a general downward movement

TABLE 7–10
PEASANT FARMS IN 25 GUBERNIYAS OF RUSSIA BY SOWN AREA (%)

| | Without Sown Area | <1 | 1–2 | 2–4 | 4–6 | 6–8 | 8–10 | 10–15 | 15–22 | >22 | Total |
|---|---|---|---|---|---|---|---|---|---|---|---|
| 1917 ........ | 11.5 | 10.3 | 18.4 | 28.9 | 14.7 | 7.4 | 3.8 | 3.9 | 0.8 | 0.3 | 100.0 |
| 1919 ........ | 6.6 | 18.0 | 24.9 | 29.3 | 12.4 | 5.2 | 2.1 | 1.4 | 0.1 | 0.0 | 100.0 |

(Table 7–10). As the table shows, we have before us a picture of the disappearance of the well-to-do and poorest groups in the countryside against a background of general impoverishment.

What has been said establishes clearly enough the mechanism of movement in the peasantry's social composition, and we urgently counsel our readers to study the quoted works by N. N. Chernenkov, P. A. Vikhlyaev, A. I. Khryashcheva, and G. A. Kushchenko. These authors have written one of the most brilliant pages in the history of Russian statistics.

After the appearance of these works, Russian economists started to attach a somewhat different significance to the *heterogeneity* of peasant farms disclosed by sown area and other quantitative economic classifications. They called this process "demographic differentiation," thus stressing that the chief cause of differences in farm size is the demographic processes of family growth as its age increases, and not social factors causing peasant farms to become capitalist and proletarianized, as we formerly supposed.

However, we consider it absolutely necessary to note that although this "demographic differentiation" has lost its social overtone for us, it thus acquires exceptional production significance. As we have more than once tried to show in analyzing the organizational plan, the size of agricultural undertakings as production machines has a very real effect on their organization, without taking it outside the usual family labor farm.

As we have seen,[2] the type of buildings, the stock of equipment, the organization of draft, the measures to use these means of production, particularly the organization of labor in farms with few or many family members, even the crops grown, their money-earning power, and sometimes the general trend of the farm—all this very flexibly reflects the labor farm's size. It was for this very reason that even before the Revolution the most perceptive agricultural officers put forward the idea of a differential agricultural program that, other than recording semiproletarianized and semicapitalist farms, would differentiate recommended improvements for different scales of labor farm at different phases of development.

Such a differentiated approach is no less significant for the practice both of cooperation and of petty credit, and for almost all forms of economic work in the countryside. Unfortunately, at this production plane the differentiation problem is only beginning to be studied,[3] and its deep analysis is evidently a matter for the future. However, because we are now inclined to treat differences in peasant farm sown areas as springing from demographic causes and not social ones, one should by no means conclude that there is no true social differentia-

---

2 See pp. 72, 80, 93, 116.

3 Studenskii, Uzhanskii, Tsil'ko, Vil'do, Anisimov, Vermenichev, and Naumov, associates at the Agricultural Economics Scientific Research Institute, carried out a number of expeditions on this plane in the summers of 1924 and 1925. The processing of these materials will undoubtedly throw much light on this question.

tion among the peasantry to distinguish one farm from another, not quantitatively but qualitatively.

Simple, everyday observation of life in the countryside shows us elements of "capitalist exploitation." We suppose that, on the one hand, proletarianization of the countryside and, on the other, a certain development of capitalist production forms undoubtedly take place there. However, in our opinion, these social processes should be sought out, not by means of classifying sown areas and so on, but by direct analysis of capitalist factors in the organization of production, i.e., hired labor on farms, not brought in to help their own, but as the basis on which to obtain unearned income, and oppressive rents and usurers' credit.

Where a general economic setting is formed suitable for such economic organization, these forms inevitably appear. As we know, the semilabor, semicapitalist "farmer's" undertaking is a very widespread type of peasant farm in the majority of countries of Western Europe and America. For example, according to the study of Swiss farms carried out yearly under the guidance of Professor E. Laur, we have Table 7–11, based on bookkeeping entries.

TABLE 7–11

| Area of Land for Use (Hectares) | Percentage of On-Farm Labor | | Percentage of All Recorded Farms in Land Use Class |
|---|---|---|---|
| | Family Members | Hired Workers | |
| <5 | 92.6 | 7.4 | 14.1 |
| 5–10 | 80.6 | 19.4 | 40.7 |
| 10–15 | 69.9 | 30.1 | 22.5 |
| 15–30 | 52.5 | 47.5 | 15.7 |
| >30 | 42.7 | 57.3 | 7.0 |
| Average | 68.3 | 31.7 | 100.0 |

On the basis of agricultural statistics, we might establish the proportion of labor and capitalist agriculture in different countries, and almost everywhere undoubtedly we would observe, together with purely labor farms, capitalist forms. In Russia, this type of farm has not become very widespread among the peasants. A special record of peasant farms using hired labor, carried out by V. G. Groman for various uezds of Penza guberniya, gave a modest 3–5 percent for these farms. According to the data of the Starobel'sk budget study, we have 9.9 percent hired labor for agricultural units, and 5.5 percent for total family economic activity (including crafts and trades). Table 7–12 is a very interesting one given by Kushchenko in his comparison of Su-razh uezd censuses for 1882 and 1911.

TABLE 7–12

| Desyatinas | Percentage of Farms Hiring Yearly and Short-Term Workers | | Number of Casual Laborers per Farm Hiring Workers | |
|---|---|---|---|---|
| | 1882 | 1911 | 1882 | 1911 |
| 0– 3.0 ...... | 1.3 | 0.4 | 1.0 | 1.0 |
| 3.1– 6.0 ...... | 1.3 | 1.5 | 1.0 | 1.0 |
| 6.1– 9.0 ...... | 2.1 | 3.3 | 1.1 | 1.2 |
| 9.1–12.0 ...... | 3.0 | 5.0 | 1.3 | 1.1 |
| >12.0 ...... | 7.1 | 6.9 | 1.2 | 1.3 |

Within the Russian peasantry, social differentiation is still in its initial stages, and we will not undertake to judge how far the semi-labor, semicapitalist "farmer" type unit will be able to improve its position with the present tendency of the Russian peasantry for en-closed farms. We must hope that the labor farm, strengthened by co-operative bodies, will be able to defend its positions against large-scale, capitalist type farms as it did in former times.

Moreover, as P. A. Vikhlyaev quite rightly pointed out in his last contribution to the Economic Scientific Research Institute, in analyz-ing the development of capitalist agriculture we must investigate dif-ferentiation not only in the peasant farms but in all agricultural units taken together. In reviewing the problem on this scale for pre-Revo-lutionary Russia, we clearly saw the process of capitalist differentia-tion, since the medium and small landowner units, a remnant of the serf period, rapidly disappeared. Their lands were taken over either by small peasant farms or by large-scale, typically entrepreneurial farms, often combined with industrial processing of agricultural produce.

However, although this goes beyond our theme, we should stress that while the elements of capitalist organization of production did not develop much among Russian peasants, the proletarianization of part of the peasantry in densely populated areas proceeded very rapidly before the Revolution. It was of a clearly industrial character and took the form of a completely regular stream of rural population pouring into industrial and urban centers. Moreover, as we are con-cerned with the labor farm, the themes we have touched on, despite their exceptionally intense and topical general economic interest, are quite to one side, so we should return to the main themes of our study.

It is important to us that the process of demographic differentiation which depends on biological family growth is, in essence, not new and is, essentially speaking, static. The dynamic processes of agricultural proletarianization and concentration of production, leading to large-scale agricultural production units based on hired labor, are developing throughout the world, and in the U.S.S.R. in particular, at a rate much slower than was expected at the end of nineteenth century. The area swept by agrarian revolutions has even, as it were, strengthened the position of the small farm. Nevertheless, it is clear to everyone working in the field of agriculture that literally before our eyes the world's agriculture, ours included, is being more and more drawn into the general circulation of the world economy, and the centers of capitalism are more and more subordinating it to their leadership.

In other words, while *in a production sense* concentration in agriculture is scarcely reflected in the formation of new large-scale undertakings, *in an economic sense* capitalism as a general economic system makes great headway in agriculture.

In what forms does this take place? Where are the social threads that bind Sidor Karpov's farm, lost in the Perm' forests, to the London banks and oblige him to feel the effects of changes in the pulse rate of the London stock exchange?

The latest studies on the development of capitalism in agriculture, particularly Lenin's works on American farming, and partly Hilferding on finance capital, Lyashchenko on trading capitalism in Russia, and others, indicate that bringing agriculture into the general capitalist system need by no means involve the creation of very large, capitalistically organized production units based on hired labor. Repeating the stages in the development of industrial capitalism, agriculture comes out of a seminatural existence and becomes subject to trading capitalism that sometimes in the form of very large-scale trading undertakings draws masses of scattered peasant farms into its sphere of influence and, having bound these small-scale commodity producers to the market, economically subordinates them to its influence. By developing oppressive credit conditions, it converts the organization of agricultural production almost into a special form of distributive office based on a "sweatshop system." In this connection, it is enough to recall the examples of capitalist exploitation which Knop, the Moscow cotton firm, applied to the Sart cotton growers, buying up their harvest in spring, giving out advances for food, and giving them credits for seed and means of production.

These trading links that convert the natural, isolated family farm into one of a small commodity producer are always the first means of organizing scattered peasant farms and of opening the first path for the penetration of capitalist relations into the countryside. Through these connections, every small peasant undertaking becomes an organic part of the world economy, itself experiences the effects of the world's general economic life, is powerfully directed in its organization by the capitalist world's economic demands, and, in its turn, together with millions like it, affects the whole system of the world economy.

The system of the local rural bazaar at which the peasant sells his harvest and buys what he needs, and around which all the countryside's economic relations crystallize, has been very little studied. The bazaar is the primary cell of this general economic organism. Recent Russian statistical works have studied these trade catchment areas. With great clarity, they have separated out these primary indivisible units of the national economy compounded at the whim of economic life and the railways, independent of natural and historical areas and of administrative boundaries. Thus, in 1915 P. A. Vikhlyaev established, for provision purposes, a peculiar system of trading connections as regards grain purchases for individual Moscow guberniya hamlets. G. I. Baskin carried out analogous work for Samara guberniya settlements as regards their grain sales, and he provided the map in Figure 7–6.

Observing local life shows that the bazaar site is a concentration of all local trading, cooperative, business, and even spiritual life for its catchment area, since the personal links of the area's inhabitants are united by the bazaar, where they invariably meet one another. In their turn, the bazaars are attracted to a larger scale center of wholesale trade, and they construct a certain national economic whole from the scattered peasant farms through the firm links of their trading machine.

In studying the structure of the trading machine for the sales markets of different agricultural produce, we can note five basic steps in the course taken by the commodity:

1. The commodity, scattered among individual producers, is collected by jobbing buyers and dealers and is concentrated in their hands.
2. Commodities collected by the buyers are roughly sorted and transferred to local wholesale trade centers.

## FIGURE 7–6
### TRADE CATCHMENT AREAS IN SAMARA GUBERNIYA BEFORE THE WAR

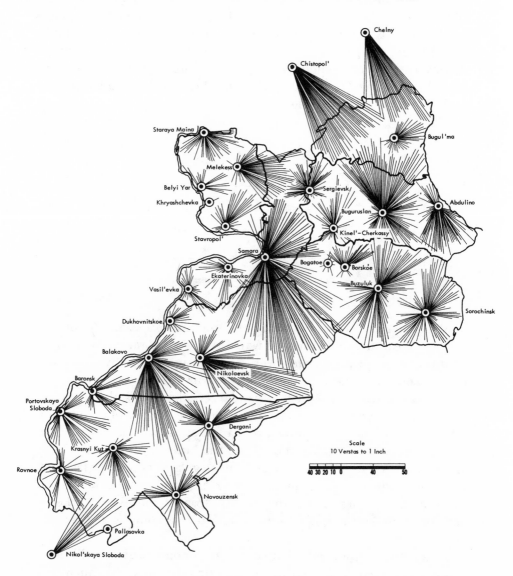

3. In the wholesale centers, commodities are sorted and distributed for onward transmission.

4. Commodities collected and sorted are transferred to local consumer wholesale centers.

5. From the local wholesale centers, commodities are distributed with the help of the trade distributive network (local stallholders and other traders).

Such is the general scheme, but according to the particular commodity it considerably changes its form and takes on individual characteristic features. For example, if we take a product such as hay we should consider the organization of its market as very much simplified. The greater part of the commodity passes directly from producer to consumer; if middlemen do exist in the supply of hay to urban markets, their number is limited. A very simple scheme will show the hay market in graphic form (Figure 7–7).

FIGURE 7–7
Market for Hay

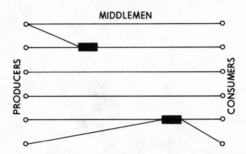

Meat sales give us quite a different picture—for example, on the Moscow meat market before the war. Livestock for meat, fattened on landowners' or peasant farms, were brought up locally by drovers or dealers and then taken to the next market in Moscow. At the market, the livestock passed into the hands of large-scale traders, the "factors." At Moscow, these factors were almost complete masters of the market. The factors resold the livestock to slaughterers, who killed the animals in the slaughterhouse and cut up the bullock into carcass, hide, and inedible offals. The offals were sent to gelatin and other factories using by-products, and the meat went to large and small butchers and to canning factories. Thus, the organization of the meat market is very complex and graphically presents quite a complicated scheme (Figure 7–8).

Hides, flax, cotton, and other similar commodities give a still more complicated picture. Moreover, it must be noted that for much produce the commodity course differs for different markets. Thus, in studying the structure of the flax market we must first note the great difference between the Western flax areas that sell abroad and the Eastern ones that serve internal demand. In the West, there are many more middlemen, and market relations are more complex and confused. Schematically, the Western type of prewar market organization

## FIGURE 7–8
### THE MOSCOW MEAT MARKET

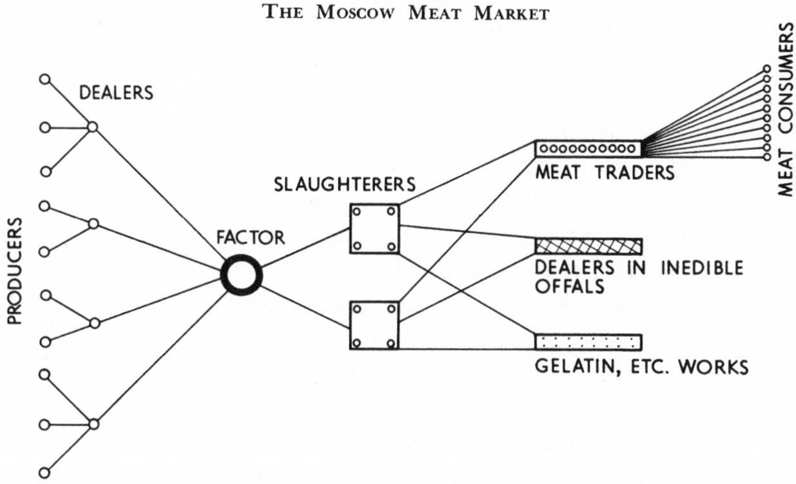

DEALERS

PRODUCERS

FACTOR

SLAUGHTERERS

MEAT TRADERS

MEAT CONSUMERS

DEALERS IN INEDIBLE OFFALS

GELATIN, ETC. WORKS

and movement of the commodity may be represented as shown in Figure 7–9.

Flax brought to the bazaar by the peasant falls into the hands of small-scale buyers who, after roughly sorting it, sell it to local town traders or agents of foreign export offices who export it, independently or through middlemen. Arriving in Western Europe, the commodity sometimes passes from hand to hand once again, and finally arrives at the mill.

The machine that has been described penetrates, with its hundreds of thousands of branches, to the full depths of the peasant farms and

## FIGURE 7–9
### THE FLAX MARKET, WESTERN GUBERNIYAS

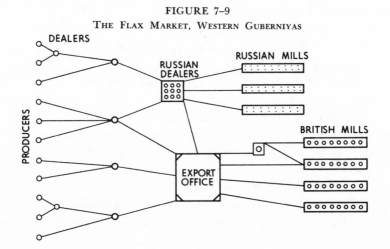

DEALERS

PRODUCERS

RUSSIAN DEALERS

RUSSIAN MILLS

EXPORT OFFICE

BRITISH MILLS

leaving them free as regards production, entirely dominates them economically. Some Gzhatsk flax-growing farm's income, level of well-being, and power to form capital begins to depend to a great extent on the purely capitalist relations of Western Europe and, at times, on how the American banks are financing the Belfast mills.

Frequently, the trading machine, concerned about a standard quality in the commodity collected, begins to actively interfere in the organization of production, too. It lays down technical conditions, issues seed and fertilizers, determines the rotation, and turns its clients into technical executors of its designs and economic plan. A characteristic example of this sort of thing here was the plantation sowings of sugar beet on peasant fields by contract with the sugar factories or contractors. After selling channels were acquired and its raw material base created, capitalism in the countryside began to penetrate into production itself. It split off from the peasant farm individual sectors, predominantly those in the primary processing of agricultural raw material and, in general, those connected with mechanical processes. Obvious examples of this are mobile commercial steam threshers in the south of Russia, small creameries in Siberia at the end of the nineteenth century, and flax-processing workshops in France and in some places in our flax-growing guberniyas.

If to this we add in the most developed capitalist countries, such as those in North America, widely developed mortgage credit, the financing of farm circulating capital, and the dominating part played by capital invested in transport, elevator, irrigation, and other undertakings, then we have before us new ways in which capitalism penetrates agriculture. These ways convert the farmers into a labor force working with other people's means of production. They convert agriculture, despite the evident scattered and independent nature of the small commodity producers, into an economic system concentrated in a series of the largest undertakings and, through them, entering the sphere controlled by the most advanced forms of finance capitalism. It is not without cause that, according to Professor N. P. Makarov, only 35 percent of farmers' incomes coming from America's wholesale exchanges goes to the farmer; the remaining 65 percent is taken by railway, elevator, irrigation, finance, and trading capital.

Compared with this vertical capitalist concentration, the transfer of farms from 10 to 100 or 500 hectares, with the corresponding transfer of a considerable number of farmers from a semiproletarian to a clearly proletarian position, would be a small detail. And if this detail does not take place, it is evidently because capitalist exploitation gives a higher percentage from vertical than from horizontal concentration. Moreover, to a considerable extent it transfers the undertakings' risk from the owner of the capital to the farmer. This form of concentration in agricultural production is characteristic of almost all young agricultural countries, which produce mass uniform produce for distant, mainly export markets.

Sometimes this vertical concentration, in accord with the general economic situation, assumes, not capitalist, but cooperative or mixed forms. In this case, control of the system of trade, elevator, irrigation, credit, and processing undertakings that concentrate and guide agricultural production in part or in whole belongs, not to the holders of capital, but to the organized small commodity producers who have contributed their own capital to these undertakings or have been able to create social capital.

The rise and development of cooperative elements in the vertical agricultural concentration becomes possible only in certain phases of this process, and a necessary precondition is the relative weakness of local capital. In this instance, we deliberately stress the word "relative," because this relative weakness of local entrepreneur capitalists may result not only from their own absolute weakness but also from the wealth of the peasant farm (Denmark) or from the fact that behind the cooperatives may stand states, which finance their resources, or large-scale export or industrial capital, which requires proper raw material. An obvious example of this process is the development of the Siberian dairying cooperatives.

At the end of the nineteenth century, after the great Siberian railway line had been laid, an exceptionally advantageous market situation came about for the development of export dairying in western Siberia, based on abundant areas of feed. In the areas of Kurgan, Ishim, and other okrugs, small entrepreneurs appeared one after the other and soon covered the area with small creameries. Thus, they started the capitalist process of vertical concentration in west Siberian agriculture. In the course of decades, Siberian dairying, created by the small speculator, took the cream off the favorable market situation, and came up against a severe crisis from the built-up excess capacity and the fierce competition both in milk purchasing and in selling butter. The creameries continued to operate for a number of years, not so much on their income from butter as on the profits of their stalls and the accounts of goods credited for milk. They dragged on a pitiful existence; then, one by one, they began to close. Peasant farms that had already transformed themselves into commodity dairying forms were threatened with heavy losses by this closure, and since they did not want to return to natural conditions, with the inevitability of history they had to face up to the question of taking over the closing factories by means of peasant artels.

The quality of the product from the cooperative factories that thus appeared was distinguished from the adulterated butter of the entrepreneurs. So, in their development, the cooperatives received financial support from trading capital in the form of the Danish and British export firms, which had Siberian offices in Kurgan and other towns, and they quickly squeezed the private entrepreneur out of dairying.

Thus, the concentration of Siberian dairying, started by small industrial capital, continues, with the support of large-scale trading capital, in cooperative forms, and as it grows rapidly it soon breaks its link with export trading capital. The Siberian union of dairying artels itself appears on the London market and, relying on bank credit, frees itself from any influence of trading capital. In somewhat other forms, but in the same type of movement with different phases of connection with the capitalist groups, other forms of agricultural cooperation also developed before the war.

What has been said is quite enough to understand the essence of agricultural cooperation as a deep process of vertical concentration in agriculture. Moreover, it must be noted that in its cooperative forms this process goes much deeper than in its capitalist ones, since the peasant himself hands over to cooperative forms of concentration sectors of his farm that capitalism never succeeds in detaching from it in the course of their struggle. Such is our understanding of the vertical concentration of agricultural production in capitalist society —a concentration that penetrates both in purely capitalist and in cooperative forms.

In expounding this concept, we have approached the basic, chief, and most important question regarding the fate of our agriculture. Everyone knows the basic fact of our economy is that our republic is an agricultural country, where more than half the national income is derived from tillage and livestock farming. In accordance with this, our agriculture is a powerful general economic factor that goes far to determine the economy of the U.S.S.R.

Processing industry, mining, and transport, the main branches of which, in our republic, are concentrated in very large undertakings, are managed by or are under the control of state bodies. Unlike them, however, the social and economic structure of agriculture is an elemental complex of 18.5 million scattered small farms, developing under pressure from elemental factors and little subject to any control.

If, speaking generally, we do not wish to risk the stability and flexible maneuverability of state capitalism, we cannot leave the chief sector of our economy in an elemental state of development. Since our agriculture is elemental in character, we shall always have to accept both our internal demand and raw material stocks, both in quantity and in quality, as something given. This also means a denial of freedom to develop planning and the processing industry. Undoubtedly, a series of general economic policy measures as regards transport, customs, tax, and other spheres might sometimes have a great indirect effect on the creation and development of peasant farms. But this influence is insufficient for the tasks of state capitalism, and we ought to aim at direct organizational control of the elemental peasant farm.

With this initial proposition before us, we should acknowledge that a basic and very complex problem in our state capitalism is with what methods we may tie in this peasant element with the general system of state capitalism and, subordinating it to the controlling influence of state central agencies, introduce it into the general system of our state planned economy. In elaborating these methods, we should, however, take into account that the basic idea of state capitalism is a recognition of it as a transitional form to a final socialist organization of the economy.

In accordance with this, when we bind the elemental peasant nature by our measures and organize it into the general system of the U.S.S.R.'s planned economy we should also have in view this final aim: we ought to introduce elements into the future organization of agriculture, the further development of which *would itself outgrow state capitalism and might be the basis for a future socialist economic system.*

Such is the most important question in the contemporary phase of our economy's development and the most urgent problem for the U.S.S.R.'s economic policy. At the present time, there are no longer two opinions on this question, and all agricultural organizers assuredly suppose that the main methods in the reorganization of our agriculture will be those of vertical concentration. We must agree with this, but for a fully conscious solution we should make clear to ourselves:

1. What internal changes should take place in the vertical concentration of agriculture and, in particular, in its cooperative forms when replacing a capitalist society regime with one of a transitional system of state capitalism and, subsequently, with a regime of socialist organization of production?

2. In today's organizational work for the peasant farm, do we need vertical concentration as an actual implement of economic policy, and in what forms?

Not much effort is required to answer the second question. Since organizational control of agricultural production processes is possible only by replacing scattered peasant farming with concentrated production forms, we should use every means to develop those processes in the life of the countryside which lead to this concentration.

The course of horizontal concentration with which we usually connect our conception of large-scale production in agriculture should in a country of small-scale peasant farming be thought of historically in forms of the elemental differentiation of peasant farms. This course is determined by the poorest part of the proletarian element in these farms, the decline of the middle peasants, and the concentration of production in well-to-do categories, run on capitalist lines and using hired labor.

As is usually supposed, in its development this process should lead to the gradual creation of large and technically quite well-organized farms. At a certain moment in the formation of the socialist economy, these are supposed to be nationalized and to form a system of "grain and meat factories."

It is self-evident that in the conditions of Soviet policy in the countryside the presence of our land code and, in general, of a regime of land nationalization, this course is completely inapplicable. Historically, further proletarianization of the peasantry can in no case play a part in Soviet policy. In the course of the Revolution, we not only could not concentrate the scattered lands into large-scale production units, but we also were historically obliged, on the contrary, to split up a considerable part of the land formerly available to the old, large-scale units.

In accordance with this, the sole form of horizontal concentration that at the present time may, and actually does, take place is the concentration of peasant lands into large-scale production units. These take the form of every sort of agricultural collective, of communalized cooperatives, artels, and partnerships for joint working of the land, as far, of course, as they are created on peasant lands, and not by taking into exploitation an old estate.

This process is taking place on a considerable scale, but it is not, and cannot be, of such a massive size that we would be able to construct on it our whole policy of agricultural concentration. Therefore, the main form for the concentration of peasant farms can be only vertical concentration and, moreover, in its cooperative forms, since only in these forms will it be organically linked with agricultural production and be able to spread to its proper extent and depth. In other words, the course of cooperative collectivization is the sole course possible in our conditions to introduce into peasant farming the elements of the large-scale farm industrialization and the state plan. This means gradually and steadily splitting off particular sectors from individual farms, and organizing them in higher forms of large-scale social undertakings.

This conception of agricultural cooperation may be almost the only method of involving our agriculture in the system of state capitalism, and at the present time this is our main task. Our agricultural cooperation originated long before the Revolution. Cooperation existed and exists in a number of capitalist countries. However, both with us before the Revolution and in all capitalist countries, it was no more than adaptation of small commodity producers to conditions of capitalist society, no more than a weapon in the struggle for survival. It was not and could not be a new social structure. The situation completely changes as agricultural cooperation and its social capital—great concentration of production and the planned nature of its work—appear in socialist society or at least in our system of state capitalism and not in capitalist society.

In this case, precisely because of great vertical concentration and centralization of the cooperative system, the network through its centers comes in contact with the leading bodies of the state economy. From a simple tool of petty commodity producers, created by them in their struggle for existence in capitalist society, the scheme is converted into one of the main components of the socialist production system. In other words, from a technical tool of a social group, or even class, it is converted into one of the bases of the new society's economic system.

This conception of the general economic significance of agricultural cooperation essentially predetermines the main lines of our agricultural policy. However, if we foresee that this process will last a long while, we should adopt a program of cooperative forms of vertical concentration for agriculture, and should attempt through a system of cooperative combines and unions to establish a direct link between each peasant farm and the central bodies of state capitalism, thus bringing it into the general stream of the planned economy. Just as capitalism passed through successive phases of development from the primary forms of elementary trading capitalism and from the home workshop to the factory and the formation of trusts embracing the whole of industry, so state capitalism, developing in its cooperative forms as regards agriculture should inevitably pass through such a series in its historical development.

Usually starting with a unification of small producers in the preparation of means of agricultural production, cooperation very rapidly proceeds to organize cooperative sales of agricultural produce. It forms gigantic unions that embrace hundreds of thousands of small producers. As operations of this middleman type acquire proper scope and stability, a smoothly working and strong cooperative machine is formed, and, what is particularly important, in analogy with the development of capitalism there takes place a primary accumulation of cooperative capital. Under pressure from the market, agricultural cooperation at this phase of its development moves with historical inevitability toward organizing primary processing of agricultural raw material (cooperatives in dairying, potato pulling, canning, flax scutching, and so on) in conjunction with its selling operations. It separates out the corresponding sectors from the peasant farm, industrializes the countryside, and thus takes over all commanding positions in its economy. In our circumstances, because of the assistance of the state and state credit, these development processes are speeded up, and may take place simultaneously and intermingle.

Having taken over sales and technical processing, agricultural cooperation thus concentrates and organizes agricultural production in new and higher forms. It obliges the small producer to change his farm's organizational plan according to cooperative selling and processing policy, to improve his techniques, and to transfer to improved methods of tillage and livestock farming, insuring a fully standard product, subjecting it to careful sorting, processing, packing, and canning according to world market demand.

However, having achieved this success, cooperation inevitably goes further in the direction of greater involvement in the production sectors of the peasant farm (machine partnerships, stud farms, control and pedigree unions, joint working, irrigation, and so on). Moreover, part of the expenditures on these cooperative production forms are met and should be met in principle from the profits on sales, purchases, and credits.

With a parallel development of electrification, technical installations of all kinds, systems of warehouses and public buildings, networks of improved roads, and cooperative credit, the elements of social capital and the social economy increase quantitatively so much that the whole system changes qualitatively. It is converted from one of peasant farms that have formed cooperatives for some sectors of their economy to one of a social cooperative economy, founded on socialized capital, that leaves in the private farms of its members the technical fulfillment of certain processes almost on the basis of a technical commission.

Such is the origin of the new forms of agriculture based on the principle of vertical concentration. In its present situation, the cooperative movement in various areas is in different phases of its gradual development. While in some guberniyas of the U.S.S.R. we see only the first beginnings of sales and purchasing cooperatives, such areas as the famous Shunga volost, the Borovichi-Valdai area, Velikie Soli, Burtsevo and Kurovo, Moscow guberniya, give us examples of cooperative concentration penetrating into the very depths of agricultural production and sales.

These are the evolutionary forms of the peasant farm, as a sector of the economy. It has already started on this course and should continue on it, come what may, unless you wish the vertical concentration of agricultural production to take the capitalist variant. This would inevitably lead to most oppressive forms of capitalist exploitation.

In the peasant farm evolution we have described, we should finally trace those changes which, with the socialization of the individual links in the organizational plan, should be completed deep within the family farm by the mechanism of the on-farm equilibrium and with its characteristic process of capital formation.

In all probability, in the first phases of the development of cooperation these changes will not be particularly great. But, undoubtedly, with the quantitative increase of elements of social economy in our countryside we will encounter the development of a new economic psychology, and we expect that the evolution of the agriculture will, in many respects, be a gradual denial of those bases of the family farm which have been established in our study of the present-day peasant farm.

# Glossary*

ADVANTAGE—On the peasant labor farm, the evaluation of comparative advantage is not based on the calculation of net income, but is arrived at by the *labor–consumer balance*.

Russian—vygodnost'.
German—der Vorteil.
French —les avantages.

BALANCE, LABOR–CONSUMER BALANCE —The calculation, not necessarily explicit or conscious, which establishes the *basic economic equilibrium* between *drudgery of labor* and *demand satisfaction*. The main economic aim is to organize the year's work to meet a single family demand, including the desire to save or invest capital if possible.

Russian—trudo-potrebitel'skii balans.
German—die Arbeits-Verbraucher balance.
French —l'appréciation de la dépense de travail et de la satisfaction des besoins.

COMMUNE, REPARTITIONAL COMMUNE —A peasant commune that practices periodical redivision or partition of the commune lands among its members.

Russian—peredel'naya obshchina.
German—die Wiederverteilungs Kommune.
French —commune pratiquant la redistribution periodique des terres.

CONSUMER RATE—The area of field cultivation with which the peasant family will meet its minimum consumption needs.

Russian—potrebitel'skaya norma.
German—die Verbrauchernorm.
French —norme de consommation.

CRAFTS AND TRADES—Economic activities, usually of primary extractive type but including cottage crafts and other forms of, often seasonal, nonagricultural work.

Russian—promysly.
German—das Handwerk.
French —métiers.

DEMAND SATISFACTION—One of the elements in the *labor–consumer balance*.

Russian—udovletvorenie potrebnostei.
German—die Bedarfsbefriedigung.

---

*The Russian and German terms given in this glossary are those used by Chayanov or his German translators. In a few cases the usage (and, consequently, the English and French versions given here) differs from that usually found.

271

**French** —la satisfaction des besoins.

**Desyatina**—A Russian unit of area measure: 2.7 acres or 1.1 hectares.

**Drudgery of Labor**—One of the elements in the *labor–consumer balance*.

**Russian**—tyagostnost' truda.
**German**—die Arbeitsbeschwerlichkeit.
**French** —la fatigue due au travail.

**Economic Expenditures**—All outlays in money and kind for production, not consumption, including expenditure on circulating capital and on capital renewal and formation.

**Russian**—khozyaistvennye raskhody.
**German**—wirtschaftliche Aufwendungen.
**French** —les coûts de production.

**Economic Unit**—A production and consumption unit, often a *farm*, but it may be in cottage industry or consist of urban artisans, for example.

**Russian**—khozyaistvo.
**German**—die Wirtschaft.
**French** —exploitation.

**Equilibrium, Basic (Economic) Equilibrium**—The result of the *labor–consumer balance* struck between *demand satisfaction* and *drudgery of labor*.

**Russian**—osnovnoe (khozyaistvennoe) ravnovesie.
**German**—das fundamentale wirtschaftliche Gleichgewicht.
**French** —l'équilibre des dépenses de travail et des besoins.

**Family, Labor Family**—A family that forms an economic unit and relies on itself for labor without recourse to wage labor. It may be engaged in agriculture on a *family farm* or in urban artisan activities.

**Russian**—trudovaya sem'ya.
**German**—die Arbeitsfamilie.
**French** —la famille ouvrière.

**Family Unit**—An *economic unit* based on the labor of a family group, not necessarily the nuclear family. Usually, the unit is a *family farm*, but it may be in cottage industry or consist of urban artisans, for example. In any case, there is no hired wage labor.

**Russian**—semeinoe khozyaistvo.
**German**—die Familienwirtschaft.
**French** —l'exploitation familiale.

**Farm**—The production and consump-

**Russian**—khozyaistvo.

tion unit which makes its living from the land, sometimes with supplements from nonagricultural sources (see *crafts and trades*). A particular form of *economic unit*.

**German**—die bauerliche Wirtschaft.

**French** —exploitation agricole.

1. FAMILY FARM—A farm normally run by a family without hired outside wage labor, sometimes in part engaging in nonagricultural crafts and trades. Since there is no wage category, analysis in terms of normal capitalist categories is inapplicable. Moreover, the motivation of such a farm is not profit but the *labor–consumer balance*. Some writers use this term for capitalist family farms, which may, of course, hire wage labor. Such a farm is called a *farmer unit* in Chayanov's terminology.

**Russian**—semeinoe khozyaistvo (see, also, *family unit*).
**German**—die Familienwirtschaft (see, also, *family unit*).
**French** —exploitation agricole familiale.

2. LABOR FARM—A farm normally relying on its own, not hired, labor, and without the category of wages. The peasant labor farm (see, also, No . 3) is a form of *family farm*.

**Russian**—trudovoe khozyaistvo.
**German**—die Arbeitswirtschaft.
**French** —exploitation basée sur le travail des membres de la famille.

3. (PEASANT) FAMILY LABOR FARM— A *peasant farm* normally run without wage labor. The family of such a farm may not coincide with the nuclear family. It may include married children, grandchildren, and also "adopted" family members (i.e., workers from other families who live in), and it may exclude members that work elsewhere. The family as a result of its year's labor receives a single labor income (see *product*) and weighs its efforts against the material results obtained (see *labor–consumer balance*).

**Russian**—(krest'yanskoe) trudovoe semeinoe khozyaistvo.
**German**—die bäuerliche Familienwirtschaft.
**French** —exploitation paysanne familiale.

4. PEASANT FARM—A peasant *economic unit* that makes a living

**Russian**—krest'yanskoe khozyaistvo.

from the land, though its activities may also take place in non-agricultural sectors, mainly *crafts and trades*. It may be capitalist in nature, a *farmer unit*, or linked to the market and employing wage labor, at least in part. Often, however, this term is used to indicate the *peasant family labor farm*, in which there is no hired wage labor and which thus differs fundamentally from the capitalist farm. Confusion may arise because of (*a*) the Anglo-American usage of the term family farm for enterprises in capitalist economy and (*b*) Chayanov's use of peasant farm rather than peasant family labor farm.

German—die Bauernwirtschaft.
French —exploitation paysanne.

5. **PEASANT LABOR FARM**—A form of the *peasant farm*, not of the semi-proletarian or semicapitalist type but, like the *family farm*, not having wage labor.

Russian—krest'yanskoe trudovoe khozyaistvo.
German—die bäuerliche Arbeitswirtschaft.
French —exploitation paysanne de main d'oeuvre familiale.

**FARM FAMILY**—A family that runs a farm (or other family-based economic unit).

Russian—khozyaistvuyushchaya sem'ya.
German—die wirtschaftende Familie.
French —la famille exploitante.

**FARMER UNIT**—A farm that in part relies on its own family labor, but uses some hired wage labor and aims at making profits; a half-labor, half-capitalist unit.

Russian—fermerskoe khozyaistvo.
German—die Farmerwirtschaft.
French —l'économie fermière.

**FARMING, PEASANT FARMING**—The economic activity of the *peasant farm*, in the narrow sense restricted to agricultural activity, but sometimes used in a broader sense to include activity in the nonagricultural sector by members of the farm family (see *crafts and trades*).

Russian—krest'yanskoe khozyaistvo.
German—die Bauernwirtschaft.
French —exploitation paysanne.

GUBERNIYA—A major administrative unit of the Russian Empire. European Russia was divided into 49 such units (and one oblast).

KULAK—A Russian word—literally, "fist"—for a richer peasant or trader who may employ outside labor.

LABOR PAYMENT—On the *peasant labor* or *family farm*, the total amount of annual income, after deducting outlays, available to the family.

Russian—oplata truda.
German—Arbeitsverdienst.
French —remunération du travail.

LABOR RATE—The amount of arable that, with normal intensity, uses the total labor force on a *family labor farm* indicates the labor rate. This amount is under constraint from the most critical labor intensive period, usually harvesting.

Russian—trudovaya norma.
German—die Arbeitsnorm.
French —norme de travail en période de pointe.

LABOR UNIT—An economic unit that operates without hired wage labor. Like the *family unit*, it may exist in agriculture, cottage industry or in urban artisan sector.

Russian—trudovoe khozyaistvo.
German—die Arbeitswirtschaft.
French —exploitation basée uniquement sur le travail de la famille.

NATIONAL ECONOMY—The economy of the state taken as a whole. In its adjectival form, this term is sometimes contrasted with the private economy, the individual microeconomic unit.

Russian—narodnoe khozyaistvo.
German—die Wirtschaft.
French —économie nationale.

PARTITION—See repartitional *commune*.

Russian—peredel.
German—die Verteilung.
French —redistribution.

PARTITION, BLACK PARTITION—Elemental peasant seizure and partition of the land.

Russian—chernyi peredel.
German—Schwartze Verteilung.
French —partage violent des terres par les paysans.

POUND—The Russian pound (*funt*) weight 0.9 pounds avoirdupois, 0.4 kilograms.

PRIVATE ECONOMIC—Relating to an economic unit or units within the

Russian—chastno-khozyaistvennyi.

national economy as a whole; micro-economic as distinct from macroeco-nomic.

**German**—privatwirtschaftlich.
**French** —d'économie privée.

PRODUCT

1. GROSS PRODUCT—Total family an-nual income, both from farming in general and from *crafts and trades.*

**Russian**—valovaya priozvoditel'-nost'.
**German**—Rohertrag.
**French** —produit brut.

2. NET PRODUCT—The gross product, less expenditures on the farm and all outlays on capital renewal. See, also, *labor payment.*

**Russian**—chistaya proizvoditel'-nost'.
**German**—Reinertrag.
**French** —produit net

PUD—A Russian weight, 36 pounds avoirdupois, 16.4 kilograms. 1 pud per desyatina = 13.3 pounds per acre.

RENT (PAYMENTS)—The amount paid for hired land.

**Russian**—arenda.
**German**—Rente.
**French** —loyer de la terre.

RENT, ECONOMIC RENT—(*a*) Unearned income due to a particular location or the quality of land. General eco-nomic factors, such as price fluctua-tions, improvements in technique, and increased fertility, may help to generate economic rent. (*b*) The German terms *Grundrente* (rent from the land) and *Bodenrente* (rent from the soil) are used, apparently in this sense, in Chayanov's article "On the theory of noncapitalistic economic systems." He uses the terms *Sklavenrente* (slave rent) and *Leibeigenrente* (serf rent) in an analogous fashion for income that results from owning slaves or serfs. (*c*) The Russian term, *renta*, is sometimes (e.g., page 39) used to translate the English term "rent" in the sense of rent payments.

**Russian**—renta.
**German**—Rente.
**French** —rente foncière.

SAZHEN—A Russian measure of length: 2.3 yards, 2.1 meters.

Sokha—The basic wooden tillage implement in the Russian countryside in the early twentieth century; it had two (or more) teeth, and, strictly speaking, was an ard, or scratchplow.

Uezd—A territorial administrative unit, a subdivision of a *guberniya*. Around 1900, an average European uezd had a population approaching 200,000, but there were wide variations.

Vedro—A Russian liquid measure, 12.3 liters, about 22 pints.

Versta—A Russian unit of linear measure, 0.66 miles or 1.07 kilometers.

Volost—A rural area administrative subdivision of an *uezd*; the primary administrative unit for the peasants in the late nineteenth and early twentieth centuries.

Worker—Someone who works, but not necessarily, as in current Soviet terminology, one who receives a wage. It includes those who work on a *family farm* and have a share in the *labor payment*.

**Russian**—rabotnik.
**German**—der Arbeiter.
**French** —ouvrier.

Zemstvo—Elective local rural council instituted at *guberniya* and *uezd* level after the liberation of the serfs in Russia.

# Bibliography of A. V. Chayanov

(Compiled by the editors, principally B. Kerblay, with the help of the Centre de Documentation sur l'U.R.S.S. et les Pays Slaves of the École Pratique des Hautes Études, Sixième Section, Sorbonne, Paris.)
The bibliography has been arranged in three sections:

I.   Economic studies (books, articles, reports).
II.  Other works (history, literature, arts).
III. Studies edited or prefaced by Chayanov.

This list has been made on the basis of Chayanov's works accessible in a number of the main European and American libraries. The bibliography does not pretend to be complete, because Chayanov's writings are widely scattered and not easy to trace. Nonetheless, the list may be useful because it is as exhaustive as we have been able to make it. We believe it includes his principal works and a wide variety of his lesser studies and articles, including some tales and a peasant utopia. To indicate where these works may be found, we have used the following abbreviations:

BDIC   Paris, Bibliothèque de Documentation
       International Contemporaine.
BM     London, British Museum.
BN     Paris, Bibliothèque Nationale.
HL     Stanford, California, Hoover Library.
LC     Washington, Library of Congress.
LL     Moscow, Lenin Library
NYPL   New York Public Library.

A few items have also turned up in the libraries of Harvard University, the University of Helsinki, the London School of Economics, and the International Labor Organization in Geneva. We have indicated these at the appropriate places in the list.

## I.   Economic Studies

1909

*Kooperatsiya v sel'skom khozyaistve Italii (Cooperatives in Italian agriculture)*. Moskva: tip. F. Burche, 22 cm., pp. 18, tab., diag.

*Sel'sko-khozyaistvennyi kredit v Belgii (Agricultural credit in Belgium).*
Moskva.
*Obshchestvennye meropriyatiya po skotovodstvu v Belgii (Social measures
relating to livestock farming in Belgium).* Moskva. In 8°, 44 pp., doklad
soedinnennomy zasedaniyu komiteta skotovodstva i komiteta o sel'sk.
ssudosberegatel'nykh i prom. tovarishchestvakh.

$$\text{LL} \quad \text{U}\frac{49}{206}$$

## 1910

*Strakhovanie skota v Belgii (Livestock insurance in Belgium).* Moskva.
*Yuzhnaya granitsa rasprostraneniya trekhpol'noi sistemy polevago khozya-
istva na krest'yanskikh polyakh k nachalu XX veka (The southern
limit of the three-course system on peasant fields at the start of the
twentieth century).* St. Petersburg.
*K voprosu o znachenii l'na v organizatsionnom plane krest'yanskago kho-
zyaistva nechernozemnoi Rossii (On the significance of flax in the organization plan of the peasant farm in non-Black Earth Russia).* Moskva.

## 1911

*Uchastkovaya agronomiya i organizatsionnyi plan krest'yanskago kho-
zyaistva (Agricultural advice in parcellated farming and the peasant
farm's organizational plan).* Trudy Moskovskogo oblastnogo s"ezda
deyatelei agronomicheskoi pomoshchi naseleniyu, Moskva, t. 2.
*Doklad S"ezda deyatelei agronomicheskoi pomoshchi naseleniyu (Report
of the Congress of Agricultural Officers [Agronomists] advising the public).* In Trudy Moskovskogo oblastnogo . . . , t. 2.
*Nekotorye dannye o znachenii kul'tury kartofelya dlya krest'yanskago
khozyaistva nechernozemnoi Rossii (Some data on the significance of
potato cultivation for peasant farming in non-Black Earth Russia).*
Moskva.

## 1912

*Krest'yanskoe khozyaistvo v Shveitsarii (Peasant Farming in Switzerland).*
Moskva: 23 cm., ott. iz zhurn "VSKh," pp. 29.

$$\text{LL} \quad \text{U}\frac{106}{257}$$

*Kooperativnoe strakhovanie skota (Cooperative insurance of Livestock).*
Khar'kovskoi sel'sk. kooperatsii, tip. Mechatnik, 23 cm., pp. 79, tab.

$$\text{LL} \quad \text{V}\frac{35}{793}$$

*Opyt anketnago issledovaniya denezhnykh elementov krest'yanskago
khozyaistva Moskovskoi gubernii (Research by questionnaire on money
items in the peasant farm in Moscow guberniya).* Moskva: Moskovskoe
obshchestvo sel'skogo khozyaistva (MOSKh). 67 + 4 pp.

BN 4° S. 5978

Helsinki, University

LL B $\dfrac{19}{519}$

## 1912–13

*Len i drugie kul'tury v organizatsionnom plane krest'yanskago khozyaistva nechernozemnoi Rossii (Flax and other crops in the organizational plan of the peasant farm in non-Black Earth Russia).* 2 fasc. Moskva: t. 1, Tablitsy. (Seminarii s. kh. statistiki Prof. A. V. Fortunatova pri Mosk. s. kh. inst.)

Vypusk 1. *Volokolamskii uezd, Moskva.* Moskovskoe obshchestvo sel'-skogo khozyaistva (MOSKh), LXXV–198 + 1 pp.

Vypusk 2. *Smolenskaya guberniya, Moskva.* Moskovskoe obshchestvo sel'skogo khozyaistva (MOSKh), 1913. LIII–209 + 2 pp.

BN 4° S.5983 (1)

LL W$\dfrac{440}{77}$ and W$\dfrac{440}{79}$

*Ocherki po teorii trudovogo khozyaistva (Essays on labor farm theory).* 2 fasc. Moskva. (MOSKh).

Vypusk 1. *Sootnoshenie proizvodstva i potrebleniya (Relations of production and consumption).* Moskva: tip. "Pechatnoe delo," 1912. 24 pp.

Vypusk 2. *Osnovy slozheniya potrebitel'skago byudzheta, (Fundamental elements of a budget of consumption).* Moskva: T–vo tip. Mamontova, 1913. 91 pp., incl. tab., diag.

BN 4° R.7939 (1)

LC RD 7035 C5 (fasc. 2 only)

Helsinki, University

LL F$\dfrac{121}{137}$ and F$\dfrac{99}{286}$

## 1913

*Organizatsiya l'novodnykh khozyaistv Moskovskoi i Smolenskoi gubernii po dannym spetsial'nykh ekspeditsii (The organization of flax farms in the Moscow and Smolensk guberniyas according to the data of special expeditions).* Moskva: tip. I. N. Kushnereva.

LL V$\dfrac{27}{721}$

*Ekonomicheskaya storona melioratsii v krest'yanskom khozyaistve (The economic aspect of amelioration on the peasant farm).* Moskva: t–vo. tip. A. I. Mamontova.

LL V$\dfrac{16}{949}$

*Proizvodstvo i potreblenie sel'sko-khozyaistvennykh produktov vo Frantsii* (Production and consumption of agricultural produce in France).

*Proekt organizatsii ekonomicheskago obsledovaniya Valuiskago uezda* (A draft proposal for organizing an economic survey of Valuiki uezd. Valuiki.

*Kooperativnoe strakhovanie skota vo Frantsii* (Cooperative insurance of livestock in France). Moskva.

*Znachenie mashiny v trudovom i kapitalisticheskom khozyaistve* (Significance of the machine in a labor farm and in a capitalist farm). St. Petersburg.

## 1914

*K voprosu o podgotovke agronomov* (On the problem of training agricultural officers). Moskva. 23 pp.

$$LL \quad W\frac{262}{1076}$$

*Voina i krest'yanskoe khozyaistvo* (War and the peasant economy). Moskva: I. N. Kushnerev i Ko. In 12°, 16 pp. (*Voina i kul'tura*, No. 31).

NYPL   Q.I. p.v. 48

$$LL \quad V\frac{154}{137}$$

## 1915

*Byudzhetnye issledovaniya i ikh znachenie* (Budget inquiries and their significance). St. Petersburg.

*Opyt razrabotki byudzhetnykh dannykh po sto odnomu khozyaistvu Starobel'skago uezda Khar'kovskoi gubernii* (An attempt to process budget data for 101 farms in Starobel'sk uezd, Khar'kov guberniya). Moskva: t. 1 Vvedenie, istoriya byudzhetnykh issledovanii, tip. V. Vengerova. 114 pp.

BN   4° V.19965 (1)

Helsinki, University

$$LL \quad V\frac{158}{17}$$

*Byudzhety krest'yan Starobel'skago uezda* (Peasant budgets from Starobel'sk uezd). Khar'kov: izd. Khar'kovskoi gubernskoi zemskoi upravy. 130–159 + 1–24 pp., errata.

BN   4° S.5982

*Normy potrebleniya sel'skago naseleniya po dannym byudzhetnykh issledovanii, predvaritel'nyi raschet* (The rural population's consumption norms according to budget inquiry data). St. Petersburg.

*Kratkii kurs kooperatsii* (A short course on cooperatives). Moskva: Lektsii, chit. na Staroobryadchesk. sel'sk. kursakh v Moskve, pod red. A. A. Zubrilina, 73 pp., ill.

LL  $V\dfrac{98}{310}$

(Cf. 1919 ed., below.)

HL   HD 3515 C 433

*L'nyanoi rynok (The flax market).* Moskva.

*Soyuzi skotovodov vo Frantsii (Unions of livestock growers in France).* Moskva.

"Dolzhen li zemskii agronom rabotat' v kooperativakh?" ("Should the zemstvo agricultural officer work in cooperatives?"), *Kooperativnoe zhizn'*, No. 1.

## 1916

*Obshchii obzor l'nyanogo rynka i ego sostoyanie v sezone 1915–1916 god (A general survey of the flax market and its condition in the 1915–1916 season).* Moskva: Izdanie Tsentral'nogo tovarishchestva l'novodov. 30 pp.

LL   $M\dfrac{141}{193}$

## 1917

*Prodovol'stvennyi vopros: lektsii, chitannyya na kursakh po podgotovke rabotnikov po kul'turno-prosvetitel'noi deyatel'nosti pri Sovete studencheskikh deputatov v aprele 1917 (The provisions problem; lectures given to trainees for cultural and educational work at the Council of Student Deputies, April 1917).* Moskva: Izd. Moskovskogo soveta studencheskikh deputatov. in 4°, 54 pp.

Harvard Slavic   1728.535

LL   $O\dfrac{16}{427}$

HL   HD 9015 R9C43

*Chto takoe agrarnyi vopros? (What is the agrarian problem?)* Moskva: "Universal'naya biblioteka." In 8°, 63 pp. (Liga agrarnykh reform, Seriya C, No. 1.)

Helsinki, University

LC   HD 715.C5

LL   $U\dfrac{5}{536}$

HL   HD 715 6434

*Osnovnye voprosy agrarnoi reformy na 2-m Vserossiiskom s"ezde Ligi agrarnykh reform (Basic problems of agrarian reform at the Second All-Russian Congress of the Agrarian Reform League)* (incl. reports by A. V. CHAYANOV, B. D. BRUTSKUS, A. N. CHELINTSEV, et al.). Moskva.

LL   $W\dfrac{65}{1125}$N.2

*Osnovnye usloviya uspekha kooperativnogo sbyta produktov sel'sko-khozyaistva (Basic conditions for successful cooperative selling of agricultural produce)*. Moskva.

1918

*Russkoe l'novodstvo, l'nyanoi rynok i l'nyanaya kooperatsiya (Russian flax farming, the flax market, and cooperatives)*. Moskva: tip. t-va. "Kooperativnoe izdatel'stvo." in 4°, 177 pp., incl. diag., tab., ill. (Tsentral'noe tovarishchestvo l'novodov).

NYPL    QCC p.v. 253

LL    $W\dfrac{440}{73}$

*Organizatsiya severnago krest'yanskogo khozyaistva (The organization of the northern peasant farm)*. Yaroslavl': Yaroslavskii kreditnyi soyuz kooperativov. in 8°, 121 pp., incl. diag., tab. (Posobiya dlya kooperativno-obshchestvennoi shkoly i kursov) pod red. V. A. KIL'CHEVSKOGO, No. 3.

HL    HD 1536 R9C43

LL    $V\dfrac{286}{387}$

LC    HD 1536 R9C43

*Osnovnyya idei i metody raboty obshchestvennoi agronomii (Basic ideas and work methods in agricultural advice to the public)* [Cf. 1924, below, *Social agronomy*]. Moskva: Moskovskoe tovarishcheskoe knigoizdatel'stvo po voprosam s.kh. ekonomii i politiki. In 8°, 123 + 1, III pp., diag.

LC    HD 1411 C434

LL    $U\dfrac{16}{139}$

$\left(\text{Cf. 1922 edition in 135 pp.—LL}\quad V\dfrac{286}{827}\right)$

*Kapitaly krest'yanskogo khozyaistva i ego kreditovanie pri agrarnoi reforme (Peasant farm capital and the granting of credits under the agrarian reform)*. Moskva: Tipo. lit. N. Zheldukovoi. In 8°, 32 pp., incl. diag. tabl.

LC    HD 715 C435

LL    $W\dfrac{262}{1981}$

HL    HD 715 C435

*Organizatsiya kooperativnago sbyta (The organization of cooperative sales)*. Moskva. In 8°, 80 pp. (Sovet Vserossiiskikh kooperativnykh s"ezdov).

LC    HD 3271 C43

LL    $W\dfrac{242}{713}$

$\left(\text{Cf. 1922 edition in 90 pp.—LL}\quad W\dfrac{242}{716}\right)$

*Priroda krest'yanskago khozyaistva i zemel'nyi rezhim (The land regime and the nature of the peasant economy)* (reports by A. V. CHAYANOV and N. P. MAKAROV) (Liga agrarnykh reform, *Trudy* III, Vseross. s"ezda Ligi agrarnykh reform, vypusk I). Moskva. In 8°, III + 10 + 45 + 11 pp.

*Ocherki po teorii vodnogo khozyaistva (An outline theory of hydraulic economy [water control] in farming).* Mosk. tovarishchestvo kn-vo po voprosam s.-kh. ekonomii i politiki, 22 cm., 25 pp.

$$\text{LL} \quad W\frac{262}{1079}$$

*Pamyatka l'novoda-kooperatora (Booklet of the flax-cooperator).* (Tsentral'-noe tovarishchestvo l'novodov. Vserossiiskii soyuz krest'yan-l'novodov). Moskva: Izd. tsentral'nogo tov-va l'novodov. In 16°, 23 pp.

## 1919

*Osnovnye idei i formy organizatsii krest'yanskoi kooperatsii (Basic ideas and organizational forms in peasant cooperatives).* Moskva: tip. T. Dortmana. In 8°, 343 (1) pp., incl. diag. tab. (Sovet Vserossiiskikh kooperativnykh s"ezdov).

LC   HD 1491 A305

$$\text{LL} \quad W\frac{242}{713}$$

HL   HD 3535 C 434

*Kratkii kurs kooperatsii (A short course on cooperatives).* Moskva: izd. 2-e pererabot. i dopolnennoe Sov. Vseross. kooperativnykh s"ezdov. In 8°, 78 pp. 2° edition, revised and enlarged.

HL   HD 3515 C433

## 1921

*Opyty izucheniya izolirovannogo gosudarstva (Attempts to study the isolated state).* Moskva: in *Trudy* Vysshego seminariya sel'skokhozyaistvennoi ekonomii i politiki, vypusk, 1, pp. 5–36.

BDIC   Q 2060

BM   8287 d4

$$\text{LL} \quad V\frac{288}{767}$$

HL   HD 1992 M891 v.1

*Nomograficheskie elementy ekonomicheskoi geografii (Nomographic elements in economic geography).* Moskva: in *Trudy* Vysshego seminariya . . . , vypusk 1, pp. 65–74.

BDIC   Q 2060

BM   8287 d4

$$\text{LL} \quad V\frac{288}{767}$$

*Ponyatie vygodnosti sotsialisticheskogo khozyaistva (The concept of advantage in the socialist economy),* pp. 5–76. In *Metody bezdenezhnogo ucheta khozyaistvennykh predpriyatii (Methods of nonmonetary accounting in economic undertakings)*. Moskva. In 8°, 98 pp., in *Trudy*, Vysshego seminariya . . . vypusk 2. (In collaboration with A. L. VAINSHTEIN.)

BM   8287 d41
BDIC

*Ekonomicheskie osnovy kul'tury kartofelya (The economic basis of potato growing)*. Moskva. In 8°, 23 pp., in *Trudy* Vysshego seminariya s.kh. ekonomii i politikii, vypusk 4.

BM   8287 d41

LL   $V\dfrac{268}{608}$

HL   HD 1992 M891 v.4

*Potreblenie g. Moskvy v 1919 godu (Consumption in the City of Moscow in 1919)*. Moskva. *Trudy*, Vysshego seminariya, vypusk 3.

1922

*Optimal'nye razmery zemledel'cheskikh khozyaistv (Optimal sizes of agricultural enterprises)*; in the collection, *Problemy zemleustroistva, optimal'nye razmery zemledel'cheskogo khozyaistva, kolichestvennyi uchet effekta zemleustroistva (Problems of land use: optimal farm size; recording the quantitative effects of land use measures)*, Trudy Vysshego seminariya sel'sko-khozyaistvennoi ekonomii i politiki pri Petrovskoi sel'sko-khozyaistvennoi Akademii, vypusk 7, pp. 5–84, Moskva, izd-vo "Novaya Derevnya."

BN   8° R.5830 (7)

*Osnovnyya idei i metody raboty obshchestvennoi agronomii (Basic ideas and work methods in agricultural advice to the public)*. Izd. 2-oe, dopolnennoe. Moskva: Izdat. Narkomzema. In 4°, 135 pp.

LL   $V\dfrac{286}{827}$

DA   (Department of Agriculture, Washington, D.C.)

*Organizatsiya kooperativnogo sbyta (The organization of cooperative sales)*. 2-oe dop. izd. Moskva: Izd. Vserossiiskogo soyuza sel'sko-khozyaistvennoi kooperatsii. 90 pp.

LC   HD 3271.C43

LL   $W\dfrac{242}{716}$

*Istoriya byudzhetnykh issledovanii (A history of budget research)*. 2-oe dop. izd. Moskva: Izd. Tsentral'nogo statisticheskogo upravleniya. In 8°, 133 pp., inc. tab., fig. (together with G. STUDENSKII).

BN   4°  V.19840
LC   HD  6987.C43
NYPL   QIP
LL   $W\dfrac{440}{75}$

"Gegenwärtiger Stand der landwirtschaftlichen Ökonomie in Russland" ("The present state of agricultural economics in Russia"), *Schmollers Jahrbuch*, 46 Jahrgang, pp. 731 ff.

1923

*Die Lehre von der bäuerlichen Wirtschaft. Versuch einer Theorie der Familienwirtschaft im Landbau (The theory of peasant economy. Test of a theory of family economy in agriculture)*. Von A. TSCHAJANOW, unter Mitwirkung des Verfassers aus dem Russischen übersetzt von FR. SCHLÖMER. Mit einem Vorwort von Dr. OTTO AUHAGEN. Berlin: P. Parey. In 8°, 132 pp., diag. tab.

Harvard Slav.   3099.23
NYPL
Paris,   Fac. Droit, 15012
LSE   London School of Economics

[This study of the theory of peasant economy was translated into Japanese by Professor Isobe Hidetoshi and was published in Tokyo in 1927 under the title, *Shonō keizai no genri*.]

"Die neueste Entwicklung der Agrarökonomie in Russland" ("The latest development of agricultural economics in Russia"), *Archiv für Sozialwissenschaft und Sozialpolitik*, Band 50, pp. 238 ff.

*Sovremennoe sostoyanie l'nyanogo rynka i vozmozhnye perspektivy sbyta russkikh l'nov (The present state of the flax market and future possibilities for the sale of Russian flax)*. London, "Tsentrosoyuz."

LL   $W\dfrac{52}{1211}$

1924

"Zur Frage einer Theorie der nichtkapitalistischen Wirtschaftssysteme" ("On the theory of non-capitalist economic systems"), VON A. TSCHAYANOFF, *Archiv für Sozialwissenschaft und Sozialpolitik*, Band 51, pp. 577–613.

*Ocherki po ekonomike trudovogo sel'skogo khozyaistva (Essays on the economics of labor farming)*. Moskva: s predisloviem L. KRITSMANA. In 8°, 152 pp. (Narodnyi komissariat zemledeliya RSFSR).

BM   SN  16/24
LL   $W\dfrac{234}{1149}$

*Die Sozialagronomie, ihre Grundgedanken und Arbeitsmethoden (Social agronomy, its basic ideas and work methods)* [cf. 1918, above]. Autorisierte Übersetzung aus dem Russischen von FR. SCHLÖMER. Berlin: P. Parey. In 4°, VIII, 96 pp., incl. diag., tab.

Geneva    ILO
NYPL    VPE p.v. 290 no. 7

[This study of social agronomy was translated into Japanese by Sugino Tadao and Isobe Hidetoshi and published in Tokyo in 1930 under the title, *Shōnō shidō no genri*.]

1925

*Organizatsiya krest'yanskogo khozyaistva (Peasant Farm Organization).* Iz rabot Nauchno-Issledovatel'skogo Instituta s.-kh. ekonomii, Moskva Tsentral'noe tovarichestvo kooperativnogo izd. In 8°, III+213 pp.

LL    W$\frac{396}{115}$ also W$\frac{234}{1146}$
HL    HD 1992 C434

[In 1957, Professor Isobe Hidetoshi, while republishing an enlarged version of his *Shōnō keizai no genri* (his translation of *Die Lehre von der bäuerlichen Wirtschaft* [cf. 1923, above]), also provided a translation direct from the Russian into Japanese of this study of *Peasant Farm Organization*, Tokyo, Taimedo.]

*Sel'sko-khozyaistvennaya taksatsiya: osnovnye idei i metody tsennostnykh vychislenii v sel'skom khozyaistve (Agricultural assessments: basic ideas and methods of agricultural calculation in value terms).* Iz rabot Kabineta sel'sko-khozyaistvennoi taksatsii i schetovodstva Nauchno-Issledovatel'skogo Instituta sel'sko-khozyaistvennoi ekonomii, Moskva, "Novaya derevnya." In 8°, 186 pp.

BN    8° R.58451
LL    W$\frac{242}{718}$
HL    HD 1294 C434

*Kak organizovat' krest'yanskoe khozyaistvo v nechernozemnoi polose (How to organize the peasant farm in the non-Black Earth zone).* Moskva: Gosudarstvennoe izd. In 16°, 45+1 pp.

HL    HD715.C436
LL    V$\frac{246}{1249}$

*Metody kolichestvennogo ucheta effekta zemleustroistva (Methods of recording the quantitative effect of land use measures).* Moskva. In 8°, 150 pp. (*Trudy* Nauchno-Issledovatel'skogo Instituta sel'skokhozyaistvennoi ekonomii, vypusk 17).

LC   S.563 M6
Union Catalog   51.54714 rev.
BM   8287 4
LL   XXIV$\frac{38}{10}$

"K voprosu ob organizatsii mel'kogo sel'skogo kredita" (*"On the organization of petty rural credit"*), *Ekonomicheskoe obozrenie* (Moskva), Vol. III, No. 1, pp. 64–78.

BDIC   4° P2273

"Zhelatel'nye formy finansirovaniya kooperativnykh zagotovok sel'skokhozyaistvennogo syr'ya" ("Desirable forms of financing cooperative procurement of agricultural raw materials"), *Ekonomicheskoe obozrenie* (Moskva), Vol. III, No. 2, pp. 46–55.

BDIC   4° P2273

"Problema traktora v narodnom khozyaistve SSSR" (*The problem of the tractor in the U.S.S.R.'s economy*), *Ekonomicheskoe obozrenie* (Moskva), Vol. III, No. 5, pp. 41–55.

BDIC   4° P2273

1926

*Sel'skoe khozyaistvo SSSR* (*Agriculture in the U.S.S.R.*). In *Entsikl. slovar' Russk. bibliogr. inst-ta. Granata.* t. XLI, chast' II, 7-e (pererab) izd. Moskva, pp. 1–42.

*Die Landwirtschaft des Sowjetbundes: ihre geographische, wirtschaftliche und soziale Bedeutung* (*The agriculture of the Soviet Union; its geographical, economic and social significance*). Berlin: P. Parey. In 4°, 40 pp., tab. (Forschungsinstitut für Agrar- und Siedlungswesen, Berlin. Der Weltmarkt für agrarische Erzeugnisse, Heft 1.)

NYPL   VPW (Germany)
Harvard Slav.   1710.100.110
LL   V$\frac{168}{235}$
HL   HD 1992.C4363

*Die volkswirtschaftliche Bedeutung des landwirtschaftlichen Genossen* (*Economic significance of agricultural cooperatives*). Kiel.

*L'évolution future de l'économie rurale* (*Future evolution of the rural economy*). Milan.

"Problema urozhaya i opyty ee razresheniya v razvitii russkoi nauchnoi mysli" ("Harvest problem and attempted solutions in the development of Russian scientific thought"), *Problemy urozhaya* (*Harvest problems*), a collection of articles. Ed. A. V. CHAYANOV. Moskva. III + 338 pp., maps and graphs. (*Trudy* Nauchno-Issled. Instituta s.-kh. ekonomii).

LL    W$\dfrac{315}{172}$

HL    HD 1992 C435

Doklad prof. A. V. CHAYANOVA v khlopkovoi sekstii osvok'a o vodnoi rente (Lecture on water rent delivered by Prof. CHAYANOV at the cotton department of OSVOK), *Khlopk. delo* (Moskva), No. 11–12 (Nov.–Dec.), pp. 903–4.

*Noveishie techeniya v oblasti ekonomicheskikh nauk na zapade* (*New trends in western economics*). (Bibliografiya po s.-kh ekonomii po materialam b-ki. Nauchno-Issled. Inst-ta s.kh. ekonomii), *Puti sel'skogo-khozyaistva* (Moskva), No. 10 (October), pp. 167–72.

1927

*Osnovnye idei i formy organizatsii sel'sko-khozyaistvennoi kooperatsii* (*Basic idea and organizational forms in agricultural cooperation*). Moskva. In 8°, VIII, 384 pp.

BDIC    02 616

LL    W$\dfrac{242}{711}$

*Osnovnye linii razvitiya russkoi sel'sko-khozyaistvennoi mysli za dva veka* (*Basic lines in the development of Russian agricultural thought over two centuries*). n.p., n.d., 40 pp.

Harvard Slav.    3085.10

*K voprosu o sebestoimosti khlopka-syrtsa v khozyaistvakh Srednei Azii* (*The problem of the cost of production of raw cotton on Central Asian farms*). Moskva: Propizdat. In 4°, 29 + 3 pp., ill. diag. (*Trudy* Nauchno-Issledovatel'skogo Instituta sel'sko-khozyaistvennoi ekonomii, vypusk 32).

LC    HD 9086 F3C4

*Ekonomicheskie osnovy polevoi kul'tury korneplodov i trav* (*Economic basis for the field cultivation of root and grass crops*). Moskva. 119 pp. (in collaboration with S. N. TUMANOVSKII), *Trudy* Nauchno-Issledovatel'skogo Instituta s.-kh. ekonomii, vypusk 21.

LL    XXIV$\dfrac{38}{10}$

*Metody taksatsionnykh izchislenii v sel'skom-khozyaistve* (*Methods of tax evaluation in agriculture*) (iz rabot Kabineta sel'khoz. Taksatsii i schetovodvstva). Moskva. 137 pp. (in collaboration with V. R. KRATINOV). (*Trudy* Nauchno-Issledovatel'skogo Instituta sel'sko-khozyaistvennoi ekonomii, vypusk 23).

1928

*Optimal'nye razmery sel'sko-khozyaistvennykh predpriyatii (Optimal sizes of agricultural enterprises)*, Iz rabot Nauchno-issledovatel'skogo instituta s.kh. ekonomiki, 3-oe dop. izd. Moskva, Izd. "Novaya derevnya." 91 pp.

$$LL \quad R\frac{194}{397}$$

"Vozmozhnoe budushchee sel'skogo-khozyaistva" ("Possible future of agriculture"), *Zhizn' i tekhnika budushchego (Life and technology in the future) (Sotsial'nye i Nauchno-tekhnicheskie utopii)* Pod red. Ark. A-na i E. KOLMANA. Moskva: Moskovskii rabochii. In 8°, 503 pp., ill.

NYPL   QI

*Sebestoimost' sakharnoi svekly (Sugar beet costs)*. Moskva: Izdatel'stvo Pravleniya Sakharotresta. In 8°, 131 pp., ill. (*Trudy* Nauchno-Issledovatel'skogo Instituta sel'sko-khozyaistvennoi ekonomii, vypusk 43).

LC   SB220.R9

$$LL \quad XXIV\frac{38}{10}$$

"Metody sostavleniya organizatsionnykh planov krupnykh sel'sko-khozyaistvennykh predpriyatii v usloviyakh sovetskoi ekonomii" ("Methods of drawing up organizational plans of large agricultural enterprises in Soviet economic conditions"), *Byulleten'* Nauchno-Issledovatel'skogo Instituta sel'sko-khozyaistvennoi ekonomii (Moskva), No. 1–4, pp. 5–14.
"L'état actuel de l'économie et de la statistique agricoles en Russie," *Revue d'économie politique* (Paris), janvier–février, pp. 82–97.
"Agricultural Economics in Russia," *Journal of Farm Economics*, Vol. X (October, 1928), pp. 543–52.

1929

*Byudzhetnye issledovaniya: istoriya i metody (Budget research: history and methods)*. Moskva: Novyi agronom. In 8°, 331 pp., diag. (In *Trudy* Nauchno-Issledovatel'skogo Instituta sel'sko-khozyaistvennoi ekonomii, vypusk 47).

Harvard   XS 56.10 (47)
LC   S567.C4

$$LL \quad XXIV\frac{38}{10} \text{ vyp. } 47$$

"Segodnyashnii i zavtrashnii den' krupnogo zemledeliya" ("Large scale farming today and tomorrow"), *Ekonomicheskoe obozrenie* (Moskva), Vol. VII, No. 9, pp. 39–51.

BDIC   4° P2273

"Tekhnicheskaya organizatsiya zernovykh fabrik" ("The technical organi zation of grain factories"), *Ekonomicheskoe obozrenie* (Moskva), Vol. VII, No. 12, pp. 95–101.

BDIC   4° P2273

"Sebestoimost' syr'evykh kul'tur" ("Costs of industrial crops"), *Sebestoimost' produktov sel'skogo khozyaistva, sbornik statei i materialov.* Pod red. prof. N. P. MAKAROVA. Moskva, pp. 118–42.

*Ekonomika sel'skogo khozyaistva kak osnova postroeniya programm opytnykh uchrezhdenii* (*The economics of agriculture as a basis for the elaboration of the program of experimental stations*). Moskva. 70 pp.

## 1930

*Die optimalen Betriebsgrössen in der Landwirtschaft* (*Optimum farm sizes in agriculture*). Mit einer Studie über die Messung des Nutzeffektes von Rationalizierungen der Betriebsfläche. Autorisierte Übertragung aus dem Russischen von FRIEDRICH SCHLÖMER. Berlin: P. Parey. In 8°, VII+98 pp., ill., diag.

LC   HD 1992 C5

[This study of optimal farm sizes has been translated into Japanese by Hayashi Hideo and Sakamoto Heiichirō under the title, *Nōgyō keiei tekisei kiboron: sono riron to keisoku.* Tokyo, 1957.]

"K voprosu o proektirovanii krupnykh sovkhozov" ("On the problem of projects for big state farms"), *Sovkhoz* (Moskva), No. 11 (November), pp. 4–8.

## II.   *Other Works (History, Literature, Arts)*

### 1912

*Lelina knizhka (stikhi)* (*Lelya's book* [*verses*]). Moskva: tipografiya "Pechatnoe slovo," 31 pp.

*Istoriya Miusskoi ploshchadi* (*K istorii Universiteta imeni A.Ya. Shanyavskogo*) (*A history of Miusskaya ploshchad'* [*about the Shanyavskii University*]). Moskva: *Vestnik Shanyavtsev,* 16 pp.

### 1917

*Moskovskie sobraniya kartin sto let nazad* (*Moscow picture collections a century ago*). Moskva: Gornaya tipografiya, 16 pp.

### 1918

(Under the pseudonym "BOTANIK X.")

*Istoriya parikmakherskoi kukly ili poslednyaya lyubov' moskovskogo arkhitektora, M. Romanich; povest', napisannaya Botanikom X i illyustrirovannaya antropologom A.* (*The history of the hairdresser's doll, or The last love of a Moscow architect.*) Moskva. 105 pp.

1920

(Under the pseudonym "IVAN KREMNEV.")
*Puteshestvie moego brata Alekseya v stranu krest'yanskoi utopii (The journey of my brother, Alexei, to the land of peasant Utopia)*. Chast' 1, with preface by . . ORLOVSKII. Moskva: Gosudarstvennoe izdatel'stvo. 63 pp.

NYPL   QCC p.v. 622

BM   8287 bb. 77

*Zodchii (The Architect)*, 2nd evening edition (11 P.M.) for Friday, 5 September, 1984 [*sic*], Moskva, 1 sheet.

1921

(Under the pseudonym "BOTANIK X.")
*Venediktov ili Dostopamyatnye sobytiya zhizni moei (Venediktov or Memorable events from my life)*. Moskva: Obraztsovaya tipografiya MSNKh, 64 pp., frontispiece, illustrations.
*Obmanshchiki (The deceivers)*, tragediya v trekh aktakh i devyati stsenakh. Sergiev: tipografiya pri Otd.Nar. Obrazovaniya Serg. Soveta, 31 pp.

1923

*Venetsianskoe zerkalo ili dikovinnye pokhozhdeniya steklyannogo cheloveka (The Venetian mirror or the wondrous adventures of a glass man)*. Berlin: "Gelikon." 46 pp.

1924

(Under the pseudonym "MOSKOVSKII BOTANIK X.")
*Neobychainye, no istinnye priklyucheniya grafa Fedora Mikhailovicha Buturlina (The unusual but true adventures of Count Fedor Mikhailovich Buturlin)*. Moskva: izd. avtora, 106 pp., illustrations.

1925

*Petrovsko-Razumovskoe v ego proshlom i nastoyashchem; putevoditel' po Timiryazevskoi sel'sko-khozyaistvennoi akademii (The past and present of Petrovsko-Razumovskoe: a guide to the Timiryazev Academy of Agriculture)*. Moskva: "Novaya derevnya." In 12° 86 pp., ill.

NYPL   Q p.v. 252

LL   V$\dfrac{221}{1338}$

1926

*Staraya zapadnaya gravyura: kratkoe rukovodstvo dlya muzeinoi raboty (Old western engravings: a brief guide for museum work)*. Moskva: Izd M. i S. Shabasnikovykh. 81 pp.

NYPL   QG P.V. 129, No. 2

1928

(Under the pseudonym "Moskovskii Botanik X.")
*Yuliya ili vstrechi pod Novodevich'im (Julia, or meetings at Novodevichii)*, Romanticheskaya povest', napisannaya Moskovskim Botanikom X i illyustrirovannaya A. Kravchenko. Moskva. 56 pp., ill.

LL    U$\dfrac{181}{806}$

III.   *Studies Edited or Prefaced by Chayanov*

1915

Paas, K. *Kratkii obzor pushnogo dela v Rossii (Brief survey of the fur business in Russia)*. Materialy po voprosam pushnogo dela izdavaemye P. K. Klepikovym, pod redaktsiei A. V. Chayanova, predislovie A. V. Chayanova. Moskva. 141 pp.

1916

*Materialy po voprosam razrabotki obshchego plana prodovol'stviya naseleniya (Materials on how to work out a general plan of provisions for the population)*, vypusk 2. Normy prodovol'stviya sel'skogo naseleniya Rossii po dannym byudzhetnykh issledovanii. Sostavleno pod redaktsiei i rudovostvom A. V. Chayanova. Predislovie V. Gromana (Ekonomicheskii otdel Vserossiiskogo soyuza gorodov). Moskva: Gorodskaya tipografiya. In 4°, 88 pp.

BN    4° V 19964
LL    W$\dfrac{245}{319}$

1917

Klepikov S. A. *Atlas diagramm i kartogramm po agrarnomu voprosu (Atlas of diagrams and cartograms on the agrarian problem)*. Pod obshchei redaktsiei A. V. Chayanova. Moskva: Knigoizdat, "Universal'naya biblioteka." In 4°, 40 pp., diag., cart.

BN    4°  S.6100 (3)
NYPL   QI p.v. 84
LOV    Mel. 8.871 (2)
HL    HD 715 K64

*Statisticheskii spravochnik po agrarnomu voprosu (Statistical reference book on the agrarian problem)*. Sostavlen Ekonomischeskim otdelom Vserossiiskogo Zemskogo Soyuza pod redaktsiei N. P. Oganovskogo i A. V. Chayanova, vypusk 1. *Zemlevladenie i zemlepol'zovanie (Landholding and land tenure)*. Liga agrarnykh reform—Redaktsionnyi komitet, P. P. Maslov, S. L. Maslov, N. P. Oganovskii, i A. V. Chayanov, Seriya A, No. 4. Moskva: "Universal'naya biblioteka." In 8°, 31 pp.

BN   4° S.6100
HL   1992 V 983

1918

*Statisticheskii spravochnik po agrarnomu voprosu (Statistical reference book on the agrarian problem)*. Sostavlen agrarnym otdeleniem ekonomicheskogo otdela Vserossiiskogo Zemskogo Soyuza pod obshchei redaktsiei YA. S. ARTYUKHOVA i A. V. CHAYANOVA, vypusk II. Sel'skoe khozyaistvo . . . , chast' 1. Sel'sko-khozyaistvennaya perepis' 1916 g. (The agricultural census of 1916), Liga agrarnykh reform, Seriya A, No. 5. In 8°, pp. 24. Chast' 2. Krest'yanskoe khozyaistvo i mirovaya torgovlya produktami sel'skogo-khozyaistva (Peasant Economy and World Trade in Agricultural Products), Liga agrarnykh reform, Seriya A, No. 6. Moskva: "Universal'naya biblioteka." In 8°, pp. 48.

BN   4° S.6100 (5 and 6)
HL   HD 1992 V983 (5 only)

1920

KLEPIKOV S. A. *Pitanie russkogo krest'yanstva* (Feeding the Russian peasant). Ed. A. V. CHAYANOV. Moskva. In 4°, XXIV + 52 pp.

BN   4° R.7868 (2)

1921

*Sbornik stat'ei i materialov po sel'skokhoz. kooperatsii I–II (Collection of articles and materials on agricultural cooperatives)*. K 9-my Vserossiiskomu s"ezdu Sovetov, V sbornike prinyali uchastie N. OSINSKII, M. SHEFFER, B. MESYATSEV, GR. KAMINSKII, BORIS KUSHNER, A. CHAYANOV, A. BITZENKO, A. MERKULOV i dr. Izd. komiteta NARKOMZEM A (kooperatotdel). MOSKVA. In 8°, 92 pp.

NIKITIN N. A. *Razdelenie Moskovskoi gubernii na sel'skokhozyaistvennye raiony (The division of Moscow guberniya into agricultural districts)*, vypusk 1. Obshchaya redaktsiya i vvedenie A. V. CHAYANOVA (Zemel'nyi otdel Moskovskogo Soveta R. K. i K. D.). Moskva: Gos. izdatel'stvo. In 4°, 160 pp., maps, tab.

BM   8287 d41
BN   4° S.5990 (1)
HL   HD 720 M6A2

1922

*Statisticheskii spravochnik po agrarnomu voprosu (Statistical reference book on the agrarian problem)*. Pod red. S. A. KLEPIKOVA i A. V. CHAYANOVA, vypusk III. Sel'skoe khozyaistvo 1918–1920 gg. (Agriculture from 1918–1920). Liga agrarnykh reform, Seriya A, No. 7. Moskva: izdatel'stvo "Novaya Derevnya." In 4°, 32 pp.

BN    4° S.6100 (7)

1926

*Problemy urozhaya (Harvest problems)*, a collection of articles. Ed. A. V. CHAYANOV. (*Trudy* Nauchno-Issled. Inst. s.-kh. ekonomii) Moskva. III + 338 pp., maps and graphs.

LL    W$\dfrac{315}{172}$

HL   HD 1992 C435

LEBEDEV V. I. *Laboratornye zanyatiya po organizatsii s.-kh. predpriyatii i tsennostnym vychisleniyam v sel'skom khozyaistve (Laboratory studies on the organization of agricultural enterprises and on agricultural calculations on value terms)*. Pod rukovodstrom A. V. CHAYANOVA. Moskva. 36 pp.

OVCHINNIKOV IU. E. *Organizatsiya strakhovaniya skota (Organization of livestock insurance)*. Predislovie A. V. CHAYANOVA. Moskva-Leningrad. 142 pp.

BRINKMAN CARL. *Ekonomicheskie osnovy organizatsii sel'sko-khozyaistvennykh predpriyatii (Economic basis of the organization of agricultural enterprises)*. Perev. s. nem. predislovie CHAYANOVA (*Trudy* Nauchno-Issledovatel'skogo Instituta sel'. kh. ekonomii). Moskva. XII + 224 pp.

1927

ANISIMOV, I. A., VERMENICHEV, I., NAUMOV, K. *Proizvodstvennaya kharakterista krest'yanskikh khozyaistv razlichnykh sotsial'nykh grupp:tablitsy schetovodnogo analiza 60 krest'yanskikh khozyaistv l'nyanogo raiona Volokolamskogo uezda Moskovskoi gubernii (A production description of peasant farms in various social groups: tables of a bookkeeping analysis of 60 peasant farms in the flax area of Volokolamsk uezd, Moscow guberniya)*. Pod obshchim rukovodstvom i red. A. V. CHAYANOVA. Moskva: Moskovskii rabochii, *Trudy* Nauchno-Issled. Instituta sel'sko-khozyaistvennoi ekonomii, vypusk 24. 440 pp.

LC   HD 9155.R93V82

*Ten years of Soviet Power in Figures, 1917–1927.* Preface by A. V. CHAYANOV. Moscow: Central Statistical Board. XIV + 516 pp., 17 cm.

HL   HD 1992 C 435

1927–28

*Statisticheskii spravochnik SSSR. God 1927–1928 (Statistical reference book on the U.S.S.R. 1927–1928)*. Pod red. A. V. CHAYANOVA. Moskva: Tsentral'noe statisticheskoe upravlenie SSSR. In 16°

NYPL  QB

# List of Tables

297

# Index

## A

Advantage: distinction between conception on the labor farm and that on the capitalist one, 86–89; its calculation in crop selection, 138

Aeroboe, Fr.: lxv; and calculation of net income in agriculture, liii; and farm organization, 45, 126; and land valuation, 227

Agrarian question: C.'s works and, xxv–xxvi, lxiv–lxv; nationalization and, xxviii; effect of the Revolution on, xxxvi; varying opinions on, xxxvi–xxxvii; regional diversities and, xxxvii–xxxviii; C. and, xxxviii ff; role of the agricultural officer, xl–xli

Agricultural Economics Research Institute, 254, 256

Agricultural Economy and Politics, Postgraduate Seminar in, 103

Agricultural enterprises: problem of their optimum size, lvi–lviii, lx, lxi, lxxiv, 90–91, 111; use of the cooperative in their integration, lviii–lx; C.'s production plan for, lxii; Marxists' attacks on C.'s thesis, lxx; definition of, 90; ratio of labor, land, and capital for all sizes of, 91; influence of family size and available capital on, 95 ff; interconnection between their elements of production, 103; effect of surplus labor and unsatisfied demand on their organization, 107; effect of land improvement on economic rent in capitalist and labor units, 237; their heterogeneity in Russia, 243–44, 254; movement towards capitalism, 257 ff; future of their organization, 265–69

Agricultural Institute of Petrovskoe Razumovskoe, C. and, xxvii, xl, lvi

Agricultural officers: interest in large estates, xxvii; employment by Zemstvo organizations, xxviii; C. and, xxx, xxxi, xxxii; accounting system for, xxxii; and the land question, xxxvi; their role in agrarian reform, xl–xli; their human role, xli; and land irrigation, l; appear-

Agricultural officers—*Cont.*
ance in remote countryside, 36; problems facing, 36–37; use of morphological static elements in peasant farms, 45; criticisms of C., 85; favor Yaroslavl' rotation, 145; suggest a differential agricultural programme, 254

Agricultural produce, its price determination, 239

Agricultural science: application to crop selection, 138–39; and restoration of soil fertility, 139–40

Agricultural Societies: Khar'kov, xxviii, xxxvi; Moscow, xxviii, xxxvi; St. Petersburg, xxviii, lxviii

Agriculture: its collectivization, xi, xxvii, lix; Marx and, xviii–xix, 36; Lenin and its capitalization, xx; changes in its economy, xxii, 36; study of the large estates, xxvii–xxviii; increased supply of specialists, xxviii; its monetization, xxxviii; dissimilarity with industry in production principles, xxxviii–xxxix, 4–5; instruments of state action for its transformation, xxxix–xl; role of the official in its transformation, xl–xli; inapplicability of labor unit, xliii; study of its regionalization, xlvii; absorption of population increases, xlviii; irrigation and, l; difficulty of calculating a net income, liii; problem of accelerating technical improvement, lvi; its vertical and horizontal integration, lviii, lix, 262–63, 266–67; C. revises some earlier positions on its evolution in U.S.S.R., lxiii–lxiv; its development dependent on industry, lxxi; social evolution before and after the Revolution, lxxiii, 36; possible domination by capitalist influence, 49, 257–64; variations in labor intensity curve, 74–75, 238; supplanted by industry, 107–8; amount of working time spent on, 179, 180; influence of its mechanism on capitalist economics, 225; effect of overpopulation on, 241; its gradual proletarianization, 257; its influence on Soviet economy, 265–66